THE BEATLES
in LIVERPOOL, HAMBURG, LONDON

pp

THE BEATLES in LIVERPOOL, HAMBURG, LONDON

PEOPLE | VENUES | EVENTS |
THAT SHAPED THEIR MUSIC

Tony Broadbent

PLAIN SIGHT PRESS | Vallejo CA

Copyright © 2018 | 2020 by **Tony Broadbent**

All rights reserved. No part of this book may be reproduced in any form, or by any electronic or mechanical means, including information storage and retrieval systems—except for use in reviews—without prior written permission.

PLAIN SIGHT PRESS
Vallejo CA 94591
www.plainsightpress.com

Cover Design: TBCBCO | Image: Slough Observer
Book Design: TBCBCO | Pulp

The Beatles in Liverpool, Hamburg, London | Tony Broadbent
ISBN 978-0-9963722-1-3
Library of Congress Control Number: 2018937756

1. The Beatles 1957-1970. 2. Great Britain & USA. Society, culture, rock 'n' roll, R&B, pop music, UK media 1956-1963. 3. History. 1. The Title

Dedicated To Bill & Virginia Harry

And All The People

Here, There, And Everywhere

Who Were Party To The Birth Of The Beatles

CONTENTS

INTRODUCTION — 1

PREFACE | The Beatles | In Brief — 3

PART ONE | People | Places | Venues

1 - LIVERPOOL PEOPLE — 19

2 - *MERSEY BEAT* — 67

3 - MERSEYSIDE BEAT GROUPS — 73

4 - LIVERPOOL VENUES — 86

5 - LIVERPOOL LANDMARKS — 101

6 - HAMBURG PEOPLE — 110

7 - HAMBURG VENUES — 130

8 - LONDON PEOPLE — 143

9 - LONDON PLACES — 185

PART TWO | The Music | The Media

1 - AMERICAN ROCK 'N' ROLL — 195

2 - AFRICAN-AMERICAN R&B — 240

3 - BRITISH ROCK 'N' ROLL — 247

4 - UK ROCK 'N' POP MEDIA — 285

PART THREE | Quintessential Beatles | Q&A ___ 315

PART FOUR | The Beatles | Timelines

Extended Timeline ___ 359

A Hard Day's Night ___ 401

PART FIVE | The Beatles and More

The Beatles - On Record ___ 409

Reading The Beatles ___ 419

Reading the Sixties ___ 433

Author's Special Thanks ___ 447

The One After 9:09 ___ 451

Other Works ___ 454

INTRODUCTION

From *'Be-Bop-A-Lula'* to *'Beatlemania'*

The Beatles rock my world. I've loved them and their songs ever since I first heard John Lennon's wailing harmonica intro to 'Love Me Do'—the precise moment that for so many was the true beginning of The Sixties. I was a teenager in London during The Beatles' seven glorious recording years and so grew up with them, you might say, as they grew in themselves. I saw them perform 'live' on several occasions and each time I twist and shouted in joyous unabashed abandon alongside everyone else in the audience. I even bought a pair of real Beatles' boots.

But as well as delighting the world with their many wondrous songs, The Beatles also brought many new ideas to light; opening doors to thought as well as perception. It's taken a lifetime to ponder everything The Beatles achieved. And it's led me to read hundreds of books; pore over thousands of newspaper and magazine articles; view countless hours of documentary film about the group. Yet, even with all that, many questions still remained, especially about the early days of The Beatles. And whatever the quest it's always somewhat sobering to have to admit to yourself that multitudes of facts don't always reveal clear truths.

Which is why, having long learned that truth can sometimes be better found in fiction, I wrote a historical-mystery novel—*The One After 9:09 - A Mystery With A Backbeat*—about the early days of The Beatles in Liverpool, Hamburg, and London, and searched for my answers there. I found them, too, at least to my satisfaction. And the book you now hold in your hands is based on all the reading and research I did over the years that enabled me to write the novel.

I've posted much about The Beatles on the '*Special Features*' website I put together to accompany *The One After 9:09*—but this guidebook to the early years of *'The Fab Four'* is much more comprehensive.

The Beatles in Liverpool, Hamburg, London concentrates on the crucial first seven years of The Beatles. | It covers the people, venues, and events from *'Be-Bop-A-Lula'*—and *'The Birth of The Beatles'*—all the way through to the truly unprecedented global phenomenon that was "*Beatlemania.*" | It looks at the birth of Rock 'n' Roll in the USA and Britain; the key originators of the 'new' sound; the huge influence African-American music had on the group; and the state of British 'pop' music in the late-Fifties and early-Sixties. | It also includes many more people and places The Beatles knew and loved in the three world-renowned cities that were the backdrop to their astonishing success. | As well as *A Brief History of The Beatles* and *Quintessential Beatles Q&A* that cover the years The Beatles were together. | Extended Timlines: *'From 1957 To 1964'* and *'The Making of A Hard Day's Night'* | *The Beatles on Record* | *Reading the Beatles* | *Reading The Sixties* | All newly curated and ordered for quick and easy reference.

This book is designed for you to dip in and out of. And I've tried to make each entry, in each and every section, whether about person or place or event, able to stand on its own Beatles' boots, as it were. So, of necessity, there's some repetition throughout.

I hope you enjoy *The Beatles in Liverpool, Hamburg, London* and come across facts and thoughts and musings about The Beatles, their music, and their times, you hadn't known of or thought about before. And should it also inspire you to delve deeper into the magical phenomenon that was The Beatles and it leads you to some of the great historians and chroniclers and bloggers of *'The Fab Four'*—all just waiting out there for you in *'Pepperland'* —then all the better—and you'll have made this labour of love more than worthwhile. And I thank you.

For as we know... in the end: *The love you take is equal to the love you make.* That's why this book is also dedicated to Beatles' fans—young and old—old and new—the world over.

Love. Love. Love.

Tony Broadbent | Unabashed Beatles' Fan
San Francisco | January 2018 | May 2020

PREFACE – THE BEATLES – IN BRIEF

The Beatles | Brief Sketches

John Lennon - Rhythm guitar

1940-1980 | John Winston Lennon | *'The Brainy One'* | Musician. Singer. Songwriter. Poet. Sometime Cartoonist. Sometime Actor. Sometime Political Activist. Always passionate, opinionated, acerbic, witty and, intellectually, often quite brilliantly wise. | The man who founded The Beatles. He invited Paul McCartney to join the band when they met at a church fete in Liverpool, in 1957; soon after which they started writing songs together. | A gifted rock singer, musician, and performer; and pop music composer of rare genius; the songs he wrote for The Beatles' credited jointly to 'Lennon/McCartney' | 1965. UK. Awarded MBE for services to music; which he later returned. | After The Beatles disbanded, he continued to record and perform, and became more politically active. His later solo work, with his wife Yoko Ono, produced some of his greatest songs. | John Ono Lennon was murdered outside his New York apartment by a deranged, supposed former Beatles' fan on 8 December 1980.

Paul McCartney - Bass guitar

1942 - | James Paul McCartney | *'The Romantic One'* | Musician. Singer. Songwriter. Sometime Actor. Sometime Poet. Sometime Fine Artist. | A hugely gifted musician and pop music composer of rare genius. His song-writing partnership with John Lennon helped power The Beatles to worldwide success. It was Paul who suggested that George Harrison, a schoolmate, join the band in 1958. | A brilliant rock singer, musician, and performer. The songs he wrote for The Beatles' credited jointly to 'Lennon/McCartney'. | 1965. UK. Awarded MBE for services to music. | After The Beatles disbanded he formed the pop group, Wings, featuring his wife, Linda, and Denny Lane, and an ever-changing roster of musicians. Wings also achieved worldwide success. | His solo work, including a symphony and a specially commissioned oratorio, has been much acclaimed. He regularly tours the world with a new band of handpicked musicians; his performances always 'sold-out'. | 1997. UK. Knighted by Queen Elizabeth II for his services to music and charity: *Arise, Sir Paul!*

George Harrison - Lead guitar

1943-2001 | George Harold Harrison | *'The Quiet, Serious One'* | Musician. Singer. Songwriter. Sometime Actor. Sometime Film Producer. Sometime Charity Activist. | 1962. It was George who first drummed up support for Ringo Starr to join the band so as to help make The Beatles better, stronger, and musically more cohesive. | Deeply spiritual, a lifelong seeker, it was George who introduced the Indian sitar into the group's music. | 1965. UK. Awarded MBE for services to music. | After the group disbanded he went on to produce a superb body of work as both singer and songwriter that put him on a par with the song-writing genius of Lennon and McCartney. | The highly acclaimed *'The Concert For Bangladesh'* he arranged, in New York, in 1971, with Bob Dylan, Eric Clapton, Ringo Starr, and Ravi Shankar, was the first such international charity event of its kind. | George Harrison died from the effects of lung cancer on 29 November 2001.

Ringo Starr – Drums

1940 - | Richard Starkey | *'The Lovable One'* | Musician. Singer. Sometime songwriter. Actor. | More famous than The Beatles, on Merseyside, when he was asked to join the group in 1962. | Ringo completed the group; helped make it truly unique. | His left-handed drumming style always had a very distinctive sound and, like George Harrison's guitar work, always seemed designed to fit the specific needs of a particular song and help make it uniquely memorable. | 1965. UK. Awarded MBE for services to music. | After The Beatles disbanded he went on to act in a number of critically acclaimed films and to tour, worldwide, with his own big band. He lives in US. | January 2018. Awarded 'knighthood' in the Queen's New Year's Honours List for services to music and charity. | 20 March 2018. Knighted by Prince William in Buckingham Palace ceremony: *Arise, Sir Ringo!*

The Beatles | A Brief History

| **1956** | The 'Skiffle' craze engulfs Britain's teenagers in the mid-1950s inspired by recording artist 'Skiffle king' Lonnie Donegan. John Lennon forms the Quarrymen—a six-man 'skiffle' band —with classmates from Quarry Bank grammar school in Liverpool. The Quarrymen forms the genesis of The Beatles.

| **1957** | Saturday 6 July. The Quarrymen perform at a church garden fête in Woolton, Liverpool. A mutual friend introduces 16-year old John Lennon to 15-year old Paul McCartney. Paul sings and plays Eddie Cochran's 'Twenty Flight Rock' and Gene Vincent's 'Be Bop A Lula' flawlessly on guitar—and follows up with a medley of Little Richard numbers. Point made—in spades. | Greatly impressed by Paul's musical ability, John later asks him to join the Quarrymen. Paul officially joins the group in October 1957. John even more impressed to learn Paul has already started writing his own songs. | The two schoolboys soon begin to compose together and—with extraordinary prescience—agree that all their future compositions will be credited to Lennon-McCartney. By the time they came to record as The Beatles some five years later the duo have written eighty or so Lennon-McCartney original songs. | John finds in Paul a partner who shares his passion for rock 'n' roll and The Quarrymen's repertoire increasingly grows to encompass the harder-edged sound. Net result is that within a year all the other original Quarrymen—skiffle-purists to a man—leave the group. | **As 1957 comes to a close John and Paul are already writing songs the world will soon come to know as 'Lennon and McCartney' originals.**

| **1958** | On Paul's recommendation and after a successful audition on the top deck of a double-decker bus—where he plays the guitar instrumental 'Raunchy' with considerable panache— George Harrison joins the group. | **As 1958 comes to a close John, Paul, and George represent the core group that will one day become The Beatles.**

| **1959** | August. The Quarrymen play opening night of Casbah Coffee Club—owned by Mona Best—in West Derby, a suburb of Liverpool. Play the Casbah six times over next couple of months. | October-November. Still minus a regular drummer—the group survive three rounds of TV talent contest in Liverpool and Manchester as 'Johnny and The Moondogs'. The band's name inspired by American DJ Alan Freed who called himself "Moondog" on his Radio Luxembourg programme they listened to religiously every weekend. It didn't help them win. | **As 1959 comes to a close John, Paul, and George refuse to give up their dream of reaching** *"the toppermost of the poppermost."*

| **1960** | Stuart Sutcliffe, close friend and fellow student of John's at Liverpool Art College, joins the group as bass player. | And so they become 'the Silver Beetles' to honour Buddy Holly and his backing band The Crickets; play lunchtime sessions at local coffee bar, the Jacaranda, owned by Liverpool promoter and would-be talent manager Allan Williams. | Make regular appearances at Mona Best's Casbah Coffee Bar in West Derby. | 10 May 1960. With added John Lennon word play the group is now called 'the Silver Beatles'. They audition, with a sit-in drummer, at another of Allan Williams's city-centre clubs for London impresario Larry Parnes and one of his stable of pop singers Liverpool-born Billy Fury. They aren't hired as Fury's backing band; nor are any of the other far more established Liverpool beat groups that audition; but they do get asked to back Johnny Gentle; another of Parnes' teen idols. | 20 May 1960. Billed as 'Johnny Gentle and his Group' begin nine-day tour of Scotland.
| 17 August 1960. Having failed to convince any other Liverpool group to do a gig in Germany, Allan Williams has just enough confidence in The Beatles, as they are now called, to book them for an 8-week season at Indra Cabaret club in Hamburg's St. Pauli 'red-light' district. | Pete Best; Mona Best's son; joins the group as full-time drummer.

| The Beatles perform at the Indra—a former strip club—for six hours every night. Bruno Koschmider—the club's owner—constantly urges them to *"Mach schau! Mach schau!"*—*"Make a*

big show!" | After an excessive noise complaint Koschmider is forced to close the Indra and moves The Beatles to his other St. Pauli club—the Kaiserkeller. He also extends the group's contract for a further 8-weeks. | The whole experience proves a baptism of fire for The Beatles. The fact they also have to share billing at the Kaiserkeller with one of Liverpool's top groups—the outrageous, always exciting, always exceedingly competitive Rory Storm and The Hurricanes—with none other than Ringo Starr on drums—another catalyst that propels The Beatles into becoming ever better musicians and performers. | During their time at the Kaiserkeller The Beatles are befriended by three avant-garde German art students—Astrid Kirchherr, Klaus Voormann and Jurgen Vollmer—each of whom will leave a unique mark—in look, manner, attitude, and style—on the group. | Their first season in Hamburg helps transform The Beatles from a rough and ready band of amateurs—all but the lowest of the low on the Merseyside beat group totem pole—into an exciting and accomplished rock band with a seemingly endless repertoire of rock 'n' roll and rhythm and blues songs—augmented by a growing number of Lennon-McCartney originals. Following an angry contractual dispute with Koschmider, which results in George Harrison's deportation from Hamburg for being underage, and the arrest of Paul McCartney and Pete Best on a trumped-up arson charge, The Beatles return to Liverpool with their proverbial tails between their legs.

| December1960. The group—minus Stuart Sutcliffe who elects to stay on in Hamburg with his now girlfriend Astrid Kirchherr—still very bruised by the experience slowly drift back together. | They play the Casbah coffee club. Local DJ and compère, Bob Wooler—a friend of Allan Williams—gets them a booking as a supporting act to the Searchers at a post-Boxing Day event at Litherland Town Hall—some five miles north of Liverpool city-centre. Wooler posts ads in the local paper. Mona Best puts up posters on the walls of the Casbah. *'Direct from Hamburg. The Beatles'*. It proves to be an auspicious turning point. | Tuesday evening, 27 December 1960. When The Beatles begin playing their hard-edged, Hamburg-honed, Pete Best 'atom-beat' driven rock 'n' roll the Litherland Town Hall audience

are stunned—and go wild—no one has ever heard anything like it—the sheer force of it hits everyone—teenagers and local promoters alike. No one has seen anything like it either—The Beatles brim with confidence, sport outrageous hairstyles, and are attired in black leather jackets, black jeans, and cowboy boots. Total knockout. | **As 1960 comes to a close The Beatles are on the point of taking Liverpool by storm.**

| **1961** | January. The Beatles are now in huge demand from local promoters such as Brian Kelly, Sam Leach, and Ray McFall. Soon regularly booked to play the City's top clubs—The Iron Door and The Cavern—for evening sessions, lunchtime sessions—even 'all-nighters'. The group works non-stop—sometimes with three separate bookings in a single day. | 21 February. The Beatles make their very first appearance at The Cavern Club | 1 April 1961. The Beatles return to Hamburg—to play Peter Eckhorn's Top Ten Club for 92 consecutive nights. The group play their own sets and then back the club's star attraction—British-born singer and guitarist Tony Sheridan. | 22-24 June. The Beatles back Sheridan at recording session for Germany's Polydor label—produced by famed German orchestra-leader Bert Kaempfert—at Friedrich-Ebert-Halle Studio. The session yields eight songs and the record that will soon lead to another important turning point in the career of The Beatles — 'My Bonnie' b/w 'The Saints'—credited to 'Tony Sheridan and The Beat Brothers'. | June - July. Stuart Sutcliffe leaves The Beatles to pursue his art studies | 2 August. The Beatles return to Liverpool. Begin long-term residency at Cavern Club. | 23 October. Polydor Records release 45rpm single 'My Bonnie' b/w 'The Saints' in Germany. George Harrison gives copy of disc to DJ Bob Wooler who repeatedly plays 'My Bonnie' at the Cavern.

| 28 October. Beatles' fans repeatedly ask for 'My Bonnie' at NEMS—one of Liverpool's top record stores. The store's manager, Brian Epstein, is intrigued enough to search out The Beatles at a lunchtime session at the Cavern and is charmed by both them and their music. | 10 November. Liverpool promoter Sam Leach launches series of 'Operation Big Beat' shows at Tower

Ballroom, New Brighton—headlined by The Beatles. Two shows—two weeks apart—draw over 4,000 fans—smashing all attendance records.

| 3 December. Brian Epstein offers to manage The Beatles—they say they'll think about it—as Sam Leach also wants to manage them. | 9 December. Sam Leach's *'Liverpool v London - Battle of the Bands'* at the Palais Ballroom, Aldershot—some 50 miles outside London—is an unmitigated disaster, as only 17 people turn up. | 13 December. Brian Epstein convinces Mike Smith, Decca Records A&R assistant, to travel up to Liverpool to see The Beatles 'live' at The Cavern.

| 17 December. Brian Epstein meets with The Beatles at Casbah Coffee Club—promises he'll help secure them a contract with one of London's 'Big Four' recording companies—Decca, Pye, Philips, and EMI—and is appointed the group's manager.

| 18 December. A&R executives from EMI's Columbia and HMV record labels inform Brian Epstein—by post—that having listened to Polydor single 'My Bonnie' they have no interest in signing The Beatles | Decca Records however offer 'Artist Test' Audition—session slated for coming New Year's Day, in London. | Mid-December. The Beatles voted 'Merseyside's Top Band' by readers of *Mersey Beat*—*'Merseyside's Own Entertainments Paper'*. | The group are now in constant demand in and around Liverpool—fans queue up for hours to see them. | 31 December. A cold and uncomfortable 10-hour road journey from Liverpool to London—all four Beatles and all their equipment all bunched together in the back of their roadie's van. | **As 1961 comes to a close everything bodes well for The Beatles—but a long and winding road still stretches out ahead of them.**

| **1962** | 1 January. The Beatles audition for Decca Records at their studio in West Hampstead, London. After repeated technical delays they record 15-songs—rock 'n' roll standards—plus a show tune or two specially selected by Brian Epstein to demonstrate the group's versatility; as well as a handful of Lennon-McCartney original compositions; all in a little more than an hour. | 5 January. Polydor Records release 45rpm 'My Bonnie' b/w 'The Saints'—now credited to 'Tony Sheridan and The

Beatles' in UK | 31 January. Despite further entreaties from Brian Epstein Decca's senior A&R executives finally reject The Beatles' audition recordings as *"old hat...as guitar groups are on the way out"* | Hugely disappointed but still determined to make good his promise to The Beatles—Brian Epstein calls upon every other contact he has in the record retail business. Makes repeated 'cold calls' to the offices of Pye, Philips, Oriole, and EMI. And is repeatedly turned down, rebuffed, or simply ignored.

| Refusing to take 'No' for an answer, Brian Epstein redoubles his efforts and—quite by chance—in the process of having the Decca audition demo-tapes transferred to 78rpm shellac disc at HMV Music Store, on London's Oxford Street is introduced to a music publisher who's very taken with John and Paul's original songs. | Music publisher Sid Colman arranges for Brian Epstein to meet record producer George Martin—Head of Parlophone—EMI's smallest record label best known for comedy and novelty records. | 9 May. Epstein meets Martin at EMI's Abbey Road Studios in London—plays the recordings from The Beatles' failed Decca audition. Parlophone represents the very last chance for The Beatles to secure an all-important recording contract. | 6 June. The Beatles undertake Artist Recording Test for George Martin at Abbey Road Studios. After the session George Martin informs Brian Epstein that Pete Best's drumming isn't good enough for recording purposes and that Parlophone will have to employ a session drummer for all future recordings.

| 26 June. Brian Epstein officially forms NEMS Enterprises Ltd. with brother Clive. | 16 August. Brian Epstein sacks Pete Best from the group at insistence of the other three Beatles after the group has managed to secure his replacement, Ringo Starr—the drummer with Rory Storm and The Hurricanes.

| 18 August. First performance of The Beatles—John, Paul, George, and Ringo—at Hulme Hall, Port Sunlight. | 23 August. John Lennon marries pregnant, long-time, art-student girlfriend Cynthia Powell in civic ceremony in Liverpool. | 4 September. Abbey Road Studios. The Beatles—with Ringo on drums—attend second recording session for George Martin. Record Lennon-McCartney composition 'Love Me Do' | 11 September. Abbey

Road Studios. The Beatles' third recording session. Re-record 'Love Me Do' and two new Lennon-McCartney compositions—P.S. I Love You' and 'Please, Please Me'—George Martin has session drummer Andy White sit in. | 5 October. The Beatles' first single—'Love Me Do' b/w 'P.S. I Love You'—released in UK | October. The Beatles appear as 'second on the bill' to rock 'n' roll star Little Richard at two concerts on Merseyside.

| 1 November. The Beatles fly to Hamburg to appear at Star-Club and return to London two weeks later. | 26 November. The Beatles' fourth session at Abbey Road Studios. Re-record 'Please, Please Me'. George Martin proclaims: "*Gentlemen, you've just recorded your first number one hit.*" | 15 December. *The Mersey Beat Poll Winners Show*. The Beatles voted 'Most Popular Group' for second year running | 18-31 December. The Beatles headline 13-nights at Star-Club—the group's third engagement and final time in Hamburg. | 27 December. 'Love Me Do' reaches No.17 in UK charts. | **As 1962 comes to a close it seems that John, Paul, George, and Ringo are at long last on their way to reaching** "*the toppermost of the poppermost*" **in the UK.**

| **1963** | 11 January. 'Please, Please Me' b/w 'Ask Me Why' released in UK | 19 January. The Beatles appear on *Thank Your Lucky Stars*; one of Britain's top 'pop music' TV shows (taped for broadcast previous Sunday). The group's first nationwide television appearance. | 2 February - 3 March. The Beatles 'First UK Tour' supporting teenage singing sensation Helen Shapiro and singer Kenny Lynch. | 11 February. The Beatles record 10 songs at Abbey Road Studios for their début LP *'Please, Please Me'* in a marathon twelve-hour session. | 22 February. 'Please, Please Me' is The Beatles' first No.1 single in most UK charts. | March 5. Abbey Road Studios. The Beatles record third single: 'From Me To You' b/w 'Thank You Girl' | 9-31 March. The Beatles 'Second UK Tour' supporting American chart-toppers Chris 'Let's Dance' Montez and Tommy 'Sheila' Roe | 22 March—'*Please Please Me*' LP album released in UK | 11 April. 'From Me To You' b/w 'Thank You Girl' released in UK | 11 May The Beatles *'Please, Please Me'* LP tops UK album charts—stays top for 30 weeks.

| 18 May - June 9. The Beatles 'Third UK Tour' with Gerry and The Pacemakers and American chart-topper Roy Orbison
| 1 July. Abbey Road Studios. The Beatles record 4th single 'She Loves You' b/w 'I'll get You' | 18 July - October 23. Abbey Road Studios. The Beatles record second LP *With the Beatles'*
| 3 August. The Beatles make thier 292nd and last appearance at the Cavern Club, Liverpool.
| 13 October. The Beatles appear on nationally broadcast *Sunday Night at the London Palladium* (equivalent to *The Ed Sullivan Show*). Over 13 million UK viewers tune in. | Newspaper photos show mobs of screaming fans outside the theatre; before, during, and after the show; national Sunday papers dub the phenomenon **"Beatlemania"**. | 17 October. Abbey Road Studios. The Beatles record fifth single: 'I Want To Hold Your Hand' b/w 'This Boy' | 24 - 30 October. The Beatles tour Sweden. | 31 October. Ed Sullivan about to fly back to New York sees 5000+ fans at London Airport waiting to welcome home The Beatles.
| 1 November - 13 December. The Beatles 'Fourth UK Tour'
| 4 November. Prince of Wales Theatre, London. The Beatles appear at *Royal Variety Command Performance*. John Lennon makes famous remark in front of Princess Margaret and the Queen Mother: **"Would the people in the cheaper seats clap your hands and the rest of you, if you'll just rattle your jewellery."** |
After the show is broadcast on national TV the following Sunday evening, *'Beatlemania'* engulfs all of Great Britain. | Brian Epstein to New York for business meetings. | 22 November. *'With The Beatles'* LP released in UK: only second album in UK chart history to sell million copies. | 29 November. 'I Want To Hold Your Hand' b/w 'This Boy' released UK | 4 December. Capitol Records at last takes note of *'Beatlemania'* and announce they've signed The Beatles for the US market | 29 December. 'I Want To Hold Your Hand' b/w 'I Saw her Standing There' released US | 24 December - 11 January. 'The Beatles Christmas Show' season of shows at Finsbury Park 'Astoria', London. | **As 1963 comes to a close; with four No. 1 Singles and two No. 1 LPs; The Beatles are the most popular recording artists in the UK and most of Europe, but as yet are all but unknown in America.**

| **1964** | January. At Brian Epstein's insistence Capitol Records launch $50,000 US marketing campaign: *'The Beatles are Coming'*
| 16 January - 4 February. Paris, France. Olympia Theatre. The Beatles in concert with Trini Lopez and Sylvie Vartan
| 1 February. 'I Want To Hold Your Hand' tops US *Billboard* Singles Chart; stays top for seven weeks. | 7 February. The Beatles fly to New York. Welcomed at JFK by 5000+ screaming fans. The group charms US press corps at airport press conference. | 9 February. New York. The Beatles appear on CBS-TV's *The Ed Sullivan Show*. Set new world record for largest-ever TV audience. 73+ million people in US watch show. | 10 - 21 February. The Beatles play the Washington Coliseum | Back to New York for two shows at Carnegie Hall | Snatch quick holiday in Florida. | February 16. The Beatles make second appearance on *The Ed Sullivan Show;* from Deauville Hotel, Miami Beach; 70+ million viewers tune in. | 22 February. The Beatles fly back to UK

| February - April. Recording sessions at Abbey Road Studios
| March. The Beatles hold 'Top 5' spots on US Singles Charts.
| 2 March - 4 April. The Beatles film *A Hard Day's Night* with the director Dick Lester. George Harrison meets Pattie Boyd—who plays a schoolgirl in the film. | Film shot and produced in 16 weeks. In profit even before scheduled July opening due to 'Special Preview' advance screenings in US and huge advance sales of soundtrack album; the real reason United Artists had originally commissioned the film.

| 9 March. NEMS Enterprises move from Liverpool to premises in London W1 | April. The Beatles have 12 songs in *Billboard* 'Top 100' | 4 June. The Beatles hold all 'Top 5' spots on *Billboard* Charts: 'Can't Buy Me Love'—'Twist & Shout'—'She Loves You'—'I Want to Hold Your Hand'—'Please, Please Me'

| June – July. The Beatles begin first leg of 'First World Tour'. 37 concerts in 27 days—taking in Denmark and Netherlands. Then Hong Kong, Australia, and New Zealand.

| 6 July. UK film premiere of *'A Hard Day's Night'*. A 'Royal Charity' event at Pavilion Theatre, Piccadilly Circus, London. Thousands of Beatles' fans outside cinema bring central London to a standstill. | 10 July. *'A Hard Day's Night'* LP and single b/w 'Things We Said Today' released in UK

| 11 August 11. US premiere *'A Hard Day's Night'* in New York | Andrew Sarris in *The Village Voice* calls it: *"...the Citizen Kane of jukebox movies."* | 19 August – 20 September. The Beatles tour US and Canada: 23 cities and 30 concerts in 30 days | 28 August. The Beatles meet Bob Dylan in New York. | Global *'Beatlemania'* erupts as film and album of *A Hard Day's Night* is released to worldwide acclaim | 9 October - 10 November. The Beatles 'Fifth UK Tour' with Mary 'My Guy' Wells | 27 November. 'I Feel Fine' b/w 'She's A Woman' released in UK | 4 December. *'Beatles For Sale'* LP released in UK | 24 December - 11 January. 'Another Beatles Christmas Show'. The group's second season of Christmas - New Year's holiday shows. This time at the Hammersmith Odeon, London | **1964 proves a truly remarkable year for The Beatles.** As George Harrison said later: *"If you look at our itinerary: we did a tour of England; a tour of Europe; a tour of America; two albums; and about 4 EPs, and three singles; and made a movie; all in the same year."*

| **1965** | 11 February. Ringo Starr marries his Liverpool girlfriend, Maureen Cox, in London | 22 February - 11 May. The Beatles fly to Bahamas to film *Help!* Directed by Dick Lester. | 22 March. Capitol Records release US LP—*The Early Beatles* | 9 April. The Beatles' ninth single: 'Ticket To Ride' b/w 'Yes It Is' released in UK | 11 April. The Beatles voted No.1 group—perform at annual *New Musical Express* poll winners' concert at Empire Pool, Wembley, London | 12 June. The Beatles notified they've each been awarded the MBE by British Prime Minister Harold Wilson. | 20 June - 3 July. The Beatles tour France, Italy, Spain. | 23 July. 'Help' b/w 'I'm Down' released UK

| 29 July. World premiere *Help!* Another 'Royal Charity' event at the London Pavilion | 6 August. *'Help'* LP released UK

| 14 August. The Beatles tape CBS-TV's *The Ed Sullivan Show* | 15 - 31 August. The Beatles tour US and Canada. The opening concert at Shea Stadium, New York—attracts a crowd of over 55,000 fans—unprecedented; a world record

| 27 August. The Beatles meet Elvis Presley at his rented Bel Air mansion in LA

| 26 October. The Beatles to Buckingham Palace to receive their MBEs from Queen Elizabeth in a formal ceremony | 1 December. *'Rubber Soul'* LP album released UK | 3 December. 'Day Tripper' b/w 'We Can Work It Out' single released UK | 3 - 12 December. The Beatles 'Sixth UK Tour' with the Moody Blues and Beryl Marsden. | **At the end of 1965 'Beatlemania' is still in full swing. The one question on everyone's lips:** *"Can the world ever get enough of The Beatles?"*

| **1966** | 21 January. George Harrison marries Patti Boyd in Esher, Surrey. | 4 March. London *Evening Standard* newspaper publishes Maureen Cleave's interview with John Lennon in which he says: *"Christianity will go...it will vanish and shrink. We're more popular than Jesus now. I don't know which will go first...rock 'n' roll or Christianity"*—a comment that will come back to haunt him. | 1 May. The Beatles perform again at *New Musical Express* poll winners' concert at Empire Pool, Wembley, London. Although never planned as such—it marks the group's last ever performance before a British paying audience. | 10 June. 'Paperback Writer b/w 'Rain' single released UK | 20 June. The Beatles return to Germany for a three-day tour that takes in Munich, Essen, and Hamburg—where they perform at Ernst-Merck-Halle. Meet with Astrid Kirchherr. | 27 June - 4 July. The Beatles tour Japan and the Philippines. Things don't go so well in Manila. Imelda Marcos—the wife of the country's president—all but commands their presence at a private party—but The Beatles refuse to play—and the group are rough handled on the way to the airport. | 5 August. *'Revolver'* LP album and 'Eleanor Rigby' b/w 'Yellow Submarine' single released in UK | 12 -29 August. The Beatles tour US and Canada | 28 August. San Francisco. The Beatles make last-ever public concert appearance at the city's Candlestick Park stadium. | 9 November. John Lennon meets Yoko Ono at the Indica art gallery in North London | **1966. The Beatles' decision to stop touring after their US Tour is unprecedented. And even though it opens the door to them becoming the first ever 'studio-based' rock band, musical pundits and fans, and many in the recording industry, can only wonder:** *"Does it signal the end of The Beatles?"*

| **1967** | 21 January. 17 February. 'Strawberry Fields forever' b/w 'Penny Lane' single released UK under mounting 'sales' pressure from EMI. Both songs originally envisioned as part of new album The Beatles are quietly working on at Abbey Road Studios. George Martin later states it was a huge mistake for him not to insist the songs should be held back as part of *'Sgt. Pepper's Lonely Hearts Club Band'* album | 1 June. ***'Sgt. Pepper's Lonely Hearts Club Band'*** album released UK—cover and 'Pop Art' insert designed by British 'Pop' artist Peter Blake—to all but universal acclaim | 25 June. The Beatles perform 'All You Need Is Love'—'live' via satellite—to a global television audience of over 200 million people—as UK's contribution to joint multi-international TV programme *Our World* | 7 July. 'All You Need Is Love' b/w 'Baby You're A Rich Man' single released UK.
| 27 August. Brian Epstein is found dead of a drug overdose at his home in London | 11 September - 3 December. The Beatles film *'Magical Mystery Tour'* | 24 November. 'Hello Goodbye' b/w 'I Am The Walrus' single released UK | 8 December. *'Magical Mystery Tour'* EP released UK | 26 December. *'Magical Mystery Tour'*—'Special Event' broadcast on BBC-TV Boxing Day programming. Critics and TV viewing audience divided in their response. | **1967. A year of unprecedented highs and an unfathomable low. The record-breaking success of *Sgt. Pepper* and the global acclaim of 'All You Need Is Love' are savagely tempered by Brian Epstein's untimely death, which leaves The Beatles all struggling to find a new way forward.**

| **1968** | 15 February - 12 April. The Beatles travel to Rishikesh, India, to study Transcendental Mediation with Maharishi Mahesh Yogi | 15 March. 'Lady Madonna' b/w 'The Inner Light' released UK | 11 May. The Beatles form new business entity: *Apple Corps Ltd.* with five separate divisions: Records. Film. Publishing. Electronics. Retail. | 17 July. World premiere of the iconic animated film *'Yellow Submarine'* at London Pavilion
| 30 August. 'Hey Jude' b/w 'Revolution' single released UK
| 8 November. John and Cynthia Lennon divorce | 22 November *'The Beatles'*—aka *"The White Album"*— released in UK

The cover and interior designed by famed British 'Pop' artist Richard Hamilton | **1968. A year of change. The group's double '*White Album*' more a collection of solo efforts; a reflection of the growing distance between each of The Beatles.**

| **1969** | 2 - 31 January. The Beatles film 'fly-on-the-wall' documentary-style *'Let It Be'* under the direction of Michael Lindsay-Hogg | 17 January. *'Yellow Submarine'* LP released in UK | 30 January. The Beatles give an 'impromptu' live performance—intended as a highlight of the film *Let It Be*—on the rooftop of Apple Corps' office on London's famed Savile Row | 12 March. Paul McCartney marries American photographer Linda Eastman at a civil ceremony in Marylebone, London | 20 March. John Lennon marries Yoko Ono in Gibraltar | 11 April. 'Get Back' b/w 'Don't Let Me Down' single released in UK | 1 May. 'The Ballad of John and Yoko' b/w 'Old Brown Shoe' single released UK | 26 September. *'Abbey Road'* LP released in UK | 31 October. 'Something' b/w 'Come Together' single released in UK | **1969. Things fall apart. The centre cannot hold. The clues are many, but only the group's inner-circle know for sure that The Beatles are now on the verge of breaking apart.**

| **1970** | 6 March. 'Let It Be' b/w 'You Know My Name (Look Up The Number)' single released UK | 10 April. Paul McCartney announces he has left The Beatles—and uses the occasion to promote the release of his forthcoming eponymous solo LP | 8 May. *'Let It Be'* LP released UK | 12 May. World premiere of documentary-style *'Let It Be'* in New York. | 20 May. UK 'double' premiere of *'Let It Be'* at London Pavilion and Liverpool's Gaumont cinema. | Following hard on Paul McCartney's announcement—the open acrimony between Beatles in the film—and Yoko Ono's seemingly constant presence throughout—confuses fans on both sides of the Atlantic—and the response is sombre to say the least. | **1970. The year the long and winding saga of The Beatles comes to an end. Each of The Beatles would go on to forge solo careers, with varying degrees of success. But everyone—here, there, and everywhere—who'd ever been a Beatles' fan—hoped and prayed for a reunion.**

A reunion that would never, could never, happen again after John Lennon was murdered—shot to death—by a deranged, supposed former Beatles' fan on the night of 8 December 1980, outside The Dakota; the exclusive apartment building on the Upper West Side of Manhattan, in New York City; where he lived with his wife Yoko Ono.

Followed then by the untimely death of George Harrison from the effects of lung cancer on 29 November 2001.

Yet—even with those twin tragedies—the magical music of The Beatles continues to live *on and on and on and on...*

The Beatles | *To The Top Of The Poppermost*

John Lennon once said that when he was a schoolboy; even when he later grew to be a teenager; he was always looking for someone to recognise him as a genius; someone who'd say 'Yes' to him. Then he realised that he had to believe it himself, first; say 'Yes' to himself, first; and not wait for others to acclaim him.

After which, he never once stopped believing that both he and The Beatles were destined for the very top. And never for a single moment did he stop urging himself and the other Beatles ever onward, to make that 'knowing' a reality:

"*Where we going to fellas?*" John would call out.
"*To the toppermost,*" the other Beatles would chorus back.
"*And which toppermost is that, fellas?*" John would shout.
"*The toppermost of the poppermost,*" The Beatles would all shout out together.

And then The Beatles would all cheer and laugh and nod their heads to one another in agreement—the pact between them remade anew.

"*We're all really the same person.
We're just four parts of the one.*"
— Paul McCartney.

Yeah. Yeah. Yeah.

PART ONE - PEOPLE. PLACES. VENUES.

1 - Liverpool People

Oh, I Get By With A Little Help From My Friends...

Aunt 'Mimi' Stanley | Julia Lennon | Mary McCartney | Mike McCartney | The Quarrymen | Ivan Vaughan | Pete Shotton | Nigel Walley | Colin Hanton | Rod Davis | Eric Griffiths | Len Garry | John Lowe | Stuart Sutcliffe | Bill Harry | Virginia Harry | Cynthia Lennon | Arthur Ballard | Allan Williams | 'Lord' Woodbine | Vinnie Ismail | Jim Gretty | Mona Best | Pete Best | Neil Aspinall | Brian Kelly | Ray McFall | Bob Wooler | 'Paddy' Delaney | Sam Leach | Terry McCann | Raymond Jones | Brian Epstein | 'Queenie' Epstein | Rex Makin | Joe Flannery | Alistair Taylor | Peter Brown | Tony Bramwell | Mal Evans | Beryl Adams | Rita Shaw | Freda Kelly | Maureen Starkey | Iris Caldwell | Cilla Black

What would the world have been like if Paul McCartney hadn't been introduced to John Lennon by a mutual friend on Saturday 6th July 1957? Or if John hadn't later tasked another friend, to ask Paul to join his 'Skiffle' group—The Quarrymen? Or if Paul hadn't then gone out of his way to ensure his schoolfriend George Harrison joined the group? Three genius musicians, singers, and composers; who would all go on to form the core of The Beatles; all come together; all the important early links in the magical chain of events entirely down to friendship.

That's why the ongoing interest in and continued relevance of all the many people The Beatles knew—and in some cases deeply loved—as they grew from schoolboys into teenagers—in Liverpool—and then evolved from teenagers into adults—in Liverpool and Hamburg and London. And why The Beatles' childhood friends—people they ran around the school playground with—larked about with—got into trouble with—are such important parts of their story. Especially the school friends John Lennon banded together to form The Quarrymen. One of whose members, Ivan Vaughan, was attending Liverpool Institute—the same secondary school as Paul McCartney—and had a strong inkling his two talented 'guitar-mad' friends should meet.

How very different things might have been if Ivan hadn't gone to Dovedale Primary School some years earlier and become best friends with John? For it was Ivan Vaughan who introduced Paul McCartney to John Lennon at St. Peter's Church Fete in Woolton, on Saturday afternoon, 6th July 1957.

So is it 'Nature' or 'Nurture' that defines us? Is it Family or Friends—*our peers*—who most influence us? Or is it a little bit of all and everything—with more than just a little help from our friends?

All the 'Liverpool People' you'll come across here brought something very special to 'The Early Years' of The Beatles. And perhaps none more so than Bill Harry, Bob Wooler, Ray McFall, Sam Leach, and Brian Epstein, all of who played unique roles in The Beatles' astonishing rise to fame, as well as being vital to the remarkable rise and rise of the whole 'Merseybeat' music scene.

But there's also Stu Sutcliffe—John Lennon's closest friend from Liverpool Art College—the immensely talented fine-artist who first played bass for The Beatles. And Pete Best—the young, brown-eyed handsome man who was The Beatles' first drummer—whose very presence helped the group get their all-important first gig in Hamburg, and who played with them for two hard-slog years before being unceremoniously pushed out of the band. And Neil Aspinall; Pete Best's closest friend; who stayed on as The Beatles' roadie and who went on to become The Beatles' most trusted confidante and the head of Apple Corps in London. Then, of course, there's the mythical Raymond Jones—the young man history tells us walked into NEMS and met Brian Epstein and set the whole magical mystery tour rolling. Every single person—Liverpudlians all—by birth or inclination—key to understanding the extraordinary early years of The Beatles.

AUNT 'MIMI' | John Lennon's aunt and legal guardian | 1903 - 1991 | Mary Elizabeth Smith née Stanley. | Respectable, elder sister of John Lennon's mother, Julia. Aunt Mimi—and her dairy-farmer husband George Smith—took John in and looked after him from the age of five when his mother went to live with another man. Aunt Mimi did everything she could to give John a loving and stable home at 'Mendips' 251 Menlove Avenue, Woolton, a suburb of Liverpool. John got on well with his Uncle George and was devastated when he died of a heart attack. John was twelve. Mimi was strict, but not unreasonably so given the circumstances; her only wish to help John stay on the straight and narrow path to what she hoped would be a proper middle-class upbringing. However, John's stubborn nature and rebellious spirit made for tumultuous times—at school as well as at home—but Mimi stood for only so much nonsense before firmly putting her foot down. Which, not unnaturally, meant that John revered, but also somewhat dreaded his Aunt Mimi. Mimi bought John his first 'proper' guitar from Hessy's Music Store—a second-hand Spanish guitar 'Guaranteed not to Split'—even though she later famously said to him in utter frustration at his decision to quit Liverpool Art College and go off to Hamburg with Paul, George, Stu, and Pete. *"The guitar's all right as a hobby, John Lennon, but you'll never make a living with it."*

Afterwards, even at the very height of *'Beatlemania'*, John never forgot all his Aunt Mimi had done for him and he always made sure to stay in touch; buying her a new home on the coast at Poole, in Dorset; and calling her on the telephone every week, without fail. She died, aged 88, in December 1991.

JULIA LENNON | John Lennon's mother | 1914 - 1958 | Julia Lennon née Stanley | Mother to John Lennon and his three half-sisters: Victoria, Julia, and Jacqui. Julia Lennon was flighty, 'off-beat', and by all accounts irrepressibly funny; a free spirit who always liked a good time and who was almost the polar opposite of her elder sister, Mimi. | Julia married Alfred Lennon, a merchant seaman, in December 1938 and gave birth to John Winston Lennon in October, 1940. When Alf, called 'Freddie' by his friends, disappeared off back to sea for almost the rest of the Second World War, Julia, like so many young women in war-torn England, took comfort wherever she could and in 1944 became pregnant by another man, a Welsh soldier. Not wanting to divorce Freddie, or re-marry, she gave the little girl, Victoria, born 1945, up for adoption.

When Julia continued to date other men and later moved in with John Dykins, her sister, the childless 'Mimi' Smith, stepped into the vacuum to take John into her home and act as responsible parent and guardian. Julia and John Dykins then lived as common-law husband and wife and had two daughters, Julia, born 1947, and Jacqui, born 1949. The family lived close to 'Mendips' and John kept in almost daily contact with his mother and in his teens would often stay the night at the Dykins' house.

The apple, it seems, doesn't fall far from the tree, for in the end it was Julia who would in many ways have the biggest impact on John. For it was she who introduced John to pop music; skiffle and rock 'n' roll; and taught him to play ukulele and banjo, and bought him his first guitar from a mail-order catalogue. John would later recall that it was his mother who first taught him to play the Buddy Holly song, 'That'll Be The Day'.

Mimi was at first very resistant to what she saw as Julia's increasingly bad influence on John, but seeing that John's love affair with music continued unabated, she and Julia came to a meeting of minds and hearts. Then came tragedy.

In July 1958, after visiting her sister, for afternoon tea and a chat, Julia was struck and killed by a motorcar driven by an off-duty policeman, mere steps away from Mimi's house.

Julia's sudden, tragic, all-too-early death was to affect John forever after and many of the songs he later composed gave clear voice to the huge and continued pain of his loss. 'Julia', 'Mother', and 'My Mummy's Dead'; three extraordinarily poignant songs where he bared his still-tormented heart to the world.

MARY McCARTNEY | Paul McCartney's mother |1909 - 1956 | Very much the heart and soul of the family; she was employed as a district nurse; uniform, bicycle, and all. And died from breast cancer within weeks of the initial diagnosis, when Paul was but 14 years of age. He was deeply traumatized by his mother's sudden death. Years later he revealed: *"That became a very big bond between John and me, because he lost his mum early on, too. We both had this emotional turmoil, which we had to deal with and, being teenagers, we had to deal with it very quickly. We both understood that something had happened that you couldn't talk about to anyone else."*

MICHAEL McCARTNEY | Paul McCartney's brother | 1944 - | Known professionally as Mike McGear. | Our Mike has always strived to stay out of Paul's giant shadow—as if. | A very keen amateur photographer, he took many iconic photos of the early days of The Beatles in Liverpool. | He's pursued a musical career of sorts; both as a solo artist and as part of the satirical comedy group, Scaffold, with acclaimed 'Liverpool poet' Roger McGough and the ever progressively acerbic John Gorman; very much a second generation 'Dissenters'. The trio scored chart hits in the Sixties with: 'Thank U Very Much' and 'Lily The Pink'.

Mike McCartney has since devised and presented a number of very popular radio shows. He's published a number of children's books. And is the author of *The Illustrated History of Rock Music*. His photographs are highly sought after by galleries and Beatles' fans the world over; many of which appear in his acclaimed books: *Mike Mac's White And Blacks... Plus One Colour. (An Intimate Portrait of Liverpool in the '60s).* | *Remember. Recollections And Photographs Of the Beatles.*

THE QUARRYMEN | John Lennon's 'Skiffle' group | Formed March 1957. | In every which way: The true start of The Beatles. The group was named after Quarry Bank Grammar School that John attended from the age of eleven. | Lonnie Donegan and 'Skiffle' were all the rage. Like thousands of teenagers the length and breadth of Britain, John responded urgently to the siren call and persuaded his Aunt Mimi to buy him a 'proper' guitar. She bought him one—*'guaranteed not to split'*—from Hessy's Music Stores. And so The Quarrymen were born.

The group comprised of whatever schoolmates John could convince or cajole into playing. The group's first gigs took place at private parties and local talent contests. The Quarrymen's repertoire, the skiffle hits of the day: 'Rock Island Line' 'Freight Train' 'Cumberland Gap' 'Midnight Special' 'Worried Man Blues'. Topped off by the old Liverpudlian sea-shanty—'Maggie May'—that John would one day reprise again atop Apple's Savile Row, London, headquarters at The Beatles' last ever appearance together.

The Quarrymen entered a qualifying round of TV show—*Carroll Levis 'Star Search'* at the Empire Theatre, Liverpool—but failed to make the grade. Undeterred, the group played on—with more and more gigs at local church and village halls, and youth clubs—including the all-important St. Peter's Church Fete on the 6th of July 1957. When Paul impressed John by not only playing and singing Eddie Cochran's 'Twenty Flight Rock' note perfectly—but also by being able to tune his guitar properly. Paul was duly asked to join the group.

The Quarrymen were booked to play The Cavern the following month—although without Paul, whose first gig with the group wasn't until that October— John being told in no uncertain terms by The Cavern's management to *"stick to skiffle and not to play anymore rock 'n' roll numbers."* | But the end of his musical beginnings was already in sight for John Lennon—he'd mined all he could—and the move from skiffle to rock 'n' roll was now inevitable. And by the time George Harrison joined, the group took their inspiration from the likes of Elvis, Little Richard, Buddy Holly, and Gene Vincent and were into playing such rockin' classics as: 'All Shook Up' 'That's All Right Mama' 'Hound Dog' 'Long Tall Sally' 'Lucille' 'Be-Bop-a Lula' 'Searchin' 'That'll Be The Day' 'It's So Easy' and 'Peggy Sue'

John and Paul started writing their own songs as Quarrymen—giving rise to such Lennon-McCartney delights as 'One After 909' 'Love of The Loved' and 'Hello Little Girl'. In the summer of 1958, The Quarrymen—John, Paul, George, Colin and 'Duff' Lowe—cut a demo disc with 'That'll Be The Day' on Side 'A' and the Harrison/McCartney original 'In Spite Of All the Danger' on the 'B' Side (Both of which can be heard on *The Beatles Anthology*).

IVAN VAUGHAN | Sometime tea-chest bass player | And later manager of The Quarrymen. | Ivan went to Dovedale Primary School—as did John. And was considered as madcap in his behaviour as ever John was—so it's no wonder the two of them got on 'like a house on fire'. It was Ivan who suggested to his schoolmate Paul McCartney; when from the age of eleven onwards he and Paul attended Liverpool Institute; that they should cycle over to see The Quarrymen perform at the St. Peter's Church Fete, in Woolton. *"It'll be a great place to chat up girls,"* Ivan promised. A momentous proposition as it turned out—as it was there, at the summer fete, on the afternoon of Saturday, 6 July 1957, that fate first played its hand when Ivan introduced Paul to John and the other The Quarrymen. And the rest, as they say, is musical history. Ivan Vaughan—remained a close friend of both John and Paul's throughout all his life. | Ivan Vaughan died from Parkinson's disease in 1994.

PETE SHOTTON | Washboard player | John Lennon's closest childhood friend; the two of them quite inseparable. Both boys attended Quarry Bank Grammar School. | It was Pete who would later approach Paul McCartney—on John's behalf—some ten days or so after Paul's impromptu Quarrymen audition at the St. Peter's Church Fete—to ask whether he'd like to join the group. | Pete's 'skiffle' career came to a sudden end when John got royally drunk one night and smashed the washboard over his head. Despite the head-banging incident Pete and John remained dear and close friends for the rest of their lives.

NIGEL WALLEY | Sometime tea-chest bass player | Playing a tea-chest bass could be such a finger blistering task—duties were often split with Ivan Vaughan. | Childhood friend of John Lennon. Attended Bluecoat Grammar School while John went to Quarry Bank. | Nigel later took on the role of the group's manager. The business card he had printed read: *Country. Western. Rock 'n' Roll. Skiffle. The Quarry Men. Open For Engagements.* | Nigel went on to become a golf professional. Enjoying a life of birdies rather then Beatles.

COLIN HANTON | **Drummer** | Joined The Quarrymen at the instigation of his friend Eric Griffiths. An apprentice upholsterer—and apprentice joiner, too, as it turned out—whose musical talent stretched to a shiny new set of drums recently acquired on hire-purchase from Hessy's. He beat time until the following year when he played at a Saturday night social club dance—emceed by none other than George Harrison's dad. The boys in the band drank a little too much free beer between sets—with somewhat disastrous results. Colin was furious and had an "all-bridges burned" argument with John—and left the group vowing never to beat time for them again.

ROD DAVIS | **Banjo player** | Met John Lennon at Sunday School when he was five years old. Pete Shotton, Nigel Walley and Ivan Vaughan were all in the same class. | Asked by his friend Eric Griffiths if he wanted to join a skiffle group he went out and bought a banjo from Hessy's for the princely sum of £5. The group's musical 'purist'—Rod left the group in September 1957 soon after their debut at The Cavern—because John insisted that The Quarrymen play more and more rock 'n' roll. Rod joined a jazz group.

ERIC GRIFFITHS | **Lead guitarist** | Eric lived in Woolton not far from John Lennon's home. He attended Quarry Bank School and was invited to join John's skiffle group when it was discovered he was the proud owner of a shiny new guitar—and had a close friend, Colin Hanton, who also happened to have a shiny new set of drums. Eric hit almost all of the right notes for well over a year until Paul McCartney—who was always pushing for the group to be better and better and better—pushed to have his chum, George Harrison, in the group. An 'impromptu' audition was arranged on the top deck of a double-decker bus—where George twanged out the tune of 'Raunchy'—a huge Bill Justis hit for Sun Records—note perfectly. Fate reared her lovely head a second time and the fourteen-year old George Harrison— joined John and Paul—to became the group's new lead guitarist. Eric was offered the position of bass guitarist, but declined, as he couldn't afford the requisite electric bass guitar or proper amplifier. With one too many guitarist already in the group, Eric faded away mid-way during 1958 by the simple expediency of never being asked again to attend any more group rehearsals.

LEN GARRY | **Sometime tea-chest bass player** | Len also attended Liverpool Institute. | Joined The Quarrymen early in 1957—at the age of fourteen—but was forced to leave the group the following year when he contracted TB. | He later recovered sufficiently to swap his tea-chest for a T-square and went on to become a successful architect.

JOHN LOWE | **Sometime piano player** | Nicknamed 'Duff'. | In the same class as Paul at Liverpool Institute. Joined in mid-1958. That same summer played on the group's demo disc, recorded and cut at Percy Phillips' home studio in Liverpool and along with his fellow Quarrymen; John, Paul, George, and Colin Hanton; duly paid his 3s 6d share of the session fee. Buddy Holly's 'That'll Be The Day' immortalised forever and a day as the 'A' Side. The Harrison/McCartney original 'In Spite Of All The Danger' forever enshrined as the future Beatles' first 'B' Side.

STUART SUTCLIFFE | **Fine Artist** | **Original Beatles' bass player** | **John Lennon's dearest friend** | 1940 - 1962 | In 1959 'Stu' Sutcliffe attended Liverpool College of Art where he and fellow art students John Lennon and Bill Harry all became very close friends. | Everyone who saw his work knew that Stu had a brilliant career ahead of him as a fine artist; especially his appointed art school tutor, Arthur Ballard, who encorged him and went out of his way to give him private lessons.

Stu's 'cool' attitude and look; dark glasses and swept back hair redolent of teenage *'rebel without a cause'* James Dean; and his utter dedication to his art impressed John greatly. | Stu was a respected member of the Student Union Committee—along with Bill Harry—and the two 'utilised' college funds to buy a public address system so their best friend's group—The Quarrymen—could play college dances; a sound idea for all concerned.

Stu later joined the fledgling Beatles after being persuaded by John to buy a Höfner electric bass guitar with the money he'd got from selling one of his paintings at the annual John Moore's Liverpool art exhibition. Stu was still struggling to learn to play the instrument when a few weeks later the group auditioned, unsuccessfully, for Larry Parnes and Billy Fury. | Urged on by John, Stu persisted with the bass, made a good show of it, but never really mastered it. His remarkable talents lay elsewhere.

In August 1960 Stu left the Art College and went to Hamburg with the group; again persuaded by John. The Beatles' line-up now strengthened by their new drummer Pete Best. | Along with the four other Beatles, Stu Sutcliffe played the Indra and Kaiserkeller clubs throughout the group's gruelling, non-stop, 16-week residency.

One memorable night, at the Kaiserkeller, Stu was introduced to the ethereally beautiful, preternaturally cool, blonde-haired, photographer's assistant Astrid Kirchherr, and her two closest male friends—art students Klaus Voormann and Jürgen Vollmer—all three of them inspired by French 'new wave' film makers and existentialist intellectuals. In honour of which, they wore black and styled themselves as 'Exis'. | The meeting proved momentous one for Stu and Astrid—a classic case of love at first sight—and the they got engaged just two months later.

Astrid Kirchherr took many of the early iconic black and white photographs of the group in Hamburg. And as her relationship with Stu deepened it was she who first cut his hair into the brushed down over the forehead style worn by young French art students of the time. The same look later universally regarded as The Beatles' iconic 'mop top' hairstyle.

When the group's second season in Hamburg at the Top Ten Club came to an end, in July 1961, Stu informed his mates he was leaving the group to stay on in Hamburg and take up painting again. His fervent hope to obtain a grant to attend the city's famed Staatliche Hochschule. His luck held. Eduardo Paolozzi, the noted British sculptor and a visiting professor, agreed to take him into his Master Class. The only concern then the sudden and increasingly severe headaches Stu had begun to suffer.

When the Beatles next returned to Hamburg—to play the newly opened Star-Club—John, Paul, and Pete Best came across a very distraught Astrid at the airport. And she informed them that Stuart had died of a cerebral haemorrhage just two days earlier, on the 10th April 1962. The result, it's long since been conjectured, of him having been beaten up and kicked in the head by a gang of Teddy Boys after playing a Beatles' gig at Lathom Hall in Liverpool, some years earlier.

John was absolutely shattered by the loss of his very dearest and closest friend. But as he supposedly told Astrid at the time— *"You have to hide your love and pain away—and move on. Live as if there is no tomorrow. Or you'll simply go under and forever be nowhere."* | Years later, John said in an interview: **"I looked up to Stu. I depended on him to tell me the truth. Stu would tell me if something was good and I'd believe him."**

BILL HARRY | *Mersey Beat* **Founder & Editor** | 1938 - |
Bill Harry attended Liverpool College of Art and was very close friends with John Lennon and Stuart Sutcliffe. | The three of them banding together—with a college friend Rod Murray—to form an 'agitprop' group they termed 'The Dissenters' whose singular aim was to make Liverpool justifiably famous for its arts: Stu and Rod with their paintings, Bill with his writing, and John with his music. | Bill, while still at art school, came up with the idea of publishing a 'What's On On Merseyside' newspaper to capture the volcanic eruption of popular music occurring all over Liverpool.

Mersey Beat - Merseyside's Own Entertainments Paper - was the first such newspaper of its kind in Britain. | *Mersey Beat*, published fortnightly, listed all the events and happenings on the local music and entertainments scene for the entire Merseyside area. | The newspaper was full of 'documentary' photos of individual artists, groups, and music events, and featured regular editorials, columnists, 45rpm and LP record chart listings and record reviewers; one of whom was Brian Epstein of North End Music Stores (NEMS) months before he claimed to have discovered The Beatles! | Bill Harry and his girlfriend, Virginia Sowry; later his wife; built the business together and did all the writing, designing, advertising, and distribution. As the demand and sales of *Mersey Beat* rose, the newspaper became known as *"the Teenager's Bible."* Local groups began calling themselves 'beat groups' and local promoters started advertising their events as 'Beat Sessions'. | *Mersey Beat* ran for four wildly successful years before merging with another pop music paper.

Bill and Virginia then followed The Beatles lead and moved to London, where Bill continued working as a rock journalist. With his unique background he was drawn increasingly into the world of PR. Clients included The Kinks, The Hollies, David Bowie, Pink Floyd, Led Zeppelin, the Beach Boys, and EMI, CBS, and Polydor record labels. | Hugely prolific; his many books on The Beatles and their 'Times'; as well as the evolving music scene; are encyclopaedic, beyond scholarly. | Today, Bill Harry runs a number of websites and 'facebook' pages dedicated to The Beatles, the Mersey Sound, and The Sixties.

At the time of writing—*Sgt. Pepper's* 50th anniversary—he's also about to publish more books. Good news all around; for as Mr. Harry so ably demonstrates in his writings and regular postings and commentaries, he still has the power to startle as well as entertain. | One of the more significant of all Beatles' people—as he was there at the very beginning of it all—in Liverpool—and knew John and Paul and George and Ringo—and Stuart Sutcliffe and Peter Best and Brian Epstein and Bob Wooler—and almost every other important player—up close and personally.

VIRGINIA HARRY née SOWRY | **Bill Harry's spouse and partner** | Virginia Sowry was Bill Harry's girlfriend while he was still at Liverpool Art College. She later became his wife. | Legend has it that the two met at Allan Williams' Jacaranda club, where it just so happened The Beatles were playing; John Lennon and Stu Sutcliffe, of course, being two of Bill's closest friends. | Virginia assisted Bill with the writing and designing of *Mersey Beat*. She ran the business, brought in advertising, did the accounts, while Bill did interviews. She also got to know most all of Liverpool's top 'beat' musicians as all the groups regarded the *Mersey Beat* office as the true centre of all that was happening around Merseyside—and increasingly the world beyond. | Bill and Virginia Harry were considered so integral to the rise and rise of 'the Mersey Sound' that a prominent London newspaper-columnist at the time dubbed them: *"Mr. and Mrs. Mersey Beat."*

CYNTHIA LENNON née POWELL | John Lennon's first wife | 1939 - 2015 | John and Cynthia met when both were students at Liverpool Art College. Cynthia's rather prim demeanour contrasted hugely with John's would-be Teddy Boy rebelliousness. But love conquered all—at least for a time. | Cynthia changed her appearance to appeal to John's oft-stated preference for Brigitte Bardot. She dutifully dyed her hair blonde, cut it into the requisite fringe style; wore tight sweaters and leather skirts; anything and everything to make John happy.

On the very cusp of Beatles fame, Cynthia discovered she was pregnant. When she told John, he simply said, "We better get married then." And they did—with Brian Epstein, The Beatles new manager, stepping in to take control of the nuptials. He arranged the civil marriage service at a local Liverpool registry office and treated the happy couple to a wedding reception lunch at a local hotel—with Paul and George—in attendance. But not Ringo, as he'd only just joined the group and was still very much the new boy. And no Aunt Mimi, either; she very much disapproved of the marriage; for obvious reasons. It limited John's future, as she saw it, and had unfortunate echoes of John's own mother—her sister—Julia's 'pregnancies out of wedlock'.

Brian Epstein gave John and Cynthia the use of his Liverpool city centre flat as a wedding gift. The whole situation made even more awkward by the established show business PR credo that young male stars should be unmarried and accessible; all the better for their fans to fantasise over; certainly never for any such teenage idol to already be the father of young child.

Cynthia gave birth to a son, Julian, but had to pretend to be nothing more than a close friend of John and the group. A newspaper eventually revealed the marriage in banner headlines and John and Cynthia—and Brian Epstein and the other Beatles—did their best to ride the ensuing publicity storm. But Cynthia and Julian had to put up with several very difficult years as John was pulled ever further and further away into the global maelstrom that was *'Beatlemania'* and they were forced to remain in the shadows.

Cynthia and John later moved to London and travelled the world together. But they divorced when John met Yoko Ono at a London art gallery reception and both fell deeply in love. Soon after which John proclaimed that he wanted to marry his new found soul mate. The couple eventually divorced and Cynthia remarried; though she was never allowed to forget that she was once married to 'Beatle John'. In 2005 she wrote her side of the story in a book simply entitled *'John'*—dedicated to Julian, and John's sisters, Julia and Jacqui, *"all three of whom have had to cope with the pain that being part of the Lennon legend imposed."*

ARTHUR BALLARD | Fine artist and Liverpool Art College teacher | 1915 - 1996 | Accomplished painter—many of his art works bought by eminent private collectors. Taught at the Liverpool College of Art from 1947 to 1980. | Arthur Ballard took a great personal interest in Stuart Sutcliffe as he considered him to be an extraordinarily gifted young artist with a brilliant career ahead of him—and would often provide his student with additional off-campus tuition when Stu skipped other tutor's classes as being boring and a waste of his 'painting' time. Not the least because Stuart also shared a passion for the works of the Dutch abstract painter Nicolas de Staël.

Arthur Ballard also took an interest in another 'gifted' but rebellious art student, John Lennon, and interceded on his behalf when the future Beatle was threatened with expulsion from the art college. The future looked hugely promising for Stuart Sutcliffe—especially when he sold one of his large canvases on display at the John Moore's Annual Art Exhibition, to none other than John Moore himself. | Arthur was disappointed, to say the least, when Stu later informed him that he'd used the prize money to buy himself a bass guitar and was giving up 'art' for the time being to go be the new bassist for John Lennon and his group, The Beatles, about to embark on their first ever season playing the riotous nightclubs of Hamburg.

ALLAN WILLIAMS | The Beatles' first ever promoter, agent, and would-be manager | Serial entrepreneur and club owner | *'The Man Who Gave The Beatles Away'* | 1930 - 2016 | Born in the Liverpool suburb of Bootle; of Welsh heritage. | Owner of Liverpool's Jacaranda Coffee Bar and Blue Angel nightclub. (We'll draw a quick veil over his co-ownership of the New Cabaret Artistes Club, where he once booked the fledgling Beatles to accompany a stripper, named Janice.) | The man who booked Gene Vincent and Eddie Cochran to headline a concert at Liverpool Stadium. | The man who arranged for 'The Silver Beetles' to audition for Billy Fury and famed London impresario Larry Parnes. | The group failed the audition but Williams arranged for The Silver Beatles to back Johnny Gentle, another of Parnes' ever-growing stable of rock singers, on a 9-day tour of Scotland. | He later arranged for The Beatles to play a residency at Indra Cabaret club in Hamburg's infamous Reeperbahn red-light district. The first of a series of engagements in the rock 'n' roll clubs of St. Pauli that would utterly transform The Beatles as a group and ultimately set them on a course that would change popular music forever. | As Mark Lewishon, the world's leading authority on The Beatles, says: *"No Allan Williams... No Hamburg. Without Hamburg... No Beatles!"*

Having seen the rise and rise of teenage coffee bars in London; the most famous example, Soho's 2i's Coffee Bar where Larry Parnes discovered Tommy Steele and Cliff Richard first sang his way to stardom; Williams opened the Jacaranda coffee bar and club in Liverpool in September 1958. He asked a couple of students from the nearby art college; one of whom was Stuart Sutcliffe, the other John Lennon; to paint the toilets and provide a mural for the cellar where he intended to feature 'live' music. The 'Jac' quickly became a key part of the local music scene.

Williams sold his share of the New Cabaret Artistes Club and he and business partner 'Lord' Woodbine, a popular West-Indian bandleader and calypso singer, visited Amsterdam and Hamburg on the proceeds to check out the club scene; ostensibly in search of new business ideas.

In Hamburg, Williams ventured down into the vast confines of the Kaiserkeller; a basement cellar club that could house five hundred people and more. A German band was doing its best to play rock 'n' roll and failing badly, the audience decidedly unmoved. Williams noticed how the audience was instantly electrified, however, whenever the sounds of Elvis Presley and Tommy Steele were played on the club's jukebox. He introduced himself to the club's owner, Bruno Koschmider, and waxed lyrical on the possibilities and profits to be made by presenting 'live' Liverpool rock 'n' roll groups. All of which, he explained, he was in the perfect position to supply. He even produced a tape he'd recorded of groups playing at 'the Jac', but the only thing that could be heard was the crackly noise of static. And so no deal. The two parted company, amiably, with the understanding that Herr Williams would soon send more tapes. Allan Williams returned to Liverpool; the seeds of 'live' rock 'n' roll as a sound business venture firmly planted. And how.

Within days Koschmider took off for London in the hopes of finding himself a real 'live' rock 'n' roll group. Which he did, at the 2i's Coffee Bar, in Soho. And he signed up a hastily formed ad-hoc group of London musicians who quickly dubbed themselves The Jets; one, of whom, was Tony Sheridan.

Meanwhile, in Liverpool, Allan Williams was busy trying to placate Liverpool group, Derry and The Seniors, when the concert tour he'd arranged for them with Larry Parnes had fallen through. Williams again eyed Soho's 2i's Coffee Bar as a place of possible salvation and travelled down to London with Derry and the group to try and arrange an audition to get them work.

Incredibly, in a one in million chance, Bruno Koschmider happened to be in the audience, having returned to London to look for more Britisher rock 'n' rollers. The Jets having already been lured away to play the newly opened rival Top Ten Club, back in Hamburg. This time Williams sealed the deal. And just three days later Derry and The Seniors were Hamburg bound to become the very first Liverpool beat group to play the Kaiserkeller. Williams also offered to supply Koschmider with other top-notch Liverpool groups and the wily Hamburg businessman just happened to own the very strip club he could repurpose; the Indra Cabaret Club; and a second deal was struck.

Back in Liverpool Williams hunted round for a group to go to Hamburg, but there were no takers. Liverpool's top group Rory Storm and the Hurricanes were set for a season at a Butlin's Holiday Camp. Gerry and The Pacemakers weren't at all interested. Back at the 'Jac' John Lennon asked "*Why not do something for us, Allan?*" "*But you lot haven't even got a drummer*," Allan retorted. "*We'll get one soon enough*," said John. And they did. In short order The Beatles; or Silver Beatles as they were still called; alighted upon novice drummer Pete Best, playing with his group, The Blackjacks, at the Casbah Coffee Club.

Not long afterwards, on a windy day in August 1960, John, Paul, George, Stu, and Pete took the ferry to the Hook of Holland and were on their way to Hamburg. Driven across Holland to the German port of Hamburg by Allan Williams himself. All five musicians; plus Allan's wife, Beryl, her brother Barry Chang, and calypso singer and Williams's business partner 'Lord' Woodbine; everyone cramped into an old Austin campervan specially hired for the occasion; with no extra seats and just the suitcases and the group's equipment to sit on. Everything so cramped and crowded by the time they reached Hamburg they'd even dropped the word 'silver' from their name. Allan Williams's express reason for driving to Hamburg; to try and talk Bruno Koschmider into giving him exclusive rights to book rock 'n' roll groups. And ever the keen-eyed businessman he simply took The Beatles with him to cut down on expenses.

Koschmider put The Beatles into the much smaller Indra Cabaret Club, a former strip club, and not his more established Kaiserkeller club. And as no hotel accommodations had been arranged for the group, he 'housed' them at the back of his porn cinema—Bambi Kino. The conditions were utterly squalid, but it didn't deter The Beatles; they just wanted to play rock 'n' roll.

The Beatles played the club for 48 nights and whenever the pace slackened Koschmider yelled "*Mach schau! Mach schau!*"— "*Make a big show! Make a big show!*"—at them. But they made so much of a show it led to a series of excessive noise complaints and the local police ordered Koschmider to cease 'live' rock 'n' roll at the Indra. He hurriedly moved them to the Kaiserkeller to work out their contract as second on the bill to the group about to take up a residency at the club—Rory Storm and The Hurricanes; the booking again arranged by Allan Williams.

Koschmider offered to extend The Beatles' contract for another two months—with various added restrictions. The Beatles wanted the work and signed the contract, but it was notes of music they focussed on far more than words on paper. Their troubles began when, in between sessions at the Kaiserkeller, they took to 'jamming' with singer-guitarist Tony Sheridan at the rival Top Ten Club. It very quickly led to a nasty falling out with Koschmider that, as November 1960 came to an end, saw underage George Harrison deported and troublemakers Paul McCartney and Pete Best ordered out of Germany.

When George Harrison turned eighteen and was officially able to re-engage in work, The Beatles returned to Hamburg to play a full season at Top Ten Club. Allan Williams sent a letter requesting the group pay him his rightful 'managerial' commission. The Beatles refused. Which led to a bitter parting of the ways. Williams never forgave The Beatles for what he regarded as gross business discourtesy.

In 1962 when Brian Epstein asked his advice about becoming the group's manager, Allan told him in no uncertain terms:

"I wouldn't touch The Beatles with a ten-foot barge pole. They diddled me. They'll diddle you."

In 1975 Allan Williams wrote his version of events in his book *'The Man Who Gave The Beatles Away'*. | Allan Williams died 30 December 2016 in Liverpool. | As a coda to all this past animosity between old Liverpool pals, it's nice to be able to relate that in 1995 Paul McCartney reflected back on those early days they all shared together:

"When we started off, we had a manager in Liverpool called Allan Williams. He was a great bloke... a real good motivator... he was very good for us at the time."

| **Side Bar** | **Eddie Cochran and Gene Vincent's triumphant UK concert tour** | The two American rock 'n' roll stars played Liverpool Empire for six days in March 1960. Following its 'sold out' success, Allan Williams made arrangements with Larry

Parnes, the British promoter of the tour, for a special one-off concert at Liverpool Stadium for that coming May. Tragically, Eddie Cochran never made the concert. He was killed in a car crash in the village of Chippenham, near Bath, on April 17—all but at the end of the first leg of the tour. Gene Vincent survived the crash and, even though severely battered and bruised, with a broken leg and on painkillers—headlined the concert in Liverpool. Allan Williams added Liverpool's top rock groups to the bill, to try make up for the newly departed Cochran, and by all accounts it was a 'Teddy Boy' stairway to heaven sensation.

| **Side Bar** | **Allan Williams' bitter parting of the ways with The Beatles** | The Beatles' first Hamburg club residency ended rather ignominiously with George Harrison's summary deportation for being underage and the police soon after speedily ordering Pete Best and Paul McCartney out of the country.

Koschmider's original contract with Allan Williams forbade The Beatles to play anywhere within a 25-mile radius—some say 40-mile—of any of his clubs without his express permission. Koschmider was therefore incensed when The Beatles—having completed their residency at the Kaiserkeller—left to play with Tony Sheridan then headlining the newly opened Top Ten Club owned by archrival Peter Eckhorn. The fact Tony Sheridan—and The Jets—had previously been the star attraction at the Kaiserkeller only made matters worse.

It was Koschmider, of course, who tipped off Hamburg police about George Harrison being underage and not having a work permit. But to ensure The Beatles really got the message he also charged Paul McCartney and Pete Best with 'setting fire' to their 'salubrious' accommodations at Bambi Kino; a veritable case of 'Hell hath no fury like a worm that's turned'.

The Beatles returned to Hamburg April 1961 to take up residency at Top Ten Club. A booking they'd initiated themselves and had completed with help from Stuart Sutcliffe and Mona Best dealing directly with club owner Peter Eckhorn. At first, simply to get Pete's hastily 'abandoned' drum kit shipped back to Liverpool—later to set up the group's return to Hamburg.

When he heard of the group's new club engagement Allan Williams wrote them a letter to demand payment of what he thought was his rightful 10% 'managerial' fee. The Beatles declined to pay him anything at all. As they saw it, Allan had simply been their first booking agent—and never their manager.

We best draw another veil over Allan Williams' expletive laden response—but he did ban the group forever afterwards from his Blue Angel nightclub in Liverpool.

When Brian Epstein later become The Beatles manager they pleaded with him to try set things right—as the Blue Angel was where all Liverpool's better groups and visiting bands went after playing a gig. Allan Williams finally relented and agreed to let them back in to his nightclub. And in the end probably got every penny he thought they owed him by 'managing' their always very hefty drinks bill.

| **Author's Note** | **Allan Williams** | I have to admit that I'd long regarded Allan Williams as being nothing but a chancer, an opportunist, even a fantasist, but a close reading of Mark Lewishon's immaculate research published in his *'The Beatles: All These Years Vol. 1 Tune In'* left me with no other choice but to rethink and re-evaluate the man. And I now place Allan Williams in the pantheon of Beatles' *'God Blessed Good Guys'*—and if not held in quite the same esteem as Brian Epstein and George Martin—certainly worthy to sit alongside such Beatles' luminaries as Bill Harry and Bob Wooler and Ray McFall and Sam Leach—and Astrid Kirchherr and Klaus Vorrmann—and, yes, even Bruno Koschmider and Tony Sheridan—as one of those very special Liverpool and Hamburg People whose influence on events you can well ponder and say…*"Without whom the world might have been a very different and far-less richer place…"*

'LORD' WOODBINE | Musician | Calypso Singer - Songwriter | Bandleader | Club owner | Entrepreneur | 1929 - 2000 | Born Trinidad | Harold Adolphus Phillips—also known as 'Woody' | Served in RAF during WWII | 1948. Sailed from Caribbean on HMT *Empire Windrush*. Arrived England. Settled in Liverpool.

Phillips formed the 'All-Steel Caribbean Band'—one of the very first 'steel bands' in Britain. He was also one of the country's first calypso singers | Dubbed "Lord" as mark of respect by fellow musicians and fans; "Woodbine" from a calypso he'd written about the British 'working class' brand of cigarettes. | He ran two clubs in Liverpool 8: New Cabaret Artistes Club and the New Colony Club. And was at various times Allan Williams' business partner. | The Silver Beetles played both of his clubs.

'Lord' Woodbine and his steel-pan band regularly performed at Williams' Jacaranda coffee bar and music club. And one night so impressed an audience of visiting German seamen they were urged to 'come' play the nightclubs of St. Pauli. The band left for Hamburg within days without informing Williams. Renamed the 'Royal Caribbean Steel Band' they were a huge hit. | He returned to Liverpool and convinced Williams to go see Hamburg for himself. Thus sowing the seeds of the Liverpool-Hamburg link.

When Allan Williams' later booked The Beatles to play Hamburg and drove them there in a hired campervan, 'Woody' travelled with them. There's a famous photo of him *en route* sitting with Paul, George, Stuart, Pete, *et al*, in front of the Arnhem War Memorial, in the Netherlands. | Ever ebullient, Woodbine also performed numerous times in Hamburg as a solo artist.

Years later Allan Williams recalled: ***"No 'Lord' Woodbine. No Beatles. I'd never have thought of going to Hamburg, otherwise."***

VINNIE ISMAIL | Musician | Singer | 1942 - 2007 | a.k.a. Vince Tow and Vinnie Tow | Somali-Irish | Born Granby, Liverpool 8 | Rhythm guitarist famed amongst both black and white Liverpool musicians of the time for his affable personality and 'natural' musical ability. | The man that taught John Lennon the magic 'string-bar-seventh' chord and, importantly, how to play rhythm-guitar, just like Chuck Berry. | 1961-63. Lead singer-guitarist Vince & His Volcanoes. | He performed with Liverpool groups the Harlems, the Valentinos, and the Handful; played guitar for The Chants, an all-male, all-black vocal group first featured—and backed—by The Beatles, at The Cavern.

| Side Bar | The Beatles and the influence of Liverpool's black musicians | Liverpool's long history as a 'multicultural' city made the sound of 'black' music part and parcel of The Beatles' cultural roots. As eager young musicians—ever hungry to learn anything and everything about their newfound passion—willing to take a bus-ride across Liverpool to go see and hear and learn how to play a new chord on their guitars—John and Paul grew up surrounded by a whole cadre of accomplished black Liverpool musicians playing sounds and rhythms unlike anything heard on BBC radio or by local dance orchestras. On steel-pans, drums, guitars, banjos, pianos, trumpets, or saxophones—anything at all that gave sound to music. Be it calypso or blues; West Indian or African-American; it was only the sound and rhythm that ever mattered to the two young would-be professional musicians and songwriters; not where a song or sound had originated from. The sound just had to be great. And even if only in this regard; singer, songwriter, steelpanist 'Lord' Woodbine; rhythm guitarist Vinnie Ismail; lead singer Derry Wilkie; the a capella group The Chants, with lead singer Eddie Amoo; and countless other black Liverpool musicians; would all have had an influence on the early musical growth of The Beatles.

JIM GRETTY | Singer, guitarist, entertainer, sometime agent and music promoter | Much loved guitar teacher | *'Country music a specialty'* | 1914 - 1992 | One of the unsung heroes of the whole Merseybeat scene according to Bill Harry—and he should know. | Chief salesman at Frank Hessy's music store in Stanley Street, Liverpool—in the late 1950s and early 1960s—he sold guitars and other musical instruments to musicians from all over Merseyside.

In 1957 he sold a Spanish guitar—*'guaranteed not to split'*—to 17-year old John Lennon (and his Aunt Mimi). | Jim gave free lessons with every guitar purchased. And although there's no record of John having ever attended the regular Monday evening sessions—Gerry Marsden and countless others did. And with as many as 20-30 youngsters all strumming away—the relevant guitar chords chalked up on a blackboard—'Singing The Blues' a rite of passage—the weekly lessons became legendary with generations of would-be guitarists. | In true affection Gerry Marsden nicknamed him *"Grim Jetty."*

Jim booked The Beatles a number of times—most notably for a charity variety show at the Albany Cinema, Maghull. The event of singular importance as it's where Brian Epstein actually first saw The Beatles perform on October 15 1961 and not, as the official history has it, at The Cavern, on 9 November.

By all accounts, unfailingly generous, Jim offered advice on music and the music business to any group that asked. To show his support he built a 'Wall of Fame'—a panorama of photographs of local bands that stretched from one end of Hessy's main showroom to the other.

Jim Gretty finally put down his guitar and left the building in 1992—at age 78.

MONA BEST | Mother of Pete Best - The Beatles' Hamburg-days' drummer | Owner of the Casbah Coffee Club | Liverpool music promoter | *De facto* **first manager of The Beatles; even if self-appointed | 1924 -1988 |** Saturday, 29 August, 1959, Mona opened one of Merseyside's first ever rock 'n' roll cellar clubs—the Casbah—in the cellars of her huge Victorian house, in Haymans Green, in the suburb of West Derby. As much a place for her 'Skiffle' and rock 'n' roll mad sons Pete and Rory to dance to music played on a jukebox, as a safe coffee-bar-style haven for other local teenagers, it fulfilled a definite need as in its first year the Casbah enrolled over 1,000 club members.

Mona's second rockin' idea was to hire live groups to play the Casbah at weekends. The Quarrymen had all but disbanded at the time—George Harrison was moonlighting in another band—but they reformed specially for the club's opening and for the next couple of months The Quarrymen were the Casbah's house band. Then a dispute over the split of the group's fee in late October caused John, Paul, and George to walk out. Even so, Bill

Harry makes an excellent case for the Casbah being *"the true birthplace of The Beatles"* as the group wasn't officially booked into the Cavern until nearly two years later.

It was Mona who urged her eldest son Pete—up to that point merely a face in the adoring crowd—to form a group to fill the vacuum left by The Quarrymen's departure. Mona bought Pete a brand new set of drums and *"Hey presto!"* the newest beat group in town, The Blackjacks, took over the club's weekend spot. | All of which meant that Pete and his drums were ripe for the plucking when the once-again 'drummerless' Beatles asked him to join them just prior to their first trip to Hamburg, in August 1960.

And when The Beatles returned to Liverpool in disarray; their first Hamburg club residency brought to an abrupt end; it was Mona who arranged to get Pete's drums and the group's other equipment shipped back. Almost everything having been abandoned when the officially 'too young to work' George and supposed arsonists Pete and Paul were thrown out of Germany.

It was Mona Best who then encouraged the group to get back to where they once belonged, got them to replay the Casbah, and who secured a series of gigs for them at local village halls—in Tuebrook and Knotty Ash—the posters proclaiming *"The Return of the Fabulous Beatles."* | Mona even tried to get the group featured on Granada TV's *People and Places* show.

It was Mona who set The Beatles up with their first ever road manager—Neil Aspinall—an accountancy-student and friend of Pete's—who was also a lodger of hers at the time.

It was Mona who took care of business, who dealt with the other Liverpool promoters and the many club and hall owners, and who made sure the group always got paid. And so to all intents and purposes she and Pete effectively co-managed the group for upwards of two years.

Mona continued to offer advice when Brian Epstein officially took over as manager of the group, which created some degree of awkwardness. | She was shocked and furious when Pete was sacked from The Beatles without warning following the group's first session with George Martin at EMI's Abbey Road Studios, London, on 6 June 1962. | Brian Epstein did all he could afterwards to set Pete up in another Liverpool beat group—Lee Curtis and The All Stars—that later evolved into The Pete Best Band. | Mona never once wavered in her support for Pete, before or after The Beatles. And even if Pete never spoke to The Beatles again, she did, as she loaned her family's army medals for John to wear on his *Sgt. Pepper's Lonely Hearts Club Band* uniform. | Mona had a son—Roag—with Neil Aspinall—but they never married. | A veritable force of nature; Mona Best was hugely instrumental in the success of The Beatles in the early years. | Mona Best died—Liverpool—9 September 1988.

PETE BEST | The Beatles' Original Drummer | 1941- | Peter Randolph Best was a member of The Beatles from August 1960 to August 1962, in Hamburg, Liverpool, and London. Although whether it was Pete's drumming ability or his brand new, blue, mother-of-pearl drum kit that first impressed the other four Beatles—John, Paul, George, and Stuart—is open to conjecture. The group needed a drummer to secure their first Hamburg gig and young Pete fit the bill—perfectly.

In the eyes of a great many Liverpool fans, Pete Best was the most popular member of the group—certainly the most handsome. Even Bob Wooler—the resident DJ at The Cavern—thought so and dubbed Pete: *"mean, moody and magnificent."* Compared to his more overtly expressive band-mates, though, Pete was quiet, shy, taciturn, and much more reserved.

Nevertheless, Pete became renowned for his atomic 4/4 beat—relentlessly kicked out on bass drum—thumped home with both drumsticks. He played drums at Indra Cabaret and Kaiserkeller clubs during The Beatles' first Hamburg residency—and at Top Ten Club during their second visit.

It was Pete who bashed the skins at the famous Litherland Town Hall gig on 27 December, 1960, that set all of Liverpool on notice that a huge new rockin' force had blown into town—*'Direct From Germany'*.

It was Pete who also played hundreds of times with The Beatles at Ray McFall's Cavern Club and played at Sam Leach's momentous 'Operation Big Beat' events at The Tower Ballroom, New Brighton.

It was Pete who played drums at the 'audition' for Decca Records, in London, on 1 January 1962, when The Beatles were rejected as being *"old hat."* He also played on the 'Artists Test' session at EMI's Abbey Road Studios, on 6 June 1962. The fateful day record producer George Martin, head of Parlophone, informed Brian Epstein that he didn't consider Pete's drumming anywhere near steady enough for recording purposes and would need to hire a session drummer for any future sessions.

Martin's decision was of such immediate concern to the other three Beatles they kept it from Pete and began to conspire to push him out of the group. And ultimately they replaced him with The Hurricanes' drummer, Ringo Starr. The only credible excuse: that John, Paul, and George; having been repeatedly rejected by Decca, Pye, Philips, and EMI—and all their various subsidiary labels; were in abject fear of losing, as they saw it, their last ever chance of winning a recording contract with a major label. | It wasn't The Beatles' finest hour and shocked Liverpool fans vented their anger. One outraged Pete Best fan going so far as to give George Harrison a black eye for his troubles.

Brian Epstein did all he could to make amends by madly pulling strings behind the scenes so Pete Best could join Lee Curtis and The All Stars. Lee Curtis later left the group. The Pete Best Band, now named, cut a disc for Decca, but it failed to chart and the record company eventually dropped the group.

Pete Best left the music business and became a civil servant. But with the break up of The Beatles, in 1970, and the murder of John Lennon, in 1980, demand to see and hear original Beatle Pete play his 'atomic 4/4 beat' grew and grew. | Pete served as a technical advisor on the TV film—*The Birth of The Beatles*—produced by Dick Clark Productions, in 1979. | In 1985 Pete (and Patrick Doncaster) authored an autobiography—*Beatle! The Pete Best Story.* | With no little coaxing—from friends and fans alike—Pete took up his drumsticks again and reformed The Pete Best Band. He started doing club dates to wildly enthusiastic audiences in England—toured the United States—and has since been all around the world. He still tours with his band—aided and abetted by his younger brother Roag.

NEIL ASPINALL | The Beatles' *'Roadie'* Road Manager | 1941 - 2008 | Neil Stanley Aspinall | Born Prestatyn, North Wales | Originally studied to be an accountant. Took up lodgings at the West Derby family home of Mona Best and became close friends with her eldest son, Pete—a friendship that ultimately led him to give up his accountancy studies and buy an old van and take on the full-time job of 'Roadie' for The Beatles.

Neil and Mona Best—who was separated from her husband—had a relationship and then a son, Roag, but they didn't marry or remain together. | When Pete Best was forced out of the group Neil, at Pete's urging, stayed true to The Beatles.

In 1963, as *'Beatlemania'* increasingly took hold, he took on Mal Evans—previously a bouncer at The Cavern—to be his assistant. And when The Beatles relocated to London later that year so did he and so did Mal. | When The Beatles gave up touring in 1996 he was made their 'Personal Assistant'.

In 1968 he married Suzy Ornstein daughter of Bud Ornstein, chief executive of United Artists Pictures (UK), the US film company that produced *A Hard Day's Night*

Ever loyal, trusted, and unfailingly discreet; he was appointed Managing Director and Chief Executive of Apple Corps Ltd, London. And after The Beatles broke up he continued to look after the group's many legacy business interests and was the moving force behind *The Beatles Anthology*.

Neil Aspinall was one of the very few people in the "inner circle" who never wrote or published a 'tell all' book about his time with The Beatles. | He died 24 March 2008, much admired, and very much missed by all who knew him.

BRIAN KELLY | Merseyside music promoter | 'Beekay Promotions' | One of the more important Liverpool promoters at the turn of the Sixties; no question; however hard-nosed, blunt, and acerbic he was in all his dealings. | Kelly was very much key to establishing the network of Merseyside venues that double-kicked the thumping sound of Merseybeat into high gear. He built his own reputation—and that of Beekay Promotions—around a number of particular venues: Litherland Town Hall; the Aintree Institute; Lathom Hall, Seaforth; Alexandra

Hall, Crosby; the dancehalls in Litherland and Lathom of particular significance in Beatles' history.

Canny businessman that he was, before booking any band on a regular basis, Kelly always had them perform "an audition" for him at one of his venues to see whether they could "cut the mustard" or not. The Silver Beetles first played at Lathom Hall on 14 May 1960—passed the audition—and, advertised as 'the Silver Beats', were 'officially' booked to play the following week. They didn't appear, however, as they were up, up, and away in Scotland, backing singer Johnny Gentle on his 9-day tour. In all their excitement they'd simply forgotten to inform Kelly of the fact. Needless to say, Kelly was not amused by their 'no show' and refused to book them ever again.

Thankfully, for all concerned, if not the history of pop music, some time in the second or third week of December 1960, Bob Wooler—who regularly worked as a compère for Beekay Promotions' events; and who later became the resident DJ and compère at the Cavern Club—persuaded Kelly to change his mind about The Beatles—now called—and newly returned from their first season in Hamburg—to play a post-Boxing Day dance at Litherland Town Hall, on 27 December 1960; the event that would change the fortunes of The Beatles forever afterwards.

RAY McFALL | Owner of The Cavern Club | 1926 - 2015 |
Liverpool accountant and businessman took over ownership of The Cavern Club in October 1959. The Cavern, which he bought from a business client, was located in the basement of a fruit and vegetable warehouse in Mathew Street, in Liverpool's city centre. It was originally a jazz-only club—with definitely no rock 'n' roll allowed. But the eagle-eyed McFall took early note of the growing wave of youngsters flocking to the city's 'jive hives' and he began to book rock 'n' roll groups. An evening residency headlined by The Swinging Bluejenes proving to be a hugely popular attraction. His breakthrough idea was to put on weekday 'work-day' lunchtime 'jive' sessions and hire Bob Wooler as resident club DJ and compère. It was Bob Wooler who then suggested, repeatedly, that he hire The Beatles to play

the lunchtime slot. The Beatles made their debut as 'Guests' of The Swinging Bluejenes, at The Cavern, on the evening of 9 February 1961—and began their lunchtime residency soon after. They proved so popular they were quickly given their own evening residency. And the rest as they say is music history.

Legend says that it was at was at The Cavern Club that Brian Epstein—the man who would go on to become their manager—first saw them. It was also where The Beatles recorded their first ever TV appearance for Granada Television. The Beatles played The Cavern 292 times—their last gig on 3 August 1963. Ray McFall travelled to New York with The Beatles—for their first US appearance—in February 1964.

Ray McFall went on to showcase many of the top beat groups and rock bands at The Cavern Club. Among them: 'Merseybeat' stars Gerry and The Pacemakers, The Big Three, The Searchers, and Wayne Fontana and The Mindbenders. As well as London's finest: The Yardbirds, The Who, and The Kinks.

BOB WOOLER | DJ | Merseyside music promoter | Resident compère & DJ at the Cavern Club | 1926 - 2002 | Frederick James 'Bob' Wooler | Ex-British Railway booking clerk. | A true music fan and aficionado; unique in that he was reputed to have the greatest collection of rock 'n' roll and R&B records in all of Liverpool, if not the entire North of England.

Bob Wooler was extremely erudite; often extraordinarily caustic; a past master of the pun and, if called for, a withering Liverpool "put-down"; his seemingly of-the-cuff alliteration-packed pronouncements, the stuff of legend. A very popular promoter of musical events, he was well regarded by all of Liverpool's groups; and very much acted as catalyst to the fast emerging Merseyside music scene. Importantly, he was a very early, very vocal, and very loyal supporter of The Beatles.

"Greetings and salutations jive fans, rockers, rollers, and on the beat clappers. Welcome to the best of the cellars, where we've got the hi-fi high and the lights down low, so let's get started with The Beatles Show!"

His exhortation to come get in the groove immediately followed by his signature introductory music for the group; the thundering sound of 'The William Tell Overture' blaring out of the public address system.

Wooler penned the first ever review of The Beatles in the regular column he wrote for *Mersey Beat*. An extraordinarily insightful and prescient piece entitled: *'What Is It That Makes The Beatles So Extraordinary'.* | Legend tells us it was Bob Wooler's incessant playing of 'My Bonnie'—the song The Beatles recorded in Hamburg—and his constant urging: *"Now all you Cavern dwellers go out and make it the best of sellers"*—that prompted Beatles' fan, Raymond Jones, to pop into NEMS to request a copy of record. The singular event that supposedly first prompted Brian Epstein to seek out The Beatles.

Bob Wooler later entered into a short-lived but highly successful business partnership with Brian Epstein and NEMS Enterprises to put on star-studded 'pop package shows' at the Tower Ballroom, New Brighton. | When NEMS moved its offices down to London, Bob elected to remain in Liverpool.

Bob Wooler died, in Liverpool, 8 February 2002.

| **Side Bar** | **Bob Wooler and 'My Bonnie'** | The Beatles' first 'official' record release was for famed German orchestra leader and record producer Bert Kaempfert—who'd scored a worldwide hit the previous year with his all-instrumental 'Winter Wonderland'—during their second club residency season in Hamburg. | Kaempfert had visited the Top Ten Club on Hamburg's Reeperbahn specifically to see the resident star attraction, Tony Sheridan—and his backing group with the funny name "Beatles"—play 'live' rock 'n' roll. He liked what he saw and heard, and hired the group to record some old songs in the 'new' sound. | The Beatles—John, Paul, and George—Pete sat this one out—accompanied by none other than The Hurricane's drummer, Ringo Starr. | The resulting 45rpm disc: 'My Bonnie' (Side A) 'When The Saints Go Marching In' (Side B) was duly released on Polydor and initially only available in Germany. The record label bore the legend: *Tony Sheridan and 'The Beat Boys'*. Not The Beatles! | The Beatles signed a contract with Kaempfert to record four more titles in the coming year.

When The Beatles next returned to Liverpool, the ever-mindful George Harrison quickly slipped a precious copy of 'My Bonnie' to Bob Wooler for him to play at the Cavern. Which Bob Wooler did—again and again and again—and the rest, as they say, is history. Or, as many people still insist, legend.

'PADDY' DELANEY | Cavern Club doorman and, if need be, bouncer | 1931 - 2009 | Not that he had to intervene over much—photos of Paddy holding back the milling crowds of young Cavern-goers show him to be a formidable and quietly commanding figure. | A former Guardsman—impressive in stature and always smartly attired in dinner jacket and cummerbund—he'd served with the Liverpool Parks Police and had worked as a doorman at the Locarno and Grafton Ballroom in West Darby—twin dance halls in 'tough' area infamous for gang violence. In 1959 Ray McFall, owner of The Cavern, hired Paddy Delaney to be the club's doorman to help keep the 'Teddy Boy' problem at bay, which he managed to do superbly well.

It was Delaney who waved Brian Epstein down the stone steps and into the club shortly after midday on 9 November 1961 to see The Beatles play a lunchtime session; thereby personally opening the door to rock 'n' roll history. | During the heyday of The Beatles at The Cavern, Paddy took a young bouncer under his wing—a gentle giant named Mal Evans who would later join The Beatles' inner circle as their second roadie.

Paddy stood guard for all 292 Cavern appearances by The Beatles. | He also stayed on post throughout the Cavern's long, slow decline—until the club was finally demolished in 1973 to make way for a proposed new underground railway line extension. | A man of hidden talents—for a time Paddy Delaney even acted as the theatre critic for *Mersey Beat*.

SAM LEACH | 'Maverick' music promoter & 'club owner' | **The Beatles' first major promoter and would-be manager** | 1935 - 2016 | Liverpool born and bred. | Rock 'n' Roll mad. Utterly irrepressible. Hugely innovative. A true original.

Sam's breakthrough promotional ideas: the first multi-group 'all-nighter' at the Iron Door Club; the first four-day multi-venue

Easter Rock Fest; his wildly popular Cassanova and Peppermint Lounge clubs; and the whole string of 'Operation Big-Beat' events at the Tower Ballroom, New Brighton—put all the other Merseyside club owners and promoters on notice... Here was an unstoppable force of business that had to be reckoned with.

After the unprecedented success of his 'Operation Big Beat' shows that had hugely impressed The Beatles and everyone else on Merseyside—well over four thousand beat-music fans regularly turned up—Sam Leach made a bid to become the group's manager. And he set about introducing them to key London booking agents by promoting a special *'Battle of the Bands'* at the Palais Ballroom, Aldershot, 50 miles outside London. It was a spectacular failure; only seventeen people turned up as the local newspaper had failed to advertise the event. Not one of the London agents Sam invited came: *"as nothing good ever comes out of Liverpool."* The Beatles—hugely disappointed with Sam—then decided that Brian Epstein should become their manager.

Regardless; along with such Liverpool luminaries as Bill Harry, Mona Best, Bob Wooler, and Ray McFall; Sam Leach played a hugely significant role in the early life of The Beatles and a signal part in the rise of the whole 'Merseybeat' music scene.

Following the tragic and untimely early death of John Lennon in 1980, Sam put on a memorable 'memorial concert' at St. George's Plateau, Liverpool, and thousands of people turned up to pay homage to the lost Beatle. | Sam gave lectures about his time with The Beatles and spoke at Beatles' Conventions around the world. For a time he even managed a Beatles' tribute band. | Sam Leach was the first inductee into the 'Merseybeat Hall of Fame'—and most deservedly so.

Sam's autobiography—*The Rocking City* (UK) *The Birth of The Beatles* (US)—puts you right there—in the clubs and on the streets of Liverpool—in the very early days of the group. There's really nothing else quite like it, certainly nothing else to touch it. It's funny, untidy, funny, irrepressible, funny, exhilarating, funny—sometimes even sad—but bubbly and boisterous in the extreme. Much, as I suspect, was Sam Leach, himself... a true 'Liverpool treasure'.

The fact that Sam Leach seems largely forgotten—his part in events all but written out of most Beatles' histories—including *The Beatles' Anthology*—is a crying shame.

But, then again, no less a person than Paul McCartney said: *"The best of The Beatles' early days in Liverpool was the Sam Leach era."* And 'Macca' is the man.

Sam Leach died in Liverpool, on 21 December 2016, still utterly irrepressible and still rockin'. He was 81 and still counting.

TERRY McCANN | **Close friend of Sam Leach and sometime 'minder'** | A London born Liverpool transplant. Sometimes referred to as a 'minder'. A good friend to have in a tight spot; ever capable of looking after himself, a friend, or his employer.

Some even say Terry McCann was the inspiration for the hero of the same name played by Dennis Waterman—'minder' to East End businessman, Arthur Daley, played by George Cole—in the popular UK TV crime series *'Minder'*. When in Liverpool, Terry acted as 'minder' and right hand man to promoter Sam Leach—of Iron Door Club and The Tower fame—truth sometimes proving stranger than fiction.

RAYMOND JONES | **Original Liverpudlian Dreamer** | Legend says it was Raymond Jones who walked into NEMS—a popular record store, on Whitechapel, in Liverpool—some time around 3 o'clock in the afternoon, on Saturday, 28th October 1961—and asked for a record called 'My Bonnie'.

Brian Epstein, the store manager had never even heard of it or the local group with the odd name who had recorded it. But fastidious businessman that he was, Epstein always wanted to ensure that customers never went away empty handed, set out to correct his mistake and went on to discover The Beatles.

Some people in Liverpool insist to this day that Raymond Jones never existed and was but a figment of the imagination of Brian Epstein or his personal assistant Alistair Taylor. Others say *"Ray Lives!"* and have old photographs to prove it.

I agree with Mark Twain: *Never let the truth get in the way of a good story*. Simply print the legend. And believe what you may.

BRIAN EPSTEIN | The Beatles' Manager | 1934 - 1967 | Born Liverpool | Brian Samuel Epstein. | The young Jewish businessman who helped steer The Beatles to worldwide fame and fortune. And who in every imaginable was utterly key to the beat group's astonishing success. But there was little or no indication of that when he first met the four original members of The Beatles—John, Paul, George, and Pete—at a lunchtime music session, at the Cavern Club, in November 1961.

At the time he was the manager of the main city-centre branch of North End Music Stores, one of a number of Liverpool stores specialising in furniture, pianos, radios, radiograms, record players, and classical records, owned by his family. Although he grew up with a love of classical music and the theatre he took especial delight in Broadway show tunes and other 'popular' music. First opening a NEMS satellite 'pop' record store that proved such a success the Epstein family's favourite son then opened an extensive 'pop' record department in the basement of the main store. As meticulous in his business dealings as he was in matters of decorum and dress, he prided himself on always having all the likely new hits, as well as all the best selling records in stock. Soon NEMS was advertised as offering *'The Finest Record Collection In The North'*.

In his autobiography—*A Cellarful of Noise*—he recalled that around 3 o'clock on the afternoon of Saturday 28 October 1961—one of his regular customers—a teenager named Raymond Jones—requested a record called 'My Bonnie' that the DJ at the Cavern had been playing and talking-up nonstop. The boy added that he thought it was from Germany. But not only did NEMS not have the record in stock, it was also supposedly by a local group he'd never even heard of, called The Beatles. He decided that both issues called for immediate further investigation.

And on 9 November 1961 he duly paid a lunchtime visit to the Cavern Club—arranged by none other than Bill Harry, founder and editor of *Mersey Beat*—to see and hear The Beatles perform. Charmed as much by their charisma as their music, he decided almost immediately to try and convince the group to let him become their manager.

For their part The Beatles were extremely flattered by the interest shown in them by the rather suave and very polished local businessman, whose NEMS record store they often frequented. But at they told Bob Wooler, the resident DJ at the Cavern, the main reason they agreed to the management deal let, even though posh Mr. Epstein had admitted he didn't know much about managing a group or even promoting shows, was he'd promised to use his business contacts to help secure them a recording contract with one of London's 'Big Four' record companies: Decca, EMI, Pye, or Philips. And the one thing they'd always dreamed of was getting a record into the charts and hearing it on Radio Luxembourg. What's more, Brian Epstein was the first person ever to ask to manage them, so, yeah, they'd all agreed to let become their manager.

Brian took immediate charge and told The Beatles they'd never get better bookings at better venues, with better fees, unless they agreed to clean up their act a little. For a start they should be punctual. And to help them he'd supply them with a weekly typewritten schedule of bookings. Next. They should stop smoking, swearing, eating and drinking on stage, and stop talking and joking with the audience. They should also stop wearing leather jackets and scruffy jeans, and wear something a little more appropriate; stage suits for instance.

And rockin' rebels though they might well have been—eyes always firmly focused on getting *'to the Toppermost of the Poppermost'*—The Beatles agreed to smarten themselves up. It started with touches of velvet on the collars of their tailor-made grey tweed jackets. And evolved into the famous collarless jackets they'd seen their art-student friends wearing in Hamburg. Their own sartorial touch; the elastic-sided Cuban-heeled boosts they bought in London. For his part, Brian Epstein also immediately put up the group's booking fees, much to the chagrin of Liverpool's many promoters. And then he got down to the tough business of getting The Beatles a recording contract.

He called every contact he had in the Sales Departments of the 'Big Four' and asked for help. Then immediately followed up with a copy of 'My Bonnie' and a covering letter to every recording executive whose name he'd been given. Executives at

EMI's two major record labels—HMV and Columbia—sent letters back to say they weren't at all interested in signing the group. But by that time he'd had a very positive response from Decca Records and had already arranged for one of their assistant A&R men to travel up to Liverpool to see The Beatles perform at The Cavern. The Beatles were duly set up for an audition at Decca's London recording studios a little over two weeks later—on New Year's Day 1962. Everything boded well. But things didn't turn out as everyone expected. After listening to the fifteen songs The Beatles recorded in little more than an hour—mostly cover songs, but with a few originals attributed to Lennon and McCartney—Decca Records turned them down flat. *"Guitar groups... especially... are on their way out, Mr. Epstein!"*

Much to the dismay of his family, who all thought he was badly neglecting his duties at the store; deeply disappointed, but still doggedly undeterred; Brian continued to take the train down to London—as many as two or three times a week—to knock on any and every record executive's door he could find. But Pye and Philips, and their various subsidiary record labels, rejected him and The Beatles outright. As did the HMV and Columbia record labels, all over again.

The whole business proving so arduous and so full of disappointment The Beatles joked about 'Embassy'—Woolworth department stores' private label—being the only option left. And they seriously considered disbanding the group for good.

Then fate intervened with a 'one-in-a-million' chance meeting. Increasingly desperate, but still resolutely determined to succeed, Brian took the failed Decca audition tapes to the vast HMV record store on London's Oxford Street—to the store's 'Personal Recording Department'—to have them transferred onto disc to make it easier for busy record executives to listen to the fledgling Beatles. And then of all people it was the transfer technician in the process of cutting a record from the Decca tapes who really liked what he heard and he called a music publisher who just happened to have an office upstairs in the same building.

The music publisher also liked the original Lennon-McCartney songs he heard. So much so that he asked to publish them. And he telephoned a friend of his—George Martin—head of Parlophone—one of EMI's subsidiary labels that specialised in classical, 'light orchestral', Trad-jazz, comedy, and quirky spoken-word albums, but that had begun to dabble in 'pop music' with a young singer called Adam Faith—to tell him about a group from Liverpool with an odd sounding name that might very well appeal to him. And he arranged for Brian Epstein to meet record producer George Martin.

A second 'one-in-a-million' meeting that in every way represented a last-minute reprieve from obscurity. An against-all-the-odds 'Hail Mary pass'—as it's called in American football—when the future rests on the outcome of a single moment. It was a meeting that would prove to be pivotal to the success of The Beatles, as it would eventually lead to them signing a contract with record producer George Martin.

All of which goes to underscore the extraordinarily vital role played by Brian Epstein—who never once gave up on "his boys" and who, however hard things got, never once weakened in his absolute belief that *"one day they'll be even bigger than Elvis Presley."* No one else had such unshakeable faith in them and their talent; no one else worked harder or more relentlessly on their behalf.

Without Brian Epstein—"Eppy" as The Beatles affectionately called him—and his many concerted efforts to ensure their success, it's hugely unlikely we'd have ever heard of The Beatles; certainly as we came to know, know, know them and love, love, love them.

Brian Epstein was found dead in his home in Belgravia, London, on 27 August, 1967—purportedly from an accidental overdose of sleeping pills. He was 32.

John Lennon remembered afterwards: *"We were in a daydream 'till Brian came along. We'd no idea what we were doing."*

And many years later Paul McCartney said of him: *"If anyone was the fifth Beatle, it was Brian."* 'Nuff said.

| Side Bar | **Brian Epstein – Businessman or no?** | Brian Epstein guided The Beatles to heights of success hitherto undreamed of by anyone in the music or entertainments business. Yet there was no 'playbook' for him to follow. There was simply no precedent for what he had to contend with; be it the seemingly never ending demands placed on him and The Beatles, the bewildering speed of events, or success on such a vast scale. And many people have since criticized and condemned him for the many mistakes he made—wittingly or unwittingly—in running NEMS Enterprises, his management company. Mistakes that cost The Beatles untold millions in lost revenue. And yet... and yet... without him there would likely have been no Beatles... no George Martin... and no *'Beatlemania'*. And 'in the end' "his boys" cost him his life and you can never put a price on that.

| Side Bar | **Brian Epstein – 'Closet' Homosexual** | Brian Epstein was a gay man—'closet homosexual'—when it was still a very serious criminal offence in Great Britain; punishable under Gross Indecency Laws by a fine and two-year prison sentence. He'd been blackmailed and had suffered innumerable beatings by sexual predators because of it. Yet he always did his best to keep it all away from his family and friends and business. Aided whenever called for by famed Liverpool family solicitor Rex Makin. And so his family never 'officially' knew or admitted to Brian's sexual leanings, although The Beatles did. But they never judged him for it and were always very supportive. | The truly sad thing was that Brian Samuel Epstein died within months of homosexuality being decriminalised in England and Wales by an Act of Parliament in 1967. One can only wonder what more he could have achieved—for himself and or on behalf of The Beatles—if he hadn't had to hide his love away. It was a tragic ending to a great and goodly man, regardless of his demons.

| Side Bar | *A Cellarful of Noise: The Autobiography of the Man Who Made The Beatles* | Published in 1964 when *'Beatlemania'* was at its height. And although ghost-written by Derek Taylor— who would later work for Epstein at NEMS and would go on to

become a trusted Beatles' confidante and Apple Corps insider—the words and thoughts are Brian Epstein's alone. With everything taken from tape recordings of their conversations together over a period of many days. As you read the book you cannot but be moved by Brian Epstein—the man—his gentle voice—and his unwavering belief in The Beatles.

MALKA 'QUEENIE' EPSTEIN | Brian Epstein's mother | 'Queenie' married Harry Epstein—whose family owned a store in Liverpool that sold furniture, electrical appliances, and even pianos—and later classical and pop records. As the business grew and expanded the name 'North End Music Stores' was shortened to NEMS. | 'Queenie' Epstein's family lived in the exclusive Liverpool suburb of Caldwell. The noted solicitor Rex Makin was her next-door neighbour.

In every respect, a proud 'Jewish' mother of two wonderful sons, Brian and Clive, she doted on her eldest son Brian and would hear nothing bad said against him. Not surprisingly, Brian always did his best to protect his mother from his private life as a closeted homosexual—a circumstance that at the time was deemed by British Law as being highly illegal and punishable by stiff fines and a prison sentence.

After a number of questionable public incidents Brian finally admitted to his family that he was homosexual. The revelation shocked his father and younger brother, Clive, but his mother 'Queenie' responded with unconditional love. Ever supportive—even when Brian appeared in court as 'Mr X' the victim of a vicious assault and robbery in a public toilet in West Derby—and the opposing councils 'discreet' pre-trial agreement not to admit in court the attacker's threatened blackmail to disclose Brian's secret sexual life—she stood staunchly by her son and never once waivered.

Years later—long after the deaths of Brian—and John Lennon—she was aghast when Brian's sexuality was fully revealed to the wider public by the irredeemably scurrilous Albert Goldman in his book *The Lives of John Lennon*.

REX MAKIN | The Epstein family solicitor | 1925 - 2017 | A 'legal legend' in Liverpool. | During the late Fifties and early Sixties, he was the Epstein family solicitor. He lived next door to the Epsteins in the exclusive suburb of Childwall. And attended to all the family's legal needs, as well as whatever "dirty laundry" the family's eldest son brought home. | He dealt very discreetly with Brian's numerous peccadilloes in London and acted as brief for the infamous Liverpool battery and blackmail incident where the victim, one Mr. B. S. Epstein, was referred to in court simply as 'Mr X'.

In 1963, Brian sought Rex Makin's advice about setting up a perpetually binding contract between himself and The Beatles. Makin told him that such an agreement would be legally indefensible and—regretfully—declined—as he'd witnessed Brian's many earlier madcap schemes go awry. Brian Epstein, as he so often did in business and life, forged ahead, regardless, and employed a different solicitor to do his bidding. The two men remained trusted friends, however. And, dutiful to the end, Rex Makin handled all of Brian Epstein's funeral arrangements following The Beatles' manager's tragic early death in 1967.

Some people also suggest it was Rex Makin who coined the term *'Beatlemania'*—while others still insist it was dreamed up by various London Fleet Street newspapers. | Rex Makin went on to enjoy a much-storied legal career and was a much-respected figure in Liverpool civic and legal circles. He was a 'Freeman of the City of Liverpool'—the first solicitor ever to receive such an honour—and held an honorary professorship at Liverpool John Moore's University. | Rex Makin died in 2017.

JOE FLANNERY | **Close friend to Brian Epstein and Beat group manager** | 1931 - 2019 | Born in Liverpool. A very close friend of Brian Epstein's; their's a strictly platonic relationship even though, like Brian, he was a homosexual when it was a criminal offence to be such in the UK. He shared Brian's passion for theatre and show tunes and fast cars; a heady mix; but it also meant that Joe was always a 'safe shoulder' for Brian to cry on when things got too rough; in both life and his secret other life.

When Brian became manager of The Beatles and experienced difficulties in dealing with the rough and tumble of local Liverpool promoters—it was Joe he called upon for help. Later, when Pete Best was unceremoniously sacked from The Beatles—it was Joe—then acting as manager for the beat group Lee Curtis and The All Stars—that got Pete set up as the group's new drummer.

Joe Flannery remained a force for good in Liverpool. | In 2016 he published *'Standing In The Wings. The Beatles, Brian Epstein and Me'*—written with Mike Brocken—with a forward by Philip *'Shout'* Norman. And better late than never, Joe Flannery's story has long needed to be told. Died 27 March 2019.

ALISTAIR TAYLOR | Brian Epstein's personal assistant at NEMS | 1935 - 2004 | 'Mr. Fixit' | James Alistair Taylor | Born Runcorn, Cheshire | Initially hired as a salesman in the record department of NEMS, Whitechapel, Liverpool city-centre branch. He was later appointed Brian Epstein's P.A. having impressed his boss with his "willingness to roll up his sleeves and help get the job done" be it stock-taking, carrying in newly delivered boxes of record releases from all the major record labels, or simply working late without complaint.

Wednesday, 9 November 1961—everything prearranged by Bill Harry—Brian Epstein made an utterly out-of-character visit to the Cavern; a cellar club on Matthew Street, hidden away as it was down a tangle of narrow lanes amidst towering warehouses, a couple of hundred yards or so from his office; to go see The Beatles play a lunchtime session. And he took Taylor, his P.A., along simply to make a good impression.

Alistair Taylor thought his boss must have gone completely mad to want to visit such a dank, dirty, foul smelling cellar in the middle of the working day or at anytime for that matter. The heat in the overcrowded club was intolerable. The noise made by the band with the odd-sounding name even more so.

Even so, as history tells us, The Beatles ended up impressing Brian Epstein more than he could ever have imagined. And a few weeks later, Alistair Taylor witnessed The Beatles—John, Paul, George, and Pete—add their signatures to their first official contract with Brian Epstein, at the offices of NEMS.

Alistair Taylor continued as executive assistant to Brian Epstein when NEMS Enterprises moved its offices to London. After Brian's death—and with the formation of The Beatle's company Apple Corps—he was appointed "office manager and chief fixer". When with the impending dissolution of The Beatles, US businessman, Allen Klein, took over management of Apple Corps—at the request of John, George, and Ringo—and began a major restructuring of the company, Alistair was summarily dismissed, along with most of the rest of Apple's employees. He later wrote—*A Secret History*—a tell-all book about his time with Brian Epstein and The Beatles.

PETER BROWN | Brian Epstein's personal assistant at NEMS | Wirral born. (That's just across the Mersey and down a bit—onto the Wirral Peninsula. It's also where Cynthia Powell—girlfriend and future wife of John Lennon was born.) | Peter was a personal assistant and then close confidant to Brian Epstein at NEMS in Liverpool—and in London when NEMS Enterprises opened offices on Argyll Street W1 in 1965.

Known for his fastidiousness, Peter was a consummate Beatles 'insider' who took on Beatles & Co. business duties when Brian Epstein was found dead from an overdose of sleeping pills in August 1967. The Beatles appointed him executive director of Apple Corps.

Peter Brown accompanied John and Yoko to Gibraltar where he acted as best man at their wedding. Peter left Apple in 1970 when John, George, and Ringo elected to hand over management to Allen Klein. In 1983 Peter (with Stephen Gaines) wrote *'The Love You Make: An Insider's Story of the Beatles'*—a seedy, 'tell-all' book which many saw as a complete betrayal of his time with Brian Epstein and The Beatles.

TONY BRAMWELL | NEMS Enterprises executive Liverpool & London | Born Liverpool. | Music mad. When a schoolboy won a *New Musical Express* competition to meet Buddy Holly in concert at Liverpool's Philharmonic Hall. | Met George Harrison on bus to school—became lifelong friends over shared passion for rock 'n' roll. | He carried George's guitar into The Beatles' first post-Hamburg gig at Litherland Town Hall—on 27th December1960—so he could get in for free (One of the many legendary Beatles' gigs I'd dearly loved to have seen; so I'm hugely envious). He would later often help out as an extra 'roadie' and was soon admitted into The Beatles' inner circle.

Tony worked for Brian Epstein at NEMS Enterprises both in Liverpool and London. Had a knack for getting things done; went from office boy to executive, then to trusted 'go-to' man. | Quickly established himself as NEMS top 'Record Promoter'. | Later travelled to the US with The Beatles.

Head of NEMS Presentations and Suba Films—produced and directed 'promotional clips' for The Beatles and other NEMS recording artists—pointing the way to the music video revolution that was MTV. | Handpicked by Brian Epstein to be the 'artistic director' of the special Sunday pop music shows at NEMS Saville Theatre, London. Jimi Hendrix among the many fabled acts that Tony helped introduce to the London music scene.

After Brian Epstein's death, Tony joined Apple Corps as Head of Apple Films. Wore many hats. Video producer. Record producer. Photographer. | Later worked for film producer Harry Saltzman and was very instrumental in Paul McCartney writing and recording the theme for James Bond 007 film—*Live And Let Die*. A true McCartney classic.

Eyes still wide-open, years later; Tony promoted the breathtakingly talented singer Eva Cassidy. | In 2005 he wrote the really rather magical book: '*Magical Mystery Tours: My Life With The Beatles*'.

MAL EVANS | Assistant Cavern Club doorman. Assistant roadie to The Beatles | 1935 - 1976 | Malcolm Frederick "Mal" Evans | Referred to by one and all as "the gentle giant", Mal Evans first stepped into the world of The Beatles when he was hired as Paddy Delaney's assistant doorman and bouncer at the Cavern. He was so effective, but unassuming, that in 1963 Brian Epstein offered him the position as Beatles' road manager Neil Aspinall's assistant. A job that called for him to help haul the increasingly cumbersome and heavy equipment used by The

Beatles onto the stage and—of course—to help keep the increasing waves of Beatles besotted fans at bay.

When The Beatles stopped touring in 1966 Mal Evans had more than proven his reliability—and discretion—and was made a personal assistant to the group and later a very much-trusted Apple executive.

Another man of hidden talents—Mal discovered Badfinger—a band who would become Apple recording artists. He even helped produce a hit single of theirs—'No Matter What'. | When The Beatles broke up in 1970—Mal continued on on the fringes of the music business in England and the US—but came to a tragic end when he was shot dead after arguing with police called to a domestic disturbance at a motel in Los Angeles in 1976.

BERYL ADAMS | Brian Epstein's secretary | NEMS (North End Music Stores) 12-14 Whitechapel, Liverpool. | The store's classical record department was situated on the ground floor—alongside the upright and grand pianos—with the basement downstairs devoted to the sale of popular music records of all genres. The second such NEMS record outlet devoted exclusively to 'pop' records, following the success of a small NEMS record store in another part of the city. And a sure sign of Mr. Brian's—as she called him—growing, and quite unexpected, success with managing the ever-increasing sales of 'pop' 45rpm discs and LPs.

When Brian later took over management of The Beatles, Beryl was involved in all aspects of the day to-day business proceedings. She helped book future engagements. Prepared detailed itineraries for the coming week—for Neil Aspinall, the roadie, as well as John, Paul, George, and Pete. Typed up a detailed accounting of all business costs to date. Prepared and handed The Beatles their weekly pay packets.

She elected to stay in Liverpool and not accompany Brian when he moved NEMS Enterprises to London. Beryl went on to manage a Merseyside beat group and marry Bob Wooler, the Cavern DJ. After that marriage, sadly, broke down she was later involved with another Liverpool legend—Allan Williams.

RITA SHAW | Shop girl at NEMS | Worked in the popular record department at NEMS in Whitechapel. | It was Rita—or so the story goes— who suggested to local promoter Sam Leach that he should first talk to her boss Brian Epstein about putting up posters and selling tickets at NEMS for his upcoming 'Operation Big Beat'—with The Beatles and four other Merseyside beat groups—at The Tower Ballroom in New Brighton. The two men went on to become friends and then bitter rivals as to which one would eventually be The Beatles' manager.

FREDA KELLY | Beatles' Fan Club secretary | Freda Kelly was a Cavern regular—and a fan of The Beatles from the very first time she saw the group. She got to know Bobbie Brown, who was running The Beatles Fan Club, and began to help with club matters. She later got a job as a shorthand typist at NEMS Enterprises. When Bobbie Brown got engaged and left—Freda took over fan club duties. She did everything so well and was so very pleasant with it all, The Beatles always used to say *"Good, Old Freda."* | When Brian Epstein moved NEMS to London, Rita stayed on in Liverpool, at the express wish of her dad, but continued as co-secretary of the National Beatles Club.

A documentary film *Good, Old Freda* was released to great acclaim in 2015. | A short story (2012) and BBC radio play (2013) by Ray Connolly has Freda Kelly as a central character in *'Sorry Boys You Failed The Audition'*. A wonderfully conceived story; even if too awful to contemplate; that explores a world in which The Beatles weren't signed to Parlophone by producer George Martin, in 1962, and what Freda does to help right the balance. A wonderful tribute to "a lovely Liverpool lass."

MAUREEN STARKEY née COX | Ringo Starr's first wife | 1946 - 1994 | Born Liverpool. | Known to close friends as 'Mo'. Maureen was a hairdresser and, from the age of 15, a Cavern Club regular and a dedicated Beatles fan. At the end of one Cavern lunchtime session, in answer to a dare by her friends, she planted a kiss on a surprised Ringo's cheek and got one in return. Ringo later met Maureen at a dance—hearts skipped a beat—and they became an item.

As other female fans of The Beatles found out about it, Maureen received numerous 'death' threats and not a few scratches to her face. A harbinger of things to come for any woman ever associated with any of The Beatles.

In September 1993—with her parent's permission—Maureen and Ringo holidayed together with Paul McCartney and Jane Asher in Greece. | When on the verge of an international tour Ringo was rushed to hospital in London with a high fever and tonsillitis, 'Nurse' Maureen rushed down from Liverpool to be at his bedside—and stayed. | Ringo Starr proposed to Maureen on her 18th birthday in January 1965 and they got married the very next month. They had a son Zak later that year—a second son, Jason, in 1967—and a daughter Lee in 1970. 'Mo' travelled with Ringo and the other Beatles to India to stay at the Rishikesh ashram of the Maharishi Yogi but the couple didn't stay long—they didn't much fancy the food or what the guru had to say.

'Mo' was great friends with fellow Beatle wives Cynthia Lennon and Patti Harrison. And was with Yoko Ono when The Beatles played their final live concert together on the rooftop of Apple Corps on Savile Row. Paul McCartney can be heard saying *"Thanks, Mo,"* after the final performance of 'Get Back'. However, life post the breakup of The Beatles took its toll, the marriage began to fail, and the couple eventually divorced in 1975. A year later Maureen moved in with Isaac Tigrett—one of the founding partners of the Hard Rock Cafe and the House of Blues. The couple had a daughter Augusta in 1987 and were married in 1989. Maureen Starkey Tigrett died 1994.

IRIS CALDWELL | Sister of the one and only Rory Storm | Rory—real name Alan Caldwell—the brilliantly flamboyant lead singer of The Hurricanes. | Iris was a stunningly beautiful blonde beauty queen. | Legend is that Iris dated George Harrison when she was 12 and he was 14. Then she dated Paul McCartney when she was just seventeen. You know what I mean.

She later also dated Frank 'I Remember You' Ifield. | How on earth could she ever *'Top of the Pops'* that? She married singer, Shane Fenton in 1964.

CILLA BLACK. OBE. | Singer, Entertainer, and British TV personality | 'National Treasure' | *"Swinging Cilla"* | 1943 - 2015 | Flame red-haired, Liverpool born singer with a voice that could knock you flat. Originally named Priscilla Marie Veronica White—she was a working-class girl from the tough Scotland Road area of Liverpool who worked as typist at a cable manufacturing company by day, who began singing with local beat groups at night.

She gained her stage-name from an encouraging report Bill Harry wrote about her in the very first issue of *Mersey Beat*. Bill remembered her surname was a colour—but inadvertently replaced 'white' with 'black'. And it stuck.

Cilla began performing regular spots with top local beat groups—The Big Three—'Kingsize' Taylor and the Dominoes—at the Iron Door and Zodiac clubs. She also sang regularly with Liverpool's then top group, Rory Storm and The Hurricanes, whose drummer Ringo Starr just happened to be dating her best friend. It was the start of Cilla's lifelong friendship with Ringo. John Lennon, also a good friend, always called her "Cyril" for the sheer delight of it.

Bill Harry later arranged for Cilla to perform for Brian Epstein at the Blue Angel Club. Brian Epstein would go on to become her manager and Cilla the first female artist to be represented by NEMS Enterprises. Record producer George Martin then immediately signed her to Parlophone. | John Lennon and Paul McCartney wrote 'Love Of The Love' especially for her, which charted in the Top Forty—a disappointment for her and Brian Epstein, but both were determined to have a No. 1 hit.

It was Brian Epstein that came up with the song that gave Cilla her first British No. 1 Hit and set her on the road to stardom. A song that he'd heard on a recent visit to the US—a haunting ballad by Hal David and Burt Bacharach's—'Anyone Who Had A Heart'.

Brian also arranged for Cilla to appear for a season at the Plaza Hotel in New York. But the supper club atmosphere didn't show the singer at her best—and despite her appearances on US television—she returned home to Britain to pursue her career.

She had a global hit with 'You're My World'. John and Paul then wrote 'It's For You' for her. She had another huge hit with The Righteous Brothers' 'You've Lost That Loving Feeling'.

In her career as a singer—Cilla Black had 11 'Top Ten' singles; 20 consecutive Top 40 hits; on the British single and EP charts. | She remained close friends with 'Eppy' until his accidental death from an overdose of sleeping pills in 1967.

It was thanks to Brian's vision for her, though, that the BBC showcased Cilla in her own TV series—simply titled *Cilla*—that aired from January 1968 to April 1976. Paul McCartney wrote 'Step Inside Love' especially for the TV series. | Her long-time love and husband, fellow Liverpudlian and songwriter, Bobby Willis assumed the role of manager. She had more hits—'Alfie' and 'Something Tells Me', perhaps the most notable. | Cilla later went on to star and/or host a number of TV programs in Britain: *Blind Date* (1985–2003) and *Surprise Surprise* (1984–2001) the most popular. She became a much-loved personality and "national treasure" and for a number of years she was the highest paid female artist on British television. | In 2003, Cilla published her bestselling autobiography: *Cilla Black - What's It All About?* Always warm and engaging, and ineffably charming, she once confessed: *"Class, I haven't. But style I've got."* | She was awarded an OBE in 1997. | Her husband, Bobby, died in 1999.

Cilla Black died, in Spain, 1 August 2015, aged 72.

In September 2014 a three-part biopic series of her life was shown on British television to great acclaim. All with Cilla's blessing and consent—as long as it showed her 'warts and all'.

Cilla starred Sheridan Smith as the young, sparky Scottie Road lass determined to succeed come what may and Aneurin Barnard as her boyfriend, husband, and manager, Bobby Willis.

Sheridan Smith does her own singing in all three episodes and does so, brilliantly. She is luminous in the role; it's a truly extraordinary performance. And well worth searching out if you ever want to get a sense of Liverpool in the midst of Merseybeat mania. | Another wonderful tribute to another lovely Liverpool lass and a *"lorra, lorra laughs"* and tears, besides.

PART ONE - PEOPLE. PLACES. VENUES.

2 - Mersey Beat

Suddenly, there was an awareness of being young...

"Newspapers, television, theatres, and radio were all controlled and manipulated by people of a different generation—who had no idea at all what youngsters wanted. Then, suddenly, there was an awareness of being young. Young people wanted their own styles and their own music—just at the time they were beginning to earn money and have real spending power. Mersey Beat was their voice. It was a paper just for them—crammed with photos and information about their own groups. Which is why—as its coverage extended to other areas—it also began to appeal to youngsters all over Britain."
— Bill Harry | Founder & Editor of MERSEY BEAT

'MERSEYSIDE'S OWN ENTERTAINMENTS PAPER'
Mersey Beat not only gave name to the thunderous, atomic, 4/4 beat sound emerging from all around Merseyside—giving it a sense of cohesion and identity that it had sorely lacked up until that point—it also helped showcase the extraordinary phenomenon that was...The Beatles.

Mersey Beat was very much the first 'What's On' music newspaper of its kind anywhere in Britain. | Published fortnightly, it covered the music scene in Liverpool, as well as everything happening on the Wirral, in Birkenhead, New Brighton, Crosby, Southport, Warrington, Widnes, and Runcorn. | It was full of photos of individual artists and groups, and music events—a 'live' documentary style of photography as pioneered by Astrid Kirchherr and Jurgen Volmer in Hamburg and quite different from the conventional studio portrait photos used by the more traditional London music press—another first. It also featured regular editorials, columnists, 45rpm and LP record chart listings and record reviewers—one of who was Brian Epstein of North End Music Stores (NEMS) months before he claimed to have discovered The Beatles!

It was Bill Harry who dubbed Liverpool—**"The Rocking City"**—and how right he was. | Bill Harry and Bob Wooler—promoter and resident DJ at the Cavern—once tried to count up the number of 'Beat' groups they encountered during the rise of the 'Merseybeat' sound. The total was close to five hundred: an astonishing amount of home-grown talent. And Beatles' fans can only give thanks it was Bill Harry—ably assisted by girlfriend, Virginia Sowry, who later became his wife—who had the wit and wherewithal, the passion and the perspicacity, to do it and do it so well. Truly, one of those instances where if it didn't exist; someone would have had to invent it.

Mersey Beat was a wonder of its Time. And even though it ran for only four years—publishing over ninety issues—before it was merged with another music publication; it was already a legend in all that it had achieved

MERSEY BEAT | Vol. 1 No. 1 | 6 July 1961
Bill Harry wrote to the *Daily Mail*—one of Britain's leading newspapers—to tell them what was happening on Merseyside—**"Liverpool is like New Orleans at the turn of the century, but with rock 'n' roll instead of jazz"**—but his observation fell on deaf ears. Undeterred, he pressed on with his idea of a Liverpool-focused music and entertainments newspaper—believing it would be sufficiently different enough from national music papers such as *New Musical Express* and *Melody Maker* that concentrated on current chart hits and established music artists. | Bill borrowed £50 from a friend of a friend and rented a small attic office, above David Land's wine merchant's shop, at 81a Renshaw Street—for the princely sum of £5 a week. Then with nothing more than a desk, a chair, and an Olivetti typewriter—also on loan—and with the assistance of his girlfriend and future wife, Virginia Sowry (who he'd met at the Jacaranda Club), and a photographer friend, Dick Matthews, he set about publishing *Mersey Beat*.

Bill did all the writing, designing, advertising, and circulation; Virginia did everything else, all the paperwork, the phone calls, the follow up with all the groups; the two of them often having to put in extremely long workweeks. | Bill named the newspaper *Mersey Beat*—based on the idea of a policeman's 'beat' (the area patrolled on foot by an on-duty policeman) and nothing at all to do with a musical 'beat'; that came later—and released the very first issue on 6 July 1961.

Such was the demand, all 5000 copies quickly sold out. Made all the more incredible, as Bill Harry was still 'officially' attending Liverpool Art College. The very same august institution of 'higher education' where he'd met his two very best friends: a very talented fine artist, Stuart Sutcliffe; and a certain disaffected youth—would be rock 'n' roll musician—John Lennon.

MERSEY BEAT | Vol. 1 No. 1. | 6 July 1961
On The Dubious Origins Of The Beatles by John Lennon
One of the many items featured within the pages of *Mersey Beat* Vol. 1 No. 1, was a wonderfully surreal little piece entitled: **Being A Short Diversion On The Dubious Origins of Beatles. Translated From the John Lennon.**

Many people ask what are Beatles? Why Beatles? Ugh, Beatles, how did the name arrive? So we will tell you. It came in a vision—a man appeared on a flaming pie and said unto them 'From this day on you are Beatles with an 'A' said Mr. Man. Thank you, Mr. Man, they said, thanking him'. And so they were "Beatles".

John was so delighted that *Mersey Beat* had published his 'origins of The Beatles' piece in its entirety; he gave Bill a huge cache of his poems, cartoons, and scribblings for the paper's future use. A veritable cornucopia of Goon-inspired imagery and glorious puns that would be featured under the inspired by-line '*Beatcomber*'—a 'Lennonesque' word play upon an influential London newspaper social column entitled '*Beachcomber*'.

MERSEY BEAT | CONTRIBUTORS | John Lennon's musings, poems, short stories, even spoof classified ads, as '*Beatcomber*', were later employed as the basis of his book: *John Lennon, In His Own Write* published to great acclaim by Jonathan Cape.

Bob Wooler, Cavern DJ and compère, wrote regular columns variously entitled: *Mr. Big Beat's Rhythm 'N' News*, *The Wandering 'I'* and *Well Now Dig This*, where he once famously described The Beatles as *"rhythmic revolutionaries."*

Virginia Sowry not only helped run the *Mersey Beat* office, she also contributed a regular column called *Mersey Roundabout: News. Views. Comments. Gossip.*

Good old Dick Matthews took photographs of all the emerging 'Beat' groups.

And Liverpool record shop owner, Brian Epstein, submitted a regular column about the coming crop of record releases—mostly featuring balladeers, big band orchestras, and show tunes—and big, established stars such as Elvis Presley and Cliff Richard and The Shadows. No mention of The Beatles, though, in his early record release columns. That, too, would come later.

MERSEY BEAT | Vol. 1 No. 13 | January 4-18 1962
'BEATLES TOP POLL!' | *Mersey Beat* held its first ever poll to find out who was the most popular group on Merseyside. When the votes were finally counted, Rory Storm & The Hurricanes were in first place. | However, on closer scrutiny of the postal votes, Bill Harry noticed more than forty votes all written in the same green ink—in the same handwriting—all from the same area of Liverpool. The questionable votes were declared void. The chief suspect none other than Rory Storm himself. Although Bill Harry could have had no idea that The Beatles—and most every other group on Merseyside—had done exactly the same thing.

MERSEY BEAT | **CIRCULATION 75,000!** | The paper's circulation rapidly increased over the next year as it started featuring stories about groups in Manchester, Birmingham, Sheffield, Newcastle, and Glasgow—and the newspaper had to move downstairs and take over a large, two-roomed office just to keep up with the demand. | As the newspaper's sales continued to rise, it became known as *"the Teenagers Bible"*—local groups began calling themselves *"Beat groups"*—venues began advertising concerts as *"Beat Sessions"*—and rival Liverpool

"Beat groups" began complaining that *Mersey Beat* featured The Beatles so often it should be re-named *Mersey Beatle*. Regardless, *Mersey Beat* could now proudly proclaim itself to all and sundry as: **'The North's Own Entertainments Paper'**

THE ALL-IMPORTANT 'EMI' TELEGRAM BRIAN EPSTEIN SENT TO: MERSEY BEAT | ROYAL 0003 | LIVERPOOL

Brian Epstein was very well aware of just how important *Mersey Beat* was to the growing success of The Beatles all around Merseyside. Which is why, directly after his first meeting with George Martin, at EMI's Abbey Road Studios, London, he immediately went in search of a Post Office, so that he could send a telegram off to The Beatles—who were already a month into their first season at the new Star-Club in Hamburg:

'CONGRATULATIONS, BOYS. EMI REQUEST RECORDING SESSION. PLEASE REHEARSE NEW MATERIAL'

And then send a second telegram: To Bill Harry c/o Mersey Beat Royal 0003 Liverpool:

'HAVE SECURED CONTRACT FOR BEATLES TO RECORDED FOR EMI ON PARLAPHONE LABEL 1ST RECORDING DATE SET FOR JUNE 6TH'

MERSEY BEAT | *'Now Over 250,000 Readers Every Issue'*

The circulation of *Mersey Beat* grew at rapid pace and even with its cover price doubling from threepence to sixpence, by late 1963, was reaching over 250,000 readers with every issue; an extraordinary growth in such a short time; and proudly able to sport the new legend: **Britain's Leading Beat Paper.**

The enormous success of *Mersey Beat* was almost without precedent in the newspaper-publishing world and when pop-culture journalist, Nancy Spain, did a special feature on it and its many imitators in the *News of the World*, Bill and Virginia—now married—were dubbed: **"Mr. and Mrs. Mersey Beat."**

MERSEY BEAT | AND AFTER

The newspaper ran for four years and published over ninety issues—in the final year even adding colour photographs—before it was merged with another music publication and then finally ceased operation. The direct consequence of the diminished demand for news of 'the Merseybeat Sound' as the centre of British pop music reverted back to London—the new home of The Beatles—and such increasingly popular acts as The Rolling Stones, The Kinks, and The Who.

In 1966 Bill and his wife Virginia followed The Beatles lead and moved to London. | Bill continued working as a rock journalist, but with his extraordinary knowledge of the whole pop music scene was drawn more and more into the world of PR. And after very successful PR campaigns involving The Kinks and The Hollies, he opened his own entertainments PR agency.

His 'own' clients included David Bowie, Pink Floyd, Led Zeppelin, the Beach Boys, Ten Years After, Jethro Tull, Procol Harum, Free, Mott the Hoople, the Pretty Things, Christine Perfect, Supertramp, Hot Chocolate, Suzi Quatro, and Kim Wilde—and record labels such as EMI, CBS, and Polydor.

Hugely prolific; his many published works on The Beatles and their 'Times', and the music and music business scene in general, are encyclopaedic—truly beyond scholarly.

Today—Bill Harry runs a number of websites and Facebook pages dedicated to all things *Mersey Beat*—The Beatles, the Mersey Sound, and The Sixties. And as with all good journalists and chroniclers of the times—his writings, and all but daily blog postings and commentaries still have the power to startle as well as delight and entertain. He continues to be involved in any number of Beatles' related projects and is readying a major new work drawn from his extensive archives.

Without doubt one of the most significant of all Beatles' people—and the one true source. As he was not only there at the very beginning of it all, he also knew John and Paul and George and Ringo—and all of the other important players—Stuart Sutcliffe, Pete Best, Allan Williams, Neil Aspinall, Sam Leach, Bob Wooler, Ray McFall, Rory Storm, Gerry Marsden, Cilla Black *et al*, up close and personally.

And what's more, he took and kept copious notes. And thank The Beatles' Gods that he did. The man has long been a veritable river to Beatles' fans the world over.

PART ONE - PEOPLE. PLACES. VENUES.

3 - Merseyside Beat Groups

The magical, mythical sound of Merseybeat...

Derry and The Seniors | Rory Storm and The Hurricanes | Gerry and The Pacemakers | The Big Three | 'Kingsize' Taylor & The Dominoes | The Searchers | The Swinging Blue Jeans | The Merseybeats | The Undertakers | The Fourmost | Lee Curtis and The All-Stars | Billy J. Kramer - With The Dakotas | The Chants

In the summer of 1961, at their very first meeting at the offices of North End Music Stores—NEMS—Bill Harry told Brian Epstein, the record store's manager, about the seemingly never ending flood of entertainment happening all over Merseyside. He said there were literally hundreds of musical groups in Liverpool—all of them providing entertainments of every kind, every single day, of every week. Countless singers, duos, trios, quartets, and combos—boy bands and girl bands—professional as well as amateur—playing every sort of music—skiffle, rock 'n' roll, country, western, folk, brass-band, Trad-jazz, modern jazz. Added to which there was an increasing demand for comedy, poetry, and reading events. A good deal of it took place in theatres, cinemas, ballrooms, and nightclubs—as was only to be expected. But demand was so great that it was overflowing into cellar clubs, jive hives—coffee bars, pubs, and workingmen's clubs—church halls, and village halls—even skating rinks. Such a huge wave of entertainments it cried out for someone to gather up all the details—about all the goings-on on Merseyside—to help keep people better informed. So he'd taken the job upon himself and—with the help of a small financial loan from a friend—had founded the newspaper *Mersey Beat*.

Mersey Beat—Merseyside's Own Entertainments Paper | Published fortnightly. Price threepence. | The newspaper became required reading for anyone and everyone involved in the local music scene and was soon dubbed 'The Teenagers Bible' by its many readers. Perhaps, even more importantly, when more and more Merseyside skiffle and rock 'n' roll bands took to calling themselves 'beat' groups, the newspaper also gave name to the unique sound coming out of Liverpool—'**Merseybeat**'.

That it was Bill Harry who saw and fulfilled the need is a singular stroke of good fortune. Few other people would have had the nerve, drive and stamina—it often required that he put in hundred hour workweeks—let alone the imagination, passion, and wit for the job. Plus—he turned out to be a pretty keen-eyed, hard-hitting journalist and—perhaps more to the point—was also good and close-friends with John Lennon and Stuart Sutcliffe. And, as they say, 'God is ever in the details.'

Mersey Beat conducted an annual poll with its readers to determine '**The Top Beat Group**'. And competition amongst groups was, of course, extremely fierce. The Beatles won the first year, as they did the second. But Rory Storm and The Hurricanes, Gerry and the Pacemakers, The Big Three, 'Kingsize' Taylor and The Dominoes, The Searchers, The Swinging Blue Jeans, The Merseybeats, The Undertakers, The Fourmost, Lee Curtis and the All-Stars, and Billy J. Kramer and The Dakotas always gave The Beatles a very good run for their money.

There were literally hundreds of other groups working all around Merseyside at the time—notable among who were The Chants—but these, arguably, were the *toppermost* groups of all.

DERRY AND THE SENIORS | Howie Casey -saxophone | Billy Hughes - rhythm guitar | Stan Foster - piano | Brian Griffiths - lead guitar | Phil Whitehead - bass guitar | Jeff Wallington – drums | Derry Wilkie - lead singer |
The very first Liverpool rock 'n' roll group hired to play Bruno Koschmider's Kaiserkeller club in Hamburg. | The Seniors were originally formed by Casey, Hughes, and Foster; who'd all played together in another group. Griffiths, Whitehead, and

Wallington completed the band. Wilkie, from the West Indies—by all accounts a superb Ray Charles look and sound-alike—then joined as lead singer. Thus was born 'Derry and The Seniors'.

May 1960. The group made an impressive showing at the Gene Vincent concert put on by Allan Williams at Liverpool Stadium. It got them an invitation to audition as the backing group for Liverpool star Billy Fury and his manager—London impresario—Larry Parnes. The Silver Beatles also tried out for the very same audition. Neither group got that job, but later—via Allan Williams—The Seniors were offered a tour backing a number of other singers managed by Larry Parnes. Everyone in the band gave up their day jobs to turn professional and then without warning Parnes cancelled.

The boys in the band were most upset and threatened to take it out of Allan Williams' hide. Instead, Williams took them down to London and to Soho's famous 2i's Coffee Bar for an audition—as he was a close friend of Tommy Littlewood, the 2i's manager. Derry and The Seniors took to the coffee bar's pocket-handkerchief of a stage and rocked the place. Allan Williams recalled them as being—*"raw, authoritative, compelling, earthy, elemental."* And then *kismet*, fate, destiny, or whatever you will, entered into the scene, because club owner Bruno Koschmider also just happened to be in the audience that night. Drawn back to the 2i's looking for more Britisher rock 'n' roll bands to play his Kaiserkeller club. And with the aid of bi-lingual waiter from a coffee bar on the other side of Old Compton Street, Koschmider and Williams quickly struck up a deal and within days Derry and The Seniors were on their way to Hamburg—where they proved a huge hit with the Kaiserkeller audience.

Allan Williams then sent The Beatles out to Hamburg. Which dismayed Howie Casey no end, as he thought them *"a no talent group that'd only go and spoil it for everyone else."* Though he later had the grace to admit how very wrong he was. Derry and The Seniors continued to rock the Kaiserkeller throughout much of the summer, but as not a single one of them had an official work permit or visa, they were forced to roll back to England in October 1960. And, in turn, Allan Williams replaced them at the Kaiserkeller with Rory Storm and The Hurricanes.

Early in 1961—now called Howie Casey and The Seniors—the band signed a recording deal with Fontana Records. And much to John Lennon's chagrin were the first Liverpool beat group to record an LP. The album *'Twist At The Top'* was issued February 1962—together with the single 'Double Twist'—but both failed to chart. | When The Seniors disbanded Howie Casey joined 'Kingsize' Taylor and the Dominoes. After which he worked as a highly regarded session musician. He played on Paul McCartney and Wings seminal album *'Band On The Run'*. And recorded and toured worldwide with McCartney throughout the 1970s.

RORY STORM AND THE HURRICANES | Rory Storm (Alan Caldwell) - vocals | Charles 'Ty' O'Brien - lead guitar | 'Lu' Walters (Wally Eymond) - bass guitar | Johnny 'Guitar' Byrne - rhythm guitar | Ringo Starr (Richard Starkey) drums | Rory Storm was a brilliantly extroverted entertainer—born way before or after his time. And despite having a serious stammer—which disappeared as soon as he started singing—people said his voice was 'right up there' with—'The King'—Elvis. | In 1958 Alan Caldwell formed a 'skiffle' group and called themselves 'Al Caldwell's Texans'. In 1959 he changed the name to 'The Raving Texans'. | Richard Starkey joined 'The Raving Texans' the same year—and with no little urging from Rory reluctantly adopted the 'stage name' Ringo Starr.

At the turn of the 1960s, Rory again changed the group's name to Rory Storm and The Hurricanes. And soon they were widely considered to be one of the top bands in Liverpool. Cilla Black once said that The Hurricanes were the very first proper group she ever sang with. And they were *"a lovely bunch of fellas."*

Dubbed 'Mr. Showmanship' by adoring fans. Always dressed to shock in bright blue or yellow suits—gold or silver lamé—his bleached blonde hair combed into an exaggerated quiff on stage with a huge plastic comb—Rory Storm was a legendary Liverpool figure who never failed to drive crowds wild. For even greater theatrical effect, Rory once jumped from an audience box down onto the stage while in full song. Always set on making a bigger splash, when The Hurricanes played New Brighton swimming baths, Rory disrobed down to his gold lamé swim trunks and, in perfect time to the beat, dived from off the top board into the swimming pool below as a finale to his song.

In 1960, the group secured a 3-month 'summer season' at Butlin's Holiday Camp in Pwllheli, Wales, and were such an "outstanding success" they were immediately booked to come back the following year.

October 1960. During their first residency in Hamburg—at the Kaiserkeller—they were billed above The Beatles; both groups alternating during each night's 12-hour set; 90 minutes on then 90 minutes off. During their time in Hamburg—as a special favour—John, Paul, and George backed 'Lu' Walters on a private recording at Hamburg's Akustik Studios—with Ringo on drums.

In 1961, the group was voted No. 4 in *Mersey Beat*'s Annual Poll. In 1962, Rory and The Hurricanes were rockin' legions of happy holiday makers "two-by-two" during their third 'Summer Season' at Butlin's; this time, at Skegness, in Lincolnshire, on the east coast of England. And it was there that John and Paul; having driven 161 long, long miles across country; turned up on the morning of Thursday 16 August to get Ringo to join The Beatles. Almost at the same moment that Brian Epstein, at NEMS, back in Liverpool, officially dismissed Pete Best from the group.

1964. With '*Beatlemania*' already in full blast, Brian Epstein entered into a management contract with Rory Storm and The Hurricanes and personally undertook the group's recording of 'America' from *West Side Story*, but it failed to chart. Brian then lost interest.

Ringo stepped into the gap; offered the group the opportunity to record in London any time they liked, but for some reason Rory never took him up on it. Perhaps, as his sister Iris Caldwell later said, because Rory was a Liverpool boy at heart and voted never to stay away too long from the city he loved the best. Add to that running for the Pembroke Harriers and supporting Liverpool football team, and there was simply never any reason to leave.

Rory Storm died, unexpectedly, in Liverpool, in 1972. And is still much missed by any and all who saw him perform—even all these years later. | A film of his life has long been mooted but as of January 2018 nothing has come to fruition. A pity. As it seems Rory Storm is still very much a Liverpool legend in the making.

GERRY AND THE PACEMAKERS | Gerry Marsden - guitar / vocals | Les McGuire - piano | Les Chadwick – bass guitar | Freddie Marsden - drums |
In the early 1960s, Gerry and The Pacemakers worked the same gruelling Liverpool-Hamburg circuit as The Beatles. | On Merseyside, the group's following was often more than a match for their good friends and rivals The Beatles and, sometimes, they even managed to best it. Which goes to explain why, in 1962, Gerry and The Pacemakers were the second group signed by Brian Epstein to be represented by NEMS Enterprises.

In 1963, with George Martin now as their producer, the group had three consecutive No.1 UK Hits: 'How Do You Do It' | 'I Like It' | 'You'll Never Walk Alone'.

Gerry Marsden also wrote most of the group's subsequent hits: 'It's All Right' | 'I'm the One' | 'Don't Let The Sun Catch You Cryin' | 'Ferry Cross the Mersey' | He also starred in the film—*Ferry Cross the Mersey*—a fun movie for dedicated fans, but one that quickly pales into insignificance when compared to The Beatles' *A Hard Day's Night*—the film it tried to emulate.

Even so, I still smile at the memory of Gerry and The Pacemakers on The Beatles–Roy Orbison 'pop-package' show that visited the Adelphi cinema in Slough—my local town—on Saturday May 18 1963. *"It's so nice to be here, down south, in Slug,"* Gerry said cheekily at the end of the group's first number; his comical mispronunciation of 'Slough' rhymes with 'now'. He brought the house down. Gerry also presented The Beatles with a Silver *Disc* for their No. 1 Hit, 'From Me To You', during the show. | A consummate entertainer, Gerry Marsden never stopped working; touring extensively to great acclaim. He began his 'Farewell Tour' in the UK in late 2017. And I thought he'd 'walk on' forever, but he officially retired in November 2018.

THE BIG THREE | Johnny Hutchinson - drums/vocals | Johnny Gustafson - bass guitar / vocals | Adrian Barber (until 1962). **Replaced by Brian Griffiths - lead guitar/vocals** | The original 'power trio'| The Big Three were regarded with awe on Merseyside. | They had the biggest bass amplifiers of any group—designed by original band member Adrian Barber—an electronics wizard. Nicknamed 'Coffin' amps—he made one for Paul McCartney. | After a successful 1962 tour, Barber stayed on at Star-Club in Germany and was replaced by Brian Griffiths, one of Liverpool's foremost guitarists. | The Big Three were signed by Brian Epstein and recorded 'Some Other Guy'—for Decca—followed in 1963 by the EP 'Live at The Cavern'—now using VOX and Fender Amps. | Record success eluded the group, however, and they and Brian Epstein parted company.

'KINGSIZE' TAYLOR & THE DOMINOES | Ted 'Kingsize' Taylor - lead guitar/vocals | Sam Hardie - piano | Dave Lovelady - drums | Bobby Thompson - bass guitar | John Frankland - rhythm guitar | 'Kingsize' Taylor and The Dominoes—named for the great Fats Domino—were one of Liverpool's most popular bands; 'Kingsize' Taylor was widely considered to be one of the best vocalists on all of Merseyside. Cilla Black sang with the group on numerous occasions. Had an all but permanent residency at the Iron Door Club.

In 1962 the group appeared at Star-Club, in St. Pauli, and proved so popular, they were offered a residency. The group later played various clubs in Hamburg, Kiel, and Berlin, before returning to the UK for Chuck Berry's 1964 Tour. | The group appeared on television, were signed by Decca—had a No.1 Hit in Germany—but failed to make any real breakthrough. As tastes in pop music moved ever forward—and the lure of the rockin' sound of 'Merseybeat' faded away—the group disbanded.

THE SEARCHERS | John McNally - guitar | Mike Pender (Mike Prendergast) - guitar | Johnny Sandon (Billy Beck) - guitar/vocals | Tony Jackson - vocals/bass guitar | Joe Kennedy - drums | Norman McGarry - drums | Chris Curtis (Chris Crummey) - drums | Frank Allen - vocals/bass guitar |

The Searchers started as a skiffle group in Liverpool in 1959 by John McNally and Mike Pender. Legend has it they took their name from John Ford's 1956 classic western *'The Searchers'*. An allusion to Buddy Holly's 'That'll Be The Day'—a song Holly had been inspired to write because of the repeated utterance of the ironic phrase by the film's main character—Ethan Edwards—played by John Wayne.

The group evolved into 'Tony and the Searchers'—with Kennedy on drums. | Then as 'Johnny Sandon and the Searchers'—with McGarry on drums—they had regular bookings at Liverpool's Iron Door Club. | Tony Sandon then left the group to join The Remo Four. | And so the 'foursome' that made up the original 'Searchers' are: McNally, Pender, Jackson and McGarry.

But then McGarry left to be replaced by Curtis; and Tony Jackson later left to be replaced by Frank Allen. | All of which is enough to make anyone's head spin. So let's just say that the last three Searchers' 'foursomes' are the ones fans search for most in regard to 60s hits.

The Searchers played every top venue on Merseyside and drew capacity crowds at The Cavern and The Tower, New Brighton. In July 1962, they began a 128-day season at Star-Club Hamburg. And played three 60-minute sets each and every night. After which they returned for a residency at the Iron Door Club.

A tape-recorded club session led to a Pye recording contract with producer Tony Hatch. Standout Hits: 'Sweets For My Sweet' 'Sugar and Spice' 'Love Potion No.9' 'Needles and Pins' 'Don't Throw Your Love Away' 'Someday We're Gonna Love Again' 'When You Walk in The Room' 'What Have They Done To The Rain'. | They were the one Liverpool beat group Brian Epstein ever truly regretted letting slip through his fingers.

THE SWINGING BLUE JEANS | Ray Ennis - lead guitar /vocals| Les Braid - bass/keyboards | Ralph Ellis - tar | Norman Kuhlke - drums | Paul Moss - banjo |
The Swinging Bluegenes began as a Trad-Jazz influenced skiffle group in Liverpool in 1957. | They played the Friday, Saturday,

Sunday evenings spots at the 'Jazz-only' Cavern Club. | In 1961 started hosting 'Swinging Bluegenes Guest Nights' on Tuesday evenings. | The Beatles played their first evening gig at The Cavern as 'guests' on 21 March 1961.

The Swinging Bluegenes were very highly regarded. In October 1961, Cavern DJ Bob Wooler, writing in *Mersey Beat*—said the group were *"in a class of their own"* and *"beyond comparison"*—even as he rated The Beatles Liverpool's No.1 beat group.

In 1962 the quintet of Ray Ennis, Les Braid, Ralph Ellis, Norman Kuhlke, and Paul Moss switched to playing rock 'n' roll and changed the group's name to The Swinging Blue Jeans. And they landed an HMV recording contract with producer Walter Ridley. | When Moss left the group they stayed a quartet—with the classic line-up of two guitars, bass guitar, and drums.

In December 1963—the band's cover of 'Hippy Hippy Shake' took them to No. 2 in the British charts. | The group best known for their hit singles on HMV: 'Hippy Hippy Shake' | 'Good Golly Miss Molly' | 'You're No Good' | 'Don't Make Me Over'

THE MERSEYBEATS | Tony Crane - lead guitar/vocals | Billy Kinsley - rhythm guitar / vocals | Aaron Williams - guitar | John Banks - drums | Crane and Kinsley formed a duo The Mavericks late 1960. September 1961 became The Pacifics. In February 1962 Bob Wooler, the Cavern's DJ, renamed them 'The Mersey Beats'. In April 1962, as The Merseybeats, they then signed a recording contract with Fontana.

In 1963, they had first their hit single 'It's Love That Really Counts'. In 1964, a million-selling gold disc 'I Think of You'.

February 1964, Billy Kinsley left to form The Kinsleys, and was replaced by Johnny Gustafson, formerly of the Big Three.

With Gustafson the group had two major hits: 'Don't Turn Around' 'Wishin' and Hopin' ' | Other recordings: 'Last Night' 'Don't Let it Happen to Us' 'I Love You, Yes I Do' 'I Stand Accused' 'Mr. Moonlight' 'Really Mystified' 'Fortune Teller' | In late 1964, Kinsley returned to the group. | Toured Germany and US in 1964 and were the stars of *'Merseybeats Show'* on Italian television. | The Merseybeats claim to have appeared at The Cavern with The Beatles more times than any other band.

THE UNDERTAKERS | Jackie Lomax - bass guitar / vocals | Chris Huston - lead guitar/vocals | Geoff Nugent - rhythm guitar/vocals | Brian Jones – saxophone /vocals | Bugs Pemberton – drums | Originally called Bob Evans and the Five Shillings. | 1959. The Vegas Five | 1961. The Undertakers. The saxophone gave them a 'unique' sound. |1962. Played Star-Club, Hamburg. | Back in UK, they rejected a management offer from Brian Epstein. | Signed with Pye Records and producer Tony Hatch—with little or no impact on the charts. | 'Everybody Loves a Lover' 'Do The Mashed Potatoes' 'What About Us' 'Money' 'Just a Little Bit' 'If You Don't Come Back' | 1965. The Undertakers split up after a tour of the US. | Jackie Lomax later recorded as a solo artist for The Beatles' Apple Corps. 'Sour Milk Sea' was his only hit, but it was a good one.

THE FOURMOST | Brian O'Hara - lead guitar / vocals | Mike Millward - rhythm guitar / vocals | Billy Hatton - bass player /vocals | Dave Lovelady - drums /vocals | 1957. Called the Two Jays. | September 1959. Expanded into the Four Jays.

1 March 1961. Play the Cavern Club for first time. | October 1962. Become The Fourmost | Played The Cavern and The Tower multiple occasions; most notably Little Richard & The Beatles Show. | Had very own Radio Luxembourg show—'*Springtime*'.

30 June 1963. Signed management contract with Brian Epstein NEMS Enterprises. | Auditioned for George Martin. Signed to EMI's Parlophone label. | 30 August 1963. The Fourmost's first single 'Hello Little Girl' (Lennon–McCartney) was released and reached No. 9 in UK singles chart. | 15 November 1963. The follow-up 'I'm in Love' (Lennon–McCartney) released and reached No. 17 in UK chart. | December 1963. Play 'The Beatles Xmas Show' | Summer 1964. The group's biggest hit 'A Little Loving' reached No. 6 in UK | Followed with Top 40 Hits 'How Can I Tell Her' 'Baby I Need Your Loving' 'Everything in the Garden' 'Girls Girls Girls' | Appeared in film *Ferry 'Cross The Mersey*' with Gerry and The Pacemakers and Cilla Black.

One singularly original feature of the group; they did impressions of other 'famous singers' as part of their stage act.

LEE CURTIS AND THE ALL-STARS | Lee Curtis (Pete Flannery) - lead singer | Frank Bowen - lead guitar | Tony Waddington - rhythm guitar | Wayne Bicketon - bass | Bernie Rogers - drums | Replaced by Pete Best - drums | Liverpool beat group led by Pete Flannery, using the stage name 'Lee Curtis', originally named Lee Curtis & the Detours. | The group managed and promoted by Joe Flannery; a close friend of Brian Epstein. | The original group appeared with The Beatles at Sam Leach's 'Operation Big Beat III' at the Tower Ballroom. Soon after which Lee put together a new backing band and named them 'The All Stars'. | Drummer Bernie Rogers left to join a new group that had a recording contract. Joe Flannery then quickly arranged, with Brian Epstein, for Pete Best—who'd just been booted out of The Beatles—to join the group.

The 'new' band appeared with The Beatles on the Mersey 'Riverboat Shuffle'; the Little Richard concert at the Tower; the 'Showdance' at the Queen's Hall in Widnes, and the Cavern. | Such was Pete Best's local popularity; the group was voted No. 2 in the second annual *Mersey Beat* poll. | When Pete Flannery left the group in July 1963 to pursue a solo career, it re-formed around Pete Best and renamed itself—The Pete Best Band.

BILLY J. KRAMER - WITH THE DAKOTAS | Born William Howard Ashton, in Bootle, a suburb of Liverpool, England, 1943. | Billy played rhythm guitar in a group, but with his good looks and million-watt smile, he cleverly switched to being a vocalist.

Brian Epstein, ever on the lookout for new talent, quickly alighted on Billy J. but was less than keen on his backing group, The Coasters, and instead teamed him up with Manchester-based group, The Dakotas, that he'd seen backing Pete MacLaine, at the Little Richard concert at The Tower Ballroom.

Billy's performing name, 'Kramer', was chosen at random from a telephone directory. And it was none other than John Lennon who then suggested that Billy add the 'J' to the name to give it *"a tougher edge."*

Billy J. and The Dakotas were both signed to Parlophone Records by George Martin. And then named 'Billy J. Kramer *with* the Dakotas'—separate identities for separate entities.

The group was offered 'Do You Want to Know a Secret?'—a Lennon-McCartney original from The Beatles' debut album *'Please Please Me'*. The record—backed on the 'B' Side by another Lennon–McCartney original, 'I'll Be on My Way'—went to No. 2 in the UK Singles Chart in 1963—although some charts did have it at No. 1. | It was soon followed up by another Lennon-McCartney song pairing—'Bad To Me' and 'I Call Your Name'—that did reach No. 1 on all charts and sold over a million copies and was awarded a gold disc. | Towards the close of 1963, yet another Beatles' cover song 'I'll Keep You Satisfied' took the group to No. 4 in the charts.

Billy J. was on a roll. And despite very strong advice to the contrary he then turned down the offer of yet another Lennon-McCartney song 'One and One Is Two' and, instead, recorded the Stateside hit 'Little Children'. It turned out to be his/the group's biggest ever hit and their second chart topper.

In 1964 Billy J. Kramer *with* the Dakotas recorded 'From a Window'—a Lennon-McCartney song that The Beatles never released and took it into the 'Top Ten' in the UK.

Billy J. *with* the Dakotas proved very popular in the US—that million-watt smile working overtime again—and made multiple appearances on the nationally televised shows: *Shindig!* | *Hullabaloo* | *The Ed Sullivan Show.*

Billy J. Kramer's cover version of Bacharach-David's 'Trains and Boats and Planes' reached No. 12. And was a swan song of sorts as all his/their subsequent record releases failed to chart. No doubt because of the fast fading appeal of 'Beat' music.

Singer and group then parted ways.

Billy J. Kramer is still smiling; still performing; with another handpicked group, also from Manchester. Still very much a favourite at concerts and clubs, and The Beatles' Festival circuit.

THE CHANTS | Joe Ankrah | Edmund 'Eddie' Ankrah | Nat Smeda | Alan Harding | Edmund 'Eddy' Amoo | Not a Liverpool 'beat' group in the strict sense, but by all accounts a group hard to beat. | The Chants were a five-piece a cappella harmony group fusing raw soul and gospel with hard driving R&B beat unique for the times. Liverpool's most popular black vocal act hailed from Toxteth, Liverpool 8. | Joe Ankrah, his brother Eddie, and friends formed The Shades in Liverpool early in 1962. Invited Nat Smeda, Alan Harding, and lead singer 'Eddy' Amoo to join to give a fuller sound and became The Chants. Regular backing band The Harlems; powered by Vinnie Ismail's driving rhythm guitar. | Managed for a short while by Brian Epstein; then took new management. | Signed with Pye. Produced by Tony Hatch. Debut disc 'I Don't Care' b/w 'Come Go With Me' released 17 September 1963. 'I Could Write A Book' b/w 'A Thousand Stars' released 1 January 1964. Two more singles in 1964 but all failed to chart. | Late 1964 saw various member changes, but The Chants kept on working; continued enchanting. | Appeared in Hamburg. Toured Ireland. | In 1976 'Eddy' Amoo left the group. Formed Liverpool soul band, The Real Thing (v.v. *Coca Cola* advertising slogan), with brother Chris, Dave Smith, and Ray Lake. Dubbed "The Black Beatles" by the press. | Landed gig backing David Essex. | June 1976. No. 1 in UK Chart with disco beat 'You To Me Are Everything' | More hits: 'Feel the Force' 'Can't Get By Without You' | 'Eddy', 'Cris', and Dave still tour as a three-piece The Real Thing 'to great acclaim. | Biggest selling all-black British 'pop' act ever.

| **Side Bar** | **The Chants and The Beatles** | 12 October 1962. Joe Ankrah met Paul McCartney at Little Richard concert at the Tower Ballroom, New Brighton. Paul fascinated when he heard that Joe was in an a cappella group. Gave Joe a signed note to produce at the Cavern when The Beatles returned from Hamburg. | Early December 1962, The Chants attended lunchtime gig and afterwards performed for The Beatles; John and George knocked out. The Beatles had The Chants perform at the Cavern that very night and backed them, much to Brian Epstein's concern; but when 'Eppy' heard them he invited The Chants to appear with The Beatles again. | On the special all-Beatles edition of *Juke Box Jury*, the first record played to them was The Chants' 'I Could Write A Book'. The Beatles voted it "a hit" but despite their fulsome praise, it turned out to be "a miss."

PART ONE - PEOPLE. PLACES. VENUES.

4 - Liverpool Venues

"There's A Place...Where I Can Go..."

> *"...and it's going on everywhere: town halls, church halls, ballrooms, ice-rinks, clubs, cellars, coffee bars... even cinemas and swimming baths. One local promoter even hired the Liverpool Stadium to put on a rock 'n' roll show..."*
> — Bill Harry | Founder & Editor of *Mersey Beat*
> as retold in *The One After 9:09*

Drums! A hard driving, hard pounding, fast and heavy, 4/4, bass-drum-laden 'Atomic' beat—*thump thud, thump thud, thump thud, thump thud*—was the very essence of what was to emerge, worldwide, as the unique sound of 'Merseybeat'. And the places the sound emerged from—the cellar clubs—jive hives—beat clubs—ballrooms—town halls—village halls—church halls—were to be found all over Merseyside.

A number of venues in Liverpool provided a unique backdrop to the story of the band we've known for all these years. And a good few of them—became places of legend in their own right—and rightly so.

The Cavern Club | The Iron Door Club | New Brighton Tower Ballroom | The Jacaranda Coffee Bar and Club | The Casbah Coffee Club | Litherland Town Hall | Lathom Hall | Knotty Ash Village Hall | Hambleton Hall | The Grafton & Locarno Ballrooms | The Rialto Ballroom | Cassanova Club | The Garston Baths | The Grosvenor Ballroom | The Neston Institute | '527' Club

THE CAVERN CLUB | 10 MATHEW STREET | LIVERPOOL |
'The Home of The Beatles'

> "By the turn of the decade, the most unlikely places had become beat clubs. At first, it had been small cafés and cellar clubs, but now even the once-jazz-proud Cavern had given way and was booking beat groups, as was another jazz castle, the Iron Door Club." — Ian Whitcomb | Musician | Singer | Author
> Rock Odyssey - A Chronicle of The Sixties

The Cavern Club first opened its doors January 1957 as a Parisian-like 'cellar' jazz club. And was situated in a multi-arched basement in the city's old warehouse district better known for its storage of fruit and vegetables and other perishable commodities. Jazz also proving a perishable commodity, Alan Sytner, the original owner, then sold the club to his accountant, Ray McFall. More attuned to the times, McFall added folk and skiffle sessions to compliment the club's jazz offerings. Business picked up. Then, ever-astute businessman that he was, sensing an ever growing demand and looking for new ways to meet it, McFall added rock 'n' roll 'lunchtime sessions' to the club's regular performance schedule.

The Cavern's rock 'n' roll 'lunchtime sessions'—featuring The Beatles—began in February 1961. And in many ways it's where and when The Beatles' local rise to fame truly began, as in a veritable heartbeat hundreds of teenagers who worked in the centre of the City regularly stood in a never less than three- or four-deep queue that stretched the entire length of Mathew Street; delivery boys and office girls, all patiently waiting to get in to see and hear The Beatles'. The 'lunchtime sessions' quickly proving such a success, the group was offered a 'highly prized' regular evening slot. Soon after which, The Cavern eschewed its jazz past and fully switched over to presenting the pounding, pulsating sounds of Merseybeat.

That the Cavern was cramped, crowded, sweaty, and dank, and the walls ran constantly with condensation deterred absolutely no one; beat music was as food and drink to everyone; manna from heaven. It certainly proved to be such for Brian Epstein, the local businessman who first saw the group perform at a lunchtime session at the club on 9 November, that same year; who within weeks would go on to become The Beatles' manager.

One of the people most responsible for The Cavern Club's enormous success was Bob Wooler, the DJ and compère. His incomparable rock 'n' roll, R&B, and Tamla-Motown record collection helped keep things bopping between live sets, but it was his brilliant use of language that kept everyone on their toes. He was a veritable past-master of 'the pun' and it was he that gave birth to the immortal line to describe The Cavern as: **"Remember all you cave dwellers, that the Cavern is the best of cellars"**, a play on the title of the LP *'The Best of Sellers'* that showcased the work of the actor Peter Sellers (produced, as it happens, by none other than George Martin).

The Cavern became synonymous with the rise of Merseybeat and at one time or another every Merseyside group of any standing played the club: Gerry and The Pacemakers, The Big Three, The Searchers, The Swinging Bluejeans, Kingsize Taylor and The Dominoes, Billy J. Kramer and The Dakotas perhaps the best known. However, The Cavern became justifiably *world famous* because of its long and storied association with The Beatles, who played at the club 292 times; the group's last performance, there, on 3 August 1963. The Beatles began their time at The Cavern as leather-jacket and jeans wearing Rockers and ended as polished performers ready to face Granada's television cameras and, ultimately, the eyes of the world.

International stars like Bruce Channel and Gene Vincent, as well as famed London groups such as the Rolling Stones. The Kinks. The Yardbirds. The Who. Queen. Elton John. All were more than eager to play at the club. Legend says singer Cilla Black worked at the club, for a time, as a coat-check girl. She certainly sang there, a number of times, with The Beatles.

The Cavern Club had its ups and down, financial and otherwise, as the pop parade inevitably moved on to greener, more profitable pastures. The warehouse building that housed the original club was pulled down in March 1973—and The Cavern dismantled, brick-by-brick—to make room for the 'Merseyrail' underground loop. The club was rebuilt, across the street, in 1984, using many of the original bricks, but closed again in 1989. It re-opened yet again in 1991, under new owners; true Merseybeat enthusiasts; and living proof that it's hard to keep a legend down. The Cavern Club is in full swing, today with as many as 40 live bands performing every week. All of which says "the Rockin' City" is still rockin'. 2017 marked The Cavern's 60th anniversary.

THE IRON DOOR CLUB | 13 TEMPLE STREET | LIVERPOOL L2 | 'The Cradle of Merseybeat'

> "There must be over three hundred groups, around Merseyside, all playing rock 'n' roll, country, western, Trad-jazz, folk. There are duos, trios, quartets, even all-girl rock 'n' roll bands. There are black vocal groups and Caribbean steel bands. There's even a flourishing poetry scene…"
> — Bill Harry | Founder & Editor of *Mersey Beat*
>   as retold in *The One After 9:09*

The Iron Door Club (née Liverpool Jazz Society—later the Storeyville Jazz Club) and The Cavern Club were originally conceived as city-centre 'jazz only' clubs—each with a strict policy of not booking rock bands for evening performances.

The Iron Door Club was founded in May 1960—in a warehouse previously used as a 'cold' factory for packing butter—by Geoff Hogarth and a business partner. The first floor was used for a cloakroom, and an office, and served as a space for band practice or selling food and drink. The upper six floors of the warehouse remained vacant. It originally served as the home of the Liverpool Jazz Society, though Sam Leach changed all that when 'his' club took over residency.

The Beatles' first appearance for Sam Leach at The Iron Door was on the night of Monday 6th March. The next, on Saturday 11th March 1961—as part of a 'Big Beat' 12-group, 12-hour, all-night session that ran from 8PM to 8AM—with a new band performing each hour. Also very significant, as it was probably the last time Stu Sutcliffe appeared with the group in Liverpool.

Among the groups said to have played that fabled night were: The Beatles, 'Kingsize' Taylor and The Dominoes, Gerry and the Pacemakers, The Big Three, The Remo Four, Rory Storm and the Hurricanes, Johnny Rocco and The Jets, The Searchers, Ian and The Zodiacs, Howard Casey and the Seniors, Faron and The Flamingoes, and Dale Roberts and The Jaywalkers.

Mark Lewisohn cites attendance capacity of the Temple Street cellar as being 1000; although he adds that as many as 2000 fans were there—at one time or another—for some or all of that famed, first 'all-nighter' event.

As locals remember it, Liverpool 'beat fans' went to one club or the other, rarely both. The Cavern experience—for bands, as well as the audience—was very much controlled by the club's resident compère and DJ, Bob Wooler. Whereas, The Iron Door Club not only permitted bands to announce themselves, but openly promoted jamming between groups, even allowing mixing of music styles. Cilla Black cut her teeth, singing with 'Kingsize' Taylor and The Dominoes, at the Iron Door. The Searchers opened there, too.

THE TOWER BALLROOM | NEW BRIGHTON | WIRRAL | MERSEYSIDE | *'The Rock 'n' Roll Venue That Changed The Name Of The Game On Merseyside'*

> "From New Brighton Tower to Garston Baths the 'beat' (beat for rhythm, not beatniks) groups thump, shout, kick, and tremble in pubs, clubs and church halls..."
> — Derek Jewell | *The Sunday Times* | September 1963

The beautiful sands that stretched for miles along England's northwest coast, made New Brighton, on the Wirral Peninsula, a hugely popular seaside resort at the turn of the Twentieth Century. It offered the *plus-perfect* setting for a world-class landmark and when the New Brighton Tower opened, in 1900, the steel lattice observation tower—567 feet high—was the tallest building in Great Britain and would have even been seen as a rival to the Blackpool Tower, some 25 miles further up the coast; as well as the Eiffel Tower, in Paris. Both of which had been completed to great public fanfare ten years previously.

To add even more to its enticement—the New Brighton Tower was set in large, beautifully landscaped grounds that boasted a boating lake, a funfair, botanical gardens, a small zoo, and a sports ground with full-size football pitch, as well as a motorcycle speedway track. Was it any wonder then that The Tower, and all it offered, was advertised as *"the finest place of amusement in the entire Kingdom."*

And yet, even with all that, and more, the New Brighton Tower was forced to close, in 1919, largely due to a downturn in business, but also a total lack of maintenance during World War One, and it was dismantled and the metal sold off for scrap. The four-storey, Gothic-style building at its base—that housed the huge Tower Ballroom—was, however, left intact and continued to prove a popular attraction during the big band era of the Thirties and Forties. But as the Fifties progressed—despite the pulling power of such star attractions as Joe Loss and his Orchestra—both the resort and ballroom fell increasingly out of fashion.

The New Brighton 'Tower' Ballroom was re-discovered, re-invigorated and later even managed by Sam Leach, the visionary Liverpool promoter. One of his many brainwaves was to present *'Operation Big Beat'*—a six-hour, one-low price, multi-group extravaganza: *'Rocking to Merseyside's Top 5 Groups'*: The Beatles, Rory Storm and The Hurricanes, Gerry & The Pacemakers, The Remo Four, and 'Kingsize' Taylor and The Dominoes. It was 'Big Beat' rockin' on a scale never before witnessed, that attracted an audience of well over 4,000 twisting, jiving, shouting, screaming, deliriously happy and ecstatic beat-fans. It smashed to pieces all previous attendance records at 'The Tower'—made all the more unbelievable when you consider it also occurred on one of the foggiest Merseyside nights in living memory.

How on earth does anyone top that? The irrepressible, indefatigable Sam Leach turned round and did it all again—two weeks later—with the same line up—and again broke his own previous attendance record.

And then to top that, he secured and booked all available, future, Friday-night dates at The Tower and launched "*The Biggest 'Beat' Programme Ever Undertaken*" by anyone, in all of Great Britain. Or so claimed the newspaper ads and posters.

But it proved true. Sam Leach's subsequent groundbreaking series of 'Big Beat' sessions continued to break attendance records and galvanized the entire Merseyside beat scene—with every group of any standing clamouring to play 'The Tower'.

Sam having shown the way, Liverpool co-promoters Brian Epstein and the DJ Bob Wooler went on to present 'pop' package shows at The Tower. In time, drawing such rock luminaries as Little Richard, Bruce Channel, Joe Brown and His Bruvvers, and the Rolling Stones to play for ever more wildly appreciative Merseyside audiences.

All of it made possible because of the towering audacity, and towering dreams, of one extraordinary man, Sam Leach.

THE JACARANDA COFFEE BAR & NIGHTCLUB |
23 SLATER STREET | **LIVERPOOL L1** | *'The One Place To Go'*
The coffee bar by day/cellar club at night opened and owned by Allan Williams; The Beatles' first booking agent-cum-manager; in a deliberate homage to the famous 2i's Coffee Bar in London's then somewhat infamous Soho district. It was one of the very first 'live-entertainment' coffee bars in Liverpool. And was a much-needed hangout for The Beatles in the very early days.

It's here that John and Paul and Stuart first saw 'Lord' Woodbine and his 'All-Steel Caribbean Band' play. Legend says that John and Stuart helped paint the basement 'cellar club' and even designed and painted a 'jazzy' mural on the walls.

Beginning 30 May 1960, The Silver Beetles, were engaged to play 'the Jac' on Monday nights, and did so a number of times, but never really to more than a handful of people.

It was also from here that John, Stu, Paul, George, and Pete; Allan Williams *et al*; set off for their very first trip to Hamburg—'Lord' Woodbine and his 'Royal Caribbean Band' steel-pan band and Derry and The Seniors already having paved the way.

THE CASBAH COFFEE CLUB | 8 HAYMAN'S GREEN | WEST DERBY

'The Cellar Club That Witnessed The True Beginnings Of It All'
This hugely popular and justifiably famous 'teenagers' club was opened in September 1958, by Mona Best, in the basement of her large Victorian-style home—way out in a suburb of Liverpool—as a place for her son, Peter, and his friends to meet, drink coffee and Coca-Cola and, importantly, jive to the latest 45rpm 'pop' records played on a Dansette record player.

The Casbah was so instantly successful they installed a jukebox and invited local groups to play 'live' on weekends. And one of the groups that played regularly was the 'Skiffle' group—The Quarrymen—John Lennon's very first group and the precursor to The Beatles.

Pete Best began playing drums and formed a group called The Blackjacks, which proved very popular with beat fans. When The Beatles were later offered a contract to play Hamburg—if they found themselves a regular drummer—they asked Pete to join them. He did—and all five Beatles—John Lennon, Paul McCartney, George Harrison, Stu Sutcliffe, and Pete Best—set off to play an 8-week residency—later extended to 16 weeks—at Bruno Koschmider's Indra Cabaret and Kaiserkeller clubs—situated off the Reeperbahn, in Hamburg's notorious St. Pauli red-light district. Light years away from the polite middle-class denizens of West Derby.

The Casbah Coffee Club had over 2000 members in its heyday. It also has the distinction of being the place where, over bottles of Coke, the savage young Beatles met and discussed the fine details of their first contract with their soon to be manager—Mr. Brian Epstein.

Now newly re-opened and fully restored to its former glory, the Casbah Coffee Club—all seven of its original interlocked cellar rooms intact—is one of the key Beatles' sites that still has something of the original rockin' vibe.

Long may it thrive.

LITHERLAND TOWN HALL | HATTON HILL ROAD | LIVERPOOL 21

'Always a Lively Time Here at the Litherland Town Hall' read the ads (typographic alliteration courtesy of itinerant DJ and compère, and inveterate punster, Bob Wooler).

Saturday night was always the biggest draw of the week, but it was here, on a Tuesday night, 27 December 1960, that The Beatles played a special post-Boxing Day dance that would turn out to be a huge and utterly unexpected 'turning point' for the group.

The Beatles had not long returned from their first 16-week stint in Hamburg. Which had ended with George Harrison being deported; Paul McCartney and Pete Best ordered to leave Germany, soon afterwards. And with Stuart Sutcliffe having decided to stay on in Hamburg with new girlfriend, Astrid Kirchherr, over Christmas and the New Year, John Lennon had had to make his way back to Liverpool, by lonesome himself.

Thoroughly downcast by the wretched turn of events, The Beatles were all but in disarray; made all the more depressing by a cold, grey, wet Liverpool December. And with or without Stu, they desperately needed work. However, their booking agent-cum manager, Allan Williams, had problems of his own; his new Top Ten nightclub, named after the club in Hamburg, had just mysteriously burned down; and he had little or no time to help them. What he did do, though, was introduce them to Bob Wooler, the local DJ, who obviously took a shine to them, as it was he who then arranged—with no little persuasion—for local promoter Brian Kelly—to book them as last minute additions to a 'Christmas Dance' scheduled to take place at the Litherland Town Hall ballroom; for what would be their very first appearance at the venue.

Posters proclaiming The Del Renas, The Deltones, and The Searchers were already up, and so Wooler and others pasted overlays saying *'The Beatles. Direct from Hamburg'* across as many of them as they could. With John, Paul, George, and Pete all dressed in their black leather jackets and trousers and cowboy boots people, not unnaturally, assumed they must be

German. What they thought of tweed-jacket wearing Chas Newby—filling in for absent bass-player Stu Sutcliffe—is anyone's guess. But right from their opening number—with Paul belting out Little Richard's 'Long Tall Sally'—The Beatles absolutely stunned the crowd. No one had seen or heard anything like it. The group's hard-hitting, cowboy boot-stomping 'Hamburg' sound was so new, so raw, so loud—and so very different—it blew everyone away. Including young accountancy student Neil Aspinall and rival promoter Sam Leach, both of whom would later play significant parts in The Beatles' story.

People in the audience just stopped dancing, or whatever else it was they happened to be doing, and rushed the stage; again, something totally unprecedented in Liverpool, let alone Litherland Town Hall. The Beatles' thirty-minute set was an absolute knockout smash; a breakout performance that immediately positioned them as being Liverpool's top 'live' draw; and effectively changed the game forever. All of which had Brian Kelly—and every other Liverpool promoter with blood in their veins—scrambling to book the group.

The Beatles played Litherland Town Hall for 'Beekay Promotions' another nineteen times over the following year, but only ever as 'top of the bill' headliners.

LATHOM HALL | LATHOM AVENUE | SEAFORTH | LIVERPOOL 21

'Jive At Lathom Hall… Every Saturday' | Lathom Hall was one of several 'prime' Liverpool venues associated with hard-nosed, local promoter Brian Kelly for both weekday and weekend promotions. Litherland Town Hall, the Aintree Institute, Alexandra Hall, among the others.

The dancehalls in Lathom and Litherland of particular significance in Beatles' history as they very much represent the group 'before and after' Hamburg. The difference between: 'don't let the doors hit you on your way out of Liverpool' and six-months later, when they 'blew the bloody doors off' and stormed their way back into the local scene.

The Silver Beetles 'auditioned' for Kelly, at Lathom Hall, by performing on the evening of 14 May 1960, for 'no fee'. A deft ploy Kelly always used to see if a group was worth booking regularly or not. The Beatles passed the audition, were 'officially' booked to play the following week—Kelly advertised them as the Silver Beats in newspaper ads—only they didn't appear. They were off backing singer Johnny Gentle on his 9-day tour of Scotland and had omitted to inform Kelly of their unavailability. To say the least Kelly was not amused by their 'no show' and refused to book them again.

Thankfully, for all concerned, if not the history of popular music, some time in the second or third week of December 1960, Bob Wooler, who regularly worked as a DJ and compère for 'Beekay Promotions' events, persuaded Kelly to change his mind about The Beatles; now called; and newly returned from their first season in Hamburg; to play the 'Christmas Dance' at Litherland Town Hall, on 27 December 1960; the event that would forever change the fortunes of The Beatles.

Following their breakout performance at Litherland Town Hall, The Beatles made nine further appearances for Bill Kelly's 'Beekay Promotions' at Lathom Hall during the months of January and February 1961.

| Side Bar | Lathom Hall and 'a kick to the head' | A particularly nasty incident occurred after one of the seven or so bookings The Beatles still had yet to play at Lathom Hall, in late January, early, or mid February, that would have seen Stu Sutcliffe on bass, again; a sad and sorry event that has subsequently loomed large in Beatles' legend. One that's still being hotly debated. | It involves the night Stu Sutcliffe, only recently arrived back from Hamburg on 21 January, was beaten up and reportedly kicked in the head by a gang of Teddy Boys. The origin; a great number of Beatles' chroniclers have since alleged; of the severe headaches and cerebral haemorrhage that eventually killed him. | The Beatles were often a prime target—as were all Liverpool's beat groups—for gangs spoiling for a fight or annoyed that one of their 'judies' appeared to fancy one or more of the musicians on stage. | Pete Best later spoke of the incident and remembers they'd finished their session, had started packing up, getting

ready to take their gear outside. Stu went out, first, and a gang of lads started picking on him. Then some girls ran back inside screaming: *"Stu's getting the living daylights knocked out of him."* Pete and John dashed out; threw a few punches; sorted things out; and pulled Stu back in again. Pete doesn't remember Stu getting his head kicked in; regardless of how some people have since sought to portray the event; but does remember John Lennon broke his little finger in the affray, which remained crooked forever after. | Of all people, Allan Williams was the first to report the event in his biography *'The Man Who Gave The Beatles Away'*—co-written with William Marshall. Marshall later admitted he'd taken the bare bones of Williams' stories and recollections and *"embellished them to make them more exciting."* Later authors simply followed his lead, most notably Philip Norman in *'Shout'*, after which it was simply accepted as gospel. | Bill Harry, one of Stu's closest friends, says that Stuart's mother was very clear on the issue: Stu's headaches had started after he took a very nasty fall down a steep flight of stairs at Astrid Kirchherr's home, in Hamburg. | Bill Harry and Pete Best, both eminently credible sources for last words on Stu Sutcliffe's tragic and untimely death.

KNOTTY ASH VILLAGE HALL | EAST PRESCOTT ROAD | WEST DERBY | *Famed home of Ken Dodd's 'Diddy Men'*

Knotty Ash is a small village, just south of West Derby, long known in the UK as the home of renowned Liverpool comedian Ken Dodd—as well as his characters, the little *'Diddy Men'*.

The Beatles played Knotty Ash village hall a half dozen times, mostly for Mona Best (Pete Best's mum) who held the regular Friday-night concession on the hall.

Although, arguably, the most legendary event ever to take place there was when The Beatles went head-to-head with Rory Storm and The Hurricanes in a hard-fought *'Battle of The Bands'* staged especially to celebrate Sam Leach's engagement party; the proceeds from which paid for the ensuing party.

Sam Leach took over the hall from Mona after Pete Best left The Beatles, and he himself had severed all ties with the Tower Ballroom, New Brighton.

HAMBLETON HALL | PAGE MOSS | HUYTON
The Beatles played this small suburban hall on St David's Road—some 10 miles east of the city-centre—ten times, in 1961. Their first gig was on 20th January 1961 and their eleventh and final appearance on the 13th January 1962.

THE GRAFTON AND LOCARNO BALLROOMS | WEST DERBY ROAD
Two very popular *'palais de dance'* venues—from pre-war days—that stood side-by-side-by-side.

Known locally as *"Da Gravvie"* and *"Da Loc"*—they were both highly favoured places for Merseyside groups to play as the acoustics were pretty good and, more importantly, they were well policed by teams of bouncers. A double win.

The Beatles played both ballrooms many, many times in the early Sixties.

THE RIALTO BALLROOM | STANHOPE STREET | LIVERPOOL 8
'Leach Entertainments' proudly presented *'The Beatles Show'* at the Rialto Ballroom on Thursday, September 6th, 1962. Billed as: *The North's Top 'Rock' Combo*, The Beatles were joined by Rory Storm and The 'All Star' Hurricanes, The Big Three, and The Mersey Beats. From 7:30PM–Midnight. And all of that knockout talent to be enjoyed for just five shillings; Sam Leach, again, determined to give the fans great value.

Only trouble, the venue was in Toxteth and *"They never mess around in Toxteth... they're as hard as effin' nails."* And so a hefty team of bouncers was always deemed a necessary addition to the cost of doing business.

The Beatles played the venue again on October 11th. This time the event, billed as a *'Rock 'n' Twist Carnival'*, was organised by none other than the students at Liverpool University. The name for the event shows how much they still had to learn; but I'd still give my eyeteeth to have been there.

Word is The Quarrymen performed at a number of skiffle contests at the ballroom, in the late 1950s; but alas to no avail.

THE CASSANOVA CLUB | SAMPSON AND BARLOW'S BALLROOM | LONDON ROAD | LIVERPOOL

February 14th 1961. Sam Leach re-opened the club—above a parade of shops—in Sampson and Barlow's Ballroom—opposite the Odeon Cinema—having had to vacate the previous Cassanova Club premises due to a vicious gang fight that'd broken out in the 'club' upstairs.

A club's reputation depended as much on its promoter, as its location, and Sam Leach was determined to get it right this time. Which he did with yet another rockin' Leach Entertainments extravaganza: '*4 Rompin Stompin Bands! Tickets just 4 shillings-and-sixpence!*' The Beatles were the closing act at the 'Cass' that night; the group having played earlier, that same evening, at Litherland Town Hall.

The Sensational Beatles were credited on posters for the event as '*The Originators of 'The Atom Beat'*—Pete Best's pounding, full on, unrelenting four/four to the bar, atomic beat!

'*The Valentine's Night Rock Ball*' poster, like so many other rockin' posters, stuck up on brick walls and in shop windows all around Merseyside, by the talented-beyond-measure, local artist Tony Booth.

The Beatles played the "Cass" on seven different occasions.

THE GARSTON BATHS | GARSTON | LIVERPOOL

The Silver Beatles played the venue a number of times and no doubt hated every single minute of it, given that the Garston Baths was also one of the most notorious spots in all of Liverpool for gang violence. The dance floor; laid over the top of the swimming pool; so often "swimming in blood", the place was known universally throughout Merseyside as "*the Blood Baths.*"

Which is really saying something given the number of gang fights that regularly broke out at almost every other Liverpool dance venue, at one time or another, in the 1960s.

The Grosvenor Ballroom, in Wallasey, being another such infamous spot for gang violence. As, too, was the Neston Institute, where a gang of rampaging Teds once booted a poor unfortunate sixteen-year old Liverpool boy to death.

THE GROSVENOR BALLROOM | WALLASEY | CHESHIRE

The Grosvenor Ballroom was another venue notorious for fights. Saturday nights were 'Big Beat' nights—an advertised headline that can be taken two ways—for local promoter Les Dodd. The featured group obliged to play on throughout whatever mayhem might ensue as a sure sign of their 'professionalism'. The Beatles performed at the Grosvenor Ballroom on 14 different occasions between June 1960 and September 1961. Their evening show there on June 6 —at the Whitsun Bank Holiday 'Jive and Rock' session—the first time they shared the bill with Gerry and The Pacemakers.

THE NESTON INSTITUTE | HINDERTON ROAD | NESTON | WIRRAL PENINSULA

The Silver Beetles played six shows at The Neston Institute—in June and July 1960—all of them for local promoter Les Dodd's Paramount Enterprises. Not a venue for the faint of heart. Around that time a gang of local Teddy Boys booted a 16-year-old boy to death at rock 'n' roll dance held there. Whether the Silver Beetles witnessed the event is still a matter of some debate—but they would have certainly been affected by it.

All six shows at The Neston Institute arranged by the group's then booking-agent-cum-manager Allan Williams prior to him arranging for them to play their first venue in Hamburg—at the Indra Cabaret Club—on 17 August 1960.

'527' CLUB | LEWIS'S DEPARTMENT STORE | LIVERPOOL

28 November 1962. The Beatles played the *'Young Idea Dance'* on the top floor of the department store. It wasn't a regular club venue; just a special set up for young staff members.

A Twist And Shout Out To: Holly Oak Hall, Penny Lane; Winter Gardens Ballroom and Wilson Hall, Garston; Orrell Park Ballroom, Aintree; Blair Hall, Walton; Peel Hall, Dingle; Aintree Institute, Mossway; Riverpark Ballroom, Hoylake; Alexandra Hall, Crosby; Plaza, St. Helens; Majestic Ballroom, Birkenhead; The Marine Club, Southport; The Queen's Hall, Widnes, *et al*

PART ONE - PEOPLE. PLACES. VENUES.

5 - Liverpool Landmarks

All These Places Had Their Moments...

Mersey Beat | The Grapes | The White Star | Ye Cracke | The Philharmonic | The Blue Angel | The Jokers | The Jacaranda | Casbah Coffee Club | Kardomah Coffee House | Punch and Judy Cafe | Joe's Cafe | NEMS Music Stores | Hessy's Music Store | Rushworths Music House | Lime Street Station | Central Station | The Adelphi Hotel | St. George's Hall | Empire Theatre | The Odeon Cinema | Lewis's Department Store | Blackler's Department Store | The Pier Head | The Mersey Ferry | The Mersey Tunnel

MERSEY BEAT | **81a Ranelagh Street L1** | The office of *Mersey Beat*—'*Merseyside's Own Entertainments Newspaper*'—founded and edited by Bill Harry—close Liverpool Art College friend of John Lennon and Stuart Sutcliffe. | Up the rickety stairs to the small attic office—above David Land's wine merchant's shop—rented for £5 a week—and with the increasing success of *Mersey Beat*, the floor below that, too. | Bill borrowed £50 from a friend of a friend. Then with nothing more than a desk, a chair, and an Olivetti typewriter—also on loan—and with the assistance of his girlfriend and future wife, Virginia Sowry; who he'd met at the Jacaranda Club; and a photographer friend, Dick Matthews—he set about publishing *Mersey Beat*.

Bill Harry did all the writing, designing, advertising, and circulation; Virginia Sowry did everything else—all the paperwork, the phone calls, the follow up with all the groups—the two of them often working twelve and fourteen hour days. | The success of the endeavour all the more extraordinary as Bill was still attending Liverpool Art College when he started *Mersey Beat*.

THE GRAPES Public House | Mathew Street | It's an ill wind. The nearby Cavern Club only served soft drinks and so every musician with a thirst popped into The Grapes for a quick one—and not-so-quick one—depending on the time of day or the gig played. And they still do, apparently. So The Grapes has definitely not lost its appeal. The much missed, much lamented, promoter and would-be Beatles' manager—Sam Leach—could often be seen here, over the years, always ready to regale you with a memorable tale of the early years of The Beatles.

THE WHITE STAR Public House | Rainford Gardens | But a stone's throw from The Grapes. And so a popular alternative watering hole for The Beatles and all the other groups that played The Cavern. They served Bass on draught; and still do.

YE CRACKE Public House | Rice Street | Close to Liverpool Art College and a favourite haunt of John Lennon, Stu Sutcliffe, and Bill Harry when they were penniless students. Hell-bent on future success, the trio formed the Dada-inspired 'art' group, The Dissenters, there. The place serves Bass, too. On tap.

THE PHILHARMONIC Public House | Hope Street | Another pub close to the Art College. Much grander, though, and with, arguably, the classiest Gents Toilets in all of Liverpool, all in different coloured marble meant to delight the eye.
    The Beatles and Brian Epstein liked to drink at 'The Phil'—and have a nosh there, too, as the food was always good. And when he at last became world famous, John would bemoan the fact he wasn't able to go to 'the Phil' for a drink.

THE BLUE ANGEL Nightclub | 108 Seel Street L1 | Formerly, the Wyvern Social Club, this is where, on the 10th May 1960, the London impresario, Larry Parnes and his star pop singer, Billy Fury, auditioned for a new backing group for a national tour. The Silver Beetles didn't make the cut, but were offered a 9-day tour of Scotland, backing Johnny Gentle—another of Parnes' stable of teen idols.

When Allan Williams re-named the club, The Blue Angel, he re-decorated it to suit 'ladies and gentlemen of taste', and over the ensuing years, it became *the* late-night watering hole for The Beatles, all the top-name groups, and any visiting personalities.

THE JOKER'S Drinking Club | Off Edge Lane | Liverpool | An after-hours drinking club that sometimes offered 'live music'. * Owned by a large black gentleman who may or may not have called himself 'The Joker'. Frequented by the good and—how shall we put it—the not so good. A favourite hangout of Liverpool CID officers and the better-connected denizens of the Liverpool underworld, it stood firmly on the intersection between the lawful and the not so lawful.

The maverick Liverpool promoter Sam Leach claimed to have taken John Lennon and Paul McCartney, and their new manager, Brian Epstein, to the club to celebrate Brian's first business engagements for The Beatles. | * Vinnie Ismail, the black guitarist and singer, sometimes performed here.

THE JACARANDA Coffee Bar and Club | 23 Slater Street L1 | The coffee bar-by-day/cellar club-by-night (just like the famous 2i's Coffee Bar in Soho, London) was originally owned by Allan Williams, the Liverpool promoter who also arranged for The Beatles to play their first 16-week season in Hamburg.

The 'Jac' was a popular hangout for the group in the early days. They played a dozen or so gigs in the basement. And it was from here that John, Stu, Paul, George, and Pete set off to play the Indra Cabaret Club owned by Bruno Koschmider, in Hamburg's notorious red-light district. | The 'Jac' has since been completely renovated—gone 'all posh'—and once again it's one of *the* places to be seen and have a drink in, in Liverpool.

CASBAH COFFEE CLUB | 8 Hayman's Green | West Derby | A second mention, too, for the Casbah Coffee Club. And why not, it more than deserves it. | A cellar club originally opened as a place for the area's many teenagers to meet, drink coffee and or Coca-Cola, and jive to the latest 45rpm records and—at the weekends—live bands—including The Beatles. Little wonder,

The Casbah Coffee Club had 2000 members in its heyday. Pete Best has said that the region's Coca-Cola supplier used to deliver over 200 '24-bottle wooden crates' of Coke a week simply to keep up with demand. That's a lot of bottle tops and empties.

Now re-opened and fully restored to its former glory, the Casbah is one of the key Beatles' sites that still has something of the original rockin' vibe. And, yes, if you ask them nicely I'm sure they'll still serve you a coffee or a Coca-Cola.

KARDOMAH COFFEE HOUSE | Corner Of Stanley Street And Whitechapel | There were Kardomah Coffee Houses in cities up and down the country, sometimes several in the same city, but none achieved the mythic proportions of one particular Kardomah, in Liverpool, that stood on the corner of Stanley Street and Whitechapel. It didn't hurt at all, that the coffee house was but a step or two away from Hessy's Music Store, and across the road from NEMS. It was *the* place to go to, *the* place to be seen. You could conduct business there; even have a coffee there. The Beatles visited the Kardomah times beyond number.

PUNCH AND JUDY CAFE | Lime Street | Situated, as it was, just outside Lime Street Railway Station, the Punch and Judy cafe was a favourite hangout for anyone waiting for someone to arrive off the London or Manchester train. The Beatles waited there countless times for their manager Brian Epstein to return from yet another trip to London, to see if he'd succeeded in securing them a recording contract. Their hopes dashed times beyond number: always a good time for a good strong cup of tea.

JOE'S CAFE | 139 Duke Street | Another firm favourite—especially on Friday and Saturday nights, as it stayed open all night; well almost. (Day 7:30AM-3:00PM | Night 10:00PM-4:00AM) Joe's Cafe as The Beatles knew it or Joe's Restaurant as it was later called was always warm and welcoming. Some say they did the best fry-up and beans-on-toast in all of Liverpool.

Joe's Cafe was witness to a somewhat unpleasant episode in Beatles' history. Having just returned from a special trip down to London, to confront Decca Records senior executives at a lunch at their Thames Embankment headquarters; it was here at Joe's Cafe that Brian Epstein informed John, Paul, George, and Pete; The Beatles having only just finished an evening gig; that Decca had finally turned them down flat.

NORTH END MUSIC STORES (N.E.M.S.) | Whitechapel & Great Charlotte Street *et al.* | The Epstein family business ever since the 1930s. The stores sold furniture, in the main; as well as radiograms and television sets, even washing machines; and then opened specialist record departments. Classical music was on the ground floor and popular music down in the basement in the Whitechapel store. | Legend has it that Raymond Jones walked into NEMS to inquire about the availability of a new record called 'My Bonnie'. The manager, Brian Epstein, hadn't heard of the disc or the group that had recorded it, but made a note to find out more, as he hated losing a sale. | He then went out of his way to find out more about the group named The Beatles and, remarkably, stumbled across his own destiny, too.

HESSY'S MUSIC STORES | 62 Stanley Street | *For All Musical Instruments Our Easy Terms Are "Easier"* | There'd been several 'Hessy's Music Stores' in Liverpool since the early 1950s, but the store located near the corner of Whitechapel, was the hands on favourite of most every musician on Merseyside. Not simply for the wealth of musical instruments always on display, but for the free music lessons Jim Gretty, the chief salesman, gave with each and every guitar purchased.

Every Monday evening he'd take the latest batch of hopefuls through three or four basic chords—chalked up on the wall—before leading them all into a heartfelt rendition of 'Singing the Blues'. | John Lennon got his first proper guitar—bought by his Aunt Mimi for £14—from Jim Gretty in 1957.

A few years later—December 1961—Brian Epstein wrote a personal cheque for almost £200 to clear all hire-purchase debts The Beatles had run up at the store. To which, John, supposedly remarked: *"Now that's what I call bloody managing."*

RUSHWORTH'S | Whitechapel | *'The Great' Music House* | The largest musical instrument store, in Liverpool, and arguably the biggest record store, too. | A great many Merseyside groups satisfied their musical needs and lusts here: drums, amplifiers, strings, plectrums, sheet music, as well as guitars of all kinds.

 The Gibson J-160E flat-top 'Jumbo' acoustic-electric guitars, much prized by John and George, were specially ordered from Chicago and hand-delivered by various members of the store's management; who knew a good thing going when they heard it.

LIME STREET RAILWAY STATION | Lime Street | The main line railway terminus that served the London-Midland Region Line and connected Liverpool to Manchester and Crewe, and then London - Euston Station. It also acted as a hub for local-railway services and was always busy. It boasted a cafe on the grand scale to serve passengers for the main-line platforms, although the Punch and Judy cafe, just outside the Lime Street entrance, did roaring trade as they not only stayed open longer, they also didn't seem to mind as much if you lingered longer over a cup of coffee. The wheels of commerce... in motion.

CENTRAL RAILWAY STATION | Ranelagh Street | Former mainline terminus. The three-storey building in the city-centre fronted onto Ranelagh Street; that ran east-west from the main entrance to junctions with Church Street and Bold Street; originally boasted a magnificent 65 feet high, arched shed behind.

 The railways were nationalised, in Britain, in January 1948. Liverpool Central became part of British Railways' London Midland Region. Yet despite the high level of traffic from Central's main line platforms—at 'High Level'—the station was listed for closure in the Beeching Report (1963). And in September 1966 almost all services were diverted to Liverpool Lime Street.

 Platforms 1, 2, 5 and 6 were taken out of use. Platforms 1 and 2 became a car park. Only platforms 3 and 4 were retained for service to and from Gateacre. The concourse of the station remained heavily in use, however, as 'Lower Level' platforms continued to be extremely busy. Who knew?

In 1971, the local rail network—now dubbed *Merseyrail*—required existing routes—including Liverpool Central to Manchester—to be electrified. This called for new underground lines to be built in the city centre and required a complete reconfiguration at Liverpool Central so that a new underground loop line at a deep level and a link line at a sub-surface level could be constructed. One of the results of which was that the site of the original Cavern Club was demolished in 1973—all in the aid of so-called "progress"—although some of the bricks were 'saved' and later used in the 'new' Cavern Club rebuilt across Matthew Street, in 1984.

ADELPHI HOTEL | Ranelagh Place | A famed Liverpool landmark for many, many years; and *the* Hotel that anyone who was anyone was obliged to stay at. Large enough to be described as 'a great Cunard liner stranded in the middle of the city'—which reflects the class of people it was initially designed to accommodate and attend to. Many famous people, including The Beatles, Bob Dylan, Gregory Peck, and George Martin have stayed here.

ST. GEORGE'S HALL | Lime Street | Built in 1842 in Greco-Roman style—an architectural statement of civic pride, the world over—it's still one of Liverpool's most impressive buildings and still very much privy to prestigious events and gatherings of the social elite and the art world.

THE EMPIRE THEATRE | Lime Street | The city's biggest and best theatre; undeniably its most glamorous.

Part of the Moss Empires chain it was designed by Frank Matcham—the architect who designed the London Palladium—and opened in 1925. It has the largest two-tier auditorium in Britain and can seat 2,350 people.

Gene Vincent and Eddie Cochran performed at the theatre in 1960. The Beatles appeared here—with the great Little Richard topping the bill—on the 28th October 1962. They also played here on several occasions, afterwards; some of which were televised.

THE ODEON CINEMA | London Road | A real picture palace, and a long-standing Liverpool institution, or at least it was.

Opened in 1934 as The Paramount, with seating for 2670, it was renamed the Odeon in 1942. In 1954 it was the first Merseyside cinema to be equipped for *CinemaScope*, and then *Todd-AO*, which made it the perfect place for young lovers to go see such big-hits as *South Pacific*, *Lawrence of Arabia*, and *The Sound of Music*. The Beatles performed here in the early 1960s.

In 1964, the cinema hosted the northern premiere of *A Hard Day's Night*. And none other than Bob Dylan played here—live—in 1965 and 1966. The cinema was later modernised and split into two, losing almost all of its unique art-deco design features. After which it was split into even more screens. The cinema has since been pulled down to make way for even more progress.

LEWIS'S DEPARTMENT STORE | Ranelagh Street | Long a landmark shopping destination, as much for Jacob Epstein's (no relation) statue of a well-endowed naked man—arms raised to heaven—that towered over the main entrance, as for the store itself. The statue's official name is 'Liverpool Resurgent', though most Liverpudlians refer to it as 'Nobby Lewis'.

It's also long been a well-known meeting place for courting couples due of its proximity to the city-centre and because nobody could miss the statue's location. John Lennon used to meet his girlfriend, Cynthia Powell, under it. Paul McCartney once worked as a 'second man' in one of the store's delivery vans (not the only time he was 'second man in').

BLACKLER'S DEPARTMENT STORE | Great Charlotte Street | Yet another 'landmark' shopping destination as, once, simply everyone shopped at Blackler's. The young George Harrison even interviewed here as a window dresser and instead was offered a job as an apprentice electrician. He took the job for a short time and then "pulled the plug on it", as he found he really wasn't very good at it. | The Beatles played the *'Young Idea Dance'* at the '527' Club—for employees only—on the top floor of the department store on 28 November 1962.

THE PIER HEAD | Liverpool's Pier Head is surely one of the most beautiful 'maritime' skylines in the world. To see it, especially from a ferry on the River Mersey, is to wonder at it all over again. The *"Three Graces"*: The Royal Liver Building, the Cunard Building, and the Port of Liverpool Building; truly outstanding for a hundred years and more.

The Royal Liver Building, arguably the city's signature landmark, adorned by two Liver Birds; one facing the river, the other facing towards the city; both marking the ebb and flow of Liverpool sailors to and from the sea.

THE MERSEY FERRY | *"Ferry 'Cross the Mersey..."*| What Paul did for Penny Lane and John for Strawberry Fields, Gerry Marsden (of Gerry and The Pacemakers) did for the Mersey Ferry. You can't even think of the words without also hearing Gerry's endearingly timeless song floating through your mind.

Passengers would board at the Liverpool 'Pier Head' and be taken across the river to either Birkenhead or Wallasey.

The ferry service has been a heritage and visitor attraction since 1990—the 50-minute round trip from the Pier Head still the only way to see the wondrous Liverpool skyline.

(And I'm sure I'm not the only to notice, but when 'the boys' set sail on their Yellow Submarine—for The Sea of Dreams—they depart from the Pier Head, where else?)

THE MERSEY TUNNELS | 'THE QUEENSWAY' | 'THE KINGSWAY' | There are three tunnels that run under the River Mersey and connect Liverpool with the Wirral Peninsula | The Mersey Railway Tunnel (opened 1886) and two road tunnels: the Queensway Tunnel (opened 1934) and the Kingsway Tunnel (opened 1971). | The Queensway Tunnel connects Liverpool with Birkenhead, as does the railway tunnel. It's this pre-war road tunnel that Neil Aspinall, Gerry Marsden, and hordes of Liverpool beat fans would have used to get to 'the Tower' at New Brighton. | The 'more modern' Kingsway Tunnel runs through to Wallasey.

PART ONE - PEOPLE. PLACES. VENUES.

6 - Hamburg People

"Oh, ich krieg's hin, mit ein wenig Hilfe von meinen Freunden..."

Bruno Koschmider | Klaus Voormann | Astrid Kirchherr | Jürgen Vollmer | The Jets | Derry and The Seniors | Tony Sheridan | Roy Young | Bert Kaempfert | Horst Fascher | Peter Eckhorn | Manfred Weissleder

The Beatles—John Lennon, Paul McCartney, George Harrison, Stuart Sutcliffe, and Pete Best—arrived in Hamburg, Germany, 17 August 1960, for the first of five club residencies that would turn out to be crucial for them; as individuals and as a band.

It's now very much accepted lore that during their first residency in Hamburg, at Bruno Koschmider's Indra Cabaret and Der Kaiserkeller clubs—on the Grosse Freiheit, in St. Pauli's notorious red-light district—the long hours and hard slog of having to perform for up to seven hours a night; night after night after night; for sixteen weeks straight; had an extraordinary effect on the sound and fury of the fledgling Beatles.

Hamburg changed them, both personally and professionally. By all accounts the raw concussive power of their music was literally breath taking. And when they returned to Liverpool and first unleashed their newfound 'Hamburg sound'—in all its hard-rocking, kick-drum thumping, foot-stomping glory—at a dance at Litherland Town Hall, on 27 December 1960, it forever changed 'pop' music, too. And would eventually also help shape popular culture in the second half of the Twentieth Century.

"I might have been born in Liverpool, but I grew up in Hamburg."
— John Lennon

BRUNO KOSCHMIDER | Owner of Hamburg's very first rock 'n' roll club - 'Der Kaiserkeller' | Also owned 'Indra Cabaret' club + 'Bambi Kino' cinema + 'Heaven and Hell' coffee bar. | 1926 - 2000 | Born Danzig, Germany. Former circus performer crippled in a trapeze accident. | Originator of the frenzy-inducing exhortation: *"Mach Schau! Mach Schau!"* ('Make a show! Make a show!') Arguably, one of the key catalysts that led to the transformation of the band of five young Liverpool lads— from rock fledglings into the savage young Beatles. (The second likely catalyst: The group's enforced rivalry with Rory Storm and The Hurricanes, at Koschmider's Kaiserkeller club.)

Bruno Koschmider flew to London early June 1960 to locate and secure a Britisher rock band to play Der Kaiserkeller; a basement club he owned on the Grosse Freiheit, in Hamburg's notorious St. Pauli red light district. Which perhaps explains why he had no qualms venturing into the heart of Soho— London's then 'capital of sin'—and to the 2i's Coffee Bar; birthplace of British rock 'n' roll. Where he signed up London group, The Jets, with star vocalist and guitarist Tony Sheridan.

When, barely a month later, Sheridan and the Jets left him to play Peter Eckhorn's newly opened Top Ten Club, Koschmider quickly returned to England and, by a million to one chance met up again with Liverpool promoter Allan Williams, down in London for the day, and contracted for Liverpool group Derry and The Seniors to play a season at Der Kaiserkeller.

Williams then urged Koschmider to sign up another Merseyside group—The Beatles. The group's contract to run for two months from 17 August to 16 October. The Beatles to receive 30DM (about £2.50) per person per day—paid every Thursday. The group tasked to perform for four and a half hours each weekday night and for six hours on Saturday nights. Koschmider also agreed to pay Williams, as booking agent, a commission of £10 for every week the group played; an arrangement that would later be the basis of a nasty disagreement; and festering bone of contention; between Allan Williams and the group.

The Beatles—all five of them—John, Paul, George, Pete Best, and Stuart Sutcliffe—stayed in Koschmider's flat their first night in Hamburg. The following night he put them up in two dark dank extremely squalid little rooms and a shared public toilet, at the back of his tiny, very grubby, porn cinema—Bambi Kino.

And if that wasn't humbling enough, rather than feature them at the Kaiserkeller, he installed The Beatles in his much smaller Indra Cabaret club, located at the wrong end of the Grosse Freiheit—'the Great Freedom'. Blocks away from the non-stop excitement of the Reeperbahn, with its copious array of cafes, bars, restaurants, and shops, and its veritable cornucopia of 'uniquely spectacular sexual entertainments' that left little or nothing to the imagination.

To pull wary punters into the Indra and keep them there, Koschmider yelled for The Beatles to "*Mach Schau! Mach Schau!*" however dead on their feet they were because of their punishing work schedule. A nightly situation that in due course led The Beatles to explore the benefits of chemically induced energy enhancement; and so Preludin first enters the scene.

The Beatles performed at Indra Cabaret Club for 48 finger-blistering, throat-shredding nights—from 18 August to 3 October 1960. Their residency brought to an abrupt halt when a noise complaint from the local police forced the club to close.

Koschmider immediately moved The Beatles down the street to his Kaiserkeller club so they could play out the rest of their contract, just as the resident band, Derry and the Seniors, were set to return to Liverpool and be replaced by Merseyside's top group, Rory Storm and The Hurricanes.

Group rivalry was intense from the start, but with everyone a long way from home, the Liverpool musicians soon became fast friends and got up to all sorts of tricks. Famously, betting which group could stomp through the wooden planks balanced atop beer crates that made up the club's decidedly rickety stage. After everyone had gone at it, for several nights in a row, Rory finally won the bet by jumping down onto the stage from the top of an upright piano.

Koschmider was not amused, but the two groups were proving to be such a huge draw, he let it be. He even extended The Beatles' contract until the end of November.

Time permitting, The Beatles, Rory, and most of The Hurricanes, often popped around the corner to go see British rock 'n' roller Tony Sheridan perform at Top Ten Club. And never ones to pass up an opportunity to learn from the best, The Beatles would jam with Sheridan up on stage. Bruno Koschmider heard about it and hit the group with a termination notice that accused them of being in clear breach of the 'performance exclusion zone' portion of their contract that precluded them from playing in any other club within a 45-mile radius of the Kaiserkeller. Specifically designed, of course, to exclude the Top Ten. The Beatles dutifully attempted to play out the remainder of their contract before moving to the Top Ten. But Koschmider was in no mood to deal and extracted his own brand of revenge by tipping off Hamburg's 'Youth-Protection Squad' that George Harrison was underage and without a proper work-permit. Which in very short order led to the youngest member of The Beatles being deported from Germany. Koschmider then accused Paul McCartney and Pete Best of arson. Legend says they set alight to a condom stuck up on a wall of their shabby little room at the rear of the Bambi Kino so they could find their few meagre belongings in the dark. Both Beatles were duly arrested, locked up for the night, and then ordered out of the country.

The Beatles in total disarray, Stu Sutcliffe decided to stay on in Hamburg, with his new girlfriend, Astrid Kirchherr, until the New Year. John Lennon—for once not the centre of trouble—stayed on with them for a week or so, but then made the long journey back home to Liverpool, all on his lonesome.

And so what then of Bruno Koschmider? The loss of The Beatles—and then Rory Storm and the Hurricanes—was but the beginning of the end. The enormous popularity of Top Ten Club, followed by Star-Club, led to a massive drop off in the number of rock crazed punters who visited the Kaiserkeller, and it wasn't long before he was forced to close it down. He later reopened it as a strip club, but under a different name.

Many years later George Harrison remembered Koschmider as: *"this old guy who'd been crippled in the war. Had a limp. And didn't seem to know much about anything, let alone music."*

| **Side Bar** | **No *"Mach Schau! Mach Schau!"* No Beatles?** | One thing that can truly never be denied, though, is that Bruno Koschmider was one of the two men responsible for The Beatles first going to Hamburg. And it was The Beatles—*'Direct From Hamburg'*—newly forged from their time in the fiery furnaces of Indra Cabaret and the Kaiserkeller that then stormed the stage at Litherland Town Hall, in Liverpool, on 27 December 1960, in a career-defining event. So if for no other reason than *"Mach Schau! Mach Schau!"* and the extraordinary effect it had on the early Beatles, Bruno Koschmider, like Allan Williams, should be considered a major figure and not just a footnote in the fabled story of the group. As the ever-magnificent Beatles' historian Mark Lewisohn has said repeatedly: *"**No Hamburg. No Beatles.**"*

KLAUS VOORMANN | **Art Student** | **'Exi'** | **Graphic Artist** | **Bass Player** | **Close friend of The Beatles** | A little more than eight weeks after The Beatles' first arrived in Hamburg, a young German art student, Klaus Voormann, was "walking off" an argument he'd just had with his long-time girlfriend, Astrid Kirchherr, and was drawn to the thunderous sound coming from a street-level window of a cellar club on Grosse Freiheit—and stepped into legend. *"What was this music... like I'd never heard. It went right through me. And it pleased me so much I wanted to get closer."*

Klaus ventured down inside the Kaiserkeller and was blown away by Rory Storm and The Hurricanes: *"**the blondest skeleton on earth tried to swing his long, bony leg over the back of the guitarist; he rocked and bobbed without dropping the mic stand.**"*

Next up on Der Kaiserkeller's rocky wooden stage were The Beatles; all five of them, John, Paul, George, Stu, and Pete; who then rocked his world with the sheer brute force of their music and their outrageous antics. The experience changed Klaus's life forever. And in so many, many ways went on to change the lives of everyone who ever came to love The Beatles.

Klaus was so knocked out by the sound and energy of 'live' rock 'n' roll he returned a few nights later with his two closest friends; his girlfriend, Astrid Kirchherr, and fellow art student Jürgen Vollmer. A trio of young self-styled Francophile 'Exis' who drew inspiration from Parisian 'Existentialists'—Albert Camus and Jean Paul Sartre—French poets, artists, and film-makers—*les chanson des vieux amants et 'le cool jazz'*—and who invariably dressed from head-to-toe, in black. The two men also sporting freshly washed mops of long hair combed down over the forehead.

The three 'Exis' woefully out of place amongst all the sailors, tourists, and 'Rockers'—the other Hamburg "teenage tribe" of the time—but everyone in the smoky cellar club banded together in a shared love of rock 'n' roll and The Beatles in particular; the trio of friends returning again and again to the Kaiserkeller, to see and hear the group play. And as eight days turned into weeks they struck up a closer and closer friendship with The Beatles that would have far reaching consequences in the lives, look, and style of the group.

Klaus Voormann went on to become a very accomplished bass player. In 1965 he formed the group Paddy, Klaus, and Gibson; managed for a time by none other than Brian Epstein. Klaus was later accomplished enough to take over from Jack Bruce as the bassist with Manfred Mann.

A gifted graphic designer and artist, he also won a Grammy for the album cover he designed and drew for The Beatles' *Revolver* LP—another Beatles' landmark. | The 'collectors edition' coffee table book *Hamburg Days* he designed, edited, and compiled with Astrid Kirchherr—published by Genesis—is a wonder—a veritable treasure trove of photographs and drawings of the people, places, and venues of the times.

ASTRID KIRCHHERR | Photographer | 'Exi' | Girlfriend of Stuart Sutcliffe | Close friend of The Beatles | Initiator of the iconic 'Beatles Haircut' | The first and still the best ever Beatles' photographer. Her photographic 'eye' for the music obsessed youth-culture emerging in Europe was utterly unique in 1960; its documentary-style much imitated since, but never surpassed.

Born in Hamburg, Germany. (20 May 1938 - 12 May 2020) An art student and then photographer's assistant, her photos of the early days of The Beatles still have the power to haunt.

Early in the third week of October 1960, Astrid's boyfriend, Klaus Voormann, urged her and his fellow art student and 'Exi', Jürgen Vollmer, to come see and hear the fabulous 'live' rock 'n' roll bands he'd just heard playing at the Kaiserkeller. All three of them, huddled together for protection, duly ventured down into the basement cellar club—and Astrid all but immediately fell in love with Stu Sutcliffe—The Beatles' then bass-player.

In a letter Stuart Sutcliffe wrote to his mother he said: *"I have found the most wonderful friends...the most beautiful looking trio I have ever seen. And the girl thought that I was the most handsome of the lot! Here was I, feeling the most insipid working member of the group, being told how much superior I looked...and this alongside the great 'Romeo' John Lennon and his two stalwarts Paul and George—the Casanovas of Hamburg!"*

Astrid took her iconic photos of the group at the Hamburg Dom Fair around this time. A real 'flash, bang, wallop' affair, as within a few short weeks, Astrid and Stu started living together. And when The Beatles were unceremoniously booted out of Germany at the beginning of December, Stu elected to stay on with Astrid over the coming Christmas and New Year holidays, which was when the two decided to get engaged.

At the end of January 1961, Stu flew back to Liverpool to explain everything to his mother, who was distraught he was throwing away his future prospects, if not his very life. Stu played a few dates in Liverpool, with The Beatles, but soon returned to Hamburg, and his real love. And this was when Astrid styled Stuart's hair into the *'Pilzenkopf'*, as then worn by both Klaus and Jürgen, that would later become such a distinct feature and signifier of The Beatles.

Stu helped Mona Best and Peter Eckhorn clear all official obstacles to The Beatles returning to Hamburg and joined the group again, 1 April 1961, at the start of their 12-week season at Top Ten Club. But his heart was elsewhere and he told his bandmates he planned to leave the group to take up art studies, again, this time in Hamburg. Stu and Astrid started planning their life together. Stu was ultimately taken on at a prestigious art school, in Hamburg, and Paul bought himself a new Höfner bass guitar.

All foreboded well. Stu began to paint striking abstracts, Astrid to take ever more striking photos, and Paul to play ever more exciting runs on his violin-shaped bass guitar.

But then the world turned, and life went on, until Stu began to experience a series of debilitating headaches and died suddenly of a brain haemorrhage on 10 April 1962; Astrid with him in the ambulance on the way to hospital. And, as fate would have it, The Beatles had only just returned to Hamburg to play the opening of Star-Club. An utterly distraught Astrid meeting them by chance at the airport, as she waited for Stu's mother to fly in from Liverpool. John Lennon completely devastated by the death of the man he called *'his closest friend, his alter ego, and his guiding force'.*

The question that's still being asked, all these many years later: Did Stu die from the trauma of having been kicked in the head a year earlier at a gang fight, in Liverpool, after a Beatles' gig? Or did he die after having suffered a serious concussion, and its increasing cascade of after effects, after a fall down a steep flight of stairs at Astrid's house?

Many years later Stu's mother told an interviewer that both she and Astrid put the blame for the awful event on the accidental fall at Astrid's home.

Astrid remained a close and dear friend of The Beatles. Her many iconic photographs from the time when it all began have been exhibited in galleries the world over and continue to draw huge crowds wherever they're shown. Both she and her Beatles-inspired works treasures to be forever treasured. | *"Astrid was the one, really, who influenced our image more than anybody. She made us look good."* – George Harrison

JÜRGEN VOLLMER | **Art Student** | **'Exi'** | **Photographer** | **Close friend of The Beatles** | Jürgen Vollmer tends to get left out of many Beatles' history books, which is a real shame.

His existentialist style; dressed from head-to-foot in black, black trousers, boots; his clean washed hair combed down over his forehead in the French 'Exi'-style; gave rise to one of the group's most important symbols and signifiers: The Beatles' Haircut. It was Jürgen, not Astrid Kirchherr, who first styled

John and Paul's hair—'Exi'-style—when they met up with him while on a brief vacation in Paris, where he was living.

Jürgen became a professional photographer. Moved to New York, then Hollywood. His photojournalism books: *Rock 'n' Roll Times* and *The Beatles in Hamburg 1961* both quite wonderful.

His iconic photograph of John Lennon standing in a doorway in Jäger-Passage, at Wohlwillstrasse 22, taken in 1960; was used fifteen years later for the cover of John's solo album *'Rock 'n' Roll'*. The magic of the moment; the place and time; echoed forever in the album's sub-title... **'You shoulda been there!'**

| **Side Bar** | **Hamburg's 'Exis' and 'Rockers'** | Hamburg's Francophile 'Exis' and Rock 'n' Roll lovin' 'Rockers'—two 'opposing' teenage tribes—very similar to the British 'Mods' and 'Rockers' youth movements. | Mods. London-birthed. The very essence of cool—with attendant Italian mohair suits and rabbit fur collar trimmed parkas and chrome-spotlight-festooned Vespa or Lambretta Italian motor scooters. Not so much modern jazz—more rhythm and blues and Motown. | Rockers. The British progeny of Elvis Presley and Gene Vincent and Eddie Cochran—and Marlon Brando in *The Wild Ones*—great rockers all. Black leather jacket, blue jeans, and white T-shirt wearing rebels without a cause—save for rebelling against conformist society—listening to Rock 'n' Roll—dancing in blue-suede shoes—and riding over 100 mph on their British-made 'ton-up' motorbikes. Raw. Edgy. Flashy. With an ever-present hint of barely contained violence all the better to attract admiring glances from the female of the species. Perhaps the oddest coincidence; the gang of 'Rocker' chicks in the film *The Wild Ones* just also happened to be called 'The Beetles'.

THE JETS | Rick Richards (Hardy) - rhythm guitar/vocals | Colin Melander (Crawley) - guitar/vocals | Pete Wharton - bass guitar | Jimmy (Del) Ward - drums/keyboards/vocals | Iain Hines - piano | Tony Sheridan – lead guitar/vocals | The first British rock 'n' roll band ever to play post-war Hamburg.

A five/six piece combo brought together by Iain Hines after meeting Hamburg club owner Bruno Koschmider at Soho's famed 2i's Coffee Bar in London. Hines had led a number of bands called 'The Jets' and so had the name of the 'new' group ready at his fingertips. (Hines missed the boat to Hamburg, for some reason, and joined The Jets again some weeks later.)

The Jets opened at Koschmider's Kaiserkeller on 5 June 1960 and were an immediate hit, drawing ever larger and larger crowds into the club. Which of course didn't go unnoticed. The Jets had played the club for little more than a month before rival St. Pauli nightclub owner Peter Eckhorn made them an offer they couldn't refuse. And the group performed their last night at the Kaiserkeller on Wednesday 6 July before beginning their residency at Peter Eckhorn's newly opened club, later called Top Ten Club, on Saturday 9 July. Where they again proved themselves a magnet for rock-thirsty punters.

Having had The Jets stolen away from under his very nose, Bruno Koschmider quickly returned to London—and Soho's 2i's Coffee Bar, again—in search of new Britisher rock 'n' roll bands to fill his now empty club. And as fate decreed, it was at the 2i's that he again met Liverpool would-be impresario Allan Williams and a Merseyside group he had "a management interest in" called Derry and The Seniors. Bruno Koschmider and Allan Williams shook hands on the deal and a week or so later Derry and The Seniors opened at the Kaiserkeller, in Hamburg. Ever one to seize a business opportunity, Allan Williams also offered to supply Bruno Koschmider with yet more Liverpool groups; the first of which would turn out to be The Beatles.

At the end of October 1960, all but one of The Jets had to return to London—a slight matter of them not having secured official work permits—and only Tony Sheridan remained on in Hamburg. Thus paving the way for The Beatles' initial all-too brief sojourn at the club, their sudden and ignominious deportation from Germany, and their eager return to the Top Ten Club, in April 1961, to fulfil their 'all-important' 'life-changing' three-month residency with *'The Teacher'*—Tony Sheridan.

DERRY AND THE SENIORS | Howie Casey - saxophone | Billy Hughes - rhythm guitar | Stan Foster - piano | Brian Griffiths - lead guitar | Phil Whitehead - bass guitar | Jeff Wallington - drums | Derry Wilkie - lead singer | The very first Liverpool rock 'n' roll group to play Bruno Koschmider's Hamburg club, the Kaiserkeller, and thus more than worth a second mention.

Derry and The Seniors were hired to replace The Jets, a London group, who'd been lured away to play the rival Top Ten Club. The Seniors' Kaiserkeller residency arranged for them by Liverpool entrepreneur, Allan Williams, following an almost inexplicably fortuitous second meeting he'd with Koschmider at the 2i's Coffee Bar, in London's Soho.

Derry and The Seniors proved to be a massive hit with the Kaiserkeller audience; especially the group's dynamic, black lead singer Derry Wilkie. Which might go to explain Howie Casey's response when Williams wrote to tell him he was next sending The Beatles out to Hamburg. Casey immediately wrote back: *"The Beatles are a no talent group that'll only go and spoil it for everyone else."* (Casey later had the grace to admit how very wrong he was.)

Derry and The Seniors continued to rock the Kaiserkeller on through the summer, until the end of October 1960, but as happened with The Jets no one had an official work permit or visa and so they had to return to England. And, in turn, were replaced at the Kaiserkeller by Rory Storm and The Hurricanes.

TONY SHERIDAN | *'The Teacher'* | Singer | Guitarist | Songwriter | Hamburg's undisputed rock 'n' roll king | Anthony Esmond Sheridan McGinnity | 1940 - 2013 | Born Norwich, Norfolk, England. | Tony Sheridan's involvement with The Beatles was pivotal. He had a profound influence—musically—on John Lennon, Paul McCartney, and George Harrison.

No less a person than Beatle Paul nicknamed him *"The Teacher."* Sheridan taught by example and, if need be, personal tuition (He greatly helped George Harrison with his guitar playing, for instance). And without doubt helped The Beatles hone their sound, stagecraft, and style of musicianship—in fact their entire performance. The 'legs apart' 'guitar positioned high-on-the-chest' stance of guitar playing—favoured by both John Lennon and Gerry Marsden of Gerry and the Pacemakers—can be directly attributed to Sheridan. He also influenced much of The Beatles' musical repertoire. Introduced them to many of the obscure rock 'n' roll and R&B songs they would later make famous.

Tony Sheridan formed his first band in 1956. In 1958, aged 18, he began appearing on the Independent Television Network's weekly pop program '*Oh Boy*'. And was the first musician ever allowed to play electric guitar on British television by the Musicians' Union (MU). In 1960 he backed Eddie Cochran and Gene Vincent on their tour of the UK (History tells us that on that fateful night Sheridan asked the two stars if they'd give him a lift to the next venue. They said 'no'. The tragic irony; he thus escaped the later road accident that left Cochran dead and Vincent badly injured.)

Sheridan came close to acquiring a UK recording contract in the early 1960s, but for various reasons—both personal and professional—one failed to materialise. | In mid-1960 when he was offered the chance to play with London group, The Jets, at Der Kaiserkeller in Hamburg, he jumped at it. The Jets were an immediate hit and were lured away to play the rival Top Ten Club even before their Kaiserkeller contract ended. Later, their own schedules permitting, John, Paul, George, Rory Storm and various Hurricanes would make pilgrimage to see Sheridan play.

In April 1961 The Beatles made their second trip to Hamburg to begin a three-month season at Top Ten, as the club's resident rock 'n' roll band and the backing group to the club's 'star attraction' Tony Sheridan. | Famed German record producer Bert Kaempfert saw them all perform at the club and offered Tony Sheridan—backed by The Beatles—a recording contract.

The 'group' recorded nine songs over two or three-days—with the first recording session on June 22-23. 'My Bonnie (Lies Over the Ocean)' 'The Saints (When the Saints Go Marching In)' 'Why' 'Cry For a Shadow' 'Ain't She Sweet' 'Take Out Some Insurance On Me Baby' Nobody's Child'. The single 'My Bonnie' b/w 'The Saints'—attributed to 'Tony Sheridan and the Beat Brothers'—was released in Germany, on the Polydor label, in

October 1961. As Sheridan later explained it, Polydor insisted on 'Beat Brothers', because "Beatles" sounded much too much like *"peedles"*—the German slang word for a small boy's penis.

The Polydor recording is of singular importance in Beatles' legend. It's the disc Raymond Jones is reputed to have sought when he walked into NEMS record store in Liverpool, on Saturday, October 28, 1961, and asked the store's smart-looking manager: *"Have you got a copy of 'My Bonnie'?"* The all-important event that would prompt Brian Epstein to search out The Beatles and, eventually, lead to him becoming their manager.

In early 1962 Ringo Starr flew out to Hamburg to play in Tony Sheridan's backing band, but found the singer and his demands not at all to his liking and quick as a flash he returned to Liverpool to play with Rory Storm and the Hurricanes. Soon after which Brian Epstein officially asked him to join The Beatles.

Sheridan continued to perform and record, in Europe and America, but never achieved the success or the recognition that many Beatle people insist he so richly deserved. He released his last album '*Vagabond*' in 2002. And in 2012 made a last appearance at 'Beatlefair' in San Diego, California. | Tony Sheridan died 16 February 2013, in Hamburg, Germany. He was 72.

ROY YOUNG | *'England's Little Richard'* | **Pianist** | **Vocalist** | Born Oxford. | Like rock 'n' roll star, Tommy Steele, a former merchant seaman. | And like Tony Sheridan, he made television appearances on UK television shows *'Oh Boy'* and *'Drumbeat'* in the late 1950s. It was his exuberant 'boogie-woogie-style' performances on TV that earned him the nickname "England's Little Richard". And in 1960-61 He released a string of singles in Britain—some of which he wrote—none of which were hits.

Young contracted to play Top Ten Club—where he proved a hugely popular solo-performer and 'gifted' backing musician. Which goes to explain why he was also one of the gifted but 'unnamed' Beat Brothers who, on many occasions, ended up backing Tony Sheridan, both on stage and on record.

Roy Young was later lured away from Top Ten Club and appeared on the bill with The Beatles, at the opening night of Star-

Club. And just as The Beatles had once done for Tony Sheridan, they did nightly duty providing vocal and instrumental backing to Roy Young and his piano, during each of their three residencies at Star-Club.

One can only wonder what influence the very talented Roy Young had on young Paul McCartney, who whenever called for could—and still does—also sing in such a way as to invite direct comparisons with the incomparable Little Richard.

BERT KAEMPFERT | Orchestra leader | Composer | Songwriter | Music producer | Multi-instrumentalist | Berthold Heinrich Kämpfert | 1923 - 1980 | Born Hamburg | Produced easy-listening, instrumental, big band, jazz records.

In 1959, he had a worldwide hit with 'Wonderland by Night'. The single topped the American pop charts and turned Bert Kaempfert and his Orchestra into international stars overnight. He went on to produce and record a number of "already-widely-loved re-made-anew" tunes such as 'Tenderly', 'Red Roses for a Blue Lady', and 'Bye Bye Blues' All of them monster hits. But he is perhaps best known for songs he composed; all of them graced by some of the world's most talented lyricists; all of which were recorded by major artists: 'Spanish Eyes (Moon Over Naples)' recorded by Al Martino and Engelbert Humperdink | 'Danke Schoen' recorded by Wayne Newton | 'Wooden Heart' recorded by Elvis Presley | 'L-O-V-E' recorded by Nat King Cole | 'Almost There' recorded by Andy Williams | 'Strangers in the Night'—a worldwide #1 hit for Frank Sinatra.

Spring 1961. Having seen Tony Sheridan and The Beatles perform at Hamburg's Top Ten Club, he offered them a recording contract; envisioning Tony Sheridan as lead singer with The Beatles as his backing group. Kaempfert's idea to catch the coming 'new' music wave, by producing a rock 'n' roll inspired single together with enough other upbeat songs to fill an album should the initial song release prove a success.

October 1961 Polydor Records released 'My Bonnie (Lies Over the Ocean)' coupled with 'The Saints (When the Saints Go Marching In)' as a single in West Germany. The album *'My Bonnie'* was then released the following year. Both the single and accompanying album were the first ever commercially released recordings by The Beatles.

To his eternal credit, Bert Kaempfert amicably agreed to Brian Epstein's impassioned request that he release The Beatles from any and all any contractual claims by Polydor; thereby clearing the way of any future impediments for George Martin to sign the group to Parlophone. | Bert Kaempfert died 21 June 1980 in Majorca, Spain. He was 56. | He was later posthumously inducted into the 'Songwriters Hall of Fame'.

HORST FASCHER | Ex-Boxer | Chief Bouncer - Kaiserkeller and Top Ten clubs | Star-Club Manager | Close friend to The Beatles | 1936 - | Born Hamburg | Bruno Koschmider hired Horst to be 'head bouncer' at the Kaiserkeller because of the fearsome reputation he had around St. Pauli's 'red light' district.

Horst was an ex-featherweight boxer who'd fought for Hamburg and West Germany. Who'd then been banned from the ring after killing a sailor in a street fight; for which he served a prison term on a manslaughter charge. On his release he formed a strong-arm team, nicknamed 'Hoddel's Gang', with former friends from Hamburg Boxing Academy. And more protector than bouncer, he later befriended The Beatles, and most of the other Liverpool beat groups that came to play Hamburg's rock 'n' roll clubs, and took them under his wing and saved them from untold horrors.

Horst began his close association with Hamburg's rock 'n' roll scene at the Kaiserkeller, but eyes ever on the prize, he later decamped to Peter Eckhorn's more upscale Top Ten Club. When the club's resident band, The Jets, who'd also been lured away from the Kaiserkeller, returned to England, lead guitarist and singer, Tony Sheridan stayed on in Hamburg as the club's new headliner. The Beatles would often watch Sheridan perform and at Fascher's urging soon began to join the singer up on stage.

When Bruno Koschmider heard about it, he was, to say the least, incensed. The Beatles were in clear breach of the performance 'exclusion zone' portion of their contract and he hit them with a termination notice.

The Beatles dutifully attempted to play out the remainder of their contract. Peter Eckhorn, again at Fascher's urging, offered them a full time gig. But then Koschmider extracted his own brand of revenge by tipping off the police that George Harrison was underage and thus not permitted to work. Which in short order led to the speedy deportation of Beatles' George, Paul, and Pete, from Germany.

Eckhorn pulled what strings he could to clear away any and all official impediments to The Beatles' returning to Hamburg. And when they finally did return, at the start of April, 1961, to begin their three-month residency at Top Ten Club, Horst let it be known to all and sundry; the police, as well as assorted gangsters, pimps, drug peddlers, and one, Herr B. Koschmider, that the group were now under his (and Eckhorn's) personal protection and that they were in no way to be troubled or trifled with. All of which then led The Beatles to enjoy a relatively charmed existence, despite John Lennon's many instances of wittingly or unwittingly pushing people and things to their very limits.

Then Manfred Weissleder, Hamburg's reigning porn-king, appeared on the scene and hired Horst to be manager of Star-Club; his new, much more upscale rock 'n' roll nightclub, newly converted from what had been a 'luxury' porn cinema. Horst duly travelled all the way to Liverpool, with Roy Young riding 'shotgun', to ask The Beatles—face-to-face—to come appear as 'Star Attractions' at the club's all-important opening night.

The demands of Hamburg's burgeoning rock 'n' roll business then being what they were, other seekers had also come to the 'mountain' that was Merseyside. And it just so happened that Peter Eckhorn and Tony Sheridan were also in Liverpool intent on securing a deal with The Beatles' then new manager, Brian Epstein. Who met, separately, with both parties, and asked for what he saw was a justifiable increase in the group's fee.

Sheridan was outraged. And Eckhorn, not at all happy, even though he offered more than he'd originally intended to try and secure The Beatles. Horst Fascher, in true knockout style, bided his time and then sealed the deal by offering considerably more than Peter Eckhorn was prepared to pay; as well as throwing in, how shall we say, a little bit more "behind the table."

Business rivalries in Hamburg never fully dormant forever, Horst always gave a 'Star' shaped pin to all his visiting Britisher rock 'n' rollers to wear on the lapels of their jackets. The 'Star' signalling to one and all, that while in Hamburg they were under the direct protection of Horst Fascher and—perhaps even more tellingly—of Manfred Weissleder.

The Beatles headlined Star-Club three times in 1962. | 13 April to 31 May | 1-14 November | 18-31 December | Much of The Beatles New Year's Eve performance recorded on a portable Grundig tape recorder by Adrian Barber; formerly of Liverpool group The Big Three. Horst can be heard belting out 'Hallelujah, I Love Her So'. Some people insist it's his brother Freddie who then sings 'Be-Bop-A-Lula' but to this author's ears and Beatles' beating heart, it sounds like Horst.

Horst Fascher was a man who always punched well above his weight. Time and time again he proved himself to be the all-important catalyst—if not the instigator—of Hamburg's always fast moving rock 'n' roll scene. A rock 'n' roller to his fingertips.

PETER ECKHORN | Owner of Hamburg's first 'classy' rock 'n' roll nightclub - Top Ten Club. | Twenty-one-year-old Peter Eckhorn inherited his family's building, at Reeperbahn 136, that had long housed The Hippodrom—an indoor circus ring; popular with boatloads of sailors, who'd flocked there for years to quaff beer and ride bulls and horses; that had gone bankrupt in 1960. A 'pleasure of past times' made all the more irrelevant by the number of brothels and sex-themed amusements easily to hand in and around St. Pauli.

St. Pauli was a small world. And when The Jets opened at Bruno Koschmider's Der Kaiserkeller club, in June 1960, as the club's 'head bouncer', Horst Fascher saw for himself the huge drawing power of 'live' rock 'n' roll. And, if he's to be believed; and why shouldn't he be; it was he who suggested to young Herr Eckhorn that there was a mountain of money to be made out of the 'new' music played 'live'. Eckhorn needed do no more than walk around the corner to see the truth of it, because he very quickly set about having the cavernous Hippodrom converted into a 'classy' music venue, which he opened in July 1960, and later called Top Ten Club. And again at Fascher's prompting and involvement, he immediately 'poached' The Jets—and Tony Sheridan—away from the Kaiserkeller.

Late November 1960, again at Fascher's prompting, he offered The Beatles a full-time gig, even though their contract with Koschmider specifically barred them from it. An irate Koschmider tipped-off Hamburg's draconian Youth Protection Squad that George Harrison was underage and not permitted to work, which in short order led to him being deported from Germany. Soon followed by Paul McCartney, and Pete Best.

However, the business link had been established and soon after George turned 18, Peter Eckhorn—aided by Mona Best and Stuart Sutcliffe—brought The Beatles back to Top Ten Club for a three-month engagement from March 27 to July 2, 1961. And this time The Beatles lived above the club, in the attic.

The Beatles—and Tony Sheridan—really rocked the place and Top Ten Club very quickly attracted hordes of new 'beat' fans. And not just drunken sailors and inquisitive tourists but, just as had happened in Liverpool, young working-class men, female office workers, and students; all of them only too eager to search out the new 'backbeat' music. None of them giving a damn the club was located down some dark, dingy Liverpool back-alley called Matthew Street or was on the seedy neon-lit Grosse Freiheit in the very heart of St. Pauli's infamous Reeperbahn. All that mattered was that they could see and hear rock 'n' roll—*"their very own music"*—being played 'live' by real rockin' groups. Little wonder then that Eckhorn extended The Beatles' contract twice over.

Top Ten Club was a huge hit and was soon renowned, far and wide, as Hamburg's premier music club. And so as the Kaiserkeller—unable to match the appeal of the new, upscale club—inevitably began to fade way, other music clubs began to spring up: Hit Club; Tanz Club; Blockhutte; Blauer Peter; Club O.K.

But then April 1962 saw the opening of the even more decidedly upscale 1000-seater Star-Club, that promised to pull in thousands more 'middle class' fans with lots more hard-earned money to spend. The added problem for young Peter Eckhorn being that Star-Club's owner, Manfred Weissleder, another St. Pauli 'businessman' suddenly turned music entrepreneur; and a much, much bigger fish; then turned round and 'poached' Horst Fascher and The Beatles away right from under his nose. | Peter Eckhorn died 1978. | Top Ten Club finally closed 1981.

MANFRED WEISSLEDER | Hamburg businessman | Porn-king | Club owner | *Star-Club News* publisher | 'Beat music' entrepreneur and evangelist | 1928 - 1980 | Born Dortmund | During the Sixties, the undisputed king of St. Pauli's red light district and controlled a dozen or more different businesses, establishments, and clubs. Having witnessed the enormous success of Hamburg's first rock 'n' roll clubs—Bruno Koschmider's Der Kaiserkeller and Peter Eckhorn's Top Ten Club—he decided to get into the game by upping the ante. He bought an entire building—Stern-Kino—that had previously housed a dancehall, restaurant, and porn cinema and converted it into an upscale nightclub that would feature live music. 'Stern' means 'star' in English and so he named the club: Star-Club. Then, clever man that he was, he hired Horst Fascher to manage the place for him.

It was Fascher who convinced Weissleder to feature only the very best 'Stars' of American and British rock 'n' roll; and that they should start with The Beatles. Fascher then went to Liverpool to negotiate a deal with The Beatles' new manager, Brian Epstein. Frank discussions were held; monies agreed to. Soon after which, The Beatles flew to Hamburg to headline Star-Club; located, as fate would have it, right across the street from the Kaiserkeller. The bright orange 'flyers' advertising the opening of Star-Club plastered around Hamburg for weeks: **"The misery is ending! The era of old fashioned farmer's music is over!"** The Beatles, now, the undisputed 'star' attraction.

For their added protection around, Horst Fascher gave 'Star' shaped lapel pins to all Britisher musicians who played Star-Club. The symbolism abundantly clear: "Hands off! Or else." But then Weissleder, in gratitude for The Beatles appearing at the club's all-important opening night, went a step further and presented each Beatle with a heavy gold-chain bracelet; suitably inscribed with each of their names. And if you look closely, in early scenes of the film, *A Hard Day's Night*—produced and released early 1964—you'll see Paul and Ringo wearing and absent-mindedly fiddling with their still 'treasured' solid-gold Star-Club chain bracelets.

In August 1964, taking his cue directly from Bill Harry's *Mersey Beat*, Weissleder began publishing *Star-Club News*. First as a 4-page newsletter, then as a 36-page 'monthly' with front and back pages in full-colour; price 50 pfennigs. In 1965 circulation grew to 100,000 and reached readers in Scandinavia, even East Germany. He also launched 'Star-Club' as a brand with its own record label and local radio program, as well as licensing 'Star-Club' in other cities. He sold a line of 'Star-Club' brand clothing and merchandise and opened a performing artists booking agency. A well thought-out brand presence that, fifty years later, is almost standard practice, but was almost unheard of back then. And an odd coupling, perhaps, but both Manfred Weissleder and Brian Epstein proved themselves to be two very gifted 'visionary' young businessmen, very much ahead of their time in the music and entertainment industries.

The Beatles played Star-Club a total of 73 nights during 1962. | First engagement: 48 nights—from April 13 to May 31. | Second engagement: 14-nights—from 1-14 November. | Third and final engagement: 13-nights—from 18-31 December. | Fab Beatles' historian and fellow Liverpudlian, Spencer Leigh, says the group got Good Friday and Christmas Day off, which will explain why some historians give the total as 75 nights.

With the inexorable rise and rise of '*Beatlemania*'—it wasn't long before the ever-canny Weissleder began widely promoting Star-Club as "*The Cradle of The Beatles.*" | And although the club underwent numerous battles with local civic authorities intent on closing it down—to protect German youth from "smut" and "gross moral dangers"—Star-Club remained Germany's premier venue for rock 'n' roll until it finally closed New Year's Eve 1969. | Manfred Weissleder later retired from the business and 'left the building' for the last and final time in 1980.

PART ONE - PEOPLE. PLACES. VENUES.

7 - Hamburg Venues

'ZUTRITT FÜR JUGENDLICHE UNTER 18 UND FRAUEN VERBOTEN'

'ENTRY FOR MEN UNDER 18 AND WOMEN PROHIBITED' warned the 'NO ENTRY' signs at the intentionally forbidding and brutally stark steel barriers that stood at the very ends of Herbertstrasse and Schmuckstrasse—the two most notorious streets, at the very heart of Hamburg's notorious 'Red Light' district. Yet it's a well-established fact The Beatles, with underage, George Harrison, in tow, often slipped through the barriers to peek at and to partake of the wealth of offerings for sale.

All in the name of Rock 'n' Roll, of course.

Hamburg has long served as Germany's 'gateway to the world'. Has long been an open door for influences of all sorts to be introduced into the country from all around the world. And in that it's a lot like Liverpool.

The denizens of Hamburg and Liverpool have also long been known for their seemingly inexhaustible appetite for entertainment. But there the two cities must part company. The immortal whore Maggie May and her lip-sticky-painted counterparts who plied for trade around Liverpool's centre of vice, Berkley Street, or who sashayed up and down Lime Street, could never have held a candle or seamed nylon stocking to the "kerb-swallows" of Hamburg's notorious red-light quarter.

Located as it was and still is along the irredeemably notorious Reeperbahn—'*Rope walk*' to such learned Beatles scholars as you and I—the 'miracle mile' that runs through the ever-beating heart of the city's portside district known as St. Pauli.

St. Pauli's popularity exploded after World War II when austerity and privations receded and Marshall Plan money poured into Hamburg and the 'economic miracle' helped rebuild the docks and the city's infrastructure. One consequence of which was that ever larger numbers of Germans of all ages, merchant seamen from all over the world, tourists from all over Western Europe, and British and US soldiers still stationed in Germany, all flooded into the area. And, how shall I put it, like the marauding hordes of old sought and fought and bled and sometimes even died to fulfil and slake their every lust and need.

Every night—Sundays included—a never-ending wave of punters converged on St. Pauli to sample a cornucopia of entertainments 'out-of-bounds' almost everywhere else in Europe. (Save perhaps for Amsterdam's own 'red-light' district of "a thousand windows.") The Reeperbahn, and the crisscross of side streets branching off it, was able to meet and satiate every want and desire. Its brothels and strip clubs ready to actualise every conceivable fantasy. Restaurants, cafes, and bars catered to every taste; however jaded.

All of it set against an ever-pulsating neon-lit riot of sex-cabarets and porn-cinemas that left little or nothing to the imagination. Prostitutes of all colours, shapes, sizes, and gender, openly solicited from 'shop' windows along Herbertstrasse; transvestites of every nationality sashayed up and down Schmuckstrasse; everyone promising the world, to every passer by, if only they would stay awhile and buy.

One particular St. Pauli side street, Die Große Freiheit—the aptly named *'Great Freedom'*—has been renowned for the last fifty years or more for its singular place in Beatles' history. And all because Grosse Freiheit 36, corner of Schmuckstrasse, is where 'live' rock 'n' roll was first introduced into Hamburg, at Der Kaiser-Keller—*'The Emperor's Cellar'*.

The 'new' music from America; played 'live' and by 'authentic' British rock 'n' roll groups at the Kaiserkeller proved to be so instantly and insanely popular, it succeeded in attracting a whole new audience to St. Pauli. Foreign sailors on shore leave, gangsters and working girls of every stripe, gangs of local working-class 'Rockers' were all perhaps only to be expected. But for 'live' rock 'n' roll also to attract hordes of art-students and young, middle-class Germans into the 'forbidden' zone, was something else entirely. But just as long as you were a fervent fan of Elvis Presley, Eddie Cochran, and Gene Vincent; and later The Beatles and Rory Storm and The Hurricanes; social class or social niceties didn't seem to matter so much.

Equally important, was that most every rock 'n' roller who ventured down into the Kaiserkeller also seemed to be a fevered consumer of vast quantities of alcohol and beer; very much the whole idea behind presenting 'live' rock 'n' roll in the first place.

The circle squared; and very profitably so, too.

So of course, it wasn't long, before other St. Pauli businessmen; eyes and ears ever attuned to new ways to make a profit; soon piled into the act. And in turn came up with their very own ideas of what a 'live' rock 'n' roll club should be, as well as the calibre of rock stars that should play there.

But it's not only The Beatles hard-rocking music we should remember the rock 'n' roll clubs of St. Pauli for. Thanks to ex-art students Klaus Voormann, Astrid Kirchherr and Jürgen Vollmer, the clubs also helped give birth to the very look of The Beatles.

St. Pauli was where Astrid Kirchherr took her first iconic black and white photos of the savage young Beatles. All five of them exhausted from long hard nights of performing. Yet each of them already distinct as they leaned up against a backdrop of heavy fairground equipment or sat on repurposed ex-army trucks at Heiligengeistfeld; the location of Hamburg Dom, the city's fabled annual winter, spring, and summer fair.

St. Pauli is also where John Lennon bought his Rickenbacker 325 guitar, and George, a Gibson amplifier, at Musikhaus Hummel; and Paul his signature Höfner 500/1 violin bass guitar, from Steinway-Haus Music Store. And where John, Paul, George, and Pete Best all bought cowboy boots, black jeans, and black leather jackets and trousers, from a tailor's shop at Thadenstrasse 6 and Paul Hundertmark's at Spielbudenplatz 9.

What a place. What excitement. And what a fabulous time it must have been to be young and utterly in love with rock 'n' roll... in St. Pauli.

THE ROCK 'N' ROLL CLUBS OF ST. PAULI

Indra Cabaret Club | Kaiser-Keller
| Top Ten Club | Star-Club

The four most famous nightclubs that first presented rock 'n' roll as a lure for sailors, tourists, and German teenagers, in St. Pauli's red-light district were all within easy walking distance of one another on the Grosse Freiheit and the Reeperbahn.

Alan Clayson, 1960's British pop musician, author, and 'beat music' historian, calls Hamburg: *"The Cradle of British Rock."* And he's not alone. One of Liverpool's most esteemed rockers, 'Kingsize' Taylor, who played St. Pauli's rock 'n' roll clubs with his backing band, The Dominoes, times beyond number, thinks very much the same: *"People think they're listening to 'the Liverpool sound', but what they are actually hearing is 'the Hamburg sound', because that's where it was created."*

"It was Hamburg that did it... That's where we really developed. To get the Germans going and keep it up for twelve hours at a time we really had to hammer. We would never have developed as much if we'd stayed at home. We had to try anything that came into our heads in Hamburg. There was nobody to copy from. We played what we liked best and the Germans liked it as long as it was loud."
— **John Lennon - 1967** - *The Beatles Anthology*

INDRA CABARET CLUB | Grosse Freiheit 64 | St. Pauli | Cabaret-style strip club opened in 1950 by Bruno Koschmider. | Named after the Indian god, Indra, the supreme ruler of all the gods and, rather appropriately as it would later turn out, the god of thunder and storms, as well as the god of war—the club had a neon-lit elephant sign outside to attract the eye and hopefully make the place even more memorable. (That's a joke.)

On a good night the club could accommodate 150 paying customers. Isolated, at the 'wrong end' of Grosse Freiheit, it's hardly surprising the Indra was increasingly eclipsed by bigger and flashier strip clubs located closer to The Reeperbahn. And despite it boasting: *'40 Minuten' 'Non-Stop Revue' 'Strip-Tease'*

'*Theater*' '*Cabaret of World Renown*', there were oftentimes fewer than a couple of dozen sailors or tourists in the club. Koschmider even installed a jukebox to keep up with the times, but it was mostly to help fill in between strippers and hopefully to entice punters to stay in the club just a little bit longer.

In 1960 Koschmider opened a second club, a music club, this time, the Kaiserkeller, down the road at Grosse Freiheit 36, closer to all the action. And as a result of a chance meeting with Liverpool entrepreneur Allan Williams began to present British bands playing 'live' rock 'n' roll. The punters poured in.

Recognising a good thing when he saw one, Koschmider immediately recast the Indra as a 'live' rock 'n' roll venue and contracted with Williams to supply another group consisting of no fewer than five Britisher musicians. No doubt hoping to duplicate the success he'd had with 'Derry and The Seniors'.

17 August 1960. The Beatles arrived in Hamburg's St. Pauli red-light district and, still shell-shocked from their 36-hour, 500 mile, road and sea journey from Liverpool, made their debut at the Indra the very same night. Huddled together on the Indra's postage-stamp-sized stage, situated at the end of a long narrow room, they played for over four hours straight, in front of half a dozen people. The club's heavy curtains, thick carpet, and shape and size made the acoustics truly awful. But the group was in no condition to care. Then things went from bad to worse.

The Beatles stayed the first night in Bruno Koschmider's flat. The following night he put them into unspeakably squalid, two-room, army-surplus bunk-bed accommodations at the back of a tiny porn cinema he owned—the Bambi Kino. They even had to share the toilets used by patrons of the cinema.

The Beatles' contract with Koschmider was for two months—from 17 August to 16 October. They were expected to perform four and a half hours each weekday night and six hours on Saturday and Sunday nights. They were given Mondays off. For which the group was paid around £100 a week—split five ways—paid out every Thursday. Koschmider also paid the group's agent Allan Williams a commission of £10 every week.

Koschmider was a hard taskmaster. He'd come to the front of the stage and shout *"Mach schau! Mach schau!"* (*"Make a show! Make a show!"*) if he thought the group wasn't giving it their all. Play louder. Jump. Shout. Lark about. Do anything and everything to keep the punters happy—and drinking. | In time the only way The Beatles could keep up with their ever more frenetic, relentlessly punishing, nightly schedule was to imbibe oceans of booze and mountains of Preludin or 'Prellies' as they were called—a prescription slimming tablet used as a pep-pill supplied 'under the counter' by Rosa, the little old lady in charge of the club's toilets.

The 'world of Beatles' again turns on a seemingly trivial event. The old lady who lived upstairs from the club lodged a series of complaints with police, as did a number of other local residents, about the dreadful noise she was forced to endure each and every night, including Sundays. Koschmider was repeatedly warned but took no notice. The net result was that 48 days and nights after opening as a 'live' venue for rock 'n' roll; and as a showplace for The Beatles; and after what would turn out to be the group's last 'Sunday-night-into-the-early-hours-of Monday-morning' appearance, the police promptly closed down Indra Cabaret Club on 2 October. And on Tuesday night, the 4th of October, Koschmider moved The Beatles to the Kaiserkeller to play out the rest of their contract.

Life being a cabaret; the Indra quickly reverted back to being a strip club after The Beatles left to play the Kaiserkeller, and so we can safely draw a veil over subsequent proceedings, as the club plays no further part in the story of The Beatles.

Never say die, however, as in the wake of *'Beatlemania'*, the Indra went through various reincarnations and is now a music club again; forever playing off the unique place it forever holds in Beatles' history.

| **Side Bar | Indra Cabaret Club - The Beatles' all-important stepping stone to the Kaiserkeller** | The Beatles racked up over 200 finger-blistering hours of rip-roaring rock 'n' roll and 'making one hell of a show' at the Indra. And many noted Beatles' historians have called it their true *"baptism of fire."* | The whole

Indra experience certainly helped transform The Beatles as a band. They were much more confident afterwards—dynamic to the point of being almost incendiary—and were already showing signs of that indefinable quality that Astrid Kirchherr said made them seem like "human magnets" and that Brian Epstein would later call "their irresistible charisma." But then—and perhaps even more remarkable given the conditions they'd endured at the Indra and Bambi Kino—over the ensuing nine months events would transpire; first in Hamburg, then back in Liverpool, and then back in Hamburg again; that would take the group's musicianship and performance capabilities to ever-higher and higher levels.

"You'd better pull your socks up because Rory Storm and The Hurricanes are coming in and you know how good they are. They're going to knock you for six." — Allan Williams' 21 September 1960 letter of encouragement to The Beatles about the imminent arrival at the Kaiserkeller of Liverpool's legendary performer, Rory Storm—'Mr. Showmanship'—and his group, The Hurricanes.

KAISER-KELLER (*'Emperor's Cellar'*) | Grosse Freiheit 36 | St. Pauli | The striking silk-screened posters said it all: *'Teenage Dance Palace'* Kaiser-Keller *'Tanzpalast der Jugend'* | Grosse Freiheit 36 | Hamburg - St. Pauli | Festival Der Rock 'n' Roll Fans | Presented by Bruno Koschmider | October-November-Dezember | Original Rock 'n' Roll Bands | *Rory Storm and His Hurican und The Beatles* | England-Liverpool

Bruno Koschmider opened Der Kaiserkeller on October 14, 1959. Located in the basement cellar of a newly constructed three-story building that housed three different clubs it even had its own 200-car parking garage. The club could hold around 500 people. Its interior decor was nautically themed; all the better to attract passing sailors in the night. All the tables and chairs could pass for sections of a lifeboat or yacht. The tables were wooden cargo barrels. Sailing paraphernalia: wooden ship-wheels, ropes, block and tackle, and all things, nautical, were hung from the ceiling or festooned around the walls.

The club boasted the very latest in jukeboxes that featured a spinning cavalcade of American and British rock 'n' roll stars. It had a purpose-fitted sound system and a proper dance floor. The one thing it lacked was a proper stage—which was constructed from wooden planks nailed atop a stack of beer crates.

When on Tuesday 4 October Koschmider moved The Beatles to the Kaiserkeller to play out the rest of their contract, Derry and the Seniors, the Liverpool beat-group Williams had first contracted to play the club, had been in residence for two months and had proved a huge success with audiences. Derry Wilkie, the group's dynamic, black, lead singer, a consummate showman every bit as exciting as Rory Storm. And so, of course, Koschmider demanded The Beatles must *"Mach shau... like Herr Derry!"* The big question: Could The Beatles measure up to Derry and The Seniors or Rory Storm and The Hurricanes?

Yet the simple truth was The Beatles had improved hand over fist, both as performers and musicians. Eight solid weeks of having to *"Mach schau! Mach schau!"* every night at Indra Cabaret Club had already produced extraordinary results. So when, on 1 October 1960, Rory Storm and The Hurricanes; now having completed their season at a Butlin's Holiday Camp; breezed in to town, ready to crush The Beatles underfoot; subsequent events could prove to be nothing but interesting.

Koschmider immediately demanded that each 12-hour nightly session be split between the two groups. 90 minutes on. 90 minutes off. No exceptions. No substitutes. No complaints. No stopping. No one to even think of leaving the club between opening and closing time. And, perhaps, not surprisingly, in the face of a shared 'common enemy' the two Liverpool groups hit it off and, if not immediately, then soon; each spurring the other on to ever greater excesses of showmanship. On one occasion betting to see which group would be the first to stomp a hole through the rickety wooden stage. Rory finally won the bet, for which a furious Koschmider fined him 65 Deutschemarks.

The 'competitive' frenzy between both groups so effective in bringing in the punters—and keeping them in—Koschmider then extended The Beatles' contract until the end of November.

It was at the Kaiserkeller that The Beatles first met Klaus Voormann, an art student, and later his two closest friends—Astrid Kirchherr and Jürgen Vollmer. All Francophiles and self-proclaimed 'Exis' who took their inspiration from French poets, writers and filmmakers, and Parisian 'Left Bank' existentialists. Astrid and Jürgen were both aspiring photographers and in the days and weeks that followed they took some of the most celebrated and iconic photos ever taken of The Beatles.

As Astrid Kirchherr said, many years later, when asked what had moved her to photograph the then completely unknown group: *"I saw their beauty, their intelligence, and their humour—and simply wanted to try and capture it."*

And it was during the eight weeks The Beatles were at the Kaiserkeller, that a deep and abiding romance—almost fairy tale like—was to blossom between Astrid and the group's bass-player, Stuart Sutcliffe. It was a relationship that would prove to have a profound and lasting effect on The Beatles; one that would help define the band's look and style and, eventually, also help shape the group's definitive line-up.

The Beatles played the Kaiserkeller for 58 nights—four and a half hours each weeknight—six hours every Saturday and Sunday night—with Mondays off—from 4 October to 30 November 1960. | The Kaiserkeller didn't fare too well, either, after The Beatles packed up their guitars, amplifiers, and drums and left for pastures new. The club simply couldn't compete with the music talent on nightly display at Top Ten Club. Within months Bruno Koschmider renamed the Kaiserkeller—the Colibri—and it reverted to being a strip tease club—with attendant jukebox. And so, somewhat sadly, given the musical alchemy that had occurred there, we draw another veil over its speedy decline and subsequent demise.

But, just as happened with the Indra, the location has gone through various reincarnations; under many different managements; and is once again a thriving music club; similarly playing off its unique place in Beatles' history... and in my decidedly humble opinion most deservedly so. *Long Live Der Kaiserkeller!*

"*In 1960, when the group first got together, we went straight off to the Kaiserkeller, in Hamburg, for a season which lasted four-and-a-half months, playing seven hours a night, seven days a week. We learned to live together... discovered how to adapt ourselves to what people wanted... and developed our own particular style. And it was our own. We had neither the time nor the wish to listen to others. We developed along the lines that we felt suited us best. And as it became obvious that the public liked us, we became more confident—and more polished. When we got back to England, The Shadows had soared right out in front with the teenagers. All around us, groups were trying to copy them. But we had our own Beatles sound—and in and around Merseyside, we began to discover that they liked us, too.*"
— John Lennon | *Melody Maker* | February 23 | 1963

"*We sang close harmonies on these little echo mikes, and we made a fairly good job of it. It used to sound pretty good, actually. We got better and better and other groups started coming to watch us. The accolade of accolades was when Tony Sheridan would come in from the Top Ten (the big club we aspired to) or when Rory Storm or Ringo would hang around to watch us.*"
— Paul McCartney

TOP TEN CLUB | St. Pauli - Reeperbahn 136 | *New Top Ten Rock 'n' Roll Club* | A definite step up from Bruno Koschmider's Kaiserkeller. | Peter Eckhorn opened Top Ten Club in July 1960 in direct competition with the Kaiserkeller. Tellingly, Eckhorn also persuaded the club's head bouncer, Horst Fascher, to come work for him at Top Ten Club. | London rock 'n' roller, singer and lead guitarist, Tony Sheridan, was Top Ten's new resident headliner; the other Jets needing to return to England as they didn't have proper work permits. The Beatles would sometimes sit in with Sheridan and The Jets, even though their contract with Koschmider expressly forbade them from doing so. It was Horst Fascher who suggested The Beatles should become Tony Sheridan's regular backing-band at Top Ten. Peter Eckhorn liked what he saw and heard and offered them a full-time gig.

Koschmider, still angry from having had The Jets snatched away by Eckhorn, served up his revenge cold by tipping-off the police that George Harrison was too young to work and accusing Paul McCartney and Pete Best of setting fire to their accommodations at the Bambi-Kino. Which quickly resulted in George, Paul, and Pete, being deported from Germany. John later making the long journey home to Liverpool, by himself, as Stu Sutcliffe stayed on in Hamburg, to be with his new love Astrid Kirchherr.

Over the intervening months, Eckhorn, working with Stu and Mona Best, smoothed over all legalities and, once George turned eighteen, The Beatles returned to Germany at the end of March 1961, to play Top Ten Club. The Beatles' contract a gruelling non-stop 13-weeks of 7-hour sessions, from 7:00 PM to 2:00 AM, each weeknight; 8-hour sessions, from 7:00 PM until 3:00 AM, at weekends; one 15-minute break allowed every hour.

Top Ten Club was one big room, the stage set along the length of one sidewall and raised a foot or so off the ground, so the audience, whether sitting, drinking or dancing, were right up close to the performers. | The club boasted a 'Binson Echo' sound system that produced a glorious reverb and repeated echo effect. George Harrison later recalled: *"You sounded just like Gene Vincent doing 'Be Bop A Lula'."* And that John and Paul absolutely loved what it did to their voices; John especially; and that they both loved singing their "absolute favourite song" so much, they'd always take turns singing lead vocal.

All in all, between 1 April and 1 July 1961, The Beatles played The Top Ten Club for 98 nights, straight, easily racking up over 500 voice-shredding, finger-blistering hours on stage.

And, as it turned out, the Top Ten was also Stuart Sutcliffe's last hurrah as bass player for The Beatles:

"Stuart was engaged to Astrid and after Top Ten decided he was going to leave the band and live in Germany. At that point I said: 'We're not going to get a fifth person in the band. One of us three is going to be the bass player, and it's not going to be me'. And John said, 'It's not going to be me, either'. Paul didn't seem to mind the idea. He went out and bought a Höfner violin bass."

— George Harrison | *The Beatles Anthology*

STAR-CLUB | Grosse Freiheit 39 | St. Pauli | Star-Club was designed to be the sparkling jewel in the business crown of Manfred Weissleder, a St. Pauli businessman and entrepreneur with even more pull than Peter Eckhorn; enough, anyway, to persuade Horst Fascher to become the club's manager.

Another telling move as it was Fascher who then arranged, after face-to-face negotiations with Brian Epstein, in Liverpool, for The Beatles to leave Top Ten Club and headline at Star-Club.

Star-Club—a re-purposed porn cinema, that could hold over a thousand paying punters—wanted The Beatles, and nothing but The Beatles, to headline the impending launch of what Manfred Weissleder intended would become Europe's premier rock 'n' roll club presenting: *'Top Class Acts From All Around Europe... and The World'*.

'DIE NOT HAT EIN ENDE! DIE ZEIT DER DORFMUSIK IST VORBEI!' screamed the hundreds of neon-orange fly-posters plastered up all across Hamburg: *'The Time For Old- Fashioned Farmers' Music Is Over!'* And it was, too. Out with the old and in with the new! Time to rock Star-Club - die Rock 'n' Twist - Parade 1962. All and everything kicked off by The Beatles.

The Beatles played Star-Club on three separate occasions in 1962. The first residency: 48 nights from 13 April - 31May. Beatles' historian and fellow Liverpudlian, Spencer Leigh, says the group were given Good Friday off! | The second: 14 nights from 1 - 14 November. Now with Ringo Starr as the group's drummer. | The third: 13 nights from 18 - 31 December. Spencer Leigh again notes that Manfred Weissleder gave the group Christmas Day off. And you know that can't be bad.

All in all, The Beatles racked up 75 rip-roarin' hard-rockin' nights at Star-Club. And as the ever-increasing wave of *'Beatlemania'* swept around the world, the ever-canny Weissleder began promoting Star-Club as **"The Cradle of The Beatles."**

Which, of course, brings us full circle to Alan Clayson's assertion that Hamburg was, indeed, **"The Cradle of British Rock."**

| Side Bar | Star-Club's "Galaxy of Stars" | *'Top Class Acts From All Around Europe... and The World'* | In time, Star-Club would host a veritable galaxy of top class rock 'n' roll talent: The Beatles, of course. But also: Ray Charles. Little Richard. Chuck Berry. 'Fats' Domino. Jerry Lee Lewis. Gene Vincent. Chubby Checker. Bo Diddley. Bill Haley and the Comets. Joey Dee. The Everly Brothers. Brenda Lee. Duane Eddy. Gerry and The Pacemakers. The Remo Four. The Searchers. Johnny Kidd and The Pirates. Joe Brown. The Walker Brothers. The Spencer Davis Group. The Pretty Things. And many, many, others.

| Side Bar | The Beatles' line-up of John, Paul, George, and Ringo—as was seen and heard at Star-Club—during those last thirteen nights in December, that brought 1962 and the group's remarkable time in Hamburg to a close, would remain unchanged until the group disbanded and the whole magical mystery tour broke apart in 1970.

| Side Bar | Ernst-Merck-Halle | Hamburg | The Beatles returned to Hamburg as part of their 1966 Summer World Tour of Germany, Japan and the Philippines. | They played concerts in Munich and Essen and then took a special train to Hamburg. | On 26 June 1996 the group played two shows at the 5600-seater Ernst-Merck-Halle. | While in Hamburg, The Beatles made sure to catch up with old friends Astrid Kirchherr, Klaus Voormann, and Jürgen Vollmer, as well as record producer, Bert Kaempfert.

"When you think about it, sensibly, our sound really stems from Germany. That's where we learned to work for hours and hours on end and keep on working at full peak even though we reckoned our arms and legs were about ready to drop off."
— George Harrison | *The Beatles Anthology*

"We were honestly never better than when we were in the thick of an all-night session—on the Reeperbahn."
— John Lennon

PART ONE - PEOPLE. PLACES. VENUES

8 - London People

How Does It Feel To Be One Of The Beautiful People?

LONDON. Capital City of the United Kingdom. The centre of British government, politics, banking, business, publishing, broadcasting—both television and radio—the arts—film, theatre, opera, ballet, symphonic orchestra—and any and all other forms of entertainment—high-brow or low. | All the top film and recording studios—film directors and record producers and recording engineers have always been located in and around London. | *"The Toppermost of the Poppermost"* in all things to do with the music business—whether recording artist, music or song composer, music publisher or performing artists' manager—were always to be found in London. | Denmark Street—at the north-end of Charing Cross Road—on the borders of Soho—was Britain's 'Tin Pan Alley'—the place where songs were composed, bought, sold, published, and plugged. The 'Big Four' record companies Decca, EMI, Philips, and Pye all had their head offices in London. As did anyone and everyone with a dream of getting a disc into the Pop Charts—everyone wishing, hoping, and praying for the ever elusive 'No.1' hit.

Spike Milligan | Peter Sellers | Mike Smith | Dick Rowe | Robert Boast | Jim Foy | Sid Colman | George Martin | Judy Lockhart-Smith | Norman Smith | Ken Townsend | Ron Richards | Andy White | Dick James | Tony Barrow | Derek Taylor | Helen Shapiro | Alma Cogan | Jane Asher | Patti Boyd | Bud Ornstein | Walter Shenson | Dick Lester | Alun Owen | Robert Freeman | Victor Spinetti

THE GOONS | BBC Radio Comedy Show | 1952-1960

SPIKE MILLIGAN | British-Irish | Radio star | Comedian | Writer | Musician | Poet | Playwright | Actor | Terence Alan Milligan KBE | 1918 - 2002 | Co-creator, writer, and performer—with Michael Bentine, Peter Sellers, and Harry Secombe—of the radical for the times, anarchic and often absurdly surrealistic BBC radio comedy show: *The Goon Show*. Bursting with madcap storylines, outrageous characters with funny voices, crazy wordplays, and ridiculous sound effects; always recorded in front of a live audience; was a long-time favourite of both John Lennon and Paul McCartney.

When Spike Milligan and Peter Sellers both later recorded comedy sketches and songs for EMI's Parlophone record label—their record producer was none other than George Martin. And it was this fact alone that gave the record producer—who George Harrison thought was *"a right toffee"* (i.e. toffee-nosed; stuck up) on first meeting him at EMI's Abbey Road studios—an immediate credibility with The Beatles.

The Goons are widely considered to have been the prime inspiration for *Monty Python*, as well as many other highly rated British comedy teams. Spike Milligan for his part was a much-loved character with all levels of British society and a great personal favourite of Prince Charles—even though Milligan once famously called him *"a right twit"* on national television. Word has it the prince laughed uproariously and took Milligan's gibe as a compliment; coming as it did from such a comedic legend.

PETER SELLERS | English | Radio star | Comedian | Impressionist | Sometime drummer and singer | Film actor | Richard Henry Sellers CBE | 1925 - 1980 | Much-lauded performer. Starred with Spike Milligan, Michael Bentine, and Harry Secombe in the 'utterly outrageous for the times' BBC radio series—*The Goon Show*—a hugely popular half-hour comedy show that ran from the early 1952 to 1960. John Lennon and Paul McCartney were huge fans of the show and the comedic genius of the actors and would listen in, religiously, every week. John cleverly imitating many of the Goon voices devised by Sellers, Milligan, and Secombe for the show's regular cast of characters—such as Eccles, Neddy Seagoon, and Major Bloodnok—throughout his schooldays and even at Art College. And as unbelievable as it may now be to anyone not alive in Britain at the time, the utterly nonsensical song often heard in the show, the 'Ying Tong Song'—the B-side to the A-side 'Bloodnok's Rock 'n' Roll Call'—was a hit for Decca Records in the UK Singles Chart in 1956—when it reached No. 3.

Later, as members of The Beatles, John, Paul, and George would often break into snippets of the 'Ying Tong Song'—a wildly popular *Goon Show* song—in between performing rock 'n' roll numbers on stage. Legend also has it that the three Beatles—having just learned from George Martin that he actually knew and had recorded Goons Peter Sellers and Spike Milligan—burst into the song's absurd refrain: "*Ying tong, Ying tong, Ying tong, Ying tong, Yiddle I po.*" Oh, to have been a fly on that wall.

Years later George Martin confirmed he was awfully glad at the time that his association with 'the Goons' gave him some sort of instant credibility with this strange bunch of lunatics from Liverpool, as he still wasn't at all sure what to do with The Beatles; turn them down flat or go ahead and record them?

Peter Sellers went on to star in many British films before his breakout international role as Chief Inspector Clouseau in *The Pink Panther* series of comedy films. He was nominated for an Academy Award three times: twice for the Academy Award for Best Actor for his performances in *Dr. Strangelove* and *Being There* and once for the Academy Award for Best Live Action Short Film: *The Running Jumping & Standing Still Film* (1959) directed by Richard Lester. The very same film that, in turn, led to Richard Lester later receiving; all because of his close association with their idols Milligan and Sellers; the immediate and absolute blessing, from each one of The Beatles, for him to go ahead and direct *A Hard Day's Night*.

As they say, it's a small world. And seemingly even smaller still when it comes to creative genius.

THE DECCA RECORD COMPANY LIMITED
| Decca House, 9 Albert Embankment, London SE1

MIKE SMITH | Recording engineer | Decca Studios, 165 Broadhurst Gardens, London | The recording engineer who oversaw The Beatles' ill-fated audition on a bitterly cold New Year's Day at Decca Studios in West Hampstead. | Mike Smith had first seen The Beatles perform at the Cavern a couple of weeks earlier—on 13 December 1961—having been invited up to Liverpool by the group's new manager Brian Epstein. Epstein even treated him to dinner before hand. | Smith was impressed enough by what he saw and heard for him to arrange an audition for the group down in London—on the 1st January 1962.

A rather fateful decision as it turned out as—still suffering from a severe hangover from a New Year's Eve party the night before—he arrived at the audition over an hour late. The Beatles having themselves endured a 10-hour journey down from Liverpool the day before—in the back of van driven by Neil Aspinall—the group's road manager—in freezing weather that'd made road conditions extremely treacherous—were also not in the best of sorts and by all accounts—and most unusual for them—were very nervous.

Brian Epstein who'd journeyed down by train to London was affronted by Smith's late arrival and start—which he took as a personal slight. | It was not a good start—for anyone. | The Beatles' amplifiers being deemed unfit for recording purposes made for a further delay. Which led to John, Paul, and George's guitars being plugged into studio amplifiers—and Pete Best and his drum kit positioned behind isolation screens. | A rudimentary 'sound' balance achieved, Mike Smith recorded The Beatles—John, Paul, George, and Pete—performing 15 songs, in a little over an hour, with no retakes; the session finishing around two o'clock. | After the session Smith told the group they'd done very well—and seemed excited about it. Told them Brian Epstein he'd hear from Decca in the very near future.

Decca Records turned down The Beatles—by a letter sent to Brian Epstein—at the end of January. | And although it was Decca Records A&R Manager Dick Rowe who forever afterwards was called *"The Man Who Turned Down The Beatles"*—it was Mike Smith who actually made the final decision not to sign The Beatles. Smith recommended that Decca sign London-based beat group Brian Poole and The Tremeloes, instead. A group Smith had also auditioned up at Decca Studios in West Hampstead on January 1st and probably within an hour or so of having said goodbye to The Beatles.

"It was a simple matter of expediency," Mike Smith would later explain. Brian Poole lived in Dagenham in Kent—as did Smith—and he and the Tremeloes could be at Decca Studios within a couple of hours at most, not days. Which would equate to considerable savings in time and money for Decca as regards future record production costs. (How wrong he was.) | But such was the North-South geographical divide before The Beatles entirely rewrote the rules of the music industry.

DICK ROWE | Decca Recording Manager and A&R (Artists and Repertoire) Manager | *"Guitar groups are on the way out, Mr. Epstein!"* **| 1921–1986. |** Forever known as *'The Man Who Turned Down The Beatles'*. Truth be told, though, all the other major London recording companies—and their many subsidiary record labels—had turned The Beatles down, too, and some more than once. At least Decca gave The Beatles an audition and later gave the actual audition tapes to Brian Epstein—which they were in no way obliged to do. And it's a matter of record (no pun intended) that a number of original Lennon-McCartney songs from the Decca audition that Brian Epstein later had transferred onto acetate disc at the HMV Record Store on London's Oxford Street would soon set in play a series of extraordinarily fortuitous chance meetings that would eventually lead The Beatles to EMI's Abbey Road Studio—and George Martin.

However, before any of that occurred, legend has it that on Tuesday, 6 February, at a luncheon meeting at Decca House, the recording company's headquarters at 9 Albert Embankment, Brian Epstein—who'd refused to take Decca's 'No' for an answer—sat with Dick Rowe and Decca's sales manager, Sidney Beecher-Stevens, in the hope of them changing their minds. The two senior Decca managers having agreed to the meeting, no doubt, for the simple reason NEMS was one of the country's top record retailers. The lunch was, by all accounts, a very cordial affair and the two executives did their best to humour Brian Epstein. They waited for coffee to be served and the table to be cleared and then Dick Rowe turned and said:

"Not to mince words, Mr. Epstein, but we don't like your boys' sound. Guitar groups, especially, are on their way out... Your boys are never going to make it... We're experts at the game...we know about these things... You'd do far better off to stick to selling records in Liverpool."

Brian Epstein's response has also become the stuff of legend: *"You...you don't know what you're talking about. These 'boys' are about to explode on the music scene... They're going to be bigger than Elvis Presley!"* (And how very right he was.)

Despite being turned down by Decca, The Beatles didn't bear a grudge. When in May the following year—with The Beatles going from success to success—George Harrison met Dick Rowe at a beat group contest at the Philharmonic Hall, in Liverpool—they were both on the jury—he suggested it would be a very good idea for Decca to sign an R&B group called The Rolling Stones who he and the other Beatles had seen play in Richmond, Surrey, just outside London, a few weeks before. Rowe did as George suggested the moment he got back to London. And so the world turns.

Personally, I think Dick Rowe should be better remembered as: *'The man who inadvertently helped The Beatles team up with record producer George Martin.'*

HMV RECORD STORE | Oxford Street, London W1 |
'The World's Largest Record Store'
EMI owned and operated | HMV - 'His Master's Voice' - an EMI subsidiary record label. | HMV - At the heart of every disc the red record label with the picture of 'Nipper' the white Jack Russell terrier staring for eternity into the bell-shaped sound-amplifier of an old wind-up record player.

ROBERT BOAST | Store Manager | Thursday, 8 February 1962 Brian Epstein visited 'His Master's Voice'—*'The World's Largest Record Store'*—on London's Oxford Street. After two days of fruitless and frustrating visits to recording companies in London's West End and, with The Beatles' Decca audition tape all but burning a hole in his brief case, he went into the store to talk to Robert Boast who he'd met on an April 1961 Deutsche Grammophon sponsored trip to Hanover and Hamburg. | Robert Boast listened to Epstein's tale of woe; wasn't in any position to help him directly; but did suggest that any future record company meetings might go that much more positively if the audition tapes were transferred onto disc. He took Epstein along to a small recording studio on the first floor—HMV's 'Personal Recording Department'—where musicians as well as members of the public could make 78rpm demonstration discs—and introduced him to the disc cutter, Jim Foy. Foy then proceeded to cut a couple of double-sided acetate discs of songs from The Beatles' unsuccessful Decca audition.

JIM FOY | **'Personal Recording Department'** | **Manager & Disc-cutter** | Jim Foy threaded the Beatles' Decca audition tape onto an empty reel on a tape machine—ready to start the transfer to acetate disc. He made a quick test for 'sound' and was immediately intrigued by the songs he was hearing. As the lathe-cutting machine then transferred magnetic tape impulses into grooves on two, separate, double-sided, black lacquer discs, he asked about them. | Brian Epstein proudly informed Foy the songs had been written by two members of the group—John Lennon and Paul McCartney—a somewhat unusual occurrence in the music recording industry of the time. | Foy asked if the songs had already been published or not. When he was told they hadn't, Foy suggested that Epstein should meet with Sid Colman, general manager of Ardmore and Beechwood, one of EMI's music publishing companies; who just happened to have an office on the fourth floor of the HMV building. | Then the immortal line: *"Should I call him to see if he has time to come down and have a listen?"* or words to that effect.

SID COLMAN | General Manager | Ardmore & Beechwood Music Publishing Company | A subsidiary of EMI

Sid Colman now steps into Beatles' history. Some chroniclers say he went down to HMV's 'Personal Recording Department'; others that Brian Epstein went up to see him. Either way, Sid Colman listened to a number of Lennon-McCartney originals on newly cut 78rpm discs and not tape; the first record executive to do so. 'Love of the Loved' and 'Like Dreamers Do' on one. 'Hello Little Girl' and 'Till There Was You' from the Broadway musical *'The Music Man'* on the other. And he expressed an immediate interest in his company publishing the songs by John and Paul. Brian Epstein replied that he was really looking to get "his boys" a recording contract and that if Colman could help secure such a deal his firm could have the publishing rights.

This is where 50 plus years of disparate memories now begin to take their toll. For years it was reported that Sid Colman picked up the phone and called the one Artist-and-Repertoire manager at EMI who he thought might best be able to deal with such a quirky sounding group as The Beatles; none other than his good old friend Mr. George Martin. And that within days Brian Epstein and George Martin's secretary were setting up a meeting—which duly led to George Martin signing The Beatles to EMI and becoming their record producer. Which is a hugely significant event in the long and winding saga of The Beatles.

However, some people now say that Sid Colman had various personal issues with George Martin and *"went around him"* to telephone his boss, EMI's managing director, L. G. Wood. And that it was that particular call that really set events into motion.

Me? I still hold to George Martin's own recollection in *All You Need Is Ears*—his autobiography written with Jeremy Hornsby—where he says: *"I got a phone call from Syd (sic) Colman, a friend and one of the music industry's nice guys, who was head of Ardmore & Beechwood, the EMI publishing company with offices above the HMV shop in Oxford Street."*

A fitting testimonial to both men's singular support for the songs of John Lennon and Paul McCartney; as it not only reflects the best of intentions, but also the best of both men.

Brian Epstein duly awarded publishing rights to The Beatles' first single—'Love Me Do' and 'P.S. I Love You'—to Ardmore and Beechwood, but was singularly unimpressed with the results. The single only reached No. 17 in the UK Hit Parade—which Brian Epstein saw as an affront to the true talent of his 'boys'. He'd expected much, much more and thought Sid Colman hadn't done nearly enough to promote The Beatles' first 45rpm record.

Brian Epstein gazed around for other options and alighted upon Hill & Range—a big US music publisher associated with Elvis Presley. However, George Martin tactfully suggested it might be better to try a smaller, hungrier UK publisher who'd move mountains to promote The Beatles. And he offered up three possible names—all known to be honest and reliable.

Brian Epstein chose Dick James because the music publisher picked up the telephone at their very first meeting and got The Beatles a spot on *'Thank Your Lucky Stars'*—a hugely influential, nationally broadcast Saturday evening TV pop show.

Brian Epstein assigned publishing rights of 'Please Please Me' and 'Ask Me Why' to Dick James—and Sid Colman and Ardmore and Beechwood were effectively cut out of the picture.

Dick James set up Northern Songs as the music publishing company for the collective works of John Lennon and Paul McCartney. | Sadly, Sid Colman died, not long after, in 1965.

The story doesn't end there. In 1969 Dick James sold his controlling shares in Northern Songs to Sir Lew Grade (ATV) without offering John Lennon or Paul McCartney a chance to buy the rights to their own songs. In the process he became a multi-millionaire.

Net result—as of January 2017*—the only two Lennon-McCartney songs ever published by Ardmore and Beechwood 'Love Me Do' and 'P.S. I Love You' are still the only two Beatles' songs owned outright by Paul McCartney.

* See Side Bar | Update | Dick James | The Beatles' Music Rights

**EMI | HEAD OFFICE - Manchester Square, Soho W1 |
ABBEY ROAD STUDIOS - St John's Wood NW8**

GEORGE MARTIN | EMI 'Parlophone' - Head of Label | The Beatles' Record Producer | Audio Engineer | Musician | Arranger | Composer | Conductor | 1926 - 2016 |
Sometimes referred to as *"the Fifth Beatle"* because he produced almost all of The Beatles' singles and albums, although he himself said, many times over, that The Beatles' roadie Neil Aspinall was far more deserving of the title.

George Martin was unique in terms of the Times and Place. England in the early 1960s was stuffy, stilted, and stultifying. Conservative. Class-ridden. Hidebound. His open-mindedness, wit, skill, imagination and, most importantly, his *'ears'* made him one of a kind. There was no better person in all the country to help cultivate The Beatles as recording artists and to produce and introduce the group and their music to the world.

After wartime service in the Fleet Air Arm, George Martin attended London's Guildhall School of Music and Drama, from 1947 to 1950, to study piano and oboe. Upon graduating he worked for the BBC's 'classical music' department. In 1950 he joined EMI's Parlophone label; very much the junior to EMI's other more prestigious recording labels, 'HMV' and 'Columbia', as assistant Artist and Repertoire Manager to Oscar Preuss. 1955 Appointed Head of Label, A&R Manager; the youngest manager and record producer of his generation. Throughout the 1950s he became known for producing comedy, novelty, and spoken-word records—working with such artists as Peter Sellers, Spike Milligan, Peter Ustinov, Flanders and Swan, Bernard Cribbins.

In 1962, he was contacted by Sid Colman of EMI-owned music publishers Ardmore & Beechwood and told about a band called The Beatles that might interest him, even though Decca had rejected them. He met with the group's manager Brian Epstein and eventually gave The Beatles an 'Artists Test'—another lucky turn in the long and winding road of The Beatles' story. The Beatles auditioned in Studio Three at Abbey Road Studios, on 6 June 1962, and duly entered into pop music history.

In the first year alone—working closely with John, Paul, George, and Ringo—fully aided and abetted by a hugely talented crew of recording engineers and technicians at EMI's Abbey Road Studios—he produced five remarkably polished 'pop' singles—four of them No. 1 UK Hits. Their first single—'Love Me Do'—released November 1962—made the 'Top 20' in the UK Charts. In 1963 they released four more singles—'Please, Please Me'— 'From Me To You'—'She Loves You'—'I Want To Hold Your Hand'—all No. 1 Hits. 'She Loves You' made No.1 on advance sales alone—and was the very first Beatles' record to sell a million copies.

Their first LP—*Please Please Me*—topped the UK Album Charts in May 1963 and stayed there for thirty weeks. Only for it to be replaced by their second LP—*With The Beatles*—in November—which stayed on top for 20 weeks—and was only the second album in UK chart history to sell a million copies.

All of which further underscores George Martin's singular act of faith in letting four unknown, untried, and untested, longhaired scruffs from Liverpool sing and record their very own songs for their first singles. Similarly, he later also let the "savage young" Beatles choose their own 'cover songs' for their first series of albums. It might seem as nothing today—but such decisions not only went against all the rules at EMI—owners of Parlophone Records—they broke almost every norm within the British recording industry. In the still very regimented Britain of the post-war years—one was always expected to abide by the rules. Conformity not individuality was the order of the day. You broke the rules at your own risk.

One further key event; after recording The Beatles' second single, 'Please Please Me' at Abbey Road Studios—and declaring from the control room that **"Gentlemen... you've just made your first number one hit"**—George Martin travelled up to Liverpool to see and hear The Beatles play the Cavern to determine whether they could record their first album 'live' at the club. And although he decided against doing so, as the Cavern would have been an acoustic nightmare for recording purposes, he couldn't have but felt the raw excitement, energy, and electricity The Beatles generated in performance. The group's charm, cheekiness, and humour had won him over during their first audition at Abbey Road, but his trip to Liverpool would have been the first time that he experienced for himself the extraordinary effect The Beatles and their music had on a live audience. And it could have done nothing but reaffirm the rule-breaking brilliance of his initial decision.

George Martin continued to bend and break rules, and effectively re-invent many of them, in his efforts to help nurture The Beatles' emerging musical virtuosity and songwriting mastery. He skilfully guided them into producing a veritable 'hit' parade of singles and long-playing albums of ever-increasing inventiveness and brilliance; even arranging for and playing piano and or harpsichord on many of their tracks. It was in every which way a working relationship made in recording heaven.

In the years 1962-1970 The Beatles released 22 singles, 13 EPs, and 12 studio albums in the UK—almost all of it produced by George Martin. | The Beatles' albums—*Please Please Me* - 1963 | *With The Beatles* - 1963 | *A Hard Day's Night* - 1964 |*Beatles For Sale* - 1964 | *Help!* - 1965 | *Rubber Soul* - 1965 | *Revolver* - 1966 | *Sgt. Pepper's Lonely Hearts Club Band* - 1967 | *The Beatles (The White Album)* - 1968 | *Yellow Submarine* - 1969 | *Abbey Road* - 1969 | *Let It Be* - 1970

Most of the orchestral arrangements and instrumentation on The Beatles' records—as well as many of the keyboard elements on the early releases—were written or performed by George Martin—in close collaboration with the group. | He composed, arranged, and produced a great many film scores, including the instrumental scores for The Beatles' films: 1964's *A Hard Day's Night*—for which he won an Academy Awards Nomination | 1965's *Help!* | 1968's *Yellow Submarine*.

1965. Not even given a bonus by EMI and denied any kind of producer royalties in recognition for his many contributions to the unprecedented success of The Beatles, George Martin left EMI, together with fellow EMI producer John Burgess, and established Associated Independent Recording (AIR); one of the UK's first independent production companies, and still one of the world's pre-eminent recording studios.

George Martin is widely considered to be one of the greatest record producers of all time. He's responsible for 30 No.1 singles in the UK and 23 No.1 singles in the US—across a range of genres from pop, rock, folk, and jazz to spoken word, classical, and film soundtracks. | He produced recordings for major artists including Judy Garland, Ella Fitzgerald, Stan Getz, Humphrey Lyttelton, John Dankworth, Cleo Laine, Alma Cogan, Matt Monro, Dudley Moore, Shirley Bassey, Tommy Steele, Cilla Black, Gerry & The Pacemakers, Billy J. Kramer & the Dakotas, The Fourmost, Elton John, Pete Townsend, Jeff Beck, Ultravox, Neil Sedaka, Kenny Rogers, Celine Dion, Paul Winter, Mahavishnu Orchestra, John Williams, The King's Singers.

To further add to his 'pop culture' *bona fides*, he also produced two of the best-known James Bond themes: 1964's 'Goldfinger' sung by Shirley Bassey. And 1973's 'Live and Let Die' by Paul McCartney and Wings.

1979. Published the memoir—*All You Need is Ears*—co-written with Jeremy Hornsby. | 1988. Appointed CBE for services to music. | 1996. Knighted in recognition for his services to the music industry and popular culture.| Mid-1990s. Compiled *The Beatles Anthology*—three double-CD sets of rarities and studio out-takes. | 1999. Inducted into the *'Rock and Roll Hall of Fame'*. | 2001. Released *'Produced by George Martin: 50 Years in Recording'*—a six-CD retrospective of his studio career. And quite wonderful it is, too. | 2011. *'Produced by George Martin'*—90-minute documentary feature film—co-produced by 'BBC Arena'—was released to critical acclaim.

The importance of George Martin's many contributions to the Beatles' music canon cannot be overstated. He was responsible for producing much of the group's unique 'sound'. He and The Beatles—working closely together—continually pushed the boundaries of what was technically and artistically possible and thereby introduced many musical elements that were entirely new to rock 'n' roll. All of which played a major role in shaping the scope and soundscape of popular music and—with AIR studios—even the nature of the music industry itself. In doing so he helped change popular music forever.

This unabashed Beatles' fan firmly believes: 'No George Martin... No Beatles'. It's all but impossible to imagine The Beatles' recording career being the success it was in the hands of any other record producer of the time—on either side of the Atlantic. | Unique and utterly irreplaceable in the long and winding story of The Beatles... George Martin should perhaps best be remembered by what he said about working with the group: *"We were a creative team...always looking for something slightly out of reach. I was merely the bloke who interpreted their ideas. The fact that they couldn't read or write music and I could has absolutely nothing to do with it. I was purely an interpreter...the genius was theirs, no doubt about that."*

| Side Bar | Derek Taylor - The Beatles' Press Officer - on George Martin | Derek Taylor has his own entry in 'London People' and deservedly so, as times beyond number he proved himself a good and trusted friend of The Beatles. His thoughts about George Martin's relationship with The Beatles are more than noteworthy as they come from someone who was not a musician, composer, or record producer, but a journalist and writer—and consummate professional—intimately involved in the day-to-day workings of The Beatles.

"George Martin had understanding, sympathy, and respect that perfectly matched their special needs and strengths. His ability was somehow the right shape... He gave The Beatles all he had. They taught him all they knew."

Wonderfully observed, the notion of George Martin being "the right shape" for The Beatles, a perfect allusion.

JUDY LOCKHART-SMITH | George Martin's secretary and later wife | When George Martin asked her into his office—at EMI's headquarters in London's Manchester Square—to hear the HMV acetates of The Beatles' Decca recording session and render an opinion—she gave 'the boys' a decided 'thumbs up'. | She later contacted Brian Epstein to arrange an EMI 'Artist Test' audition—and was always very supportive of the group.

NORMAN SMITH | The Beatles' original Recording engineer | Record producer | Musician | Songwriter | Recording artist | 1923-2008 | Played a key role for the Parlophone label at EMI's Abbey Road Studios. | John Lennon nicknamed him "Normal" Smith. | He was The Beatles' recording engineer from their original 1962 'Artists Test' all the way through the group's early single releases and LPs; from *Please Please Me* to 1965's *Rubber Soul*—a total of almost 100 Beatles' songs.

1966. Promoted to Head of Parlophone—George Martin having left EMI the previous year to set up Associated Independent Recording Studios (AIR). | Smith also went on to produce important albums for Pink Floyd: *The Piper at the Gates of Dawn*, *A Saucerful of Secrets*, *Ummagumma*. And The Pretty Things: *S.F. Sorrow*.

Norman Smith was also an accomplished musician, song composer, and—under the alias 'Hurricane Smith'—in the early 1970s—a successful recording artist. He scored a US No.1 Hit with 'Oh Babe, What Would You Say?'

KEN TOWNSEND - MBE | Sound engineer | Recording engineer who played a unique role at Abbey Road Studios by helping to shape the 'sound' of The Beatles. | He worked on several Beatles' albums, such as *Rubber Soul*—*Revolver*—and *Sgt. Pepper's Lonely Hearts Club Band*.

In 1966, during a recording session for the album *Revolver*—when The Beatles were working on the recording of 'Tomorrow Never Knows', John Lennon said how much he hated having to do a perfect 'second take' to double the sound of his vocals. And how increasingly frustrated both he and the other Beatles were by continually having to re-record vocals to create multi-layered vocal effects; always a key component of The Beatles' sound. It was not only time-consuming but a waste of a valuable track on the 4-track tape machine, which at the time was 'state of the art' recording technology.

Townsend, the technical manager at Abbey Road Studios', got to thinking and created the world's first 'artificial double tracking' system—ADT—by taking the signal from the playback and recording heads—delaying them slightly—thereby creating two 'sound images' from the single original signal. | By altering the speed and or the frequency he found that he could also create a variety of other 'new-sounding' tape effects—which The Beatles were only too eager to explore during the rest of the *Revolver*—and later—recording sessions.

The introduction of ADT is regarded as being a milestone in the history of sound recording—for which Ken Townsend later received an MBE for services to the recording industry.

Ken Townsend spent his entire working career at Abbey Road Studios—and retired as the Chairman of the Studio Group after 42 years of service. In yet another example of Lennon wordplay, he's said to have nicknamed ADT: *"Ken's Flanger"*; the sole reason *'flanging'* is still used as the standard technical term for 'artificial double tracking' in recording studios around the world. | *"Thank-You-Thank-You-Mister-Mister-Ken-Ken."*

RON RICHARDS | **Recording engineer** | **Record producer** | **Manager** | **Promoter** | 1929-2009 | Richards was the recording engineer for, and helped produce, The Beatles' 'Love Me Do' and Gerry and the Pacemakers' 'You'll Never Walk Alone'—recording milestones for both groups. | 1952. Ron Richards began working in London's 'Tin Pan Alley'—Denmark Street—as a 'song plugger' for Chappell music publishers. In 1958 he joined EMI's Parlophone label as a promotions man. George Martin, head of label, spotted his talent for music and moved him into production, where he would rise to recording engineer and record producer. *Rubber Soul*; UK release date 3 December 1965; was the final Beatles' album Ron Richards worked on as recording engineer before EMI promoted him to record producer.

Richards is perhaps better known for discovering and signing The Hollies, the beat group from Manchester, to a recording contract with Parlophone. From 1963-1975 he produced all of The Hollies' music, during which time the group enjoyed seventeen 'Top Ten' hit singles in the UK and worldwide success.

He later left EMI to join former EMI producers George Martin and John Burgess at Associated Independent Recording (AIR) one of the UK's first independent production companies.

ANDY WHITE | Drummer | Session Musician | *"A steady pair of hands"* | Andrew 'Andy' White |1930 - 2015 | Born Scotland | From the late '50s until the mid-'70s one of London's busiest 'session' drummers. Best known for being called in to EMI Abbey Road Studios for the re-recording of The Beatles' first UK single, 'Love Me Do', when he replaced Ringo Starr. White also played drums on 'P.S. I Love You'—the single's B-side.

Ringo Starr had recorded 'Love Me Do' at Abbey Road the previous week—4 September 1962—but unknown to him or the other Beatles, his drumming had been deemed unacceptable and a session musician hired for the group's next recording session. That's why Ringo was so surprised when he arrived at Abbey Road—11 September 1962—for the 7:00 PM scheduled start of a three-hour recording session—to find Andy White already setting up his drum kit in the studio. It being only second his recording session with The Beatles, Ringo went along with everything, but was visibly upset by the unexpected turn of events, as he felt he'd been ambushed and the group were about to 'do a Pete Best' on him and fire him before he'd even had a chance to prove himself. Which is probably the only reason the record producer that night, Ron Richards; George Martin's assistant; later asked Ringo to play tambourine on 'Love Me Do' and maracas on 'P.S. I Love You'. The 4 September version of 'Love Me Do' with Ringo playing drums—no tambourine accompaniment—was used on the UK single released 5 October 1962. The 11 September 1962 'Andy White on drums' versions of both songs—with Ringo Starr on tambourine and/or maracas—appear on *'Please Please Me'*—The Beatles' UK debut album. And were used again for the US single released 27 April 1964.

In his lengthy career as a session drummer Andy White worked with a number of prominent artists, in the UK and US, including Anthony Newley, Tom Jones, Rod Stewart, Billy Fury, Lulu, and Herman's Hermits; and Chuck Berry, Louis Armstrong, Marlene Dietrich, and Burt Bacharach.

He married Lyn Cornell of the UK all-female vocal group Vernons Girls. | And later moved to the US to live. | He died in New Jersey in 2015—aged 85.

DICK JAMES MUSIC LTD. | Denmark Street, London WC2

DICK JAMES | The Beatles' music publisher | 1920–1986. Recording artist and music publisher. | Dick James was a 1950s pop-singer of UK hits Robin Hood (TV theme) and The Ballad of Davy Crockett. He later set up as a music publisher—Dick James Music. But business was hard going and he was in definite need of a lucky break.

At that moment in time Brian Epstein; hugely dissatisfied with what he regarded as Ardmore and Beechwood's paltry efforts to help 'Love Me Do' climb the pop charts; began looking for a different musical publisher for John Lennon and Paul McCartney's growing list of original songs. And he informed George Martin that he intended to approach Hill & Range; the big US music publisher associated with Elvis Presley. George Martin tactfully suggested it might be better to find a smaller, hungrier UK publisher who'd move mountains to promote The Beatles and offered up three possible names; all people known to be honest and reliable.

Dick James immediately impressed Brian Epstein by securing The Beatles a spot on ATV's hugely popular, Saturday evening, nationally-televised pop show *Thank Your Lucky Stars*. | Brian Epstein duly assigned Dick James, the publishing rights of 'Please Please Me' and 'Ask Me Why'. | Dick James then set up Northern Songs as an independent music publishing company to specifically handle The Beatles. John Lennon and Paul McCartney and Brian Epstein all each had a block of shares—but Dick James and his business partner retained the controlling interest.

In 1969 Dick James sold his controlling shares in Northern Songs to Sir Lew Grade (ATV) without giving John or Paul a chance to secure full rights to their own songs. | John Lennon had long dismissed Dick James as being just "another one of the men in suits who got rich off us" and over time the relationship had soured somewhat. And as The Beatles began to break apart, Dick James read the signs and broke away first and in the process became a multi-millionaire.

| Side Bar | Update | The Beatles' Music Rights | Dick James sold music rights to Northern Songs—effectively all the songs of Beatles John Lennon, Paul McCartney, George Harrison, Ringo Starr—to Sir Lew Grade (ATV)—who later sold them to pop star Michael Jackson, who later sold 50% rights to Sony Music—Jackson's estate selling the remaining 50% in 2016. For fifty years, neither Paul McCartney, nor John Lennon's estate has owned the rights to the songs of Lennon-McCartney.

January 2017. McCartney sued Sony Music in US Court for the return of the songs of Lennon-McCartney; as US copyright law decrees all rights revert to the creators of such after 50 years. | July 2017. The suit didn't go to court. McCartney and Sony Music came to a private settlement; the details sealed; but it was widely reported that Paul has at long last retrieved the rights to his part of the Lennon-McCartney songbook.

NEMS ENTERPRISES | Monmouth Street, London WC2 | Argyll Street, London W1

TONY BARROW | Record reviewer | Writer | Public Relations man | Tony Barrow was born in Liverpool. However, he was based in London during the early days of The Beatles. He wrote a regular record review column for the *Liverpool Echo* under the by-line 'Disker'. His full-time job was writing album-sleeve copy for Decca Records. Brian Epstein, manager of NEMS record stores, was very familiar with 'Disker' and wrote to ask the man behind the pseudonym to plug The Beatles in his column. Tony Barrow demurred; said unfortunately he could do nothing to help as the Liverpool group with the very odd-sounding name had yet to actually release a record.

When The Beatles did eventually release 'Love Me Do', Brian Epstein went on the hunt for a Press Officer and at first offered the job to young, aspiring PR whizz Andrew Loog Oldham, soon to become manager of the Rolling Stones, who declined. Brian next offered the job to Tony Barrow; who again turned him down. This time Brian wouldn't take 'no' for an answer and countered by offering to pay Tony double whatever salary Decca Records was paying him.

In 1962, Tony joined NEMS Enterprises, at their 13 Monmouth Street, Covent Garden office, as Senior Press and Publicity Officer where, as well as attending to ever-increasing demands for The Beatles he paid close attention to the PR needs of Cilla Black and Billy J. Kramer, and oversaw the rest of Brian Epstein's fast-emerging stable of Liverpool superstars.

When Brian moved NEMS Enterprises from Liverpool to London—in the wake of *'Beatlemania'*—and opened an office in Argyll Street W1—next door to the London Palladium—Tony set up a PR office there. And it was Tony who dreamed up The Beatles' nickname..."*The Fab Four.*" He wrote the sleeve notes for many of The Beatles' album covers. He toured extensively with the group—set up all their major press conferences—and was always on hand to smooth the way with the world's press.

Very late on the night of August 27, 1965—with The Beatles in Los Angeles preparing to give two concerts at the Hollywood Bowl—Tony was one of the very few people permitted to accompany John, Paul, George, and Ringo when they were driven in a convoy of large black limousines to meet Elvis Presley, at his rented mansion in Bel Air. Elvis was in town having just finished shooting yet another forgettable movie, *Paradise, Hawaiian Style*. The single stipulation by Colonel Tom Parker, Elvis's manager: no press, no pictures, no recording. *Oh, to have been a fly on that wall.*

Tony worked for NEMS until 1968 when The Beatles set up their own management company—Apple Corps—in the wake of Brian Epstein's death. | He then established his own PR firm—Tony Barrow International. In 2005 Tony Barrow authored the book: *John, Paul, George, Ringo & Me—The Real Beatles Story.*

DEREK TAYLOR | Journalist | Writer | Publicist | Record producer | 1932-1997 | Born Liverpool | Best known for his role as The Beatles' Press Officer and later as Press Officer for Apple Corps. | Close friend to all The Beatles—most especially George Harrison. | 30 May 1963 working as a journalist for the *Daily Express* newspaper was assigned to write a review of a Beatles' concert at the Manchester Odeon and was enchanted by what he saw and heard. His glowing review of the group attracted the attention of their manager Brian Epstein and he was invited to meet The Beatles personally. | As The Beatles gained national attention, Taylor's editors at the *Daily Express* conceived of an idea to boost circulation—a regular column ostensibly written by George Harrison but ghostwritten by him. The collaboration between the Beatle and the journalist on subsequent articles was the start of a lifelong friendship.

1964. Brian Epstein asked Derek Taylor to assist in writing his autobiography: *A Cellarful of Noise*. Taylor interviewed Epstein over several days at a seaside hotel in Torquay and shaped the audio recording transcriptions into a singular narrative—retaining almost all of Epstein's words. | Brian Epstein was so pleased by the experience he hired Taylor away from his newspaper job—put him in charge of The Beatles' press releases—and had him take on the role as media liaison for both himself and the group. Taylor was later appointed Brian Epstein's personal assistant. He served as Press Officer for The Beatles' first US concert tour in the summer of 1964. But resigned that September—at the end of the tour—after a major falling out with Brian Epstein. A stickler for details, Epstein demanded Taylor still had to work out his three-month notice period. He went to work at the *Daily Mirror*.

1965. Derek Taylor left the UK and moved to L.A. California with his family, where he started his own public relations company. His clients included the Byrds, the Beach Boys, The Mamas & The Papas and he became: *"probably, the most famous rock publicist of the mid-'60s."* | June 1967. He was co-founder and publicist of the Monterey Pop Festival. | August 1967. George Harrison flew to California—wrote 'Blue Jay Way' while still 'jet-lagged' and waiting for Derek Taylor and his wife Joan to find their way to his rented home on Blue Jay Way in the fog-ridden Hollywood Hills. | Taylor later accompanied George Harrison on a visit to San Francisco's Haight-Ashbury—epicentre of 'Hippy' culture—where Patti Boyd-Harrison's sister lived. | That same year Derek Taylor was also a singular catalyst in Harry Nilsson's musical career when he introduced Nilsson's album *'Pandemonium Shadow Show'* to The Beatles—who were so impressed by the singer's talent they invited him to London. Which led to Nilsson becoming a collaborator and close friend of both John Lennon and Ringo Starr.

1968. Derek Taylor returned to England in April; at the express request of George Harrison; to work as the Press Officer for The Beatles' newly created Apple Corps. In August oversaw the public launch of the company's record label, Apple Records; marked by the release of The Beatles' single 'Hey Jude'.

Taylor left Apple Corps—in late 1970—when Allen Klein was brought in to manage the company after the breakup of The Beatles. | He joined WEA UK—later Warner Music Group—and worked with the Rolling Stones, Yes, America, Neil Young, Carly Simon, Alice Cooper, and others. He also co-produced Harry Nilsson's album: *'A Little Touch Of Schmilsson In The Night'*.

He returned to America in the mid-1970s to become VP Marketing for Warner Bros. Records. One his projects—the worldwide marketing campaign for the TV film and album release of *The Rutles 'All You Need Is Cash'*—a spoof on The Beatles, that featured George Harrison in a bit part. Taylor left Warner's in 1978. | In 1978-79. He collaborated with George Harrison, again, on his autobiography, *'I Me Mine'*, published in 1980. He wrote his own autobiography: *'Fifty Years Adrift' (In An Open Necked Shirt)*—published December 1983—with the introduction written by George Harrison.

He returned to England and worked for George Harrison's film company Handmade Films. | 1987. Derek Taylor wrote *'It Was Twenty Years Ago Today'* to celebrate the twentieth anniversary of the release of The Beatles' *'Sgt. Pepper's Lonely Hearts Club Band'* | Early 1990s, Neil Aspinall asked him to re-join Apple Corps to direct the compiling and marketing for the coming wave of Beatles' legacy projects that included *'The Beatles - Live at the BBC'* and the three double CD compilation-albums linked to the TV series and coffee-table book *'The Beatles Anthology'*.

Derek Taylor died of cancer—8 September 1997—and at the time of his death was still employed by Apple Corps. | George Harrison, Neil Aspinall—Michael Palin, and Eric Idle and Neil Innes of *'The Rutles'* fame—all attended his funeral.

SINGERS, ACTORS, GIRLFRIENDS... AND A MODEL WIFE

HELEN SHAPIRO | Singer | Actor | 1946 - | Born Bethnal Green London | England's early-Sixties teenage "pop music queen." | The youngest female singer ever to top the UK Singles Charts. | Voted Britain's 'Top Female Singer' before she was even sixteen. | Age 9 she began singing and playing a ukulele in her brother's youth club 'Skiffle' group. | At 10 she was a singer in the school band 'Susie and the Hula Hoops'. But had such an unusually deep voice for a girl not yet in her teens—school-friends nicknamed her "Foghorn." | At 13 she started singing lessons at The Maurice Burman School of Modern Pop Singing, off Baker Street, in London. Singing star Alma Cogan had attended the same school. Burman was so taken with the young Helen's voice he waived the tuition fee and was later instrumental in bringing her to the attention of Norrie Paramor of Columbia Records—one of EMI's top pop producers; the man responsible for signing Cliff Richard & The Shadows. Helen Shapiro's 'mature-sounding' voice, with its unforced and rich intonation, turned her into an overnight sensation.

1961. At 14 her first record—'Don't Treat Me Like a Child'—hit No. 3 in UK Singles Charts. Her next two UK singles—'You Don't Know' and 'Walkin' Back to Happiness' were both No.1 Hits. | 'Walkin' Back to Happiness' selling 40,000 copies a day at one point during its record-breaking 19-week chart run. Her fourth single release—'Tell Me What He Said'—reached No. 2. Her next hit single—'Little Miss Lonely'—peaked at No. 8.

March 1962. She made her film debut as the female lead in *It's Trad, Dad!* Directed by Richard Lester; it was his first feature film; it also helped set him up to direct *A Hard Day's Night*.

March 1962. She appeared as 'her singing self' in the Billy Fury film *Play It Cool*. | Her fourth single release—'Tell Me What He Said'—reached No. 2. | 1962. She made the UK Top 40 with 'Keep Away From Other Girls'—the first song by Burt Bacharach to make the British charts.

1963. She headlined a UK. 'Pop Package' Tour—with The Beatles fourth on the bill. | The rise and rise of The Beatles and the 'Merseybeat' sound increasingly labelled her as "old fashioned" and she was eclipsed by the new wave of female singers—Dusty Springfield, Cilla Black, Sandie Shaw, and Lulu—and her career as a pop singer declined.

Helen branched out as a performer to broaden her audience—regularly undertook cabaret tours of workingmen's clubs around the country; did theatre work; began to sing jazz, her particular love. | 1984 - 2001 she toured extensively with legendary British jazz trumpeter Humphrey Lyttelton and his band. | 1986. She appeared as a 'regular' character on the television soap opera *Albion Market*. | She played the role of 'Nancy' in Lionel Bart's musical *Oliver!* in London's West End. | Her one-woman show *'Simply Shapiro'* ran from 1999 until 2002—after which she bid farewell, so long, and goodbye to show business.

| Side Bar - Helen Shapiro and The Beatles | 2 February - 3 March 1963 | *"She was only sixteen"*—but she headlined a UK 'Pop Package' Tour—with The Beatles as one of her supporting acts. The Beatles were 'fourth' on an eleven-act bill. It was the group's first national tour of Britain. | The Beatles having been booked by promoter Arthur Howes for a series of national tours following their breakthrough 19 January performance of 'Please Please Me' on the hugely influential, nationally syndicated, Saturday night TV pop show *Thank Your Lucky Stars*. | She had a very unassuming, not at all 'Star-like', manner and used to travel on the same tour bus as The Beatles and all the other acts. She and the group enjoyed each other's company. John Lennon and Paul McCartney wrote the song 'Misery' especially for her, but she never recorded it. | Years later she said her managers had declined the song without ever even asking her opinion—as they thought The Beatles were a passing fad. And then Kenny Lynch went and had a big hit with the song. 'Misery' indeed.

ALMA COGAN | **Pop Singer** | **Songwriter** | *"The Girl with the Giggle in Her Voice"* | 1931 - 1966 | The highest paid female entertainer in Britain during the late 1950s–early 1960s. | Born Whitechapel, London—of Russian-Romanian Jewish descent—though convent educated. | Began singing at an early age—

competed in charity shows and talent contests—began appearing in musical revues—then was spotted by a record producer from HMV. | Her first release—'To Be Worthy of You' b/w 'Would You'—recorded on her 20th birthday—led to her appearing regularly on the BBC radio show—'*Gently Bentley*'—and becoming the star vocalist for the enormously popular BBC radio comedy series— '*Take It From Here*'.

Her voice was often likened to Doris Day's; pure, powerful, and loaded with personality. Many of her recordings were covers of US hits. One such song—'Bell Bottom Blues'—her first hit—reached No. 4 on 3 April 1954. | In the 1950s she made the UK Singles Chart eighteen times—'Dreamboat' reaching No. 1. Her other 1950s hits include 'Why Do Fools Fall in Love', 'Sugartime', and 'The Story of My Life'.

She was one of the first UK recording artists to appear frequently on television, where her strong singing voice, bubbly, effervescent personality, and dramatic, full-hooped, sequined skirts—complemented by her figure-hugging tops—could be showcased to perfection. She topped the Annual *NME* Reader's Poll as 'Outstanding British Female Singer' four times between 1956 and 1960.

The UK musical revolution of the 1960s, signalled by the rise and rise of The Beatles, cast Alma Cogan as out of fashion and "square." | Her highest 1960s chart ranking in UK was at No. 26—with 'We Got Love'—all her successes now increasingly abroad—in Denmark, Sweden, Germany, and Japan. | She started to write more and more of her own songs—some of them hits—but again only abroad. | She continued to be a popular figure in UK show-business circles, however, and was offered the part of 'Nancy' in the stage production of *Oliver!* |1964. She appeared on the hit, teenage TV pop-show *Ready Steady Go!* | She even headlined at one of London's premier cabaret venues—Talk of the Town. | There never seemed to be any stopping her.

| **Side Bar** | **Alma Cogan and The Beatles** | Alma Cogan lived with her widowed mother in Kensington High Street, London, in a lavishly decorated ground floor flat, which was a legendary party venue. Regular visitors included Princess Margaret, Noël

Coward, Cary Grant, Audrey Hepburn, Michael Caine, Frankie Vaughan, Roger Moore and a host of other celebrities; including Brian Epstein and The Beatles. She tried to update her 'image' by recording The Beatles' songs 'Eight Days a Week b/w 'Help!' but her career never really took off again.

Alma was really close with all The Beatles. Paul McCartney first played the melody of 'Yesterday' on her piano. He also played tambourine on her recording of 'I Knew Right Away'. John Lennon had long thought Alma Cogan was unhip and way out of date; had mocked her savagely from afar. But after they met in 1964 on the ATV pop show *Ready Steady Go!* that changed, dramatically, and they became very close and, indeed, intimate friends.

It was long rumoured the pair had had a serious and deeply felt romance; kept secret because of Alma's mother's strict Jewish faith. Although it now appears John's wife Cynthia was only too aware of the depth of feeling that existed between Alma and John—something she later confirmed to one John Lennon's biographers—but that was only publicly acknowledged after her death in 2015. | In the last year of Alma Cogan's life it became increasingly clear that her health was failing and she died from ovarian cancer in London—26 October 1966—aged just 34. Those that knew them both said John was truly inconsolable.

JANE ASHER | Actor | Author | Entrepreneur | 1946 - | Born London into an upper middle class English family—her father was a noted doctor and consultant—her mother a professor of music. | She was Paul McCartney's girlfriend and muse from 1963 until 1968. | The inspiration for a number of songs Paul wrote and composed when in The Beatles. | Both she and her family were a major influence on Paul's life and lifestyle. | Jane Asher—began her acting career at the age of five and over the next ten years appeared in a number of successful British films and numerous television series.

18 April 1963. Having previously appeared as the 'resident teenager' on the BBC TV's weekly 'pop music' show *Juke Box Jury*—17-year-old Jane interviewed the group at a photo shoot for

The Radio Times—the BBC's weekly-listings magazine—prior to a performance by The Beatles at the Royal Albert Hall, London. At a reception afterwards—she and Paul McCartney were smitten with one another and they began their 5-year relationship. And as Paul and Jane grew closer and closer and The Beatles ever more famous, and privacy of any sort difficult to find or maintain, Jane suggested that Paul should regard her family's house as his London home and her 'modern-minded' mother agreed to let him move into an empty attic room.

Paul moved into the Asher family's six-floor townhouse on Wimpole Street, and stayed for three years—happily ensconced in a top-floor room next to Jane's brother Pete. Paul remembers his time at the house as being *"kind of perfect!"* Living with a doctor's close-knit, well educated, and culturally aware family greatly broadened his own social horizons. It's perhaps telling that Paul's close friendship with Jane's brother, Peter, despite all the later ups and down, has endured to this very day.

Paul and Jane often went on holiday together when their busy schedules allowed. In September 1963 they spent two weeks in Greece with Ringo Starr and his future wife Maureen. They holidayed again with Ringo and Maureen—yachting in the Bahamas. Everyone who knew them expected them to get married. In 1966, Jane helped Paul find a house in Cavendish Avenue, St John's Wood London—close to Abbey Road Studios—and they moved in together. That same year she also persuaded Paul to buy High Farm, in Campbeltown, Scotland as a retreat far away from the public eye. All of which is to say that without Jane's influence, it's likely Paul McCartney and Wings' song 'Mull of Kintyre' would never have hit the airwaves.

And yet however idyllic it might all have seemed to the outside world Jane was never one to simply accept the role of girlfriend of a world-famous Beatle; her true passion was for acting. And she made it very clear from the start that she was unwilling to sacrifice her career for Paul—which not surprisingly was a continuing cause of friction during their relationship. After all, Paul was a Northern lad, born and bred, and they do—or did—things differently 'oop North, and perhaps too chauvinistic for today's world, but par for the course in Sixties Britain.

1967. Jane embarked on a five-month tour of America—with the Bristol Old Vic Company—and performed in *Romeo and Juliet*—in a number of major East Coast cities. When she returned to London—Paul and the other Beatles were already experimenting with LSD—experiencing new inner worlds—that, of course, she hadn't been party to—and was even jealous of. | The new spiritually infused dynamics altered everything and slowly—inexorably—Paul and Jane—began to grow worlds apart. | Even so—the couple got engaged on Christmas Day 1967. | In February and March 1968 Jane accompanied The Beatles and each of their partners to Rishikesh, in India, to attend an advanced Transcendental Meditation training session with the Maharishi Mahesh Yogi. | In the end it was the young pop star's dalliances with other girls—sophisticates as well as groupies—that proved the couple's undoing. Returning earlier than expected from acting in a play in Bristol—some two hours by train from London—Jane walked in on one such affair—and immediately walked out. Jane and Paul subsequently tried to retrieve their own relationship—but by July 1968 it was all over.

Jane announced the end of the engagement on *Dee Time*, a hugely popular BBC TV Saturday evening chat show; and that really was the end of it. Other then a few reminiscences to Hunter Davis in late 1967—for the official biography of '*The Beatles*'—Jane has never written or divulged another word about her time with the ever beguiling, endlessly charming Beatle Paul. And—other than Neil Aspinall—she's the only person that was once inside The Beatle's inner circle never to have done so. | Paul wrote 'Things We Said Today', 'You Won't See Me', 'We Can Work It Out' and 'I'm Looking Through You' about his relationship with Jane Asher. He also wrote 'And I Love Her' and 'Here, There And Everywhere' especially for her. Jane Asher—surely one the great 'muses' of our time, and in that perhaps only rivalled by Pattie Boyd-Harrison and Yoko Ono.

Jane Asher went on to pursue an illustrious acting career—appearing in countless films, television plays, and theatrical productions. She married the supremely gifted, gimlet-eyed British political cartoonist and illustrator Gerald Scarfe in

1981—after they'd lived together for almost ten years. They have three children. Jane Asher is still in great demand as an actress. She's written novels, numerous lifestyle books, and, to top it all, developed a best-selling range of 'Jane Asher' cake mixes.

A true 'Lady Jane'... by any and every measure.

| Side Bar | The Asher family and The Beatles | Margaret Asher, Jane's mother, was a professor of the oboe at the Guildhall School of Music and Drama. George Martin, The Beatles' famed record producer, studied piano and oboe at the school between 1947 and 1950 and was one of her pupils. | Margaret Asher later gave private lessons in a music room in the basement of the family's Wimpole Street house —John and Paul wrote a number of songs down there—the two of them playing the same piano— including 'I Want To Hold Your Hand'. Paul eventually managed to get a small upright piano of his own into his attic room and wrote, or rather dreamed, 'Yesterday', up there.

Peter Asher—Jane's brother—has remained a lifelong friend. He's the 'Peter' of the 1960s pop duo 'Peter and Gordon', who recorded a number of Beatles' songs, all of them hits: 'A World Without Love', 'Nobody I Know', 'I Don't Want To See You Again', 'Woman', and 'If I Fell'. Peter Asher subsequently became head of A&R for Apple Records.

And lastly, it's long been mooted that, one day, while Spring-cleaning the house she and Paul shared together on Cavendish Avenue, Jane inadvertently threw away a notebook containing the handwritten lyrics to a number of early Lennon-McCartney songs. *Oh, oh, darling.*

PATTIE BOYD | *"The face of the '60s"* | Model | Photographer | Author | One-time film extra | George Harrison's first wife | Eric Clapton's first wife | Patricia Anne Boyd | 1944 - | Born Taunton, Somerset, England | 1962. Convent school educated Pattie moved to London and worked as a 'shampoo girl' at Elizabeth Arden's salon. A client who worked for a fashion magazine told her she should be a model. Photographers loved her 'look' and she was soon snapped up by the great David Bailey and Terence Donovan. Pattie modelled in London, New York, and Paris and appeared on the cover of UK and Italian *Vogue* magazine. In 1963, she appeared in a TV commercial for Smith's crisps (US - potato chips) shot by film director Dick Lester; who later cast her for a walk-on part as 'blonde schoolgirl on train' in 1964's *A Hard Day's Night*. And during the filming she met; yes, you've guessed it; George Harrison. And George, being no mug, asked her for a date. Pattie declined as she was already seeing someone. Several days later George asked her out again and this time she said 'yes'. Brian Epstein chaperoned them on their first date.

Later that year Pattie moved into *'Kinfauns'*; a house, in Esher, Surrey, George had purchased in 1964. The couple got engaged on Christmas Day 1965 and married on 21 January 1966 in a ceremony at a register office in Epsom. Paul McCartney was best man. The couple honeymooned in Barbados.

1966. George and Pattie flew to Bombay in September and stayed for six weeks so George could take lessons from sitar master Ravi Shankar. It was the start of the couple's interest in Eastern philosophy. In 1967, in the true LSD-inspired spirit of the times, the couple had the outside of *'Kinfauns'* painted in psychedelic patterns, along with several of The Beatles' musical instruments and George Harrison's Mini and John Lennon's Rolls Royce.

25 June. Pattie attended the *'Our World'* broadcast when The Beatles played 'All You Need Is Love'. She then attended a lecture on Transcendental Meditation at Caxton Hall, London—subsequently joined the Spiritual Regeneration Movement. Inspired by her experience she encouraged all four Beatles to attend a lecture to be given by the Indian mystic Maharishi Mahesh Yogi, at the Hilton Hotel, in London, on 24 August. This resulted in everyone, as well as Mick Jagger and Marianne Faithful, all piling into a first class railway compartment the following day to attend the Maharishi's 10-day seminar in Bangor, North Wales. In twin strange twists of fate Cynthia Lennon was barred from the train by an over zealous policeman. Neil Aspinall later drove her to Bangor. And it was that very same weekend that Brian Epstein, The Beatles' manager, who was due to join The Beatles in Bangor on the Monday to meet the Maharishi, died

from an accidental overdose at his London home. The Beatles and all the women in their lives understandably utterly devastated, but all took some measure of comfort from the practices of TM that Pattie had introduced them to. February 1968. Pattie accompanied George and the other Beatles when they flew out to the Maharishi's ashram in Rishikesh, India.

March 1970. The couple moved to Friar Park—a Victorian neo-Gothic mansion—near Henley-on-Thames. But in 1973, Pattie and George's marriage began to fail—both had affairs with other people. | 1974. The couple separated. Pattie flew to Los Angeles to stay with her younger sister Jenny; married at the time to Mick Fleetwood. Eric Clapton was in Miami recording *461 Ocean Boulevard*, his post-heroin addiction, comeback album. Even being on opposite coasts the attraction proved irresistible. He called her on the telephone: *"Come join me on tour... see what it's like."* She did. It was *"exhilarating, sexy, and great fun."* Eric *"the perfect playmate."* And they began living together. | Pattie's divorce from George Harrison was finalised 9 June 1977. | 2007 Pattie Boyd published her autobiography: *Wonderful Today* in the UK *Wonderful Tonight: George Harrison, Eric Clapton, and Me* in the US. | After her divorce from Eric Clapton she set up as a professional photographer with a studio in Fulham, London. *'Through the Eye of a Muse'*, an exhibition of her photographs of her times with George Harrison and Eric Clapton has been seen in major cities throughout the world.

| **Side Bar** | **Pattie Boyd** | **Musicians' Muse** | Pattie Boyd inspired George Harrison, her "soulmate", to write a number of songs: 'For You Blue', 'It's All Too Much', and 'Something'—the song Frank Sinatra hailed as being the best Beatles' song he'd heard and the greatest love song ever. George wrote 'So Sad' the same year he and Pattie separated. George Harrison and Eric Clapton became close friends in the late 1960s and began writing and recording music together. Eric was a regular visitor to Friar Park Clapton—and fell deeply in love with Pattie. His 1970 album— *Layla and Other Assorted Love Songs*—recorded as being by 'Derek and the Dominos'—was written to proclaim his love for her—the hit song 'Layla' a cry of unrequited love.

Pattie rebuffed each and every one of his many advances. The reason given for Clapton's descent into heroin addiction and a self-imposed exile that lasted for three years.

Her divorce to George Harrison having been finalized 9 June 1977—Pattie married Eric Clapton in Tucson, Arizona 27 March 1979. He wrote 'Wonderful Tonight' and 'Bell Bottom Blues' about their time together. | Over time the marriage became a struggle; marred by Clapton's continued alcoholism and infidelities and her own drinking problem. Pattie left Eric Clapton in April 1987. And he wrote 'She's Waiting' to mark their separation. The couple officially divorced in 1988. A year later he wrote 'Old Love'... *"about love getting old."*

A HARD DAY'S NIGHT - THE FILM

NOEL RODGERS | **United Artists Records Representative for the UK** | British born | Based in London | As happened with Sid Colman, at EMI music publishers Ardmore and Beechwood, yet another largely unsung 'hinge' of Beatles' history.

Noel Rodgers witnessed the rising tide of *'Beatlemania'* in Britain; how could he not; but what made him unique at the time was he was utterly convinced 'the sound wave' would ultimately hit the USA with hurricane force. And was dumbfounded by Capitol Records—EMI's American subsidiary label—continued refusal to release The Beatles' records in the US.

He delved deeper into the issue and discovered that EMI had neglected to secure any provision regarding film soundtracks in their contract with The Beatles. It provided the perfect opening for United Artists and he approached 'Bud' Ornstein, 'Head of Production' for United Artists European film division, also based in London, with the idea that UA should offer The Beatles a three-picture deal in order to obtain the rights to three, potentially, extremely lucrative, soundtrack albums. Which later had the requisite effect on Capitol Records, I'm sure, when Brian Epstein flew to the US in November 1963 to inform them that the UA film and soundtrack deal had already been "green lit."

'BUD' ORNSTEIN | Film Producer | George 'Bud' Ornstein | 1918 - 1978 | Born America | Based in London | 'Head of Production' for United Artists European film division that'd opened in 1961 with the brief to produce half a dozen low-budget films a year. 'Bud' Ornstein already had an impressive track record; he'd financed *Dr. No* (1962) and *Tom Jones* (1963); both films 'British made' that'd been box office successes in the US.

And so when Noel Rodgers of United Artists Records approached him in late summer 1963—he'd also witnessed '*Beatlemania*' first hand and immediately saw the possibilities of making a quick low budget rock 'n' roll exploitation movie or three with The Beatles—and of course the potential windfall from the films' soundtracks.

'Bud' Ornstein approached Brian Epstein, in September, and negotiated a three-picture deal. And in October film production got under way. He turned to fellow-American Walter Shenson; an independent film producer also based in London he'd worked with previously and tasked him with producing a Beatles' film; director, script, and title yet to be determined; with enough new songs to make up a soundtrack album. With the single proviso the film had to be ready for release by July 1964. Ornstein then had United Artists draft a very modest production budget for the 'music exploitation' film; capped at £200,000.

The accepted film industry model for such a film was that it should recoup its production and distribution costs while also generating as large a profit as possible from teenage fans before the featured pop star(s) faded away into obscurity. Only, The Beatles never did fade away. And *A Hard Day's Night* entered into the annals of film history as one of the only films ever to recoup its total production costs *before* its release. Still able to draw crowds into movie theatres 50 years *after* its release.

After the massive success of The Beatles' first film, Ornstein left United Artists in to go into partnership with Brian Epstein in a new company called Pickfair Films to produce even more Beatles' films, but unfortunately nothing ever came of it.

30 August 1968, Beatles' road manager, close friend, and confidante, Neil Aspinall, married Ornstein's daughter, Suzy.

WALTER SHENSON | **Film Producer** | 1919 - 2000 | American born. San Francisco. | Best known for producing The Beatles' films: *A Hard Day's Night* (1964) and *Help!* (1965) | Attended Stanford University. | During World War II served for two years in the United States Army. Started as a publicist for Paramount Pictures; then Columbia Pictures. Worked on *From Here to Eternity* (1953) and *The Caine Mutiny* (1954) before turning to producing. | 1955. Moved to London. Spent two years as head of publicity on Columbia's European film productions. Then set up as an independent film producer.

He produced a couple of low budget UK films; the Peter Sellers' comedy hit *The Mouse That Roared* (1959) and its sequel; without Sellers, but directed by Dick Lester; *The Mouse on the Moon*. In October 1963, he was approached by 'Bud' Ornstein—'Head of Production' for United Artists European film division—who'd financed *The Mouse on the Moon*—and tasked to produce a 'quick, down, and dirty' musical comedy starring the rising British pop group The Beatles before they faded back into obscurity. United Artists having just secured the film's soundtrack rights planned to recoup the film's very modest production cost; capped at £200,000, approximately $500,000; and make a tidy profit by promoting a UA soundtrack album of new Beatles' songs. Director, script, and title yet to be determined; the film set for July 1964 UK release.

Walter Shenson, to his eternal credit, tapped Dick Lester to direct. Lester then brought in noted Liverpool playwright, Alun Owen, who'd worked with him on an earlier comedy TV series. The team went to see The Beatles. Everyone thankfully hit it off. And the impossible happened. The team Walter Shenson brought together produced, wrote, shot, and completed post-production work on what turned out to be a brilliant, breathtaking, breakthrough film; shot in less than seven weeks; produced from start to finish in sixteen weeks.

The film premiered in London in July 1964, and was released the following month in the US, and was a huge hit on both sides of the Atlantic—with a box office take of about $8 million in the first week alone.

A Hard Day's Night is one of the only films ever to recoup its total production costs before its release due to advance album sales and 'special' pre-release screenings. (Percentage-wise, it's still one of the most profitable films of all time.) So when United Artists; eyes resolutely fixed on the prize of a second Beatles' soundtrack album; immediately asked Shenson to produce a second Beatles' feature film, he negotiated for the film rights to both movies to revert to him 15 years after their initial release dates. And they agreed to it; an extraordinary piece of negotiation on Shenson's part; but then again, no British 'pop music' film had ever made the slightest dent in the US market before. And nobody thought The Beatles would last for more than another year or two, at best. Or had any idea that any 'product' to do with The Beatles would be of any further interest to anyone, ever. UA still had no inkling of the worldwide phenomenon The Beatles' and their first film would become. And, remember, in September 1963, when the very idea of 'a Beatles film' was first mooted, The Beatles' life-and-career changing appearance on the nationally televised *Ed Sullivan Show,* in the US in February 1964, wasn't even a distant thought in anyone's mind; even the always questing mind of The Beatles' manager, Brian Epstein.

| Side Bar | **Walter Shenson and Ringo Starr's wondrous malapropism...** *"It's been a hard day's night"* | United Artists began pressuring the film's producers to come up with a film title. Some of the not-so-memorable working titles: '*The Beatles*' and '*Beatlemania*'. With everyone almost at their wit's end John Lennon recalled one of latest word-mangling off-the-cuff 'Ringo-isms' uttered by Ringo after an exhausting all day and night studio recording session, and he mentioned it Walter Shenson, or Dick Lester, or the other Beatles; or whoever, as memories differ. The important thing is the producer thought Ringo's soon to be immortalized phrase—about it having been *"a hard day's night"*—would make a terrific film title. And it was he who duly called senior executives at United Artists back in the US and told them of the proposed title; and was met with stony silence. Undeterred, he suggested the executives should ask the secretaries and any other young employees at UA, in Hollywood;

who just might already be Beatles' fans; just what they thought of it. They just loved the idea and the title was accepted.

| Side Bar | United Artists' soundtrack album of *A Hard Day's Night* | After all their plotting, planning, and producing to get their hands on a soundtrack album of original Beatles' songs, United Artists Records released their 'original soundtrack' version of *A Hard Day's Night* in the US on 26 June 1964. It contained all seven songs from the film and 'I'll Cry Instead'; which had been written for the film but cut at the last minute; plus four orchestral instrumentals of Beatles' tunes arranged and conducted by George Martin. In comparison, the '*A Hard Day's Night*' LP released in the UK had all eight 'soundtrack' songs; plus five more Lennon-McCartney originals.

All of the new Beatles' songs on the UA soundtrack album were also released as 45rpm singles by Capitol and later on the Capitol album '*Something New*'. Nevertheless, the UA strategy did work. The UA Beatles' soundtrack LP went straight to No.1 on the US *Billboard* chart, and stayed there for 14 weeks; the longest run at 'the top' for any album in 1964. Interestingly, when some years later UA decided to exit the record business, altogether, they sold their entire music catalogue to Capitol; who promptly reissued "the missing album" on the Capitol label.

And in added irony, The Beatles' record producer George Martin got an Academy Award nomination for 'Best Score' (Adaptation) for *A Hard Day's Night*, but The Beatles didn't get nominated for any of any of their seven wonderful original songs; not a one. The Academy of Motion Arts and Pictures—in all its wisdom—awarded 1964 'Best Original Song' to 'Chim, Chim Cher-ee' from the film *Mary Poppins*.

RICHARD 'DICK' LESTER | **Film Director** | Richard Lester Liebman| 1932 - | American. Born Philadelphia, Pennsylvania | Child prodigy—started University of Pennsylvania age 15—to study 'Psychology'. Gifted pianist. | 1951. Graduated—then started in local CBS television station as floor manager—made assistant director—then director in first year. | 1953. Directed half-hour 'western' TV series that aired 'live' on CBS. | 1953. Travelled to London; just as the independent commercial television network was being launched; and began work as a television director on episodes of *Mark Saber*, a half-hour detective series. He also began directing musical comedy shows, one of which, *The Dick Lester Show*, caught the eye of Peter Sellers. Lester then began collaborating with Sellers and Spike Milligan to translate BBC Radio's long running hit comedy series, *The Goon Show*, for television. The first show: *The Idiot Weekly, Price 2d*, was a hit. As were two follow-up shows: *A Show Called Fred* and *Son of Fred*.

In 1959, this led directly to Lester and Sellers co-directing an 11-minute comedy short, *The Running Jumping Standing Still Film*; starring Sellers and Milligan; that was nominated for an Oscar. Perhaps, even more importantly to later events, The Beatles, particularly John Lennon, absolutely loved the film.

Lester also began to be hired as TV commercials' director. In 1962, he directed his first feature, *It's Trad, Dad!—Ring-A-Ding Rhythm* in the US—a 'pop music' film with a boatload of British and American pop stars, including Helen Shapiro, Craig Douglas, Acker Bilk, Del Shannon, Gene Vincent, and Chubby Checker. And in 1963, directed the comedy *Mouse on the Moon* for independent producer Walter Shenson; a fellow American living in London; that did reasonably well at the UK box office.

When in 1964 Bud Ornstein, Head of United Artists UK, asked Shenson to produce an as yet untitled Beatles' film, he tapped Dick Lester to direct. United Artists initially viewed it as just another low-budget rock 'n' roll exploitation movie before The Beatles faded away into obscurity. Thankfully the Fates decreed otherwise. Shenson and Lester met with Brian Epstein and The Beatles and the fact that Dick Lester had worked closely with both Milligan and Sellers gave the director instant credibility with the John, Paul, and George, fervid 'Goons' fans all.

Playwright Alun Owen, who'd worked on *The Dick Lester Show*, and had written a hit play, *No Trams To Lime Street*, was hired as the screenwriter. The Beatles were absolutely insistent that it be nothing like the standard "*bloody awful Elvis rock 'n' roll flick.*" Owen went on tour with the group for a few days; was both startled and inspired by what he saw; and he proposed *"an exaggerated day in the life of The Beatles"* as the film scenario.

A Hard Day's Night brought a fresh take on the rebellious spirit of rock 'n' roll to the movies; what's more it was great fun to watch and to listen to. It was shot in black and white; the film company didn't want to pay for film colour stock; but that's now widely seen as a blessing in disguise. The film is notable for the *cinéma vérité*, documentary-style, fly-on-the-wall, hand held camera-work and quick-cut editing techniques—inspired by French 'New Wave' filmmakers. Film critic Andrew Sarris, in the *Village Voice*, memorably described *A Hard Day's Night* as being "the *'Citizen Kane'* of jukebox musicals."

In 1965, Lester directed the second Beatles' film *Help!* That same year he also directed the "Swinging Sixties" cult film *The Knack ...and How to Get It*—with Michael Crawford—that won the Palme d'Or at the Cannes Film Festival. | 1966. *A Funny Thing Happened on the Way to the Forum*. | 1967. Directed the anti-war movie *How I Won the War* with Michael Crawford and John Lennon. | 1968. *Petulia* with Julie Christie. | 1973. *The Three Musketeers* and its 1975 sequel *The Four Musketeers* | 1974. *Juggernaut* | 1976. *Robin and Marian*, with Sean Connery and Audrey Hepburn | 1979. *Cuba*, with Connery again. | 1983-84. *Superman II (part) & III* | 1989. *The Return of the Musketeers*.

Lester then 'unofficially retired' from 'directing', but returned in 1991 to direct the Paul McCartney concert tour chronicle: *Get Back*. | NB: Andrew Yule's biography of Dick Lester, *'The Man Who Framed the Beatles'*, is a fun and enjoyable read; well worth seeking out.

| **Side Bar** | **Dick Lester and Pattie Boyd** | In 1963, a year before he directed *A Hard Day's Night*, Dick Lester shot a series of TV commercials for Smith's crisps (US - potato chips) and cast the model Pattie Boyd. | They met again—by chance—at an audition for the film and he cast her for a walk-on part as *'Jane – blonde schoolgirl on train'*—where as fate would have it she met and fell in love with George Harrison during the filming of the movie.

ALUN OWEN | Actor | Screenwriter | Playwright | 1925 - 1994 | Alun Davies Owen | One of the 'new wave' of British playwrights to emerge in the late 1950s—early 1960s—predominantly active in television—perhaps best remembered for writing the screenplay for The Beatles' debut feature film *A Hard Day's Night*. | 1925 Born Anglesey, Wales, to Welsh parents. His family moved to Liverpool when he was eight. | Served in the Merchant Navy. Later did a couple of years' stint as a 'Bevin Boy'—a 'wartime service' coal miner. | He joined a northern repertory company as an assistant stage manager. Moved into acting. Joined Birmingham Repertory Company for the 1943-44 Season. After which he progressed to Sir Donald Wolfit's Shakespeare Company, the London Old Vic Company, and the English Stage Company at London's Royal Court.

Mid-1950s Owen had small roles in films: *I'm All Right Jack* and *The Servant* | 1955-56. He enjoyed a spell as a comedian; appearing in *The Dick Lester Show*; *Idiot Weekly, Price 2d*; *Son of Fred*; all directed by "the young American prodigy" Dick Lester. 1956-58. Played 'stooge' to celebrated British comedian Arthur "Ay-Thang-Yew"Askey, in the TV series *Before Your Very Eyes*.

Mid-to-late-1950s. He began turning increasingly to 'playwriting'. Submitted his first scripts to BBC Radio. | 1958. His first full-length play for radio, *Progress to the Park*, was such a hit it was produced for the stage by the Theatre Royal, Stratford East, and later transferred to London's West End. | 1959. His second play, *The Rough and Ready Lot*, was staged at the Lyric Opera House, Hammersmith.

In 1959, he followed up with his first work written directly for television and ABC's *Armchair Theatre*; the highly successful, Liverpool-based 'slice-of-Northern-life' drama '*No Trams to Lime Street*' starring Billie Whitelaw. | 1960. Wrote the screenplay, from an existing storyline, for Joseph Losey's gritty crime film, *The Criminal*, starring Stanley Baker. | 1961. Won *UK Guild of Television Producers and Directors'* Writer's Award and UK Scriptwriter's Award.

1963-64. American film producer Walter Shenson assigned to produce the first Beatles film and tapped Dick Lester to direct. Lester, in turn, hired Owen to write the screenplay that went on to be the basis for *A Hard Day's Night*. | 1964. Owen also wrote the 'book' for Lionel Bart's hit musical *Maggie May*—a story of Liverpool's dockland—that opened at London's Adelphi Theatre that same year. | Alun Owen continued writing for British television throughout the 1960s, 70s, and 80s. During which time his original trio of 'Liverpool' plays were recast and reproduced for television. | He wrote plays for BBC2's *Theatre 625* and ITV's *Saturday Night Theatre* | 1990. His last work was an adaptation for ITV of R. F. Delderfield's novel *Come Home, Charlie, and Face Them*.

| Side Bar | Alun Owen and The Beatles | 1963-64 | Johnny Speight—acclaimed British TV hit writer was director Dick Lester's first choice as screenwriter The Beatles' first film. 'Thankfully'—*Ed. comment*—Speight was unavailable and Lester turned to Alun Owen who he'd previously worked with on a number of BBC TV comedy shows. | For their part The Beatles were very keen on having Owen write the screenplay as they'd all been most impressed with his Liverpool-based TV play—*No Trams to Lime Street*. | Walter Shenson—the film's producer—suggested the film be about: **"An exaggerated day in the life of The Beatles"** and Alun Owen flew to Dublin with The Beatles, on their Autumn Tour, to observe them up close and to "get a feel" for their individual characters and manners of speech. After three days and nights of 'shadowing' the group Owen returned to London with the 'vision' of the as yet untitled film's screenplay planted firmly in his head. | *"The Beatles are prisoners of their success. They go from airport to hotel to theatre or stadium or concert hall—back to the hotel—then straight back to the airport. It's the same in every city they go to. They travel in a little cocoon—of Liverpool. There's the manager, the road manager, the publicity man, the car driver, the guy that sets up and breaks down their equipment. That's all they ever see. Because they'd be mobbed—all but torn to pieces—the moment they got out of the car or hotel room or off the concert stage."*

His script for *A Hard Day's Night* earned him a nomination for the 1965 Academy Award for 'Best Original Screenplay'.

ROBERT FREEMAN | Photographer | Designer | 1936 - | Renowned for the cover photos he took for five of The Beatles' albums: *With The Beatles, A Hard Day's Night, Beatles For Sale, Help!* and *Rubber Soul.* | His design work for the end credit sequence of *A Hard Day's Night*, reprised on posters for the film and front cover of the soundtrack LP, was truly inspired; even the sound effects of an SLR camera's motorized shutter clicking away, capturing one Beatle's headshot after the other, was brilliantly effective. He also designed all the graphics for *Help!*

Robert Freeman first came to prominence as a photojournalist for *The Sunday Times* newspaper. | His portfolio of black-and-white photographs of John Coltrane, Cannonball Adderley, Dizzy Gillespie and other noted jazz musicians—taken at a music festival in London—much impressed Brian Epstein and The Beatles and led to his first commission to photograph the group.

22 August 1963. The photo session for *With The Beatles* took place in the Palace Court Hotel, Bournemouth. As Robert Freeman later recalled: *"They all had to fit into the square format of an LP cover. So rather than have them all in a line, I put Ringo in the bottom right-hand corner... since he was the last to join the group... he was also the shortest."* The Beatles in severe close-up; looking moodily straight to camera, not smiling; shot in black and white and lit only by natural light; was unlike anything ever seen on an LP cover before. It was thoroughly new and startling. The extraordinary impact of the *With The Beatles* cover photo led to a commission to shoot the first-ever Pirelli Calendar in its entirety; soon to become one of the most prestigious and sought-after photo assignments in all of commercial photography.

Robert Freeman published a giant-size coffee table book of his many photographs of the group: *The Beatles: A Private View.* The book's cover, the starkly iconic black and white photo from *With The Beatles*, printed from edge to edge; sans title, sans words; the eyes of the savage young Beatles staring at you forever into eternity; as had been his original idea for the LP cover. Only, EMI, in all its wisdom, had vetoed the idea on the grounds that The Beatles weren't yet famous enough to carry a cover with no name or title. Such are the tribulations of an artistic life.

VICTOR SPINETTI | Actor| Author | Playwright | Raconteur | Poet | Vittorio Giorgio Andre Spinetti | Born Cwm, Ebbw Vale, Wales | 1929-2012 | Attended the Royal Welsh College of Music and Drama in Cardiff. | Immediately took up a stage career. | Joined Joan Littlewood's Theatre Workshop based in the East End of London. Among the theatre company's famed productions: *Fings Ain't Wot They Used T'Be* (1959) and *Oh! What a Lovely War* (1963). When the production transferred to Broadway, Victor Spinetti won a Tony Award for his performance. He appeared in countless theatre productions in the UK and later in his career was a member of the Royal Shakespeare Company at Stratford-upon-Avon. He appeared in over 30 films, including films as varied as *Sparrows Can't Sing* (1963); *Becket* (1964); Franco Zeffirelli's *The Taming of the Shrew* (1967); *Under Milk Wood* (1972); *The Return of the Pink Panther* (1975); *Voyage of the Damned* (1976); *Hardcore* (1977); *Under the Cherry Moon* (1986); *The Krays* (1990); and significantly for the purposes of this book, The Beatles' very first film, *A Hard Day's Night* (1964). In 2008, his one-man show *A Very Private Diary* was a hit in London's West End and later toured the UK.

Victor Spinetti died of prostate cancer, in 2012, aged 82.

| **Side Bar** | **Victor Spinetti and The Beatles** | Spinetti had the distinction of appearing in *A Hard Day's Night*, *Help!*, *Magical Mystery Tour*. The best explanation for their long-running collaboration and continued friendship given by George Harrison who said to Spinetti when they first met on the set of *A Hard Day's Night*: "You've got to be in all our films... if you're not in them me Mum won't come and see them... because she fancies you." Years later George also told him: "You've got a lovely karma, Vic."

Spinetti co-wrote *In His Own Write*, with John Lennon, the play adapted from John's book of poetry and verse. He also directed. The play premiered at London's National Theatre in June 1968 to mostly glowing reviews. Spinetti described the play as being **"about the growing up of any of us...the things that helped us to be more aware."** Paul McCartney later described Victor Spinetti as **"the man who makes clouds disappear."**

PART ONE - PEOPLE. PLACES. VENUES.

9 - London Places

LONDON TOWN... Brought Its Own Special Something To The Act We've Known For All These Years

Palais Ballroom - Aldershot | 2i's Coffee Bar - Soho | Decca Recording Studios - West Hampstead | The Decca Record Company Ltd - Albert Embankment | HMV Record Store - Oxford Street | EMI House - Manchester Square | EMI Recording Studios - Abbey Road | Jennings Music Shop - Charing Cross Road | Dick James Music - Denmark Street | NEMS Enterprises - Argyll Street | London Palladium - Argyll Street | Prince Of Wales - Haymarket | London Pavilion Cinema - Piccadilly Circus | Empire Pool - Wembley | Scala Theatre - Scala Street | The Astoria - Finsbury Park | BBC Radio & Television Studios: Paris Studios - Lower Regent Street | Rex House - Lower Regent Street | Piccadilly Studios - Piccadilly | Playhouse Theatre - London W1 | The Aeolian Hall - New Bond Street | Maida Vale Studios - Maida Vale | Lime Grove Television Studios - Shepherd's Bush | BBC TV Theatre - Shepherd's Bush Green | BBC Broadcasting House - Langham Place W1 | Associated-Rediffusion TV Studios - Kingsway & Wembley | Euston Railway Station | Paddington Railway Station | Marleylebone Railway Station

The Beatles, and their manager Brian Epstein, all moved down to London after the success of the group's early single record releases: 'Love Me Do' and their first LP *Please Please Me*. However, this 'London Places' section begins, almost a year earlier, with a remarkable near miss, in Aldershot, long famous as a military town, some 30 miles south-west of London, at The Palais Ballroom, the site of the infamous *"The Battle of The Bands"* that never was.

London also provided the scene of another near miss; certainly for Decca Records, at Decca's Recording Studios in West Hampstead. Euston Station makes an appearance because of the countless times Brian Epstein travelled down to London by train from Liverpool's Lime Street Station to try and convince the UK's 'Big Four' recording companies: DECCA | EMI | PYE | PHILIPS; all based in London; even to listen to The Beatles.

The sequence then moves to a veritable hit at The HMV Record Store, on London's famed Oxford St. W1, where Brian Epstein had the tapes of The Beatles' failed Decca audition transferred onto 78rpm acetate demo discs. A key event that directly led to Brian Epstein meeting Sid Colman, General Manager of Ardmore & Beechwood, one of EMI's many music publishing companies. The man who then turned round and introduced him to George Martin, Head of Parlophone Records, one of EMI's recording labels. The result of which led to George Martin working as The Beatles' record producer at EMI's Abbey Road Studios in North London. From there—The Beatles would go on to appear at The London Palladium and The Prince of Wales Theatre, and the nationally televised events that marked the very start of the phenomenon that became known in Britain, then America, and then all around the world, as *'Beatlemania'*.

PALAIS BALLROOM | **Queens Road** | **Aldershot** | Saturday 9 December 1961 | Sam Leach—rock 'n' roll mad Liverpool promoter and would-be Beatles' manager—had the marvellously inventive idea of getting The Beatles to play in front of some of London's top impresarios, so they could see for themselves the scenes of frenzy the band were generating, nightly, on Merseyside. After yet another massive turn out for the group at the Tower Ballroom, New Brighton, on the Friday night, he hired a specially equipped van—seats for everyone—and a driver. | The next day The Beatles were driven all the way down to London for their debut. Almost. The venue—the Palais Ballroom—turned out to be in a small town; better known for the huge regular army camp situated on its outskirts. A town situated more than thirty miles from the show business capital—the West End of London. | Worse, proposed advertising for the event hadn't appeared in the local newspaper, as Sam's cheque had yet to clear. So no one even knew The Beatles were coming! Fly posters were hurriedly handed out or pinned up around the town:

BIG BEAT SESSIONS AT The Palais Ballroom ALDERSHOT
Every Saturday commencing this Saturday 9th December
Presenting a "Battle of the Bands" LIVERPOOL v LONDON
Liverpool's No. "1" Band   Direct from Their German Tour
THE BEATLES VERSUS IVOR JAY & the JAYWALKERS
Plus Two Other Star Groups.
7-30 p.m. to 11.30 p.m. Bar. Buffet. Admission 5/-
Everyone Welcome—Tell Your Friends

Even worse, Sam had failed to mention that the big London impresario—Tito Burns—that everybody hoped to meet had already declined the invitation to come be impressed by The Beatles. And so, after scurrying around the town—trying to drum up interest—and even giving away free tickets to the show—The Beatles managed to attract no more than 18 people. Even so, they put on a show as wildly rockin' as any they'd ever performed at the Cavern or the Tower. | Photos of the night's event taken by Dick Richards—the *Mersey Beat* photographer—can be viewed online courtesy of *The Savage Young Beatles* website. 'PART FIVE: Reading The Beatles' has the link. | Personally, I've always wondered what happened to Ivor Jay & the Jaywalkers—and the two other star groups—who were advertised as playing, but never showed up. Their presence alone would have almost doubled the size of the audience that night.

2i's COFFEE BAR | 59 Old Compton Street, Soho W1 | The birthplace of British rock 'n' roll. The 2i's attracted hopefuls by the busload. Tommy Steele was discovered here. | Hamburg nightclub owner, Bruno Koschmider, came here on a mission to find genuine Britisher rock 'n' rollers to play his Kaiserkeller Club, back in St. Pauli, and signed The Jets—with Tony Sheridan. When The Jets got lured away, he returned to the 2i's in search of more talent and quite by chance met up again with Liverpool promoter Allan Williams—down in London for the day—to try and get work for Derry and The Seniors. The group got up and performed. Koschmider was impressed and immediately agreed a deal with Williams. | Derry and The Seniors thus became the first Liverpool 'beat' group to do a season in Hamburg; thereby paving the way for Allan Williams to later send out The Beatles.

DECCA RECORDING STUDIOS | **165 Broadhurst Gardens, West Hampstead** | January 1, 1962 | A bitterly cold and snowy New Year's Day. After a bone-rattling ten-hour road journey from Liverpool—and having got lost on the way—The Silver Beatles began their Decca audition late. They run through some 15 songs in little over an hour. Mike Smith—Associate A&R man—recorded 10 songs direct to tape. Afterwards he had one or two songs cut onto 45rpm 10" discs for Dick Rowe, Decca's senior A&R man, and others, to hear and to pass judgment on.

THE DECCA RECORD COMPANY LIMITED | **Decca House** | **9 Albert Embankment SE1** | At the end of January 1962, Decca Records officially turned down The Beatles; their manager informed of the decision by post. Decca Records sign London group, Brian Poole and The Tremeloes, instead. Brian Epstein refuses to take 'No' for an answer and travels down to London to see Dick Rowe, in person, at Decca's Thames-side headquarters. Over lunch, in Decca's executive dining suite, Rowe reputedly tells him: *"Pop groups are on the way out... guitar groups, especially. Your Beatles just won't sell, Mr. Epstein."*

HMV RECORD STORE | **363-367 Oxford Street W1** | After yet another frustrating trip to London, with no one at all interested in hearing The Beatles' Decca sessions tapes, Brian Epstein went into HMV Record Store—*The World's Largest Record Store*—on Oxford Street and had them transferred onto 78rpm acetate demo discs in the store's 'Personal Recording Department' studio. Jim Foy, the HMV store's disc-cutter, liked what he heard and cut two double-sided 10" discs. | 'Hello Little Girl' | 'Til There Was You' | 'Love of The Loved' | 'Like Dreamers Do'. It's these two discs that initially open up the door to EMI. On learning that three of the songs were original compositions, Foy suggested that Epstein should meet Sid Colman, general manager of Ardmore & Beechwood, one of EMI's music publishing companies, with offices on the top floor of the building. Sid Colman also liked what he heard and asked if he could publish the three original Lennon-McCartney songs.

Brian Epstein replied that he wasn't just looking for a publishing contract, but if Colman could perchance help secure a recording contract for the group, Ardmore & Beechwood could publish the songs. Sid Colman immediately picked up the phone to EMI's head-office, in nearby Soho, and arranged for Brian Epstein to meet with a business colleague, George Martin, Head of Artistes & Repertoire at Parlophone Records; owned by EMI.

EMI HOUSE | 20 Manchester Square W1 | Made famous by the shot of The Beatles looking down over the stairwell inside EMI's London headquarters, taken for the cover of *Please Please Me* LP, by legendary theatre photographer Angus McBean.

EMI RECORDING STUDIOS | 3 Abbey Road NW8 | Famed the world over because of The Beatles' *Abbey Road* album. Brian Epstein was most unimpressed when he first set eyes on the place. He thought it more resembled a solicitor's law office. It's where he first got to meet record producer George Martin, and where on 6 June, 1963, The Beatles were given an Artists' Test. They barely passed the audition, apparently, due as much for their 'Goonish' humour, as their musical abilities. Over the next seven years, The Beatles record all of their subsequent studio albums and singles at Abbey Road, invariably in Studio Two.

DICK JAMES MUSIC LTD. | Shaldon Mansions | Suite Two | Denmark Street W1 | The office of Dick James Music, on the corner of Denmark Street; London's 'Tin Pan Alley'. Brian Epstein, dissatisfied with what he saw as Ardmore & Beechwood's paltry efforts to help 'Love Me Do' climb the pop charts, looked for a different musical publisher for John Lennon and Paul McCartney's growing list of original songs. Dick James immediately impressed Brian Epstein by securing The Beatles a spot on the hugely popular Saturday evening television show *Thank*

Your Lucky Stars. Epstein then assigned Dick James, the publishing rights of 'Please Please Me' and 'Ask Me Why'. Dick James later set up Northern Songs as The Beatles' music publishing company; but then later sold the rights out from under them.

| Side Bar | Denmark Street | Britain's 'Tin Pan Alley'
Denmark Street was the heartbeat of the British music industry in its glory years. | The first music related business on the street was the music magazine *Melody Maker* founded 1926. | *The New Musical Express* was founded there in 1952. | By the end of the 1950's Denmark Street was known as Britain's 'Tin Pan Alley' and was home to almost all of the most successful British music publishers and songwriters, as well as various other music related businesses; musical instrument shops; and recording studios such as Regent Sound and Southern Music.

NEMS ENTERPRISES | Sutherland House | 5-6 Argyll St. W1
March 9 1964 | NEMS Enterprises—now with a staff of twenty-five people—moved into new premises in Argyll Street, London | It's no accident that the new NEMS office was situated right next door to the world famous London Palladium.

JENNINGS MUSIC SHOP | Charing Cross Road W1
Having passed their 'artist test' with George Martin, at EMI's Abbey Road Studio, by the skin of their teeth, it was clear to Brian Epstein that The Beatles were in desperate need of new amplifiers. It wasn't just that the motley collection of second-hand single speaker amplifiers and jerry-made 'coffin' bass amp, that'd worked night in and night out in the clubs of Liverpool and Hamburg, weren't suitable for recording purposes; being as horribly bashed about as they were; they didn't look at all good. Brian Epstein had noticed an advertisement in the musical trade-papers proclaiming that The Shadows *only* used VOX Amplifiers. And, so, rather than simply buying a new set of amplifiers, he contacted VOX to arrange a similar exclusive advertising deal for The Beatles. Jennings Music Shop, on Charing Cross Road, was VOX's main London showroom.

THE BEATLES IN LIVERPOOL, HAMBURG, LONDON

THE LONDON PALLADIUM | 8 Argyll Street W1
13 October 1963. The Beatles topped the bill on *Sunday Night at the London Palladium*, Britain's most prestigious and popular, nationally broadcast TV variety show. More than 13 million viewers watched the show. The wildly enthusiastic scenes of the 'hundreds' of Beatles' fans, in the theatre; and it the streets outside; before, during, and after the show. The following day, the event made headlines in most every London newspaper. *The Daily Mirror* christening the affair: *'Beatlemania'*.

Tellingly, the NEMS office of Brian Epstein, the Beatles' manager, was on the 5th floor of Sutherland House, at 5-6 Argyll Street, right next door to the London Palladium.

The Beatles played the Palladium three times: 13 October 1963 | 12 January 1964 | 23 July 1964

THE PRINCE OF WALES | Haymarket W1
4 November 1963 | The Beatles appeared at the 'Royal Command Performance' in the presence of Her Majesty Queen Elizabeth The Queen Mother and Her Royal Highness Princess Margaret. This was the occasion of John Lennon's famous remark, when he stepped forward to introduce the band's final number, 'Twist and Shout'. *"For our last number I'd like to ask your help. Would the people in the cheaper seats clap your hands and the rest of you, if you'll just rattle your jewellery."*

After the show was broadcast to the nation, the following Sunday evening, *'Beatlemania'* engulfed all of Great Britain.

THE LONDON PAVILION | Piccadilly Circus W1
The film *A Hard Day's Night* had its World Premier at this famed central London cinema. Giant photographic 'cut-outs' of The Beatles' faces adorned the entire front of the building.

Piccadilly Circus and Central London was all but brought to a complete standstill, as the Metropolitan Police battled to control huge, surging crowds of Beatles' fans before, during, and after the film's showing. Some hope. But other than girls fainting, here, there, and everywhere, no one was hurt. Other than for the fact that only a very select few got to see then in person.

EMPIRE POOL - WEMBLEY ARENA | Wembley | The Beatles appeared at the *New Musical Express' NME Poll Winners' Concert* at 'The Empire Pool and Sports Arena, Wembley' on four separate occasions | 21 April 1963 | 26 April 1964 | 11 April 1965 | 1 May 1966. The latter highly significant, because it turned out to be the group's very last concert appearance in the UK.

SCALA THEATRE | W1 | Interior and exterior shots of *A Hard Day's Night* were filmed here. Including the 'rehearsal' scenes for the later 'television show', as well as the wonderfully riotous end sequences showing the audience of young fans, all screaming and shouting and whaling and cheering and stamping and clapping and, generally, going absolutely bonkers over The Beatles. And who could ever blame them? I'd have done the same.

THE ASTORIA | Finsbury Park | East London | The venue for *The Beatles Christmas Shows*—for two years in a row

BBC PARIS STUDIOS | 12 Lower Regent Street | BBC Radio comedy programmes requiring a live audience were broadcast 'live' from the Paris Studios. It was also was used for recording pop artists and a live audience. | The Beatles recorded their own BBC radio show *Pop Go the Beatles* from here on numerous occasions. | Other stars that recorded at BBC Paris Studios include: David Bowie, Jeff Beck, Deep Purple, Fleetwood Mac, Genesis, Led Zeppelin, Pink Floyd, Rod Stewart, and Joni Mitchell.

REX HOUSE | Lower Regent Street W1 | November 1962 - July 1964 | Directly adjacent to the BBC Paris Studios. The Beatles record twelve radio programmes in the studio for later broadcast

BBC PICCADILLY STUDIOS | 201 Piccadilly W1 | 21 March 1963- 26 May 1965 | *Saturday Club*—the hugely popular weekly radio show, hosted by Brian Matthews, was recorded here. | 26 May1965. The date of The Beatles' fifty-second and final recording session for the BBC took place here.

BBC PLAYHOUSE THEATRE | London W1 | *Easy Beat*—BBC Radio pop music program recorded here—for later national broadcast on the 'Light Programme' | During 1963, The Beatles easily made four appearances on *Easy Beat*.

THE AEOLIAN HALL | New Bond Street | May 1963 | The Beatles recorded their first *Pop Go the Beatles* here.

BBC MAIDA VALE STUDIOS | Maida Vale | 17 June-2 July 1963 | The Beatles recorded their very own radio show *Pop Go the Beatles* from here. Always a 'must-listen-to' for all teenagers.

BBC LIME GROVE TELEVISION STUDIOS | Shepherds Bush W11 | 1 January 1964. The Beatles appeared on the very first broadcast of the BBC pop show *Top of The Pops*. As holders of that week's No.1 spot, 'I Want to Hold Your Hand', the group were the last artists to appear on the show; always the big finale. The Beatles appeared on the show several more times; always featured as *"the Toppermost of the Poppermost"*.

BBC TV THEATRE | Shepherd's Bush Green W11 | *Juke Box Jury* 7 December 1963 | Saw all four Beatles as 'Jurors' on *Juke Box Jury*. | Later—on different occasions—George Harrison and Ringo Starr appeared as 'Jurors'. As, too, did The Beatles' manager Brian Epstein, who actually appeared twice.

BBC BROADCASTING HOUSE | Portland Place & Langham Place W1 | Headquarters of the BBC. | The first radio broadcast from the building was made on 15 March 1932 | The first musical programme, by bandleader Henry Hall and the BBC Dance Orchestra, on 15 March 1932 | When first built, Broadcasting House included 22 studios and the BBC Radio Theatre—where music and speech programmes could be recorded in front of a studio audience. | Between March 1962 and June 1965, The Beatles were featured performers in no less than 52 different BBC radio programmes; recorded and/or broadcast from here, as well as everywhere else, the BBC had studios in London.

ASSOCIATED-REDIFFUSION | Television Studios | Kingsway WC2 & Wembley | 4 October 1963 - 20 March 1964 | The Beatles made a number of appearances on the highly rated, must-see, Friday evening, 'live' audience always dancing in the studio, pop music show, *Ready Steady Go!* (And, truly, the weekend really did "start here" for any self-respecting London Mod.)

And, in the beginning, like every other recording star, The Beatles always had to mime to their trending or existing 'hit' record. Later, when the Musician's Union decreed that any music that was broadcast also had to be played 'live', the show moved to larger TV studios in Wembley, west of London.

Any of the show's legion of fans, lucky enough to still be invited to attend the fully 'live' broadcast, dutifully trekked out all the way to Wembley, to dance their way into the weekend.

EUSTON RAILWAY STATION | Euston Road NW1
The famous towering Euston Arch had not long been dismantled and taken down, in 1963, when Brian Epstein began making his regular journeys from Lime Street Station, Liverpool, to Euston Station, just north of London's West End. I can only imagine the number of taxi journeys he made, over the endless weeks and months, trying to secure a recording contract for The Beatles from the Big Four: Philips, Decca. Pye, and EMI.

PADDINGTON RAILWAY STATION | Westbourne Terrace NW8 | The train featured in *A Hard Day's Night* leaves from here. The scenes where The Beatles' train arrives in London and they dash into the open doors of a line of London black cabs, and they push on through and into their waiting, big, black, ever so posh, Daimler limousine, was also filmed here.

MARLEYLEBONE RAILWAY STATION | Euston Road NW8
The madcap scenes of fans chasing The Beatles in the opening scenes of *A Hard Day's Night* were filmed here. Dick Lester also employing a hand-held camera, stealing shots as and when he could.

PART TWO—MUSIC INFLUENCES. THE MEDIA.

1 - American Rock 'n' Roll

"Awopbopaloobop Alopbamboom!"

Elvis Presley | Buddy Holly | Chuck Berry | Little Richard | Bill Haley | Eddie Cochran | Gene Vincent | Jerry Lee Lewis | Carl Perkins | The Everly Brothers | Roy Orbison | Ray Charles | 'Fats' Domino | Arthur Alexander | Bo Diddley | DJ Alan "Moondog" Freed

ROCK 'N' ROLL! The 'Big Bang' that ultimately gave rise to The Beatles. And just as it did for teenagers John Lennon, Paul McCartney, George Harrison, Ringo Starr, and countless other young people here, there, and everywhere, it all began with four world-shaking talents: Elvis Presley; Buddy Holly; Chuck Berry; and Little Richard.

The *'King'*—Elvis Presley—was of signal influence, in both voice and style, and no other recording artist impacted the early Beatles quite as much as the electrifying, young, rockabilly, rock 'n' roller from Tupelo, Mississippi.

Buddy Holly—from Lubbock, Texas—a sublimely gifted singer-songwriter—and his backing group—The Crickets—not only helped inspire the song-writing talents of Lennon & McCartney—but also the very name 'Beatles'.

As for writing brilliantly memorable songs—and delivering them with brilliantly original musicianship—few artists from either side of the Atlantic could come close to *'the preeminent poet of rock 'n' roll'* from St. Louis, Missouri—Chuck Berry.

And as for writing and performing the very quintessence of rock 'n' roll—*Awopbopaloobop Alopbamboom!*—there was simply no one to touch the unstoppable force from Macon, Georgia—*'the Quasar of Rock'*—the one and only Little Richard.

There were, of course, other American artists, both black and white, who influenced The Beatles in the early days; namely Bill Haley, Eddie Cochran, Gene Vincent, Jerry Lee Lewis, Carl Perkins, the Everly Brothers, Ray Charles, 'Fats' Domino, and Bo Diddley; brilliant exponents all of rock 'n' roll, rhythm & blues, rockabilly, country, gospel, and soul.

There were other artists, too, both male and female, whose music won favour with The Beatles and the group went out of their way to cover their 'stand-out' songs. There was also an American disk jockey who had his own unique part to play in introducing The Beatles to the sounds of authentic rock 'n' roll.

But it was mainly Elvis Presley and Buddy Holly and Chuck Berry and Little Richard who first provided the bedrock of what would eventually become The Beatles' very own sound.

'Hail, Hail... Rock 'n' Roll'

ROCK 'N' ROLL

ELVIS PRESLEY | *The undisputed 'King' of Rock 'n' Roll*
Singer | **Guitar Player** | **Film Star** | **American Icon**

That's All Right | *Heartbreak Hotel* | *Hound Dog* | *Don't Be Cruel* | *Blue Suede Shoes* | *I Got a Woman* | *I'm Gonna Sit Right Down And Cry* | *Shake, Rattle and Roll* | *Lawdy, Miss Clawdy* | *All Shook Up* | *Teddy Bear* | *Jailhouse Rock*

Elvis Aaron Presley. | 8 January 1935 - August 16, 1977 | Born Tupelo, Mississippi, USA | The absolute embodiment of Rockabilly and Rock 'n' Roll. A 'pop' music phenomenon: utterly inimitable; although imitated times beyond number. | Elvis Presley has sold more than a billion records—and counting. Some of them still as shockingly brilliant as the day they were first heard—most all of them timeless. | 1956. 'Hound Dog' b/w 'Don't Be Cruel' has to be the best double-sided jukebox record of all time. Rockin' just doesn't get any better.

For millions of fans Rock 'n' Roll was born in 1954 when producer Sam Philips first recorded Elvis Presley at his Sun

Records storefront recording studio in Memphis, Tennessee. | 'That's All Right', written by Arthur Crudup, a black, blues musician, and 'Blue Moon of Kentucky', written by Bill Monroe, a white, bluegrass-country singer; music from both sides of the 'colour line' reinterpreted, reimagined, and reinvented for a whole new generation of suddenly gone wild white teenagers.

Accompanied by guitarist Scotty Moore, bass-player Bill Black, drummer D.J. Fontana—his Sun-blessed 'rockabilly' trio—in an up-tempo, backbeat-driven mix of country and rhythm and blues—everything stripped down and direct—with just enough added reverberation to catch the ear and not let go.

It was his voice that hit you first—an unbelievably rich baritone and crystal clear tenor: *"We-e-ell since my ba-by left me..."* So knowing. So yearning. So downright real; it couldn't ever be denied. It was raw. It was passionate. It was emotive. And it resonated down deep. It spoke truth—to you—understood what it meant to be young and restless—how it felt to win and lose in love—and in life. And, oh, yes, Elvis sounded so damn sexy. Elvis didn't just sing. He *was* the music. Listening to him, made you want to leap up out of your seat and just go rock 'n' roll. It sometimes felt angry, sometimes dangerous, but it was always such a blast; such full on excitement.

And then once you actually got to see Elvis himself; it was game over; you could do nothing but surrender; you were gone man gone. Forever hooked. The look—the clothes—the shiny sweptback blue-black hair—that face—those eyes—that smile—that curl of the lip—those struts—those moves—the slow, sensual swivel of the hips—even the hang of his great looking guitar.

He brought something entirely new; something utterly unprecedented; to small town theatres, county fairs, local television, and then US Network TV. And followed all that up with a whole slew of Hollywood films that showed him off, worldwide, and made Elvis Aaron Presley an indelible part of youthful rebellion; the personification of the hopes and the dreams, and the unfathomable angst of teenagers the world over. Looking back to the time when he first heard Elvis, as a teenager, John Lennon said: **"Before Elvis, there was nothing."**

In 1955, Elvis was signed to RCA-Victor. | January 1956. His very first single for RCA-Victor—'Heartbreak Hotel'—No.1 Hit in US—Elvis's first million-seller. | July 1956. His next single—'Don't Be Cruel' b/w 'Hound Dog' released. Within weeks 'Hound Dog' was No. 2 on Pop Charts with sales of over one million. The only force capable of topping Elvis; more Elvis. 'Don't Be Cruel' overtook 'Hound Dog' and took the No. 1 spot on all three music charts: Pop, Country, and R&B. A totally unprecedented event in pop music, but it was only just the beginning for Elvis.

All the rest, as they say... all the singles, the albums, the films, the live concerts, are all history made and recorded for eternity. 'Pop culture' history; 'Social' history; Elvis is no longer simply confined to Rock 'n' Roll; Elvis Presley has long left that building. He is a legend for the ages and unquestionably, one of the most celebrated and influential musicians of the 20th Century.

Still the best-selling solo artist in the history of recorded music; with estimated record sales, worldwide, of over a billion records; Elvis *is* 'The King' and forever will be.

| Side Bar | What musicians said about Elvis: *"Elvis Presley is the greatest cultural force in the 20th century. He introduced the beat to everything and he changed everything—music, language, clothes, it's a whole new social revolution—the '60s came from it."* — Leonard Bernstein. Composer. Conductor - The New York Philharmonic | *"Hearing him for the first time, was like busting out of jail"* — Bob Dylan | **"Nothing really affected me until I heard Elvis. If there hadn't been Elvis, there wouldn't have been The Beatles."** — John Lennon

BUDDY HOLLY | *The Prince of Rock 'n' Roll*
Singer | Guitar Player | Songwriter

That'll Be The Day | *Peggy Sue* | *Heartbeat* | *Everyday* | *It Doesn't Matter Anymore* | *It's So Easy!* | *Love Is Strange* | *Maybe Baby* | *Not Fade Away* | *Oh, Boy!* | *Raining in My Heart* | *Rave On!* | *Words of Love* | *True Love Ways*

Charles Hardin Holley | 7 September 1936 - 3 February 1959 | Born Lubbock, Texas, USA | Buddy Holly made a major and lasting impact on popular music on both sides of the Atlantic.

He was one of the first rock 'n' roll musicians who wrote, recorded, and produced his own songs. Also one of the first recording artists to employ the then 'advanced' studio technique of 'double-tracking'. He also introduced, and helped make popular, the now standard two guitars, bass, and drums rock-group line-up. His trademark horn-rimmed glasses and pleasing vocal 'hiccup' singing style made him instantly recognisable.

1952. Buddy made his first appearance on local television. | 1953. Formed the group 'Buddy and Bob'. | 1955. Holly and his band opened for Elvis Presley three times—the experience turned him into an ardent rock 'n' roller. *"We owe it all to Elvis,"* he said later. | Opened for Bill Haley & His Comets—and was spotted by Nashville talent scout who helped him gain a contract with Decca Records.

1956. Recorded demos and singles for Decca under the name Buddy Holly and the Three Tunes. | 1957. Unhappy with Decca, Holly teamed up with producer Norman Petty; who became his manager. | Wrote 'That'll Be the Day'. The song's title and refrain a reference to a line uttered by John Wayne in the film *The Searchers* (1956). Buddy and his band record a demo of 'That'll Be the Day'. Brunswick Records were impressed enough to release the song without re-recording it and, as Holly's name was still linked with Decca, credited the single to 'The Crickets'. But when he first set out on first tour, he did so as 'Buddy Holly and The Crickets'. | September 1957. 'That'll Be the Day' made No. 1 in US and No. 1 on UK Singles Chart.

1957 - 1958. Buddy Holly and The Crickets had seven hits in 'Top 40' Singles Charts. | October 1957 'Peggy Sue' reached No. 3 in US chart and No. 6 on UK singles chart. | November 1957. His album *Chirping Crickets* reached No.5 on UK Albums Chart. | January 1958. Following his second appearance on nationally syndicated TV's *The Ed Sullivan Show*, he embarked on a tour of Australia. | Then in February 1958, he toured the UK; as part of which he played Liverpool Stadium—to thunderous acclaim.

December 1958. Holly parted company with Norman Petty, his manager, and his band The Crickets, over non-payment of royalties and other financial irregularities. Beset by legal and financial problems following the break-up, Holly reluctantly agreed to embark on a 'Winter Dance Party' 'pop' package bus tour of the US Midwest and formed a new touring band. Having just completed a show in Clear Lake, Iowa, on February 3, 1959, rather than travel in a cramped tour bus that'd repeatedly broken down or have to endure the subfreezing weather any longer, Buddy Holly elected to charter a private plane to take him onto the next gig in Moorhead, Minnesota. He and fellow rock 'n' roll stars Ritchie Valens and J. P. 'The Big Bopper' Richardson were killed in a plane crash, soon after take off. Forever immortalised as 'The Day The Music Died'. He was just 22 years of age when he died; still a huge tragic loss to American music.

1986. Buddy Holly was one of the first musicians inducted into the *Rock and Roll Hall of Fame*. | His influence not only confined to The Beatles; The Hollies were another British group to take inspiration from his name. In 1964 the Rolling Stones had their first 'Top 10' hit in Britain with Holly's 'Not Fade Away'.

| Side Bar | Buddy Holly and The Crickets and The Beatles | The first song John Lennon ever learned to play and sing was Holly's 'That'll Be The Day.' | John's first group, The Quarrymen, had a number of his songs in their repertoire: 'Words of Love' and 'It's So Easy' particular favourites. It was John's close Liverpool Art College friend, and The Beatles' first bass player, Stu Sutcliffe, who first conjured the name 'Beetles' in homage to Holly's backing group, The Crickets. It was John who then changed the letter 'e' to a letter 'a' as a pun on the word 'beat'.

1964. The Beatles recorded 'Words of Love' for *Beatles for Sale* and 'Crying, Waiting, Hoping' for *Live at the BBC* (1994) | 1975. John Lennon recorded 'Peggy Sue for *Rock 'n' Roll* | 2012. Ringo Starr recorded 'Think It Over' for *Ringo 2012* | 1975. Paul McCartney acquired all thirty-eight songs of the Buddy Holly music catalogue and every year—since 1976—has promoted a 'Rave On Buddy Holly Week' in the UK.

CHUCK BERRY | *The Preeminent Poet of Rock 'n' Roll*
Guitarist | Singer | Songwriter

Maybellene | School Days | Rock and Roll Music | Roll Over Beethoven | Sweet Little Sixteen | Reelin' And Rockin' | Johnny B. Goode | Memphis Tennessee | Little Queenie | Back In The USA | Bye Bye Johnny | Jaguar And Thunderbird | Nadine | You Never Can Tell | No Particular Place To Go | Come On

Charles Edward Anderson Berry | 18 October 1926 - 18 March 2017 | Born San Jose, California. Brought up St Louis, Missouri, USA | Chuck Berry *is* Rock 'n' Roll. His influence as a songwriter and guitarist is truly incalculable. A brilliantly original electric guitar player, his ringing four-bar introductions were the perfect set-ups for his sharp-eyed, quick-fire lyrics.

He wrote "teenage anthems" that embraced adolescent love and lost love, rebelliousness and angst; and that celebrated late 1950s, early 1960s Americana. High school hops, teen record parties and dances, soda fountains, jukeboxes, juke-joints, telephones, automobiles, drag-races, open roads, and interstate highways—even the joyous liberating power of rock 'n' roll itself. A kaleidoscopic reflection of the growing 'pop' culture that would not only shape teenage aspirations, expectations, and mind-set in the US, but also in the UK, Europe, and much of the rest of the world for the rest of the twentieth century.

Chuck Berry began playing concerts at local high school. Then bar bands and club bands. He was influenced by black 'blues' musicians; especially Muddy Waters and T-Bone Walker; as well as white 'hillbilly' and country artists; though he admitted his singing style owed much to the cool, clearly enunciated delivery of Nat King Cole. And in that respect not at all odds with his later trademark hot-lick 'duck-walk', a virtuoso display of showmanship that only served to underscore his effortless guitar artistry and commanding stage presence.

1955-1960. Chuck Berry had a string of 17 R&B Hits on US Charts. | 1955. Signed with Chess in Chicago. His first release 'Maybellene'—first ever *bona fide* rock 'n' roll hit—reached No. 1 on US R&B Chart and No.5 on the 'Pop' Chart. | 1957. Scored second 'Top 10' Hit with 'School Days - Ring! Ring! Goes The Bell'. | Followed by a run of destined to be rock 'n' roll classics: 1957. 'Rock 'n' Roll Music', 'Roll Over Beethoven', 'Too Much Monkey Business'. | 1958. 'Sweet Little Sixteen', 'Reelin' And Rockin', 'Johnny B. Goode', 'Carol', 'Around and Around', 'Memphis, Tennessee'. | 1959. 'Little Queenie', 'Back In The USA', 'Let It Rock' | 1960 'Bye Bye Johnny', 'Jaguar And Thunderbird'. | 1964. 'Nadine', 'You Never Cab Tell', 'No Particular Place To Go'.

Appeared in several rock films including: 1957. *Rock, Rock, Rock* and *Mr. Rock and Roll.* | 1959. *Go Johnny Go* | 1960. *Jazz on a Summer's Day* | 1963. He kept touring; playing one-night concerts just about everywhere. | Had more hits with 'Nadine (Is It You?)', 'No Particular Place to Go', and 'You Never Can Tell'.

Always endeavouring to keep up with times he did cover versions of songs by Buddy Holly, Elvis Presley, the Rolling Stones—and The Beatles. 'My Ding-A-Ling' was his only No. 1 single; laden with *'double entendres'*; but still a rather sad reflection on his earlier 'poetic' genius.

But never one to be kept down, he continued touring, even if without new hits, and survived for the next three decades as an esteemed 'Oldies-but-Goldies' revival act. And then, from out of the cinematic blue, he was fittingly celebrated, and introduced to new generations in the film *Back To The Future*.

January, 1986. Chuck Berry one of the first musicians inducted into the *Rock and Roll Hall of Fame*. The citation: **"While no individual can be said to have invented rock and roll, Chuck Berry comes the closest of any single figure to being the one who put all the essential pieces together."** | 1988. Published *Chuck Berry: the Autobiography*. Tells as much about mid-twentieth century America as his life as a musician—talks about "race" and about "being black"—about his run-ins with the law and the three times he spent in prison—yet throughout remains surprisingly upbeat—one might even say un-embittered. Although ever the pragmatist that might be no more than a public "smile and a grin" and a further example of his genius as a showman—as he was still a working musician at the time.

There can be little doubt that as one of the driving forces, and faces, of early rock 'n' roll he was deliberately targeted by authorities under the guise of 'defenders of the public morals', and so had every right to feel bitter. He was, after all, not afraid to make his feelings known. His sometimes pointed, often very caustic and abrupt dealings with music promoters, as well as other rock musicians, was legendary in the business. No way was he ever going to get fooled again. (And a quick tip of the hat here to The Who—who else?). To the eyes and ears of this lifelong Chuck Berry fan, his lyricism throughout his autobiography is often as compelling as his otherwise matchless lyrics.

In 2008, quite astoundingly, Chuck Berry embarked on a European tour at the tender age of 82.

18 March 2017. Chuck Berry died, aged 90, still rockin' and a rollin'. His final album—his first in 38 years—was announced on his 90th birthday in 2016. Simply entitled 'CHUCK'—it was dedicated to his wife Thelmetta 'Toddy' Berry and was released posthumously. And, boy, could he still rock 'n' roll.

| **Side Bar** | **Chuck Berry and The Beatles** | Chuck Berry had a profound influence on The Beatles—and the Rolling Stones. Both bands covered many of his songs at the start of their careers. | The Beatles recorded Chuck Berry's 'Roll Over Beethoven'—*With The Beatles* and 'Rock 'n' Roll Music'—*Beatles For Sale* | 'Too Much Monkey Business', 'Carol' 'Johnny B. Goode', 'Memphis, Tennessee', 'Sweet Little Sixteen', 'I Got to Find My Baby'—*Live at The BBC* | 'I'm Talking About You'—*On Air - Live at the BBC Volume 2* | 1975. John Lennon also recorded Chuck Berry's 'You Can't Catch Me' and 'Sweet Little Sixteen'—for his album *Rock 'n' Roll* | 1988. Paul McCartney recorded Chuck Berry's 'Brown Eyed Handsome Man'—*Paul McCartney's Снова в СССР* | All of which goes to underscore the fact there'll probably never be a rock 'n' roll band—anywhere in the world—ever—that doesn't start out by playing Chuck Berry numbers. He was and will forever be *"the founding father and preeminent poet of Rock 'n' Roll."* | *"If you tried to give rock 'n' roll another name, you might as well call it 'Chuck Berry'."* — **John Lennon**

LITTLE RICHARD | *The Architect of Rock 'n' Roll*
Singer | Piano Player | Songwriter | Actor

Tutti-Frutti | Long Tall Sally | Good Golly, Miss Molly | Lucille | Baby Face | The Girl Can't Help It | Rip It Up | Keep A Knockin' | She's Got It | Whole Lotta Shakin' Goin' On | Ready Teddy

Richard Wayne Penniman | 5 Dec 1932 - 9 May 2020 | Born Macon, Georgia, USA | Rock 'n' Roll pioneer: seamlessly combined boogie-woogie, gospel, and New Orleans R&B. | Electrifying. Dynamic. Explosive. Irrepressible. Charismatic. Flamboyant. Inimitable, though many have tried and, save for Paul McCartney, few have ever come close. Little Richard's frenetic piano playing with its distinctive beat and rhythm; his absolutely phenomenal singing voice; his croons and wails and screams; his whoops of unabashed delight and ecstatic trills are altogether spine-tingling in effect and all but defined 'live' performance dynamics of rock 'n' roll. Huge influence on everyone that followed: most notably James Brown, Otis Redding, Jimi Hendrix, Rolling Stones, Elton John. Hence the additional sobriquet: *'The Quasar of Rock'*

Born into a deeply religious family. Began singing in church at young age. Influenced by gospel performers Mahalia Jackson and Sister Rosetta Tharpe. | Sang in travelling medicine show and vaudeville groups as solo artist on the 'Chitlin' club circuit. | 1951. Signed with RCA-Victor—to little or no effect. Learned to play boogie-woogie piano. | 1952. Formed Tempo Toppers band and joined 'blues' package tours in clubs across the South. | 1953. Signed Peacock Records, to little or no effect, disbanded Temp Toppers. | 1953-4. Formed the 'Upsetters'. Sent demos to Specialty Records. | 1955. Signed Specialty Records. Bought out contract with Peacock. Partnered with producer Robert 'Bumps' Blackwell. | September 1955. Recorded 'Tutti Frutti' at J&M Studios, New Orleans. Single released in November; an instant hit. No. 2 *Billboard* R&B Chart. No. 17 *Billboard* 'Top 100' in US and No. 29 UK Singles Chart. Million-seller—worldwide hit. | 1956. Next hit single, 'Long Tall Sally, reached No. 1 R&B Chart. 'Top-Ten' Hit in US and UK Singles Charts. Another million seller.

Little Richard began performing in package tours across US. "Dynamic, uninhibited, unpredictable, wild." During a time of deep racial segregation his music and concerts "opened the door—brought the races together." And anyone with a gay bone in his body saw the rainbow colours of his stage 'pancake' make-up, flamboyant stage clothes, and uninhibited and unafraid personality as signals of longed for freedom.

1956. Little Richard had nine 'Hits' in US Five 'Hits' in UK: 'Slippin' and Slidin'', 'Rip It Up', 'Ready Teddy', 'The Girl Can't Help It', and 'Lucille'. | His songs covered by Pat Boone, Elvis Presley, Bill Haley, Jerry Lee Lewis, The Everly Brothers, Gene Vincent, and Eddie Cochran. | He appeared in the films: *Don't Knock the Rock*, *Mister Rock and Roll*, and *The Girl Can't Help It*.

1957. More international hits: 'Jenny, Jenny', 'Keep A-Knockin', 'Good Golly, Miss Molly'. | May 1957. *Here's Little Richard*, Little Richard's first album, reached No. 13 *Billboard* Top LPs Chart. | In October 1957, he undertook a package tour of Australia with Gene Vincent and Eddie Cochran. At the end of which he announced he was giving up rock 'n' roll to follow a life in 'evangelical' ministry. | 1959. Parted with Specialty Records. (All of Little Richard's songs later bought by Michael Jackson.) | He married. Recorded gospel songs. Signed to Mercury records. And released the album *King of the Gospel Singers*.

1962. UK concert promoter Don Arden persuaded Little Richard to tour Europe; with Sam Cooke second on the bill. Signed on thinking it was a Gospel Tour. First house; sang gospel, to little or no effect. Second house; Little Richard and organist Billy Preston launched into 'Long Tall Sally' and the crowd went wild; tore down the house. Same response wherever he played. October 12, 1962, Little Richard headlined Tower Ballroom, New Brighton; with The Beatles second on the bill. Two weeks later, on October 28, he played Liverpool Empire; again with The Beatles | November 1-14. Little Richard appeared the opening season Star-Club, Hamburg; starred alongside The Beatles; as later did Ray Charles. | He returned to the US. And to keep all future options open, recorded for Little Star Records, under the name 'World Famous Upsetters'. Otis Redding joined the band. In 1963, he returned to tour the UK, with The Rolling

Stones as his opening act. Starred in TV special, *The Little Richard Spectacular*, for Granada Television; a huge ratings success.

1964. Recorded with Specialty, again. The single 'Bama Lama Bama Loo' reached UK Top 20; but only No. 82 in US | Signed with Vee-Jay Records. Issued the album *Little Richard Is Back*. | Jimi Hendrix (Maurice James) joined the Upsetters band. | 1965. Little Richard, with Billy Preston and Jimi Hendrix, recorded soul ballad 'I Don't Know What You've Got, But It's Got Me'. Made No. 12 R&B Chart | Signed with Modern Records; a mix of rock and soul singles; the only hit, 'Do You Feel It?'

1966. Signed with Okeh Records. Produced studio album *The Explosive Little Richard* | 1967. *Little Richard's Greatest Hits: Recorded Live!* hit the 'Pop Album' chart; his first in ten years.

1967-69. Toured US—casinos, resorts, music festivals—often stealing the show from headliners. |1970. Signed Reprise Records. *The Rill Thing* album—produced several chart singles. | 1973. Rocked triumphant in film documentary *'Let The Good Times Roll'* | 1973-77. Signed with various independent record labels. Performed as guest instrumentalist and or vocalist on recording sessions—anything to keep on rockin'. | 1977 Little Richard departed rock 'n' roll for evangelism—again. | 1979. Released *God's Beautiful City* gospel album.

1986. Little Richard was one of the first musicians inducted into the *Rock and Roll Hall of Fame*. The citation: "*He claims to be 'the architect of rock and roll', and history would seem to bear out Little Richard's boast.* **More than any other performer; save, perhaps, Elvis Presley; Little Richard blew the lid off the Fifties, laying the foundation for rock and roll with his explosive music and charismatic persona.** *On record, he made spine-tingling rock and roll. His frantically charged piano playing and raspy, shouted vocals on such classics as 'Tutti Frutti', 'Long Tall Sally' and 'Good Golly, Miss Molly' defined the dynamic sound of rock and roll.*"

2003. Songwriters Hall of Fame. | 2010. 'Tutti Frutti' into Library of Congress' National Recording Registry | No. 8 *Rolling Stone—100 Greatest Artists of All Time*. | Here's Little Richard— No. 50 *Rolling Stone '500 Greatest Albums of All Time'*. | 'The Girl Can't Help It', 'Long Tall Sally', 'Tutti Frutti'—*Rolling Stone '500*

Greatest Songs of All Time'. | 'Long Tall Sally', 'Tutti Frutti', 'Good Golly, Miss Molly'—Rock and Roll Hall of Fame's *'500 Songs that Shaped Rock and Roll'*. | 'Tutti Frutti' topped *Mojo—'The 100 Records That Changed the World'*.

| **Side Bar** | **Little Richard and The Beatles** | A huge influence on The Beatles, especially Paul McCartney who'd idolized the singer since he was a schoolboy. Little Richard's 'Long Tall Sally' was one of Paul McCartney's all-time favourite rock 'n' roll songs; one of the very first songs he performed in public. Little Richard's vocal-style a later inspiration for his own up-tempo rockers. In Liverpool—every musician worth his salt considered Little Richard a rock 'n' roll god. | 1962. Maverick Liverpool promoter Sam Leach negotiated with Don Arden for Little Richard to play Tower Ballroom, New Brighton, but was outbid by Brian Epstein who wanted to position his group as second on the bill to Little Richard to give them instant added credibility. And on Friday 12 October, Little Richard, *'The Quasar of Rock'* 'With A Sensational Line Up of 10 Top British Rock Groups *including* The Beatles' was such a success Brian Epstein negotiated a second Liverpool show to take place two weeks later. An on Sunday 28 October, Little Richard starred in 'A NEMS Enterprises *'Pop Package Show'* at the Empire Theatre, Liverpool; with The Beatles again second on the bill. Brian Epstein's rapport with Little Richard was such that he offered the singer 50% of The Beatles' management contract if he could help break the group into the US market and help secure them a recording contract. Little Richard, regretfully, had to demur. | November 1-14. The Beatles play Star-Club, Hamburg, for a two-week residency and shared the bill, again, with Little Richard. | During The Beatles' induction into the Rock and Roll Hall of Fame, George Harrison thanked all the rock 'n' rollers present and pointed to Little Richard, sitting in the audience: **"If it wasn't for Little Richard... there... It was really all his fault we amounted to anything at all."** | John Lennon once said that when he heard 'Long Tall Sally' for the first time: **"I was that impressed I couldn't bloody well speak for days."**

| Side Bar | Little Richard's 'Long Tall Sally' and The Beatles
The song neatly brackets The Beatles' 'live' career. It was one of the medley of Little Richard numbers Paul McCartney sang the day he first met John Lennon at St. Peter's Parish Church Garden Fête, in Woolton, Liverpool on 6 June 1957. | It was also The Beatles' opening number at their all-important breakthrough gig at the Christmas Dance at Litherland Town Hall, in Liverpool, on 27 December 1960—when Paul McCartney belted out the opening words to 'Long Tall Sally' before compere and DJ Bob Wooler could even finish his introduction—and The Beatles stunned the crowd with their hard rockin' Hamburg sound. And it literally established them overnight as the top 'live' group on Merseyside. | And years later, when The Beatles decided to give up touring for good at what would be the end of the very last US Tour, the very last song, of the very last 'live' public concert they'd ever give, on 29 August 1966, at San Francisco's Candlestick Park, was, yes you've guessed it: 'Long Tall Sally'. And no mere coincidence, I'm sure.

| Side Bar | Little Richard recorded by The Beatles
1964. 'Long Tall Sally'—*Long Tall Sally* (EP) | 'Lucille' and 'Ooh! My Soul'—*Live at the BBC* (1994) |
1975. John Lennon recorded: 'Rip It Up'/'Ready Teddy' medley and 'Slippin' and Slidin'—*Rock 'n' Roll* | 1988. Paul McCartney recorded: 'Lucille'—*Paul McCartney Снова в СССР*

| Side Bar | Little Richard and British Rock 'n' Roll | Cliff Richard, one of Britain's very first successful rock 'n' roll singers—changed his name from Harry Webb in tribute to his musical hero. | Mick Jagger said Little Richard was *"the originator and my first idol."* | Keith Richards said that when he heard 'Tutti Frutti' *"it was if, in a single instant, the world changed from monochrome to Technicolor."* | David Bowie once called Little Richard his *"original inspiration"* and that upon listening to 'Tutti Frutti' for the first time he knew he'd *"heard the voice of God."* | 'Nuff said.

ROCK 'N' ROLL | ROCKABILLY | COUNTRY

BILL HALEY | *The Father of Rock and Roll*
Singer | Songwriter | Guitarist | Bandleader

Crazy Man, Crazy | *Rock Around The Clock* | *Rock A Beatin' Boogie* | *See You Later, Alligator* | *Shake, Rattle and Roll*

William John Clifton Haley. July 6, 1925 - February 9, 1981 | Born Highland Park, Michigan, USA | American singer and musician widely regarded as being the first 'white' US artist to popularise rock 'n' roll. | Prime exponent of what gifted rock chronicler Charlie Gillett called 'Northern band rock 'n' roll':
  "High-spirited, hard-charging jump blues coupled with a danceable backbeat; heightened by careening solos and stomping stop-time breaks."
  1932. Bill Haley's family moved to Philadelphia, Pennsylvania | 1938. Began performing guitar and singing songs at local venues. | 1940. Left home—went out on the road with his guitar. | Began working in radio. | 1951. Recorded cover of 'Rocket 88' with his group—the Saddlemen. | 1952. Renamed as Bill Haley with Haley's Comets; they record 'Rock the Joint'.
  1953. Haley's 'Crazy Man, Crazy' was the first rock 'n' roll record to enter US charts; peaking at No.15 on *Billboard* 'Pop' singles chart. | Followed later in 1953 with 'Rock Around the Clock' that peaked No. 23 on *Billboard*, then re-entered again at No.1. | 1954. Haley had another worldwide hit with million-seller 'Shake, Rattle and Roll', his first Gold Record; notable as it was the first ever rock 'n' roll record to enter UK 'Singles' charts. 1955. 7 August. Bill Haley and His Comets were the first rock 'n' roll act to appear on the iconic *Ed Sullivan Show*.
  1955. 'Rock Around the Clock' used as the theme song for the film *Blackboard Jungle*, a gritty drama about life in a big city high school, starring Glenn Ford and Sydney Poitier. The single charted first in UK; then soared to top of US *Billboard* chart again. The film made the record notorious—and a teen-magnet.
  The event now regarded by many rock historians as: ***"The Record That Started the Rock Revolution"*** and the demarcation

line between "The Rock Era" and all of the popular music that had preceded it. Tellingly, after the record rose to No.1 Bill Haley was dubbed *"Father of Rock and Roll"* by the industry media and white teenagers alike.

1956. Bill Haley starred in the first rock 'n' roll musical films *Rock Around the Clock* and *Don't Knock the Rock*. | 'Rock Around the Clock', 'See You Later, Alligator', 'Shake, Rattle and Roll', 'Skinny Minnie', 'Razzle Dazzle' were all million-seller hits.

Bill Haley had 37 'Hit' records. Sold over 25 million records worldwide | At the height of their popularity—Bill Haley and The Comets had guaranteed advance sales of 100,000 copies on every recording released in UK | Bill Haley toured UK multiple times—first in 1957—then eight more times between 1964 and 1979 | 'Rock Around the Clock' entered UK 'Pop' charts nine times between 1957 and 1974 | 1981. Bill Haley died 9 February—aged 55—Texas USA | 1987. Bill Haley posthumously inducted into the *Rock and Roll Hall of Fame* | 2005. Bill Haley and His Comets inducted into the *Rockabilly Hall of Fame* | 2012. The Comets were inducted into the *Rock and Roll Hall of Fame* as a group.

"People associate the beginning of rock 'n roll with 1954. Actually, it had been gathering momentum and when we made 'Rock Around the Clock'... it just exploded. That's when the mob scene started...thousands of kids at the stage door. It wasn't because we were so great. The hysteria wasn't for us. It was for the music. This was a new music for kids who hadn't had any of their own." — Bill Haley

| **Side Bar** | **Bill Haley and British Rock 'n' Roll** | 1956. 'Rock Around the Clock' was the first single ever to sell over one million copies in both Britain and Germany. | Haley's album—*Rock Around The Clock* —for Decca Records—was also a massive seller in UK | 1957. Bill Haley was the first major American rock singer to tour Europe. | 5 February 1957. British Rock 'n' Roll fans mobbed him and his band on arrival at Waterloo railway station in London—having earlier arrived by ocean liner *Queen Elizabeth*, in Southampton—to commence their first UK Tour.

THE BEATLES IN LIVERPOOL, HAMBURG, LONDON

National tabloids splashed full-page pictures of the 'groundbreaking' event on newspaper front covers.

"The birth of rock `n roll was seeing Bill Haley and The Comets when they came to England." – Pete Townshend - The Who

| Side Bar | Bill Haley and The Beatles | 1957. Some six months before fifteen-year old schoolboy Paul McCartney first met sixteen-year old John Lennon, he went to see Bill Haley in concert at the Liverpool Odeon during his totally sold-out UK Tour: *"The first time I really ever felt a tingle up my spine was when I saw Bill Haley and The Comets on the telly... Then I went to see them live. The ticket was 24 shillings, and I was the only one of my mates who could go, as no one else had been able to save up that amount. But I was single-minded about it... I knew there was something going on here."* | 1963. Bill Haley and His Comets appeared at Star-Club in Hamburg; six months or so after The Beatles' final performance there; caught up in the comet-like trail of rock 'n' roll revitalised and remade anew by 'The Fab Four' from Liverpool

EDDIE COCHRAN | Singer | Guitarist | Musician | Songwriter

Twenty Flight Rock | Summertime Blues | C'mon Everybody | Jeannie, Jeannie, Jeannie | Somethin' Else | Three Stars | Teenage Heaven | Three Steps To Heaven

Edward Raymond Cochran | October 3, 1938 - April 17, 1960 | Born Albert Lea, Minnesota, USA | 'Summertime Blues', his all but matchless commentary on teenage life, then as now, his signature song. The first great Rock'a'Billy Rocker; a great-looking one, too; mean, rebellious, and sultry; with a grooving gravelly voice that just reached out and grabbed you. He was the full package, the real deal. Eddie had the look, the sound; knew just how to stand. He knew how to rock a song and knew how to play rock 'n' roll guitar, both rhythm and solo. He played an orange-coloured Gretsch semi-hollow body electric guitar; one of the first ever seen in the UK; that really was "somethin' else", and the envy of every would-be guitarist the length and breadth of Britain; especially a young George Harrison.

1952. Eddie Cochran's family moved to southern California. He took up the guitar. | 1954. Eddie joined songwriter Hank Cochran—no relation—in a local country-western band called 'The Cochran Brothers'—and too young to play in bars —they played dance halls, country fairs, and schools. | 1955. Recorded two 'hillbilly' records for Ekko Records. Did a promotional tour. Met Elvis Presley. Auditioned for Sun Records in Memphis—but to no avail and the duo broke up. Hank departed for Nashville—to become a songwriter. | 1956. Eddie landed a contract with Crest—a minor Hollywood label—and released 'Skinny Jim'. During which time he also worked as a session musician and recorded backing vocals for other artists.

An executive at Liberty Records impressed by Eddie's looks and talent saw him as Liberty's answer to Elvis and got him a cameo role in *The Girl Can't Help It*, starring Jayne Mansfield. Eddie sang 'Twenty Flight Rock' in the film and showed the world he could more than hold the stage with the likes of co-stars Little Richard and Gene Vincent. He also later appeared in *Untamed Youth* (1957) and *Go Johnny Go* (1959).

1957. Eddie Signed with Liberty Records, but was always far more than just a good-looking face on film, he was an extremely accomplished musician and producer, an early adopter of over-dubbing; many times playing multiple instruments on his own records. His first single for Liberty, 'Sittin' in the Balcony', made the 'Top 20' pop charts. He quickly followed up with 'Drive-in Show' and his first album *Singin' to My Baby*. | 1958. He recorded and released 'Summertime Blues' that became one of Liberty's biggest ever successes. | 1959. Released 'C'mon Everybody'—UK Top Ten hit. | Met songwriter Sharon Sheeley, who wrote Ricky Nelson's No.1 hit 'Poor Little Fool', and the two collaborated on writing 'Somethin' Else' which Liberty released as a single September 1959. | Recorded 'Three Stars'—a tribute to Buddy Holly, the Big Bopper, and Richie Valens who'd died in plane crash.

1959-1960. Eddie Cochran toured US and Australia. And after entreaties from London impresario Larry Parnes—agreed to co-headline a UK Tour with Gene Vincent. It was the country's first ever 'All-Rock Package Tour' and would have a huge influence on British rock 'n' roll. The demand for tickets was so high the originally scheduled tour was extended by ten weeks.

16 April 1960. Late on a Sunday night, after completing a week-long engagement of *'A Fast-Moving Beat Show'* at the Bristol Hippodrome, Eddie hired a private taxi; a cream-coloured Ford Consul normally used for weddings; to take him and his fiancée songwriter Sharon Sheeley, and Gene Vincent, to Heathrow Airport to catch a flight for a brief trip back to the USA before resuming the second leg of their UK Tour.

Tour-manager Patrick Thompkins also hitched a ride and sat in the front passenger seat. The taxi, travelling at speed, along a winding two-lane road, blew a tyre. The driver lost control, the car spun around backwards and crashed into a concrete lamppost. Eddie Cochran's head smashed against the roof of the taxi and he was thrown bodily from the car out onto the road.

Rushed by ambulance to hospital in the nearby town of Bath, he died the following afternoon from his massive head injuries. The taxi diver, unbelievably named George Martin, and Patrick Thompkins walked away from the crash without injury. Gene Vincent fractured his collarbone. Sharon Sheeley suffered a broken pelvis.

Eddie Cochran died April 17, 1960, a tragic loss to popular music. He was 21 years of age. The irony being, he'd just released a single, co-written with his brother Bob, entitled 'Three Steps to Heaven'. The song reached No. 1 in the UK charts.

| **Side Bar** | **Eddie Cochran and The Beatles** | Eddie Cochran's 'Twenty Flight Rock' arguably the 'audition piece' that began The Beatles. | 6 July 1957. The day Paul McCartney met John Lennon at the Woolton Parish Church Garden Fete, Liverpool. John was with The Quarry Men Skiffle Group, singing Gene Vincent's 'Be Bop A Lula', Paul in the crowd already struck by John's charisma. After the Quarrymen finished their afternoon set, a mutual friend introduced Paul to John. Paul showed John how to tune his guitar properly; as opposed to G-banjo tuning; and then sang and played Eddie Cochran's 'Twenty Flight Rock' flawlessly. John was impressed enough to invite Paul to join The

Quarrymen. | George Harrison saw Eddie Cochran perform in Liverpool during his final tour and was hugely impressed by the American rock 'n' roller's guitar-playing and stage persona. As George later recalled for *The Beatles Anthology*: "*He was standing at the microphone and as he started to talk he put his two hands through his hair, pushing it back. And a girl, one lone voice, screamed out, 'Oh, Eddie!' and he coolly murmured into the mike, 'Hi honey'. And I thought, 'Yes! That's it—that's rock and roll!'* "

GENE VINCENT | Singer | Guitarist

Be-Bop-A-Lula | *Dance to the Bop* | *Race With Devil* | *Bay Blue* | *Blue Jean Bop* | *Git It* | *Who Slapped John?*

Vincent Eugene Craddock. | February 11, 1935 - October 12, 1971 | Born Norfolk, Virginia, USA | Rock 'n' Roll and 'rockabilly' pioneer. | 'Be-Bop-A-Lula', his debut single, sold 200,000 copies the very first month of its release. | Gene began playing the guitar at an early age, influenced by *Grand Ole Opry* on the radio and 'gospel' of local black churches. | 1952. Age 17 he dropped out of school, enlisted in the United States Navy. Never saw combat but completed Korean War deployment. | 1955. He shattered his left shinbone in a motorcycle crash. It left him with a limp and in constant pain and he wore a steel sheath around the leg for the rest of his life. | Took up as a 'country' singer. Billed as 'Gene Craddock and the Virginians'. Appeared on local 'country' radio stations and live shows. Became local recording star. | 1956. Name change to: 'Gene Vincent and *His Blue Caps*' | Capitol Record's executives thought Gene and his sidemen looked like "a motorcycle gang"; even so their demo disc of 'Be-Bop-A-Lula' won him a contract with the label. | Capitol release 'Woman Love' as 'A' side, with 'Be-Bop-A-Lula' on the 'B' side. Gene's lyrics and moans on 'Woman Love' just too damn suggestive for radio stations, so they flip the disc. 'Be-Bop-A-Lula' becomes Top Ten Hit for 20 weeks on *Billboard* Chart. Launches Gene Vincent's career big time. | 1956. 'Bluejean Bop'—No. 49 on *Billboard* chart.

1956. Gene Vincent co-starred in the rock 'n' roll film classic, *The Girl Can't Help It*, starring Jayne Mansfield; co-starring Eddie Cochran, Little Richard, 'Fats' Domino, The Platters, and Julie London | 1957. Top Twenty Hit 'Lotta Lovin'' spent almost another 20 weeks on *Billboard* chart. And Vincent was awarded gold records for his hits. | November 17 1957 Gene Vincent and His Blue Caps performed 'Dance to the Bop' on US nationwide television's *The Ed Sullivan Show* | 1958. 'Dance to the Bop' reached No. 23 on *Billboard* chart, but was Gene Vincent's last American hit single. His popularity started to wane.

1958-9 Appeared regularly on local US TV and radio music shows. But an on-going dispute with US Tax Authorities and American Musicians' Union led him to leave US for the UK.

December 15, 1959. Gene Vincent's first appearance in England on Jack Good's breakthrough TV pop music show, *Boy Meets Girl*. Vincent arrived in a lumberjack shirt and blue jeans. Not exactly the tough rockin' image Good was hoping for. And so Shakespearean trained actor that he was, Good re-staged his star act and transformed Gene Vincent into *"a rock 'n' roll version of Laurence Olivier's Richard III"*; clothed him from head to foot in black leather jacket, trousers, and boots; with matching black leather gloves.

Everything a perfect match to the black iron calliper Vincent wore on one leg as the result of his motorcycle accident. Vincent topped it off with big medallion on a chain and stood brooding; hunched over his microphone; left leg stuck out behind him; stiff and unbending; a rock 'n' roll god undiminished by all the troubles life had thrown at him. The 'encased in a carapace of black leather' rockin' image; later echoed in The Beatles' Hamburg days; Jim Morrison of The Doors; and even Elvis in his Las Vegas shows; entirely the brainchild of "hip to the cool" British TV producer Jack Good.

After his British TV appearance Gene Vincent toured France, the Netherlands, Germany, and the UK—a huge star with every UK Teddy Boy and European Rocker. And then toured Australia on same bill as Eddie Cochran and Little Richard.

April 16, 1960. Almost at the end of another UK 'pop package' tour, having just appeared in Bristol, Gene Vincent and fellow rock 'n' roller Eddie Cochran—and songwriter Sharon Sheeley—were involved in a car crash in Chippenham, Wiltshire. Vincent broke his ribs, his collarbone, and further damaged his left leg. Sheeley suffered a broken pelvis. But Cochran was thrown from the car—suffered serious head injuries—and died the next day. Vincent returned to the United States immediately after the accident.

1961. Promoter Don Arden persuaded Vincent to return to the UK to do an extensive tour in theatres and ballrooms. And in 1963 Vincent moved to Britain to tour the UK again, this time backed by British instrumental group Sounds Incorporated. On later tours, backed by The Outlaws; as well as other groups. | 1966-9. He attempted to resurrect his recording career, on different labels, on both sides of the Atlantic, but met with little success. Then financial pressures aplenty; personal and tax related; forced a return to the US | Died October 12, 1971, aged 36, from a ruptured stomach ulcer—in California.

1997. The first inductee into the 'Rockabilly Hall of Fame' | 1998. Inducted into the 'Rock and Roll Hall of Fame' | 2012. Gene Vincent's original rockabilly backing band, The Blue Caps, were inducted into the Rock and Roll Hall of Fame, retroactively, to back their lead singer into eternity, by special committee.

| **Side Bar** | **Gene Vincent and The Beatles** | April-May 1962. The Beatles first got to meet their idol Gene Vincent at Star-Club, Hamburg. Little Richard was also one of the featured acts, and Beatles' idols, during the group's first 7-week residency at Star-Club. Club owner Manfred Weissleder making good on his promise: only to feature the *'Brightest Stars of Rock 'n' Roll'*.

Sunday 1 July 1962. Gene Vincent appeared at The Cavern Club, Liverpool; backed by Sounds Incorporated. The Beatles second on the bill. It was the group's 189th appearance at The Cavern. Mike McCartney, Paul's brother, took some great black and white photos of the meeting of rock legends; Paul and John in "full leather gear" just like their idol Gene Vincent.

| Side Bar | Gene Vincent, 'Be-Bop-A-Lula', and John Lennon | One of John Lennon's all-time favourite songs, he sang it, stood on the back of a lorry, backed by The Quarrymen, at St. Peter's Church fete in Woolton, the very first time Paul McCartney saw him play; the all-important day that John met Paul. And later that same day Paul sang and played his version of 'Be-Bop-A-Lula'; and songs by Eddie Cochran and Little Richard; when he 'auditioned' for John. The ever-intrepid Beatles' historian Mark Lewisohn states that The Quarrymen and The Beatles, in their early days, featured a dozen or more Gene Vincent songs in their live shows; though few of the tunes were ever recorded.

September 13, 1969. *'Toronto Rock and Roll Revival'*. A one-day, 12-hour music festival, held at Varsity Stadium, University of Toronto, Ontario, Canada. Over 20,000 attend. Among the listed performers Rock and Roll icons: Bo Diddley, Chuck Berry, Jerry Lee Lewis, Little Richard, and Gene Vincent; and leather-clad Vincent clones, The Doors. The one-time, only appearance, of John Lennon, Yoko Ono, and The Plastic Ono Band was a total surprise, no advance-notice was ever given. Gene Vincent was to be backed by The Doors, but in the end Alice Copper's band did the honours. After an emotional rendering of 'Be-Bop-A-Lula', John Lennon came on stage and embraced his long time idol, the very public reaffirmation, causing Gene Vincent to weep with joy. The *'Toronto Rock and Roll Revival'* also notable for a rockin', riotous, comeback *"as if reborn"* performance by Little Richard; another of Lennon's Rock 'n' Roll idols

In 1975 John Lennon opened his album *Rock 'n' Roll* with his own cover of 'Be-Bop-A-Lula' | *Rolling Stone* magazine listed 'Be-Bop-A-Lula' as No. 103 on its '500 Greatest Songs of All Time'. John Lennon had it as one of his 'Top Twenty Best Rock Songs of All Time' on his 'personal' portable jukebox he took with him on his later travels in America. | As John Lennon once told Barry Miles: *"'Be-Bop-A-Lula' is without a doubt the Gene Vincent song that influenced the Beatles the most... That beginning...'We-e-e-e-l-l-l-l-l!'... always made my hair stand on end."*

JERRY LEE LEWIS | *The Killer*
Singer | Piano player | Songwriter | *Great Balls of Fire* – et al

Born September 29, 1935. Ferriday, Louisiana, USA | Rock 'n' Roll's first real wild man known for his piano pumping, heart-pounding mix of rock 'n' roll and rockabilly—and in later years for his own take on country, gospel, honky-tonk, and blues. | 1956. Recorded 'Crazy Arms' for Sun Records, Memphis Tennessee—huge hit way down South. | 1957. 'Whole Lotta Shakin' Goin' On'—huge hit—catapulted Jerry Lee Lewis to worldwide fame. | Followed up with 'Great Balls of Fire', 'Breathless', 'High School Confidential'. | Then the wheels came off the wagon in the wake of his "scandalous" marriage to his 13-year-old first cousin (once removed) when he was 23 years old. And he very quickly all but faded into obscurity.

Jerry Lee slowly climbed back up the mountain again with updated versions: What'd I Say, I Got a Woman, Sweet Little Sixteen, Good Golly Miss Molly, Money | 1964. Jerry Lee Lewis's live album *'Live at the Star Club, Hamburg'* widely regarded as one of the greatest 'live' rock albums ever recorded. | 1968. Jerry Lee made a transition into 'Country Music'—had huge hit with 'Another Place, Another Time'—which reignited his career.

Late 1960s—into the 1970s—regularly topped 'Country-Western' charts. | No. 1 country hits include: To Make Love Sweeter for You', 'Would You Take Another Chance on Me', 'Me and Bobby McGee' | The he uncovered his rock 'n' roll roots again with his cover of the Big Bopper's fabled 'Chantilly Lace'. | His album *Last Man Standing* his best seller—with over a million copies sold worldwide. | Jerry Lee Lewis won numerous Grammys—including a 'Lifetime Achievement Award'. | 1986. Inducted into the 'Rock and Roll Hall of Fame'. | 1997 Inducted into the 'Rockabilly Hall of Fame'. | 2004. *Rolling Stone* ranked him No. 24 on their list of the '100 Greatest Artists of All Time'.

Jerry Lee Lewis is the last living member of Sun Records' Million Dollar Quartet—the others rock 'n' roll rockabilly superstars Johnny Cash, Carl Perkins, Roy Orbison, and Elvis Presley. | 2017. Unbelievably, the great 'wild man of rock' is still touring, still pumping and pounding the piano, still hollering: *"You shake my nerves and you rattle my brain..."*

| Side Bar | Jerry Lee Lewis and Ringo Starr | Tower Ballroom, New Brighton | Thursday, May 17th, 1962 | First ever *'Thank Your Lucky Stars – The Rhythm & Blues Spectacular'* stage show—Britain's Mightiest Ever Non-Stop Big Beat Show Dance!—A Bob Wooler Rockerscope '62 Presentation—took place at the Tower Ballroom in New Brighton. | Starring *'Mr. Rock 'N' Roll' Himself. The Fabulous JERRY LEE LEWIS and the Echoes* | Also on the bill were The Big Three, Kingsize Taylor & The Dominoes, The Undertakers, Billy Kramer with The Coasters—and a handful of other Merseyside acts. | That Thursday night the Echoes were without a drummer and—as Rory Storm and The Hurricanes didn't have a gig—none other than Hurricanes' drummer Ringo Starr sat in to back 'The Killer'.

CARL PERKINS | *The King of Rockabilly*
Singer | Songwriter | Guitarist

Gone Gone Gone | *Blue Suede Shoes* | *Honey Don't* – *et al*

Carl Lee Perkins | Born Tiptonville, Tennessee, USA | April 9, 1932 - January 19, 1998 | Carl Perkins learned to play on homemade guitar. Inspired by Grand Ole Opry broadcasts on radio and Bill Monroe's guitar playing style and vocals. | 1946. Age 14 got first paying gig—with his brother Jay—at tavern outside of Jackson—Bill Monroe's 'Blue Moon of Kentucky a crowd pleaser. | Brother Clayton took up bass so the Perkins Brothers got more work. Became locally famous. Began performing on local radio stations. | 1954. Carl Perkins recorded songs on a borrowed tape recorder—sent tapes to Columbia and RCA—got no reply. | October 1954. Auditioned for Sam Phillips at Sun Records, Memphis, Tennessee. | March 19, 1955 Released 'Movie Magg' and 'Turn Around'—a regional success—led to tour appearances with Elvis Presley—and later Johnny Cash. | October 1955. Sun released 'Gone Gone Gone'—another regional success. | He then wrote 'Blue Suede Shoes'. | December 19, 1955.

Carl and his band recorded the song at Sun Studio. | January 1, 1956. Released 'Blue Suede Shoes' with 'B' side 'Honey Don't'—a massive chart success. | Reached No. 1 *Billboard* 'Country Music' chart | No. 2 *Billboard* 'Hot 100' popular music chart. | Top Ten hit in UK | 'Blue Suede Shoes'—first record by a Sun artist to sell a million copies. | 'Boppin' the Blues' reached No. 9 on *Billboard* 'Country Music' chart. | February 1957. Released 'Matchbox'—an instant rockabilly classic.

1958. Carl Perkins moved to Columbia Records | 1959. Wrote 'The Ballad of Boot Hill' for Johnny Cash | 1962 -1963 Performed Las Vegas casino. Toured Germany. | May 1964. Toured Britain with Chuck Berry. The Animals backing group for both performers. | 1969. Co-wrote 'Champaign, Illinois' with Bob Dylan. | 1969 -1979. Opening act for the *Johnny Cash* US touring revue—played Folsom and San Quentin prison concerts. Also appeared regularly on TV series *The Johnny Cash Show*. | 1987. Inducted into Rock and Roll Hall of Fame | 'Blue Suede Shoes' chosen as one of the Rock and Roll Hall of Fame's *500 Songs that Shaped Rock and Roll*. | 1989. Co-wrote and played guitar on the Judds' No. 1 country hit 'Let Me Tell You About Love'. | 1996 Published autobiography—*Go, Cat, Go!*—in collaboration with music writer David McGee. | 1997. Inducted into the Rockabilly Hall of Fame | 2004. *Rolling Stone* ranked Carl Perkins No. 99 on its list of the *100 Greatest Artists of All Time*

| **Side Bar** | **Carl Perkins and The Beatles** | On the last night of the 1964 UK tour with Chuck Berry, Perkins was at a party with The Beatles; sharing stories, playing guitar, singing songs. Ringo Starr asked if he could record 'Honey Don't'. "*Man, go ahead. Have at it,*" Perkins chuckled. | The Beatles went on to record 'official EMI' covers of Perkins' 'Matchbox', 'Honey Don't', and 'Everybody's Trying to Be My Baby'. And for the BBC: 'Lend Me Your Comb', 'Sure to Fall (In Love with You)', and 'Glad All Over' (And, no, not the Dave Clark Five hit). | 1981 Recorded 'Get It' with Paul McCartney, playing guitar and providing vocals, released on McCartney's 1982 album—*Tug of War* | October 1985. George Harrison, Ringo Star, Eric Clapton, Dave

Edmunds, and Rosanne Cash appeared on stage with Perkins for *Blue Suede Shoes: A Rockabilly Session* television special, taped live at Limehouse Studios, London for BBC Channel 4, the show transmitted 1 January 1986 | 1996 Carl Perkins' last album *Go Cat Go!* featured Carl singing duets with George Harrison, Paul McCartney, Ringo Starr, and many others including Johnny Cash, Willie Nelson, Tom Petty, Paul Simon, and Bono.

THE EVERLY BROTHERS | *The* Close-Harmony Duo Singers | Songwriters

All I Have to Do Is Dream | *Bye Bye Love* | *Let It Be Me* | *Wake Up Little Susie* | *Cathy's Clown* | *Crying in the Rain* | *Walk Right Back* | *When Will I Be Loved?* | *Ebony Eyes* | *Claudette* | *Love Hurts* | *Bird Dog* | *Lucille*

Isaac Donald 'Don' Everly | Born in Brownie, Kentucky, USA. February 1, 1937 | Phillip 'Phil' Everly | Born Chicago, Illinois, USA. January 19, 1939 | Rockabilly and rock 'n' roll singers born and bred out of country music. | Mid-1940s. Their father—acclaimed 'country music' guitarist Ike 'Pa' Everly'—had Phil and Don singing on his Shenandoah, Iowa, radio program | 1953 Family moved to Knoxville, Tennessee. The brothers caught the attention of family friend **Chet Atkins**—manager RCA Victor's studio Nashville | 1955 Don and Phil moved to Nashville, Tennessee. | Early 1956. Chet Atkins arranged for Everly Brothers to record for Columbia Records. Dropped by the label when their first record 'Keep a-Lovin' Me', written and composed by Don, flopped. | Late 1956 signed to Acuff-Rose as songwriters.

1957 Signed to Cadence Records. First song they recorded, 'Bye Bye Love', written by **Felice and Boudleaux Bryant**, had been rejected by 30 other music acts. Don and Phil's recording reached No. 2 on 'Pop' charts, right behind Elvis Presley's 'Let Me Be Your Teddy Bear'. No. 1 on 'Country' chart; No. 5 on R&B chart; the Everly Brothers' first million-seller. | Their 'crossover' success, in blending US 'country' and 'rock', helped put Nashville on the map as a major music and recording centre.

1957 - 1958. Don and Phil toured with Buddy Holly. Became close friends. Both brothers devastated when Holly died in a plane crash. | 1960. Signed with Warner Bros. Records. Their first hit for the label, 'Cathy's Clown', written and composed by Don and Phil, sold eight million copies. It was the duo's biggest-selling record. And then the brothers' enlistment in United States Marine Corps Reserve in October 1961 took them out of 'the spotlight' until; following their discharge from active duty; the Everlys resumed their singing and recording career.

1960-1962. Had a string of 'Pop' hits in US, some on Cadence Records from the recording vaults, culminating in 'Crying in the Rain' at No. 6 and 'That's Old Fashioned at No.9. | 1963–1970. Of their 27 singles on Warner Brothers label only three made the *Billboard* 'Hot 100'; none higher than No. 31.

1960-1968. It was a different story in the UK. The brothers remained very popular in Britain and had 10 'Top Ten' hits—18 of their singles in the 'Top 40' | 1968. The brothers returned increasingly to their 'country' origins and their album *Roots* was widely hailed by critics, but they enjoyed little other success.

1970. Live album—*The Everly Brothers Show*—was unsuccessful and their contract with Warner Brothers lapsed. Don released first solo album—also not a success. | 1971 Don and Phil resumed performing together—signed with RCA Victor Records—issued two albums that "went nowhere"—and broke up July 14, 1973. | 1973 - 1983. The brothers then pursued solo careers in US and UK with some, but not overly great success.

September 23, 1983. The brothers performed a reunion concert at the Royal Albert Hall. London. | 1984. The brothers returned to the studio as a 'duo' for the first time in over a decade—recorded the album *EB '84*—produced by Dave Edmunds. The lead single—'On the Wings of a Nightingale'—written and composed by Paul McCartney—put them in the US *Billboard* 'Hot 100' again. | 1986. The Everly Brothers were among the first acts inducted into the *Rock and Roll Hall of Fame*. | Grammy Lifetime Achievement Award recipients

The Everly Brothers continued to record—increasingly with other artists—until 2006 | 'Phil' Everly died January 3, 2014

| Side Bar | The Everly Brothers and The Beatles | American rock 'n' roll was dominated by solo acts—Chuck Berry, Little Richard, Buddy Holly, and Elvis—when the Everly Brothers first hit it big with 'Bye Bye Love'. | Close 'fraternal' or 'sororal' harmonies were commonplace in country music and bluegrass—but were totally without precedent in rock 'n' roll. | Don and Phil—both accomplished guitarists—used vocal harmony based mostly on diatonic thirds—Don sang the baritone part and Phil the tenor harmony. | Their close harmony singing style was hugely influential on 'the sound' that distinguished The Beatles as group—especially in the particular ways John and Paul—and George—sang and harmonised together. | Most Beatles' songs followed standard triadic three-part harmony: with John's baritone taking the main melody; Paul's tenor taking the higher part, a third above John; George singing in-between John and Paul, sometimes, even singing a note below John. | In their later studio-as-instrument based recordings The Beatles, never averse to non-standard harmonies, experimented more and more with overdubbed harmonies; sometimes purposefully clashing; other times reaching for ever more complex multi-part tonalities. | The Everly Brothers were also a huge influence on Simon & Garfunkel and rock groups such as The Beach Boys, The Byrds, The Hollies, and The Bee Gees.

ROY ORBISON | *'The Big O'*
Singer | Songwriter | Guitar player

Only the Lonely | *Blue Angel* | *Running Scared* | *Crying* | *Dream Baby* | *In Dreams* | *Falling* | *Blue Bayou* | *It's Over* | *Oh, Pretty Woman*

Roy Kelton Orbison | April 23, 1936 - December 6, 1988 | Born Vernon, Texas, USA | Rock 'n' roll. Rockabilly. Country. Pop. | 22 songs on *Billboard* 'Top 40'. | A very distinctive, tremulous voice. He sang broken-hearted emotional ballads. His songs; extremely well crafted, often quite complex in structure; conveyed a quiet, almost desperate, vulnerability in their impassioned reflections upon lost love and loneliness; the eternal cornerstones of teenage angst. | During performances he projected an air of mystery; wore black clothes to match his jet-black hair and dark sunglasses; would stand stock-still, unmoving, his dark rich baritone sliding effortlessly to a crystal clear tenor and beyond, reaching the very highest notes without always needing to resort to falsetto, in a three, possibly four, octave range. When witnessed in performance, the effect was astounding.

Roy Orbison began singing in high school in a country and western–rockabilly band that would later become The Teen Kings. | 1956. The Teen Kings signed by Sam Phillips, Sun Records. Toured with Carl Perkins. Band disbanded. Roy Orbison stayed on in Nashville. | Introduced to Elvis Presley. | Wrote 'Claudette'—about his girlfriend and later wife. Sold song to Everly Brothers who recorded and released it as B-side to their smash hit 'All I Have to Do Is Dream'. | 1959-60. Worked as songwriter at Acuff-Rose Co. | 1960. Signed with Monument Records | 1960. Wrote and recorded 'Only The Lonely'. Single shot to No.2 on *Billboard* 'Hot 100' and hit No.1 in UK and Australia. | Toured US with Patsy Cline. | Next song—'Blue Angel'—reached No. 9 in US and No. 11 in UK | Wrote and recorded 'Running Scared'—reached No.1 on *Billboard* 'Hot 100' chart and No.9 in UK | 1961. 'Crying' b/w 'Candy Man' reached No. 2 | 1962. 'Dream Baby...How Long Must I Dream?' made No. 4 in US and No. 2 in UK | 1963. A string of hits: 'In Dreams' No. 7 in US and No. 6 in UK | 'Falling'—No. 22 in US and No. 9 in UK | 'Mean Woman Blues' c/w 'Blue Bayou' No. 5 in US and No. 3 in UK | 1963-4. 'Pretty Paper'—a Christmas song written by Willie Nelson—No. 15 in US and No. 6 in UK

Spring 1963. Toured UK with The Beatles. | Fall 1963. Toured UK, Ireland, and Canada. Toured Australia and New Zealand—with the Beach Boys. Returned to tour Britain and Ireland. Toured Australia again—with the Rolling Stones. | 1964. Roy Orbison started writing songs with Bill Dees. The duo wrote 'It's Over'—No.1 Hit in UK (June) | He and Dees followed up with 'Oh, Pretty Woman'— No.1 in the US and UK charts (October). The single sold over seven million copies.

1965. Signed to MGM Records (US) and Decca Records (UK) | Continued to tour throughout late 1960's and to record albums in the 1970s; but to little or no chart success. | 1973. Signed to Mercury records. | Faded into the background; even as more and more artists began to cover his songs and have hits. | January 1976 *Roy Orbison Greatest Hits* album—No. 1 in UK | 1987. Released album of re-recorded hits: *In Dreams: The Greatest Hits.*

1987. Inducted into the Rock and Roll Hall of Fame and Nashville Songwriters Hall of Fame. | 1987. Began collaborating with Electric Light Orchestra lead vocalist and bandleader Jeff Lynne—who was completing production work on George Harrison's *Cloud Nine* album. He was asked to sing on one of Harrison's songs—which led to an impromptu teaming up with Bob Dylan and Tom Petty—and the 'super' group and album—*The Traveling Wilburys, Vol. 1* | The album spent over year on the US charts—peaking at No. 3. It was No. 1 in Australia and reached No. 16 in the UK. It then won a Grammy for 'Best Rock Performance by a Duo or Group'. *Rolling Stone* included it in the *Top 100 Albums of the Decade.*

1987-88 Developed solo album—*Mystery Girl*—co-produced by Jeff Lynne. Biggest hit 'You Got It' written with Lynne and Tom Petty—that would reach No. 9 in the US and No. 3 in the UK | Toured US and Europe. Returned home to Nashville after a hectic and exhausting promotional schedule. He died of a heart attack—aged 52. | February, 1989. Roy Orbison had two solo albums in UK Album chart—*Mystery Girl* at No. 2 and *The Legendary Roy Orbison* at No.3 | April, 1989. The first deceased musician since Elvis Presley to have two albums in the US 'Top Five'—*The Traveling Wilburys, Vol.1* at No.4 and *Mystery Girl* at No. 5 | 1989. Inducted into Songwriters Hall of Fame | *Rolling Stone* placed Roy Orbison at No. 37 on list '*Greatest Artists of All Time*' and No. 13 on list of '*100 Greatest Singers of All Time*'

| **Side Bar** | **Roy Orbison and The Beatles** | While in no way as influential on them and their music as Elvis Presley, Buddy Holly, Chuck Berry, Little Richard—or even Carl Perkins or The Everly Brothers—The Beatles were fully aware of Roy Orbison and came to admire him greatly. | The very first song they ever

sang on radio—BBC Manchester's *Teenagers' Turn*—was Roy Orbison's 'Dream Baby'. | Roy Orbison was also the inspiration for The Beatles' first No.1 record—'Please Please Me'—written by John Lennon immediately after listening to 'Only The Lonely'. The Beatle later recalled: **"That was my attempt at writing a Roy Orbison song."**

18 May 1963. Roy Orbison was booked to replace original headliner Duane Eddy on The Beatles' third UK Tour; also starring Gerry and The Pacemakers. Orbison flew into London Heathrow from the US and headed straight for the Adelphi Cinema, in Slough, Bucks, some 20 miles from London, for the first night of the tour. Notable for the first time he ever wore his prescription sunglasses on stage—that soon after became his trademark. | The Beatles were riding high in the British charts—'Beatlemania' was starting to erupt all across the country—the big question: "Who should close the show?"

Roy Orbison—the advertised 'headliner'—gave way to the inevitable and agreed instead to close the first half. Booked to perform for 15-minutes—on that first night of the tour he played a full 30-minute set that set the place on a roar—resulting in a standing ovation entirely without precedent. (And I know that to be true because I was there in the audience—and on my feet—clapping and cheering and yelling for more. The photo on the cover of this very book, taken that very evening, when The Beatles were presented with a Silver *Disc* for 'From Me To You' by Gerry Marsden of Gerry and The Pacemakers.) |

Roy Orbison later recounted how The Beatles—John and Paul—grabbed him by the arms and held him back; not allowing him to take that first curtain call in Slough. **"So there I was...held captive by The Beatles...John saying 'Yankee Go Home'...after that we had a good time together".** | He went on to become a lifelong friend of The Beatles—his later career given a much-deserved boost when George Harrison invited him to join The Traveling Wilburys.

A truly original talent and, by all accounts, a truly nice guy.

BLUES | R&B | GOSPEL | SOUL

RAY CHARLES | *'Genius'*
Singer | Songwriter| Musician | Composer

I Got a Woman | What'd I Say | Georgia on My Mind | Hit the Road Jack | Unchain My Heart | I Can't Stop Loving You

Ray Charles Robinson | September 23, 1930 - June 10, 2004 | Born Albany, Georgia, USA | Major figure in R&B, Soul, Blues, Gospel, Country, Jazz, Pop, and Rock 'n' Roll | Cited Nat King Cole as primary influence. | Called "Brother Ray" by friends and fellow musicians | Frank Sinatra called Ray Charles—"the only true genius in show business". | Ray Charles came from a poor sharecropper family. Abandoned by his father. Brought up by his mother. His love of music sparked at the age of three by the sound of 'Boogie Woogie' played on an old upright piano by family friend Wylie Pitman—the man who first taught the boy how to play piano. | Ray Charles began to lose his sight at age four and was blind from the time he was seven—when he attended a special school for the deaf and the blind. | 1937-1945 He was taught how to read music using braille and to play piano compositions of Bach, Mozart, and Beethoven by 'gifted' music teacher—Mrs. Lawrence. | He developed interest in jazz, blues, and country music he heard on the radio. Began to perform at school functions and on local radio. | Graduated to playing in and writing arrangements for local bands—moved to Orlando—then Tampa—and ultimately followed a fellow musician to Seattle, Washington

March, 1948. Met 15-year-old Quincy Jones—beginning of lifelong friendship. | April, 1949. Recorded 'Confession Blues'—with trio he'd formed—that reached No. 2 *Billboard* R&B chart—his first nationwide hit. | 1950. Moved to Los Angeles. | Toured as musical director for various blues-based bands. | Recorded a number R&B 'Top Ten' hits | 1953. Signed to Atlantic Records by Ahmet Ertegün. 'Mess Around' his first hit for Atlantic. | 1954. Had a hit with 'It Should Have Been Me'. | Wrote and recorded 'I Got a Woman'. Reached No. 2 R&B chart. | Continued writing and recording R&B hits until 1959's miraculous 'What'd I Say' stormed into *Billboard* 'Top Ten'. | 1958-9. Headlined Apollo Theater, New York—Uptown Theater, Philadelphia—Newport Jazz Festival | 1959. Released cover of Hank Snow's 'I'm Movin' On'—his first 'country' hit. | Recorded three more albums for Atlantic: *The Genius After Hours*—a jazz album released 1961—*The Genius Sings the Blues*—a blues record also released 1961—and *The Genius of Ray Charles*—a 'pop themed' big band record—his first 'Top 20' album.

1960. Signed with ABC-Paramount Records—in a cannily well-crafted lucrative deal—one of the first black musicians ever to be granted artistic control by mainstream record company—and ownership of his original recording tapes. | 1960 'Georgia on My Mind'—first hit single for ABC-Paramount—received national acclaim—won four Grammy Awards | 1961. Expanded his small 'road' ensemble into a full-scale big band. Released 'Hit the Road Jack' and 'Unchain My Heart' | 1962. *Modern Sounds in Country and Western Music* and—its sequel album—*Modern Sounds in Country and Western Music, Vol. 2*—helped usher 'country' into the musical mainstream. | 1962. 'I Can't Stop Loving You' topped both US 'Pop' and R&B charts—gave him his only No.1 record in UK.

1962. Founded his own record label—Tangerine Records—promoted and distributed by ABC-Paramount. Released 'I Can't Stop Loving You'. | 1963. Top 10 'Pop' Hits with 'Busted' and 'Take These Chains from My Heart' | 1967. Top 20 Hit with 'Here We Go Again' | 1967-1983 continued to record singles and albums across all genres. | 1975. His cover of Stevie Wonder's 'Living for the City' won him yet another Grammy. | 1977-1980. Re-signed with Atlantic. | 1983. Signed with Columbia Records | 1986. One of the first inductees into the *Rock & Roll Hall of Fame*. Same year—received 'Kennedy Center Honors'. | 2002. *Rolling Stone* ranked Ray Charles No.10 on its list of '*100 Greatest Artists of All Time*' | 2008 No.2 '*100 Greatest Singers of All Time*' | Ray Charles died—June 10, 2004—aged 73.

| Side Bar | Ray Charles and The Beatles | A major influence on The Beatles—and just about everyone else in pop music. | One of the great 'Stars of Rock 'n' Roll' who also appeared at the 'opening' of Star-Club, Hamburg—during the group's initial 7-week season. | The Beatles' early repertoire included many Ray Charles' 'standards': 'I Got A Woman', Don't Let The Sun Catch You Cryin', 'Hallelujah, I Just Love Her So', and the incomparable 'What'd I Say'—which the group would sometimes make last for a good half an hour and more all the while driving the audience into a state of unreleased frenzy.

'FATS' DOMINO | *The Fat Man*
Piano Player | Singer | Songwriter

The Fat Man | My Blue Heaven | Reelin' 'n' Rockin' | Blueberry Hill | Walking To New Orleans | Blue Monday | Jambalaya | Whole Lotta Loving | Ain't That A Shame | I'm Walkin'

Antoine 'Fats' Domino, Jr. | 26 February 1928 - 24 October 2017 | Born New Orleans, Louisiana, USA | Of French Creole descent. | In 1950s and 1960s—unquestionably one of the biggest and most influential rhythm and blues and rock 'n' roll artists. | During his recording career—sold sixty-five million singles—had thirty-five 'Top 40' singles in US Charts. Twenty-three records went gold. Twenty-two of his singles for Imperial Records were double-sided hits. | His exuberant, bouncy, 'boogie-woogie piano' style coupled with a warm, amiable, "instantly likeable" voice helped him sell more records than any other rock 'n' roll act in the 1950s—save for Elvis Presley. | During a time of deeply entrenched racial segregation he was also one of the first R&B artists to gain popularity with white audiences.

'Fats' Domino grew up in a musical family. His father was a violinist. Learned piano from his brother-in-law—jazz banjo player—Harrison Verrett. | Began playing New Orleans 'honky tonks' as a teenager. Given nickname "Fats" by bandleader Bill Diamond who likened young Antoine's piano-playing technique to 'Fats' Waller and 'Fats' Pichon. | Mid-1940s. 'Discovered' by trumpeter, bandleader, and Imperial Records A&R man Dave Bartholomew. | 1949. 'The Fat Man'—a rock 'n' roll 'backbeat' first—released by Imperial Records in December—and widely considered the first rock-and-roll record ever—went on to sell over a million copies by 1951. | 1955. His breakthrough record 'Ain't That A Shame' reached 'Top 10'—but Pat Boone's "milksop" cover version hit No. 1.

1956. His version of 'Blueberry Hill', written in 1927 and already recorded by Gene Autry, Louis Armstrong *et al* reached No. 1 R&B Charts and No. 2 US 'Top 40'. Said 'Fats': *"I just sing it the way it would fit me and it came out great for me."* By the following year 'Blueberry Hill' had sold more than 5 million copies worldwide. |1956-62. Followed up with a series of what would become rock 'n' roll classics: 'Walking to New Orleans,' 'Blue Monday' *et al.* | 1956. One of the first black artists to appear on '*The Ed Sullivan Show*' where he performed 'Blueberry Hill' with his signature twinkle and smile. The very same year he also appeared in the film '*Shake, Rattle & Rock*'. And co-starred in '*The Girl Can't Help It*' with Little Richard, Eddie Cochran, Gene Vincent, and a milk-bottle erupting Jane Mansfield.

1963. Imperial Records was sold. 'Fats' signed to ABC-Paramount Records. Released 11 singles for the label but only one 'Top 40' entry—'Red Sails in the Sunset'. | 1965. Signed to Mercury Records—reuniting with producer co-writer Dave Bartholomew. | 1968. His final 'Top 100' single was a cover of The Beatles' 'Lady Madonna' | 1986. One of the first 'stars' inducted into *Rock and Roll Hall of Fame* | 1987. Received Grammy lifetime achievement award | 1998. National Medal of Arts. | 2004. *Rolling Stone* ranked 'Fats' Domino No. 25 on its list of '*100 Greatest Artists of All Time*'. | 'Fats' Domino died of natural causes—aged 89—at home in Harvey, Louisiana. Much lamented.

| **Side Bar** | '**Fats' Domino and Elvis Presley** | Elvis—"*The King*"—introduced 'Fats' at his very first Las Vegas concert: *"This gentleman was a huge influence on me when I started out."* He pointed to 'Fats': *"That's the real king of rock and roll."* (And you know what John Lennon thought about Elvis.)

| Side Bar | **'Fats' Domino and The Beatles** | The Beatles were hugely influenced by 'Fats' Domino. | George Harrison said the first rock 'n' roll song he ever heard was 'Fats' Domino's 'I'm in Love Again'. | John Lennon and Paul McCartney recorded a number of his songs. | Paul McCartney said 'Fats' Domino was one of his all-time favourite rock 'n' roll singers: *"He thrilled us in our early days in Liverpool. His hit records like 'Ain't That A Shame', 'Blueberry Hill', 'I'm In Love Again' and many others introduced us to the sounds of New Orleans rock 'n' roll. His voice, piano playing, and musical style was a huge influence on us and his appearance in the film 'The Girl Can't Help It' was truly magnificent."*

Paul also said 'Fats' Domino was the inspiration for him writing 'Lady Madonna'. The one and only 'Fat Man' then returned the compliment by recording the song. His 1968 cover of 'Lady Madonna'—for his Reprise album *Fats Is Back*—his last 'Top 100' single. The album also featured his cover of The Beatles' 'Lovely Rita'. | 1969. 'Fats' did a real rock 'n' rollin' cover of John Lennon's 'Everybody's Got Something to Hide Except For Me and My Monkey'—from *The White Album*.

1975. John Lennon covered 'Fats' Domino's composition 'Ain't That A Shame' on *Rock 'n' Roll*—his tribute album to the musicians who'd influenced him. | 2007. *Going Home: A Tribute to Fats Domino*—John Lennon's 1975 cover of 'Ain't That A Shame' opened an album made up of newly-recorded versions of 'Fats' Domino songs. Paul McCartney performed 'I Want To Walk You Home'. | Other musicians paying and playing tribute on the album included B.B. King, Norah Jones, Willie Nelson, Tom Petty, Neil Young, Elton John, Herbie Hancock.

| Side Bar | **The Beatles meet 'Fats' Domino** | 16 September 1964. The Beatles were huge fans of 'Fats' Domino and very much wanted to meet him—if at all possible—while in New Orleans during their gruelling 25-concert, 30-day tour. | It was New Orleans' own Clarence 'Frogman' Henry—one of the opening acts for the City Park Stadium concert—having just replaced the Righteous Brothers—who managed to track down the ever reclusive 'Fat Man' and his manager, Bob Astor—and quickly

and quietly ferried them to a trailer parked behind the stadium being used as 'green room'. (There's a great photograph of 'Fats' and The Beatles, in their concert performance clothes, jamming together.) | As John Lennon would later recall: *"We hung out for about an hour... took pictures for his kids... had a sing-song with him."* | When 'Fats' Domino was later asked by a local TV station interviewer if he got to meet The Beatles when they were in New Orleans, 'Fats' replied: *"No, they got to meet me."* Shades of when The Beatles met another legend, the great Muhammad Ali.

BO DIDDLEY | *'The Originator'*
R&B Singer | **Guitarist** | **Songwriter** | **Music Producer** | **Technical Innovator**

I'm a Man | *Bo Diddley* | *Pretty Thing* | *Mona* | *You Can't Judge a Book by the Cover* | *Before You Accuse Me* | *Who Do You Love?* | *Before You Accuse Me* | *Road Runner* | *Hey Bo Diddley*

Ellas Otha Bates. | December 30, 1928 - June 2, 2008 | Born in McComb, Mississippi, USA | Bo Diddley played key role in the transition from the blues to rock 'n' roll. | Invented a 'signature' beat that forever changed rock music. | 1955. The legendary American DJ Alan Freed—the man who coined the phrase "rock 'n' roll"—considered Bo Diddley the first true exponent of the style. Playing the song 'Bo Diddley'—the musician's first ever single for Chess Records—Freed declared: *"Here's a man with an original sound...an original beat...that's gonna rock 'n' roll you right out of your seat."*

Bo Diddley was adopted and raised by his mother's cousin and so became Ellas McDaniel. | The McDaniel family moved to South Side of Chicago | Studied trombone and violin—so proficient on violin Chicago's Ebenezer Baptist Church musical director invited him to join orchestra. Performed with them until he was 18; then took up the guitar. | Inspired by John Lee Hooker. As well as Gene Autry, the singing cowboy. *

THE BEATLES IN LIVERPOOL, HAMBURG, LONDON

Played music on street corners to supplement income as carpenter and mechanic. | Formed a band called the Hipsters—later the Langley Avenue Jive Cats—in high school. | 1951. Landed regular spot at 708 Club, on Chicago's South Side. Repertoire heavily influenced by Louis Jordan, John Lee Hooker, and Muddy Waters. | Took stage name "Bo Diddley" | 1954. Teamed with fellow musicians to record demos of his compositions 'I'm a Man' and 'Bo Diddley'.

1955. Signed with Checker label—subsidiary of Chess Records, Chicago. A contemporary of Chuck Berry, Howlin' Wolf, and Muddy Waters. | Re-recorded his demo songs at Chess Studios with backing ensemble—Otis Spann (piano)—Lester Davenport (harmonica)—Frank Kirkland (drums)—Jerome Green (maracas). | Resulting record released March 1955—with 'Bo Diddley' as the A-side—sure-fire No.1 R&B hit. | That same year was the first black artist to appear on CBS-TV's *The Ed Sullivan Show* | Top 20 R&B hits with 'Pretty Thing' (1956), 'Say Man' (1959), 'Road Runner' (1960), 'You Can't Judge a Book by the Cover' (1962).

Checker Records released eleven full-length Bo Diddley albums between 1958 and 1963 including *Bo Diddley Is a Gunslinger* and *Have Guitar, Will Travel*. All of which helped the musician break through as a "crossover artist with white audiences" | He wrote many songs for himself and others. 1956 co-wrote 'Love Is Strange' with guitarist Jody Williams—a hit for Mickey & Sylvia in 1957 and the Everly Brothers in 1965. | Moved to Washington, DC—set up recording studio in basement of his home; produced and recorded commercial releases. Marvin Gaye, member of a local Doo Wop group, the Marquees, was one of his 'finds'.

His signature 'Bo Diddley beat', variously described as: *"a bump-and-grind shuffle" "a deceptively simple but repetitive five-accent; one-two-three, one-two; 'hambone' rhythm"* with *"a relentless syncopated beat drawn from a West African drum pattern and later African-American clapping rhyme"*—soon became a cornerstone of rock 'n' roll and rhythm and blues music.

Many of Bo Diddley's most famous songs have no chord changes—musicians play the same chord throughout—the music reduced to its basic rhythmic core; allowing the pulsing rhythm alone to create 'pure' driving' excitement. | His hard-pick, muted-string, choke-neck style rhythm guitar is utterly distinctive. As he once said: *"I play drum licks on the guitar."*

Pioneering electric guitarist—his incorporation of a 'tremolo' effect within his unique rhythmic playing style made him an icon to all would-be rock guitarists. | Also developed special guitar effects—including distortion and feedback—that brought 'new sounds' to 'live' performance as well as sound recording.

Bo Diddley is also justly famous for his many uniquely shaped 'signature' guitars, all of which he designed himself. From his first cigar box-shaped 'Twang Machine'—to his famous 'Flying-V'—and his rectangular-bodied 'Turbo 5-speed' with its own built-in envelope filter, flanger and delay.

A man ahead of his time in other ways—he included women musicians in his band—all of them top flight. And it's beyond questions that Bo Diddley influenced The Beatles—as well as many other rock luminaries such as Elvis Presley, Buddy Holly, the Rolling Stones, Eric Clapton, the Who, the Yardbirds, and Jimi Hendrix—and did so across many dimensions. As a number of rock historians have all attested: *"Bo Diddley's influence was so widespread; it's hard to imagine what rock 'n' roll would have sounded like without him."*

Indeed, Bo Diddley was a huge influence on British teenagers intent on discovering rhythm and blues and early rock 'n' roll records—especially after he toured the UK in 1963 with Little Richard and the Everly Brothers. The Rolling Stones—a relatively unknown band at the time—famous only in and around London—were the opening act for the tour. As Mick Jagger said years later: *"Bo Diddley was an enormous force in music and was a big influence on the Rolling Stones. He was very generous to us in our early years, and we learned a lot from him".*

1987. Inducted into the *Rock and Roll Hall of Fame.* | June 2, 2008. Bo Diddley died—age 79—at his home in Archer, Florida

| Side Bar | Bo Diddley and The Beatles | February 1964, at The Beatles' first ever press conference in the United States, having just landed at New York's JFK airport, a reporter yelled out: *"What are you most looking forward to seeing here in America, John?"* Without a moment's hesitation John Lennon shot back: *"Bo Diddley!"* | John Lennon was always intent on learning hot to play rhythm guitar with substance and force. He sought out Vinnie Ismail—a highly respected Somali-Irish musician in Liverpool—to help him get down to the nitty-gritty of playing rhythm guitar like the great Bo Diddley and Chuck Berry.

Buddy Holly used the Bo Diddley rhythm in 'Not Fade Away' and if was good enough for Buddy, you can bet your life it was good enough for John Lennon who, as a musician; and like his band-mates Paul McCartney and George Harrison; was always searching for ways to play harder, stronger, better.

1972. John Lennon and Yoko Ono produced the *Elephant's Memory* track 'Chuck & Bo' as a tribute song to Chuck Berry and Bo Diddley. | * Bo Diddley wasn't the only future rhythm and blues, rock 'n' roll, or rockabilly star to be influenced by the singing cowboy Gene Autry; Johnny Cash, Willie Nelson, Waylon Jennings, Kris Kristofferson, and James Taylor were, too. Though perhaps of greater relevance to this 'Side Bar', Ringo Starr, was as well. He's often said that Gene Autry was his first musical influence: *"I remember getting shivers up my back when he sang, 'South of the Border'"*

ARTHUR ALEXANDER | 'Soul' singer | Songwriter

Anna (Go To Him) | A Shot of Rhythm and Blues | Soldier of Love (Lay Down Your Arms) | Sally Sue Brown | You Better Move On | Every Day I Have to Cry Some

May 10, 1940 - June 9, 1993 | Born Sheffield, Alabama, USA. | Arthur Alexander's wonderful songs were covered by The Beatles, Gerry and the Pacemakers, the Rolling Stones, the Hollies, Dusty Springfield, Jerry Lee Lewis, Otis Redding, Tina Turner, Bob Dylan, Ry Cooder | 1960. Recorded first single 'Sally Sue Brown' under name of 'June' Alexander—short for 'Junior'. |

1962. First hit for Dot Records—'You Better Move On'—also first hit single recorded at famed Muscle Shoals studio. Released LP—*You Better Move On*. | While other artists continued to cover his songs his own career floundered. | 1965. Changed record labels—Sound Stage 7—to little or no avail—success still eluded him. |1972. Recorded album for Warner Brothers. Not a success. | 1975. 'Every Day I Have to Cry Some'—hit on US 'Pop' Charts for Buddah Records. Success short lived. Follow-up single 'Sharing The Night Together'—written by Ava Aldridge and Eddie Struzick—reached No. 92 on US R&B Charts. Again, success short lived. | Left the music business. Incredible as it may seem for such talent—he drove busses—the best way he could keep movin' on. | 1990. Inducted into Alabama Music Hall of Fame. | 1993. Began to perform again. Signed new recording and publishing contract. Recorded album *'Lonely Just Like Me'*. Performed in Nashville with new backing band. Suffered fatal heart attack just a few days later; a tragic ending to so talented a singer and songwriter.

| Side Bar | The Beatles and Arthur Alexander | The Beatles covered 'Anna (Go to Him)'—'Top Ten' Hit on US R&B Charts. | The Beatles also did 'live' recordings of 'Soldier of Love' and 'A Shot of Rhythm and Blues' for BBC Radio | 'Where Have You Been' was "unofficially" recorded 'live' on a portable tape-recorder at Star-Club, Hamburg, 1962.

"If The Beatles ever wanted a sound...it was R&B. That's what we used to listen to, what we used to like, and what we wanted to be like...'Black'...that was basically it...Arthur Alexander..."
— Paul McCartney

ROCK 'N' ROLL

ALAN FREED | *'King of the Moondoggers'* | American disc jockey | Rock 'n' Roll evangelist and promoter | The man who gave name to *"Rock 'n' Roll"* and who, in all probability, inspired the pre-Beatles group name, 'Johnny and The Moondogs'

THE BEATLES IN LIVERPOOL, HAMBURG, LONDON

The first white DJ in America to champion African-American rock 'n' roll and R&B artists. | Alan Freed's *'Rock 'n' Roll'* radio show—taped in US—air-mailed to Europe from New York—and broadcast to Britain via independent commercial radio station Radio Luxembourg. The star turn of each Saturday night's two-hour *Jubilee* 'teen-programming' segment—the last half-hour from 9:30 PM until 10:00 PM the only reliable source of authentic American rock 'n' roll. | Essential listening—it was where Little Richard or Chuck Berry were first heard in Britain—and one can only surmise that John Lennon and Paul McCartney tuned-in religiously—as did every other British teenage would-be rock 'n' roller with a pulse.

Albert James 'Alan' Freed | December 15, 1921 - January 20, 1965 | Born Windber, Pennsylvania, US. | Served US Army in World War Two. Disk jockey for Armed Forces Radio. | After the war worked at radio stations in Pennsylvania and Ohio. | 1951. Hosted radio show on WJW Cleveland sponsored by 'hip to the jive' local record-store owner Leo Mintz. Began playing original R&B records by African-American artists rather than white pop 'cover' versions. | He dubbed the mix of blues, rhythm and blues, and country music he played over the radio and in dance halls: *"Rock 'n' Roll"* *

Billed himself: *"King of the Moondoggers"* | Upbeat—yet up-close and confiding—he addressed his listeners as *"fellow hipsters"* all banded together in the love of truly authentic 'black music'. | The breakthrough—his radio-show—*Moondog's Rock 'N' Roll Party*—attracted a huge audience of white teenagers. | 1952. Promoted 'rock 'n' roll' dances and live concerts. His 'Moonglow Coronation Ball' in Cleveland attracted thousands—selling more tickets than there was space—caused a near riot. A 'breakout' event—now considered to have been the very first rock 'n' roll concert—it also attracted the attention of a major New York radio station. | 1953. Moved to New York and top radio station WINS but had to relinquish name 'Moondog' after a court case involving locally famous NY street musician of same name. | Undeterred he continued on with his evangelism for 'Rock 'n' Roll' and loudly championed artists such as Chuck Berry and 'Fats' Domino. | Put on big-name 'live' rock 'n' roll shows at the Paramount Theatre, Times Square—to racially mixed audiences—small steps that did much to bridge the segregation gap; the ticket demand always huge. | 1957-59. Hosted television pop shows: *Dance Party* on WNEW-TV and then *The Big Beat* on WABC-TV

1959. Out of the blue—the US Congress—never known for their love of rock 'n' roll—opened an investigation into 'payola' inside the broadcasting industry. Freed was charged with accepting cash and/or publishing rights to give airplay to specific records—mostly by small, independent labels. (Think about whose business that might have impacted. And start with the major record labels and their lobbyists. Just sayin') The resulting scandal and negative publicity—coupled with later charges of tax evasion—effectively destroyed Freed's career. He lost his radio show and was fired from his TV show. No major metro TV or radio station would then employ him. | 1960. 'Payola' was made illegal. | 1962. Freed pleaded guilty to two charges of commercial bribery. Received fine and a suspended sentence. | 1960-64. Managed to get work at small radio stations in Miami and Los Angeles—but the glory days were over.

Alan Freed appeared in a number of rock 'n' roll themed movies. 1956: *Rock Around the Clock*; *Rock, Rock, Rock* | 1957: *Mister Rock and Roll*; *Don't Knock the Rock* | 1959: *Go, Johnny Go!* | 1986. One of first group of people inducted into *Rock and Roll Hall of Fame* | 1988. Posthumously inducted into *National Radio Hall of Fame* | 1999. Story of his life told in made-for-TV movie: *Mr. Rock 'n' Roll: The Alan Freed Story* | Alan Freed died January 20, 1965, Palm Springs, California. He was 43 years old. | Thus are prophets treated in their own land.

| **Side Bar** | So who did come up with the term "rock 'n' roll"? *
A musician and close friend of longstanding; suffice to say I've long called him 'Bluesman'; points to The Boswell Sisters—a white, New Orleans Jazz inspired, close-harmony trio who recorded a song called '*Rock and Roll*' way back in 1934—although in allusion to the rock and rollin' motion of the sea. Which gives

us 'the words' admittedly but not 'the beat'. It's not until 1947 and 1948 that black artists Roy Brown and Bill Moore recorded *'Good Rockin' Tonight'* and *'We're Going To Rock, We're Going To Roll'*—the first in a full-on, post-war outpouring of the 'new' country-blues infused sound and arguably the true beginnings of *'Rock 'n' Roll'* as a 'style of music' and 'idea'. And it was Alan Freed who first, as it were, lassoed 'the sound' and who then helped popularise the term. So he deserves recognition for that, otherwise, academics and music aficionados none-withstanding, the very term *'Rock 'n' Roll'* might well have been lost to history.

And in that much like British Trad-Jazz musician, Ken Colyer, who alighted upon the slang term 'Skiffle' when he immersed himself in New Orleans Jazz and folklore. (Such a Jazz devotee; he signed on as a merchant seaman just to get his post-war British self across the Atlantic to go visit *"the Big Easy."*) Which is how any of us ever found out that 'Skiffle' was originally used to describe spontaneous 'rent' music parties in Chicago in the 1920s and '30s. 'Skiffle', the term he repurposed to describe the simplified form of Jazz; as expressed in 'black' country-blues songs; that took Britain by storm in the 1950s.

| **Side Bar** | John Lennon on Rock 'n' Roll | *"It's the music that inspired me to play music. There's nothing conceptually better than rock 'n' roll... because the best stuff is primitive enough and has no bullshit. It gets through to you; it got through to me, the only thing to get through to me of all the things that were happening when I was fifteen. Rock 'n' roll then was real; everything else was unreal. The thing about rock & roll, good rock 'n' roll... is that it's real. And realism gets through to you despite yourself. You recognize something in it, which is true, like all true art."*

| **Foot Note** | 'Jazz', 'Skiffle', and 'Rock 'n' Roll' were also well worn euphemisms for joyful and heated sexual congress between consenting adults, regardless of race, creed, or gender. Sex, of course, like the ever-ebullient primal 'beat' found in all African-American-derived music, another *"river from which all else flows."* Yet another reason to... **'Hail, Hail... Rock 'n' Roll'**

PART TWO – MUSIC INFLUENCES. THE MEDIA.

2 - African-American R&B

THE RIVER WITHOUT END...
Rhythm & Blues | Rock 'n' Roll | Motown | Soul *et al*

AFRICAN-AMERICAN MUSIC
African-American culture was the fount of all the greatest popular music forms of the Twentieth Century. An astonishing stream of inspired musical invention and expression: Ragtime; Dixieland; New Orleans Jazz; Big Band; Swing; Stride; Gospel; Jive; Jump Blues; Delta Blues; Chicago Blues; Rhythm and Blues; Boogie-Woogie; Do-Wop; Rock 'n' Roll; Modern Jazz; Bebop; Soul; Motown; Funk; Disco; House; Hip-Hop.

There's no question the early Beatles' sound owed much to black artists—musicians, singers, and songwriters. Yet, initially, like most young people in 1950s Britain—John Lennon, Paul McCartney, and George Harrison wouldn't have known the sound of American rock 'n' roll was really black 'rhythm and blues' being performed by white artists. Or that R&B, as it increasingly came to be called, had evolved from a blending of jazz, gospel, and blues. They could have cared less that *"Rock and Roll"* had been so named by a white American radio DJ named Alan Freed. The only thing that mattered was that Freed's pre-taped Saturday night *'Rock 'n' Roll'* radio show on Radio Luxembourg; featuring original black artists such as Little Richard and Chuck Berry, as opposed to anodyne cover versions by Pat Boone or Bill Haley; came through loud and clear over the family wireless-set in Liverpool. Mass produced portable transistor radios for every teenager still a few years away in UK.

Britain also didn't have sales charts separated by music genre or audience ethnicity; "Race" records as they were called in the United States from the 1930s through the early 1950s. So in the early days the group of young British teenagers who made up

The Beatles—or indeed the Quarrymen—wouldn't have focused on whether a recording artist was black or white. What mattered most was the sound; be it rock 'n' roll, rockabilly, country and western, or rhythm and blues. The records all spoke for themselves; to British ears the accents were 'all American', with no regional or racial or even gender bias. The cultural context of the music—whatever its origin—would have been as a mystery to them. They wouldn't have known The Angels who sang 'My Boyfriend's Back' were 'white' or that The Chiffons who sang 'He's So Fine' were 'black'. They were simply all-girl singing groups from—*"that great shining city on the hill"*—America. And just like The Cookies with 'Chains' or The Shirelles with 'Boys' or 'Baby It's You', it was the quality of the song in performance that caught their ear and got their attention. *Sans* colour. *Sans* race. *Sans* gender. The only questions: Would the song work for them? Would it lend itself to their style of harmonising? Would it add something truly distinctive to their performance song set? The fact they chose mostly 'black' music told its own story and The Beatles were quick to read between those lines and to learn.

The Beatles began as a cover band... and in the main chose to cover the very best African-American music they could find.
The early Beatles were first and foremost a cover band and were always on the look out for great songs—always listening for that something special. Be it a new rhythm pattern, different song structure, intriguing lyric, compelling harmony, or a single guitar riff—anything that could help them stand apart from all the other Liverpool groups. | They expanded their repertoire—song-by-song—finding that 'something special' as often as not on the 'B'-side of a 45rpm import disc from the US based Chess, American, Scepter, Cadence, Dot, or Motown record labels. | The group's constant desire to be different also being an early driver to John and Paul wanting to write their own songs. | Mid-1959. The Quarrymen skiffle group—comprising just John, Paul, and George—with Stuart Sutcliffe about to join as the group's bass guitarist—boasted a working repertoire of over 200 cover songs; a quarter of them covers of songs by black artists. Much of it rock 'n' roll by Little Richard and Chuck Berry—but increasingly

R&B songs by Ray Charles, 'Fats' Domino, Larry Williams, The Coasters, and Sonny Terry and Brownie McGhee.

Mid-1960. The Beatles—now with Pete Best on drums—underwent their baptism of fire in Hamburg's Indra Cabaret and Kaiserkeller clubs—playing almost every night for 16-weeks straight—racking up almost 500 performance hours on stage. | And by the time the group returned to Liverpool—and gave their earth-shaking performance at Litherland Town Hall on 27 December 1960—'rhythm and blues' cover songs comprised more than half of their working repertoire. The growing emphasis as much a reflection of John, Paul, and George's growing proficiency as musicians as the unique appeal of original songs by a whole coterie of black artists: The peerless vocal artistry of 'Soul' singers Smokey Robinson, Sam Cooke, and Arthur Alexander. The soulful sounds of the Miracles, the Isley Brothers, and the Donays—and Richie Barrett Lenny Welch, and Barrett Strong. Not to forget, of course, The Beatles always really love, love, loved the magical, close-harmonied, gospel-infused, ultra-cool sounds of the 'call-and-response', all-girl singing groups the Cookies, the Shirelles, the Chiffons, the Chantels, the Crystals, the Marvelettes, and the Ronnettes.

The Shirelles' 'Boys' one of The Beatles' all time favourites. John always used to sing 'Boys' before it became a signature song for Ringo. The Beatles simply didn't care it was originally a song about 'boys' sung by a group of girls. Spirit and soul trumped gender. As Paul McCartney later said: ***"We loved the song... loved the record so much. What it said was irrelevant; it was the spirit, the sound, the feeling; the sheer joy when you did that 'Bab-Shoo-Wap. Bab-Bab-Shoo-Wop'. That was the great fun of doing 'Boys'—there was really nothing else to touch it."***

R&B. Gospel. Rock 'n' Roll. Motown. Soul. In time The Beatles absorbed it all—and very consciously so—because they loved the spirit—the sound—the feeling—and the sheer joy of the music so very, very much. And who can blame them—there really was no other music that even came close to matching it.

The Beatles' choice of cover songs was no mere serendipity. The Beatles knew what worked with audiences and what didn't; feedback was immediate and the song-lists they compiled contributed massively to the group's early success on stage; as it did when they came to record professionally. They drew from a well of music that was full to the brim and overflowing.

In hindsight it may seem inevitable The Beatles increasingly "found their thrill" in R&B, Motown, and Soul, but the fact remains they first had to locate each artist—each song—then elect to cover it and make it their own. And in doing so they laid the framework of what would become their very own sound—as each cover song brought its own special colouring and shading to The Beatles' own evolving skills as song composers. How could it not? Every great artist; whether composer, painter, or writer; is influenced by who or what has gone before.

The Beatles always made a point to acknowledge their debt to black musicians, singers, and songwriters. The group's unabashed admiration for the music is evident from the many cover versions of rock 'n' roll and rhythm and blues songs written and recorded by black artists that they not only specifically chose to play 'live' in the clubs and dance halls of Hamburg and Liverpool—but also later recorded for EMI's Parlophone label and the BBC. And it's long a matter of record that no one was more pleased than The Beatles that their own growing success helped introduce many black artists—and their songs—to a worldwide audience.

It's been estimated that from 1960 to 1962 The Beatles added a cover song to their working playlist, on average, every eleven days; old songs discarded as new ones were adopted. Cover songs from all genres: Rock 'n' Roll; R&B; Soul; Rockabilly; Country—even a song from a Broadway musical—made up six tracks on each of three of the group's earliest albums: *Please Please Me*; *With The Beatles*; *Beatles For Sale*. And by the time they recorded their last ever cover song in 1965; Buck Owen's 'Act Naturally' for their album *Help!*; they'd amassed well over 300 songs by other artists in their performance repertoire; the majority of the songs originally by African-American artists.

"We didn't sing our own songs in the early days—they weren't good enough," John Lennon wrote in response to an opportunistic and deliberately provocative article published in the *New York Times* a couple of months after the breakup of The Beatles. The premise of—'So In The End, the Beatles Have Proved False Prophets'—was that The Beatles had forsaken the revolutionary promise of rock 'n' roll and, in the end, had merely ripped off black music. "Not so," said John. *"The one thing we always did was to make it known that they were black originals...we loved the music and wanted to spread it in any way we could."*

The Beatles weren't the only British band to cover African-American Rock 'n' Roll and R&B and Soul. | Many people in the US still refer—with no little awe—to "the British Invasion" of 'Beat' groups that occurred in 1964—after The Beatles had "conquered" America—but the simple truth is African-American music had long conquered the British Isles. | New Orleans Jazz brought joy to the Twenties. The 'swing' of the Big Bands—with or without crooners—helped alleviate the depression of Thirties and the uncertainties of world war during the early Forties. During the post-war years in Britain—with everyone determined to brush off the *"everything's on ration"* austerity blues and get out from under the unrelenting greyness of it all—nothing could come close to matching the siren call of "freedom from all your cares and woes" that came from America. There was a distinct hunger for "something to enjoy" and whatever your 'music fancy' the USA had it all and in abundance. In 1950s Britain there was a whole new generation of young people—the first ones ever with real money to spend—just ready and waiting to become avid devotees for every single style of American popular music.

The most diverse music scene in Britain at the time wasn't to be found in London, but in Liverpool. Hundreds of music groups of every kind—amateur and professional—burst onto the scene to fulfil the ever-growing demand. And every day—of every week—there were solo singers, duos, trios, quartets, combos, boy bands, girl bands playing every kind of music. Trad-Jazz.

Swing. 'Skiffle'. Rock 'n' Roll. Country. Western. Modern Jazz. Folk. Brass band. Merseyside had it all. And even though Merseyside could boast the greatest concentration of 'cowboy-inspired' country and western bands in the entire country, it was Rock 'n' Roll that ultimately came to the fore. And it was that, with copious sprinklings of R&B, that laid down the foundation of what would become the signature, tough-sounding, guitar and "atomic" drum-driven 'Beat' music—later known all around the world as 'Merseybeat'.

The whole rockin' 'Merseybeat' music scene: driven by Rory Storm and The Hurricanes | Gerry and The Pacemakers | The Big Three | 'Kingsize' Taylor & The Dominoes | The Searchers | The Swinging Blue Jeans | The Merseybeats | The Undertakers | The Fourmost | Lee Curtis and The All-Stars—and a host of other lesser-known groups. And The Beatles, of course, let's not forget The Beatles.

Bill Harry—founder and editor of *Mersey Beat*—and Bob Wooler—music promoter and resident DJ at the Cavern Club—once tried to estimate the number of 'Beat' groups they'd each encountered during the rise of the 'Merseybeat' sound. It came close to five hundred—a truly astonishing amount of 'homegrown' talent. | UK Tours by American and British 'stars' of rock 'n' roll were staged in theatres, cinemas, and stadiums. | Local 'star' groups appeared in ballrooms, nightclubs, and working-men's clubs—overflowed into Jazz cellar clubs, coffee bars, pubs, local cinemas, church halls, village halls—impromptu jive hives—even skating rinks.

The 'blues' and growing R&B scene was mostly London-based: with big 'blues' pockets as far afield as Birmingham, Newcastle, and Belfast. And just as happened with rock 'n' roll in Liverpool; it grew out of smoky Jazz cellars and small over-crowded clubs. | Among the first London blues bands of note; the ones that paved the way for everyone else: Alexis Korner Blues Incorporated | John Mayall's Bluesbreakers | The Cyril Davis All Stars.

Followed hard on, of course, by The Rolling Stones. And The Yardbirds; featuring Eric Clapton, then Jeff Beck, and then Jimmy Page. | The Who or The High Numbers as they originally called themselves. | Long John Baldry and the Hoochie Coochie Men, that with the later addition of Rod Stewart, Julie Driscoll, and Brian Auger became 'Steampacket'.

Also not forgetting, Mod-London's finest, the one and only Georgie Fame and The Blue Flames. And the countless other 'blues' groups to be found up and down the country, arguably the most outstanding: The Spencer Davis Group from Birmingham | The Animals from Newcastle | Them from Belfast.

Specialist pure 'blues' and R&B clubs sprung up in and around London: 100-Club | The Marquee | The Flamingo all in central London. | The 'Ealing Jazz Club' out on the western fringes of the city. | Eel-Pie Island out in Twickenham. | The Crawdaddy in Richmond. | The Ricky-Tick Club in Windsor.

As for 'Soul': One of the first and most exciting 'Soul' groups on the London scene were Geno Washington and The Ram Jam Band. Geno Washington, a black USAF serviceman based in England—who moonlighted in various London clubs—proved to be so popular with audiences that when he was discharged, from active service back in the US, was immediately invited to return to England to front The Ram Jam Band again. As it was felt the only proper way to present and interpret the authentic sound of African-American 'Soul' music was with an American-born singer and 'front-man'. Such was the respect 'the kids' in Britain had for the authentic sound of 'Soul'—as in R-E-S-P-E-C-T.

All of it only made possible by the all-embracing, life-affirming sounds of African-American Jazz in all its many forms, all the many manifestations of the Blues, R&B, Rock 'n' Roll, Soul *et al*.

"Praise the Lord, oh, praise the Lord"

PART TWO—MUSIC INFLUENCES. THE MEDIA.

3 - British Rock 'n' Roll

THE TEN RESTLESS, REBELLIOUS, ROCKIN' YEARS THAT PRECEDED THE BEATLES

'C'mon pretty baby let's a'move it and a'groove it...'

We have to start with **'Skiffle'**, once described by the great Pete Frame as: *"the bastard offspring of traditional, New Orleans-style jazz."* And hugely important, as Britain's own homegrown Rock 'n' Roll revolution evolved from out of it. So there's also a bit on Ken Colyer, the British jazz musician who, at the turn of the 1950s, first alighted upon the name 'Skiffle'.

As 'Skiffle' led directly to Rock 'n' Roll; we next visit—**The 2i's Coffee Bar**—*the* coffee bar cellar 'club' in London's Soho, where 'Rock 'n' Roll' first started in Britain.

All of which leads us straight to the man who all but single-handedly paved the way for British Rock 'n' Roll—'The Skiffle King', himself, **Mr. Lonnie Donegan**, the man Queen guitarist Brian May once eulogized as having been *"the very cornerstone of English blues and rock."*

All followed hard on by some of the key names in British Rock 'n' Roll and Rock 'n' Pop including: Britain's first real Rock 'n' Roll manager; Britain's first Rock 'n' Roll TV producer; Britain's first *bona fide* genius audio engineer cum record producer. As well as many of *"the toppermost of the poppermost"* singers and backing bands who always tend to pop up when you start delving into *"the ten restless rockin' years"* before The Beatles burst out of Liverpool and onto the British Rock 'n' Pop scene.

'It's rhythm that gets into your heart and soul... Well let me tell you baby it's called rock 'n' roll'

'SKIFFLE' | ***The Birth of British Rock 'n' Roll*** | 'Skiffle'—one contemporary British music critic wrote: *"is just a simplification of Jazz."* Written, somewhat surprisingly given the times, not to dismiss *"the simple form of rhythmic music"* but rather to explain one of the main reasons for 'Skiffle's extraordinary popularity and success. And that 'Skiffle' in doing away with the need of expensive musical instruments—when music-making was entirely in the hands of a small group of professionals—and important this: *"The poor man's Jazz was made available to everyone."* So 'Skiffle' didn't just come from out the blue, it grew out of a post-war British jazz scene that had moved away from Big-Band 'swing' music; popular before and during the war; and stepped back to the more halcyon days of authentic traditional New Orleans 'Dixieland' jazz.

Among the 'Trad-Jazz' bands around London in the early 1950s; trumpet, trombone, clarinet, banjo, bass, drums—and the odd piano; all blowing up a storm; were Ken Colyer's Jazzmen. Formed in 1953 when Colyer, having not long returned from New Orleans, was invited by Chris Barber and a group of musicians to be trumpet 'chair' and become leader of the band. | It was Ken Colyer who then plucked the name 'Skiffle' from out of jazz folklore to describe the much simpler, but still totally authentic American country-blues music the band's resident banjo player, Lonnie Donegan, performed during intervals between sets. A necessary sleight of hand meant to mollify the duffle-coated Trad-Jazz purists in the audience; of which there were many in tradition-bound Britain. (Something John Lennon had to contend with when The Quarrymen skiffle group first played The Cavern and also when he attended Liverpool Art College.)

During the 'Skiffle Breaks' as they were called Lonnie Donegan would put down his banjo and pick up his guitar and—accompanied on washboard and tea-chest bass—would sing a variety of *"charming and intimate ballads, Blues, and work-songs."* Audiences lapped it up—with the songs of Huddy 'Leadbelly' Ledbetter becoming particular favourites. So much so 'Skiffle Breaks' began to rival the Trad-Jazz music sets in popularity. | As a result Ken Colyer, a noted Jazz purist, left the band in the

Spring of 1954; although others in the band insist they left him; and trombonist Chris Barber resumed the leadership and Pat Halcox replaced Colyer on cornet and trumpet.

In late 1955 Chris Barber's Jazz Band, under the name the 'Lonnie Donegan Skiffle Group', released a fast-tempo version of Leadbelly's 'Rock Island Line' with 'John Henry' on the B-side. The record spent eight months in the UK Top 20—peaking at No. 6 (No. 8 in the US). It was the first debut record to go gold in Britain—went on to sell over a million copies worldwide—and single-handedly (a deliberate pun) set off the skiffle craze.

It's no exaggeration to say 'Skiffle' hit the youth of post-war Britain like a whirlwind of Biblical proportions. Some commentators even referred to it as *"a plague."* True. As it caught on, it helped sow the seeds of a seemingly very un-British rebellious attitude; a 'new-style of freedom' in lifestyle, clothes, hairstyles that to many was the very antithesis of the country's age-old system of class deference and its *'Keep Calm and Carry On'* stiff-upper-lip wartime spirit. Yet to the coming generation, anything that helped get you out from under the drab unrelenting austerity of post-war Britain was all to the good.

The key take-away in all this—as it touches on The Beatles—'the Skiffle boom' made an entire generation of British working-class kids realise music wasn't strictly the preserve of professional musicians or only for the middle and upper classes to indulge in—they could make music themselves; by and for themselves. And once that particular cat was out of the proverbial bag, it was never ever going to be stuffed back in again. | No music theory necessary—no music teaching required—all anyone needed to play 'Skiffle' was a banjo—maybe a guitar—a tea-chest bass (with attendant broomstick handle and length of string)—a washboard and supply of metal thimbles—a very rudimentary grasp of rhythm—someone with a passable voice—and the urge to get up and have a go. And you had yourself a 'Skiffle' group. Even if only in unwitting preparation for a magical moment one summer afternoon on the back of a lorry at a village church fête in a leafy suburb of Liverpool—when skiffle-crazed John Lennon met rock 'n' roll mad Paul McCartney.

It's been estimated there were as many as 50,000 'Skiffle' groups in Britain at the time. Little wonder then that 'Skiffle' was the genesis of almost every 'Beat Group' that ever played on Merseyside—or anywhere else in Britain—during those hallowed times in rock history. | And even as Elvis Presley, Gene Vincent, Eddie Cochran, Buddy Holly—and Rock 'n' Roll—grew and grew in popularity and influence and 'Skiffle' faded away to be all but eclipsed forever—and all the banjos, tea-chests, and washboards were cast aside—the kids were alright—they still had a firm grip on their guitars—they still had a firm hold on the extraordinarily freeing idea of *"three chords and a dream."*

Rave on.

| Side Bar | 'Skiffle' and The Quarrymen | If 'Skiffle' did nothing else, it encouraged amateurs to have ago at making music and one of many 'Skiffle' groups that got together in the wake of Lonnie Donegan was The Quarrymen—formed in March 1957 by John Lennon. | John Lennon - vocals, guitar, Eric Griffiths - guitar, Rod Davies - banjo, Pete Shotton - washboard, Colin Hanton - drums, Len Garry - tea chest bass | Lonnie Donegan's single 'Puttin' On the Style' b/w 'Gamblin' Man' was high in the UK Charts and soon to hit No.1—when The Quarrymen performed at St. Peter's Parish Church fête, in the village of Woolton, in Liverpool, 6 July 1957. The day 16-year old John Lennon met 15-year old Paul McCartney. | In between The Quarrymen's afternoon performance and evening performances—Ivan Vaughan, a mutual friend—and sometime Quarryman tea-chest bass player—introduced Paul to John. | Paul showed John how to tune his guitar—not in G-banjo tuning but in E-A-D-G-B-E standard tuning. | Paul then not only ripped through Gene Vincent's 'Be-Bop-A-Lula' and Eddie Cochran's 'Twenty Flight Rock'—singing and playing note perfectly—but a whole medley of Little Richard hits. John was suitably impressed and—through another mutual friend—later invited Paul to join his 'Skiffle' band—"to make it stronger...make it better". | The move from 'Skiffle' to Rock 'n' Roll now all but inevitable—prompted banjo player Rod Davies to leave the group in February 1958.

This gave Paul McCartney the perfect opportunity to introduce his friend and former schoolmate, George Harrison, to John Lennon, to help fill the gap in the Quarrymen's line-up. And the rest—as they say—is history. A surely a moment to pause and ponder another Beatles' 'What if?' equation: *No 'Skiffle', No Quarrymen. No Quarrymen, No Beatles.*

"There was this big 'skiffle' craze happening for a while in England, which was Lonnie Donegan. He set all them kids on the road. Everybody was in a 'skiffle' group. Some gave up, but the ones who didn't give up became all those bands of the early '60s...

All you needed was an acoustic guitar, a washboard with thimbles for percussion, and a tea chest; you know, a box that they used to ship tea in from India; and you just put a broom handle on it and a bit of string, and you had a bass...

You only needed two chords... jing-jinga-jing–jing-jinga-jing–jing-jinga-jing–jing-jinga-jing... and I think that is, basically, where I've always been at; I'm just a skiffler, you know. Now I do posh 'skiffle'. That's all it is."
— George Harrison

THE 2i's COFFEE BAR | SOHO, LONDON W1
The Birthplace Of British Rock 'n' Roll

The 'Revolution' Starts Here! | The 2i's Coffee Bar opened on Old Compton Street, in Soho, London, in 1956. | Most every major British rock 'n' pop music star of the late Fifties—including Tommy Steele and Cliff Richard—was discovered while performing there. It was very much the birthplace of the British rock 'n' roll—if not its entire pop music industry and culture. The coffee bar featured 'live' music in its cellar basement—performed on a tiny, 18-inch wide stage made of milk crates with wooden planks set on top of them.

It all started with skiffle groups, but the place really took off when it began to feature rock 'n' roll artists and for a time it was 'the most famous music venue in all of England' and attracted talent spotters and music promoters such as Jack Good, Larry Parnes, and Don Arden.

The coffee bar—at street level—boasted a long serving counter with a Gaggia espresso coffee machine—a sparkling attraction in itself in austerity-ridden post-war London—an orange juice dispenser—ditto—a sandwich display case—'meat paste' a speciality—and a bright, shiny jukebox spinning everyone's favourite US and UK rock 'n' roll platters. It had a few fixed seats but at evenings and weekends that parlayed into standing room for about 20 people—all the better to stand tall and look cool. At the rear of the coffee bar a narrow stairway led down to a 'dark and dismal cellar about the size of a large bedroom—approximately 25ft x 12ft—lit by a couple of fly-specked light bulbs. There was a single microphone—ex-army surplus kit from some forgotten war—and some speakers up on the wall.'

British rock stars who were discovered or that performed at The 2i's Coffee Bar include: Tommy Steele, The Vipers Skiffle Group, Cliff Richard, Hank Marvin, Bruce Welch, Brian Bennett, Tony Meehan, Jet Harris, Vince Eager, Terry Dene, Adam Faith, Joe Brown, Wee Willie Harris, Clem Cattini (The Tornados), Eden Kane, Lance Fortune, Tony Sheridan, Albert Lee, Johnny Kidd, Screaming Lord Sutch, Mickie Most (as one of the Most Brothers), and Big Jim Sullivan.

The BBC TV pop program *'Six-Five Special'* once broadcast live from The 2i's. Lionel Bart—who wrote many a Top Ten Hit and who composed the hit musical *'Oliver'* was once a waiter at The 2i's. Peter Grant—who went on to become Led Zeppelin's manager—also worked there as a bouncer.

And, of course, The 2i's was where Bruno Koschmider first met and hired Tony Sheridan—and the other Jets—to perform at his Kaiserkeller club in Hamburg. And where, a month or so later, in a desperate search for new rock 'n' roll talent, he bumped into Allan Williams, again, in a million to one chance meeting. Williams, down in London for the day to try get work for Derry and The Seniors. Koschmider saw the group perform, was most impressed, and immediately arranged with Williams for them to come play the Kaiserkeller. And so they became the very first Liverpool 'beat' group to go out to Hamburg; paving the way for the very next group to seek their fortune there... The Beatles.

THE MOVERS AND THE SHAKERS

Lonnie Donegan | Larry Parnes | Jack Good | Joe Meek | Norrie Paramor | Tommy Steele | Cliff Richard and The Shadows | Billy Fury and The Tornados | Adam Faith | Marty Wilde and The Wildcats | The Vernons Girls | Johnny Gentle and the Silver Beetles | Joe Brown and The Bruvvers | Johnny Kidd & the Pirates | Brian Poole and The Tremeloes

LONNIE DONEGAN | *'The King of Skiffle'*
Musician | Singer | Songwriter | Entertainer

Don't You Rock Me Daddy-O | *Cumberland Gap* | *Puttin' on the Style* | *Gamblin' Man* | *I'm Just a Rolling Stone* | *Jack O' Diamonds* | *Midnight Special* | *Tom Dooley*

Much of 'Skiffle's impact was due to Lonnie Donegan—who's since been called "Britain's first musical superstar". Before The Beatles—he was Britain's most successful recording artist. And it well could be argued that The Quarrymen 'Skiffle' group—the all-important precursors to The Beatles—might never have come into being without him and his 'Skiffle' recordings. And in that he was also a singular influence on many other British rock 'n' pop stars of the 1960s. | Anthony James Donegan MBE | Born Glasgow, Scotland. 29 April 1931 - 3 November 2002 | Son of a musician—his family moved to East Ham, London when he was two years of age. | In the early 1950s he joined Ken Colyer's Jazzmen as a banjo player and guitarist. When the band took a break between sets of 'authentic' New-Orleans-style 'Dixieland' Jazz—Donegan picked up his guitar and—with two other band members on washboard and tea-chest bass—and sang a selection of American-style country-blues, folk and work-songs. The intervals—called 'Skiffle Breaks' on posters for the Jazz band's appearances—proved to be such a hit with audiences they began to rival the advertised main-attraction—the 'Dixieland Jazz' sets. | The band's leader—Ken Colyer—a brilliant Jazz trumpeter but also very much a music purist—left the group and Chris Barber—another very accomplished trumpet player—took over.

December 1955. The Chris Barber Band—under the name the 'Lonnie Donegan Skiffle Group'—released their version of Leadbelly's 'Rock Island Line' b/w 'John Henry'. It was a huge hit. The first debut record to go gold in the UK. It ultimately sold more than three million copies. | Lonnie Donegan was also the first British male singer to have two 'Top Ten' hits in the US *Billboard* Charts. | His first records with the Chris Barber Jazz Band were for Decca—and then EMI's Columbia label. After which he left the band and signed with Pye Records—his next single 'Lost John' reached No. 2 in the UK Singles Chart. | He travelled to the United States. Appeared on *The Perry Como Show* and other television shows.

Returned to the UK, recorded his debut LP album, '*Lonnie Donegan Showcase*' which sold over a quarter of a million copies. | From 1956 to 1962 he had three UK No1 Hits—32 Singles in the UK Top Thirty; 24 of them in a row. Including: 'Does Your Chewing Gum Lose Its Flavour', 'Battle of New Orleans', 'My Old Man's A Dustman', 'I Wanna Go Home'. | He kept on touring almost to the very end. An extraordinary, although at times a somewhat prickly, individual, he's still very much revered by the countless British musicians who followed in his wake.

| **Side Bar** | **Lonnie Donegan and The Beatles** | 1956. When Lonnie Donegan appeared in a variety show at Liverpool's Empire Theatre—Paul McCartney sat in the audience captivated—enraptured. So much so it inspired him to want to learn the guitar—and his dad duly went out and bought him one for £15. | George Harrison borrowed money from his mum and dad to go the same show—only he went to every single show Lonnie Donegan played at the Empire. And when he fond out Lonnie Donegan was staying near where he lived—he went round and banged on the door until he got the performer's autograph. | When weeks later George went round Paul's house to sneak a peek at his 'Teach yourself to play the guitar in a day' book—one of the very first songs they managed to play was Lonnie Done-

gan's 'Don't You Rock Me Daddy-O' | John Lennon heard Lonnie Donegan on the evening pop station Radio Luxembourg— thought it sounded easy enough to play and asked his Aunt Mimi if she could buy him a guitar. He also went out and bought a 78-rpm disc of Lonnie Donegan's 'Rock Island Line'—all of which prompted him to form The Quarrymen. | And the last shall be first. The Beatle who took up 'Skiffle' first—much earlier than all the other Beatles—was Ringo Starr—who joined the Eddie Clayton Skiffle Group in 1957—the very same group that would go on to become Rory Storm and the Hurricanes.

"*Lonnie Donegan and 'Skiffle' just seemed made for me... it was easy music to play...and if you knew two or three chords...you were on your way.*"
— George Harrison

"*Lonnie Donegan was the first person we had heard of from Britain to get to the coveted No. 1 in the charts in America, and we studied his records avidly. We all bought guitars to be in a 'skiffle' group. He was the man.*"
— Paul McCartney

LARRY PARNES | *The Very First Rock 'n' Pop Impresario*
Show-business entrepreneur | Theatrical Producer

Laurence Maurice Parnes. 1930-1989. Born Willesden, London. | Britain's first major rock 'n' roll manager; famous for having discovered Tommy Steele at Soho's 2i's Coffee Bar in London in 1956—and then uncovering and grooming an entire stable of 'homegrown' teen idol talent that, pre-Beatles, were viewed as the cream of British male pop singers. | Early 'trademark touch' was to give each of 'his boys' a striking, ear-catching 'stage name'; image, more than content always being his order of the day. And so Tommy Hicks turned into Tommy Steele, Reg Patterson was re-christened Marty Wilde, and Ron Wycherley became Billy Fury; all of whom went on to enjoy considerable success in the British 'pop charts' of the late Fifties, early Sixties.

Parnes also handled Johnny Gentle (John Askew), Vince Eager (Roy Taylor), Dickie Pride (Richard Knellar), Duffy Power (Ray Howard), Lance Fortune (Chris Morris), Terry Dene (Terence Williams), Nelson Keene (Malcolm Holland), and Georgie Fame (Clive Powell). Also managed Tommy Bruce and the Cockney singer Joe Brown—the latter the only one of Parnes' stable of singers who flatly refused to change his name and said he'd rather give up the guitar than adopt the name 'Elmer Twitch'. (And who can blame him.)

With all that moody talent on his hands Larry Parnes pioneered and developed the idea of the 'rock 'n' pop package tour' in 1958 and sent his 'galaxy of stars' playing one-night stands all around Britain—everyone travelling through time and space on the same hired coach.

Parnes also promoted 'Stellar Name' concerts—including the 1960 Gene Vincent and Eddie Cochran UK tour. Their appearance at the Liverpool Empire was such a huge success that local entrepreneur Allan Williams arranged with Parnes for the two US rock stars to return to the city to do another show—this time at the much larger Liverpool Stadium. Tragically, before the Jacaranda Enterprises concert could take place, Eddie Cochran was killed in a road crash outside Bristol. But Gene Vincent recovered enough from his injuries to appear in Liverpool supported by a number of Merseyside's top beat bands—Rory Storm and The Hurricanes all but blowing the roof off.

Parnes was so impressed by all the Liverpool talent he asked Allan Williams to arrange an audition for a new backing band for Billy Fury. None of the groups that attended the audition got the job, but Parnes did later hire the Silver Beetles to back one of his singers, Johnny Gentle, on a nine-day tour of Scotland. | The pre-Hamburg Beatles gave it their all, but the tour wasn't anywhere near the stellar success they or Johnny Gentle had hoped for. And even Tommy Moore, the drummer they'd all but press-ganged to join the group, walked out of the Silver Beetles after constant disagreements with John Lennon.

Larry Parnes, ever eager to find new ways to get bums on seats, always had another teen idol and another rock tour to promote and he began to put on 'Summer Season' pop variety shows at popular British seaside resorts—another huge success. | All of which earned him the nickname of "Parnes, Shillings and Pence" within London show business circles—a direct allusion to the British currency of the time, which consisted of 'pounds, shillings and pence'—as he had a definite knack of making money and being extremely tight-fisted with it—all the better to keep his business empire growing. | In 1964 Parnes produced the film '*Mods And Rockers*' and in 1965 wrote and produced the story for the Billy Fury pop music film '*I've Gotta Horse*'. Larry Parnes and Brian Epstein never did do business together; Parnes having rebuffed an early offer to stage Beatles' concerts as being unprofitable. (A rather big mistake on his part.)

Parnes was later smart enough to realize the inexorable rise and rise of The Beatles—and other top-line beat groups such as The Rolling Stones, The Kinks, and The Who—meant that his own star in the 'pop world' could do nothing but wane and he abruptly changed course and devoted himself instead to London's West End theatre.

In 1967 he put on the play '*Fortune and Men's Eyes*'. He later helped produce the musical '*Half A Sixpence*' and staged a pantomime at the London Palladium—'*Cinderella*'—both of which starred Tommy Steele as a "superb all-round entertainer"—always the peek of achievement for any 'star' ever managed by Larry Parnes. And in 1972 he bought the Cambridge Theatre on a 12-year lease and began to promote shows that he thought better reflected his own distinct flamboyant style—among them the musicals '*Charley Girl*' and '*Chicago*'—the latter production starring the young, but already luminous Judy Dench.

As was the case with Brian Epstein—Larry Parnes was a homosexual at a time when being such was a criminal offence in Britain. But, unlike Brian Epstein, it seems Parnes accepted his condition as but a fact of life and wasn't overly tormented or tortured by it. Thankfully, a person's sexuality is no longer a relevant indicator of their character. And—like Brian Epstein—Larry Parnes should be remembered and applauded for the 'galaxy' of popular music, film, and theatre entertainments he brought to generations of people in Britain.

JACK GOOD | *Visionary Architect of British Rock 'n' Roll Television Producer* | *Musical Theatre Producer* | *Record Producer* | *Artist Manager* | *Musician* | *Sometime Painter*

Born Greenford, Middlesex, London. 7 August 1931 - 24 September 2017 | One of most influential people in British rock. | Grasped rock 'n' roll's essential 'revolutionary' appeal from the very start—then spearheaded the revolution. | All but invented the way 'pop music' is presented on television. | Produced Britain's first ever fast-paced TV 'teenage' pop music shows *Six-Five Special*, *Oh Boy!*, *Boy Meets Girls*, *Wham*. He also managed some of the UK's first real rock 'n' roll stars—Tommy Steele, Marty Wilde, Billy Fury, Jess Conrad—and Cliff Richard.

Completed 'National Service' in RAF. | Attends Oxford University to study philology. Becomes president debating society and Balliol drama society | Brief career as stage actor and comedian | Joins BBC as trainee producer | 1956. Saw audiences' wildly energetic reaction to *Rock Around the Clock* as sign of social revolution to come.

In 1957, he persuaded BBC to put on 'pop show' as if it was a teenage hop. *Six-Five Special*—his first TV show—mix of Trad-jazz, skiffle, rock 'n' roll—very first to target Britain's emerging 'youth' culture. | Show transmitted 'live'—"*over the points...over the points*"—Saturday evenings at 6:05 pm. Exciting new format—no studio sets—just performers and studio audience as part of non-stop spectacle—all seemingly impromptu—everything flowing from one performance to the next. | *Six-Five Special* quickly attracts 12 million viewers.

Still on low, basic salary despite huge success; shades of what would later happen with George Martin at EMI; Jack Good leaves to work for independent television and more money.

In June 1958 he launches *Oh Boy!* for ITV franchise holder ABC (Associated British Corporation). After trial broadcasts in Midlands, the new TV show goes national in direct competition with *Six-Five Special*. The BBC's *Six-Five Special* sticks to its established time and mix, but Jack Good goes full-on rock 'n' roll with *Oh Boy!*

The programmes were broadcast 'live' from the Hackney Empire, London. Each show lasting for just 26 minutes and—*Oh Boy!*—with no song lasting for more than a minute.

The TV show catches the hearts, minds, and souls of rock-thirsty British youth. Showcases Marty Wilde and Billy Fury—but makes star of Cliff Richard | Good directly responsible for Cliff Richard's breakthrough by resurrecting 'Move It'—the discarded B-side of the singer's latest single. 'Move It' becomes Cliff's—and the UK's—first *bona fide* rock 'n' roll hit | September 1959. ITV replaces hit show with "middle of the road" *Boy Meets Girls* fearing rock 'n' roll is on the way out.

1960. Follows up with TV pop show *Wham!*—featuring Billy Fury, Joe Brown, Jess Conrad | 1960. Produces Billy Fury's top-notch *The Sound of Fury* album | Member of Lord Rockingham's XI—band made up of seasoned London session players. | Recorded and backed other singers on a number of UK Chart hits. | Early 1960s. Writes column for *Disc* weekly UK pop magazine.

1962-64. Moves to New York. And then Los Angeles. Works as an actor. Appears in *Father Goose* with Cary Grant and Trevor Howard. *Strange Bedfellows* with Rock Hudson and Gina Lollobrigida. Sets up Jack Good Productions | April 1964. Produces *Around The Beatles*—60 minute TV special for ITV in London. | September 1964 - January 1966. Produces wildly successful US TV show *Shindig!* for ABC | *Shindig!* features The Beatles, the Beach Boys, the Supremes, James Brown, Bo Diddley, the Everly Brothers, Marvin Gaye, the Animals, Manfred Mann

1968. Enjoys great success as London theatrical producer. Created West End shows: *Catch My Soul*, based on Shakespeare's *Othello*; both musical and film (1974) | *Oh Boy!* | *Elvis the Musical*. (1977) | Produces TV specials for Mary Tyler Moore and Tina Turner | 1992. Jack Good's own life becomes the 'story' of West End musical: *Good Rockin' Tonite*

He sets up homes in New Mexico US and Oxfordshire UK | Then to top it all; takes up art, develops a talent for painting icons; not pop stars, religious themes; in line with also having a late-life conversion to Catholicism.

| Side Bar | Jack Good and The Beatles | 1964. *Around The Beatles*; a 60 minute TV special produced by Jack Good for ITV-Rediffusion London. | 28 April. Taped show ITV's Wembley Park Studios, London. | 6 May. Broadcast UK on ITV network. | 15 November. Broadcast in the US on ABC network.

The Beatles enact satirical version of Pyramus and Thisbe, 'a play within a play'—*Act V Scene I*—from Shakespeare's *A Midsummer Night's Dream*, in full Elizabethan costume and tights, no less. | The Beatles later performed 'Twist And Shout', 'Roll Over Beethoven', 'I Wanna Be Your Man', 'Long Tall Sally' 'Can't Buy Me Love'—and medley of 'Love Me Do', 'Please Please Me', 'From Me To You', 'She Loves You', 'I Want To Hold Your Hand'. Then finished off the show—and the audience—with rockin' version of The Isley Brothers' 1959 hit 'Shout'. | The show's working title—*John, Paul, George And Ringo*—not nearly all encompassing enough to hold Shakespeare as well as all the supporting acts; all shown in the round as if from the very Globe theatre itself; Cilla Black, P.J. Proby, Long John Baldry, the Vernons Girls, Millie, The Jets, and Sounds Incorporated | Last but not least—Brian Epstein—The Beatles' manager listed on 'end titles' as 'Production Associate'.

JOE MEEK | *Recording Pioneer and Audio Marvel*
Audio engineer | **Record producer** | **Songwriter**

Robert George 'Joe' Meek | 5 April 1929 - 3 February 1967 | One of the most innovative audio engineers and pop record producers of the Fifties and Sixties. The first British independent music producer of note. | Genius. Madman. Paranoid. Pioneer. Renegade. Tone deaf. Unable to read music. Truly one of the most enigmatic figures in 'British pop'. | Responsible for such soundbreaking Top Ten hits as 'Telstar', 'Johnny Remember Me', and 'Have I the Right'.

There was never anything meek about Joe Meek; he was always as relentless with himself as he was with others. And he pushed his singers and studio musicians; and whatever was the standard recording equipment and procedures of the time; to their very limits and beyond. And in the process pioneered many new recording techniques. So much so that his influence can still be very much heard today. Electronics mad; after having completed two-years of National Service at a radar station; in 1951, he was one of the first professional audio engineers to experiment with sound-on-sound overdubbing techniques. And, arguably, was one of the first; if not *the* first record producer; to exploit the use of the recording studio as an instrument.

In 1954 he was the first to put a microphone directly in front of—and sometimes even inside—the sound sources. The first to overload preamplifier inputs intentionally and print "in the red" sound signals to tape. He was also the first to use compressors and limiters creatively rather than as audio corrective tools.

In 1957 he was the first to build a compact spring reverb unit and to "flange" sounds using two synchronized tape recorders. | In 1959 the first to employ tape loops on commercial recordings. | In 1960 he set up his own recording studio, on Holloway Road, in North London and began an unfettered exploration of 'new sound' possibilities in which he utilised and fully embraced the use of early electronic keyboards.

In 1962 he had a worldwide hit with 'Telstar'; his 'electronic' sound and mind-bending composition designed to celebrate the first ever telecommunications satellite.

Joe Meek was a true audio visionary who made sonic breakthroughs that were uniquely his own and although not always scalable or even repeatable within the recording profession they were brilliant achievements all the same.

And even though at times he may have been as mad as a hatter—driven to whatever heights of fantasy or depression—it's truly sad to report that in the end he went out with a bang.

He killed his landlady and then himself—with a shotgun; the true circumstances of which are still in question. Such a tragic ending and such a terrible waste of such unfettered talent.

In 2009 the Music Producers Guild (UK) created 'The Joe Meek Award for Innovation in Production' in *"homage to the remarkable producer's pioneering spirit in recording music."*

| Side Bar | Sounds Familiar | As the Sixties progressed, and The Beatles demanded ever more and more from the "white-coated boffins" up at EMI's Abbey Road studios, the group unwittingly pushed the 'steeped in tradition' sound engineers—and their brilliant young successors—to reinvent many of Meek's revolutionary recording techniques. You only have to read the recollections and books by people such as Norman Smith, Ken Townsend, Ron Richards, and the excellent Geoff Emerick to realize it was more a case of 'great minds thinking alike', than any systematic process of copying Meek's earlier inventions.

NORRIE PARAMOR | *The record producer's record producer*
Head of A&R for EMI's Columbia Label

Norman William Paramor | 15 May 1914 – 9 September 1979 | One of London's most prolific, successful, and influential Artists & Repertoire—Heads of Label—and record producers in the late Fifties and early Sixties.

Paramor famously signed the singer, Cliff Richard and his backing band The Drifters; later renamed The Shadows, and they didn't do at all too badly in their recording career. But Cliff Richard went to become the third-top-selling artist in all of UK Singles Chart history, bested only by The Beatles and Elvis Presley; to an exclusive contract with Columbia Records. And just like, George Martin, worked out of EMI's head office at Manchester Square, in Soho, W1, and EMI Abbey Road Studios, up in St. John's Wood.

There's simply no getting around the fact that Paramour was "the Big Cheese" at EMI; the producer that everyone looked up to. So, there's little doubt that George Martin, the lowly head of EMI's offbeat, comedy, spoken-word Parlophone label, would have been constantly working in his shadow. Especially, as at the turn of the Sixties, George Martin—who'd already missed out on Cliff Richard and had almost passed up on Adam Faith—could have only thought to himself: *"Where on earth am I ever going to come across any artist or group to top Cliff Richard?"*

BRITISH ROCK 'N' ROLL SINGERS & THEIR BACKING BANDS

TOMMY STEELE | Singer | Guitar player | Actor | Entertainer | Composer | Conductor | Director | Novelist | Painter | Sculptor

Rock With the Caveman | *Singing the Blues* | *Knee Deep in the Blues* | *Come On, Let's Go* | *Elevator Rock* | *Rebel Rock*

Britain's first *bona fide* teen idol and "overnight" rock 'n' roll star As a young would-be pop singer he was initially turned down by none other than record producer George Martin—but irony of ironies—Decca stepped in and made Tommy Steele a huge star with a series of 'Top Ten' hits.

Born Thomas William Hicks. Bermondsey, London, England. 17 December 1936 | One time merchant seaman; heard Buddy Holly records on lay over in US; flipped from 'skiffle' to rock 'n' roll in a heartbeat. | His 'cheeky chirpy Cockney chappy' personality made him an instant hit with all who saw him. | Formed his first band, the Cavemen, with Lionel *Oliver!* Bart and Mike Pratt. | Discovered by photographer John Kennedy singing and playing at the legendary 2i's Coffee Bar, in Soho. | Kennedy teamed up with famed London promoter Larry Parnes to manage the hot young singer. | 1956. First single 'Rock With the Caveman'—with his band the Steelmen—reached No.13 in UK Singles Chart. | Followed up with covers of American hits such as 'Singing the Blues' and 'Knee Deep in the Blues' | 1957. At the start of the year his cover of 'Singing the Blues' reached No. 1 the week after Guy Mitchell's version hit the top of the charts.

A film of his life—*The Tommy Steele Story*—went into production four months later. He wrote 12 songs for the film in 7 days, with collaborators Lionel Bart and Mike Pratt. 'A Handful of Songs' became a signature hit for the singer. *The Tommy Steele Story*—first ever album by UK act to reach No. 1 in UK charts. | Almost immediately starred in *The Duke Wore Jeans*

1959. The film *Tommy The Toreador* gave him massive hit record 'Little White Bull' (Not exactly rock 'n' roll but mums and kids loved it as much as they did "our Tommy"). | From which point there never seemed to be any stopping him and remarkably there still isn't.

Steele moved more and more into stage work—did 'Summer Season' musical and variety shows—annual 'Christmas Season' pantomimes. He was invited to join the Old Vic Company and appeared in *She Stoops to Conquer* in London's West End. Played title role in stage musical *Hans Christian Andersen*. Played lead role in *Half A Sixpence* in the West End and on Broadway | A knack of always going from success to success to success.

1967. He co-starred in Disney's film version of *Half A Sixpence* and then *The Happiest Millionaire* | 1968. *Finian's Rainbow* with Petula Clark and Fred Astaire | 1969. Excellent as the notorious 18th-century Cockney criminal Jack Sheppard up against dastardly "Thief-Taker General" Jonathan Wild in *Where's Jack?*

1971. Starred in his own show *Meet Me in London* at London's Adelphi Theatre | 1974. Composed and recorded twelve autobiographical songs for '*My Life, My Song*', the album cover illustrated by twelve of his paintings; those and other works on display in a one-man exhibition at the Christopher Wade Gallery, London.

1983. Directed and starred in stage production of *Singin' in the Rain* at the London Palladium. | Published *The Final Run*—World War Two novel about the evacuation of Dunkirk. | 1991. Toured with the stage version of *Some Like It Hot*. | 1979-80 *An Evening With Tommy Steele* at Prince of Wales Theatre one of West End's longest running one-man shows. | Toured UK with another one-man show: *What A Show!* | 2003-5. Toured UK as Ebenezer Scrooge in production of *Scrooge: The Musical*—then moved into London Palladium for final Christmas season | 2008. Toured in stage musical *Doctor Dolittle*. | 2009. Reprised *Scrooge*—became annual Christmas season event. | Tommy Steele is very much regarded as a British 'national treasure'—and deservedly so. His autobiography: *Bermondsey Boy: Memories of a Forgotten World*—a nice treat.

"The overnight sensation bit was true. It was the first time rock 'n' roll had ever been seen in Great Britain, and because it was never seen before, you couldn't make any mistakes. It was all so new people just wanted to see more. And no one else played guitar...especially country guitar...except me." — Tommy Steele

| Side Bar | **Tommy Steele and The Beatles** | It can be argued that the singer's huge and continued success essentially funded Larry Parnes' entire stable of pop singers. One of the very best of them, Billy Fury, was the cause of the audition in Liverpool; set up by Allan Williams; to find himself a backing band. The very same audition that ultimately set The Beatles on the road to Scotland; backing another of Parnes' latest teen idols; Johnny Gentle. | After which Williams had just enough confidence in The Beatles to send them over to Hamburg to play the Indra and Kaiserkeller clubs for Bruno Koschmider. | Tommy Steele; man of many talents; sculpted the bronze statue of 'Eleanor Rigby' that stands in Stanley Street, Liverpool, not far from the Cavern. He donated the statue to the City of Liverpool as a tribute to The Beatles—saying he was one of the group's biggest ever fans.

CLIFF RICHARD | Pop Singer | Musician | Performer | Actor *Move It* | *Livin' Doll* | *Travellin' Light* | *Please Don't Tease* | *Theme for a Dream* | *Gee Whizz It's You* | *Summer Holiday* | *The Young Ones* | ad infinitum

Sir Cliff Richard OBE | Born Harry Rodger Webb. 14 October 1940 | Cliff Richard is Britain's Elvis Presley—even though he took his stage surname from his rock idol Little Richard | Dominated the pre-Beatles British pop charts in the late Fifties and early Sixties. In his more than 50-year career—has had 14 UK No.1 singles—67 UK Top Ten singles—more than 130 hit singles, albums, and EPs in the UK Top Twenty. He has recorded over 70 albums. Sold more than 250 million records worldwide. He's the third-top-selling artist in UK Singles Chart history—behind The Beatles and Elvis Presley. And is undoubtedly the biggest British solo singer of all time. He's still as popular today as when he made his debut.

Discovered at the 2i's Coffee Bar in Soho in 1958—singing as Cliff Richard with backing group The Drifters. | Signed a contract with EMI's Columbia label and record producer Norrie Paramor. | Appeared on *'Oh Boy'*—Jack Good's wildly popular TV show—performed 'Move It'—which reached No.2 in the UK charts. **None other than John Lennon credited 'Move It' as being Britain's first truly authentic rock 'n' roll song.** | Cliff's next record—'Livin' Doll'—was his first No.1 hit and his first million-selling disc. The success of which prompted his backing group to change their name to The Shadows so as to avoid confusion with the American group—The Drifters.

Cliff followed up with such No.1 hits as—'Travellin' Light', 'Please Don't Tease', 'A Girl Like You', and 'Theme for a Dream'. | In 1962 'The Young Ones'—the title song from his hit movie of the same name—went straight to No.1—as did the movie's soundtrack album. Cliff was also voted that year's top box office draw in British cinemas. | 'Bachelor Boy' coupled with 'The Next Time'—taken from his next film *'Summer Holiday'*—also reached No.1. | As a direct result of performing at the 2 i's Coffee Bar Cliff made his screen acting début in a minor supporting role as a singing teenage delinquent in 1959's *'Serious Charge'* and then as one of the main leads in *'Expresso Bongo'*—a film based on a Wolf Mankowitz satirical play about Soho's lurid rock 'n' roll culture—starring Laurence Harvey. However, serious acting was never Cliff's forte and he came into his own with a series of feature film musicals: *'The Young Ones'*, *'Summer Holiday'*, *'Wonderful Life'*, and *'Finders Keepers'*. | In April 1965 he topped the charts again with 'The Minute You're Gone'.

In April 1968 'Congratulations' was the British entry for the Eurovision Song Contest, yet another hit No.1, and his 27th million-selling record. | Some ten years later Cliff hit the No.1 spot again with 'We Don't Talk Anymore'; the song became his biggest-ever hit, with over five million sales worldwide. | He's the only singer to have had a No.1 single in the UK in five consecutive decades: 1950s, 1960s, 1970s, 1980s, and 1990s. | Success in the US always eluded Cliff Richard and The Shadows; even though they've always had a small but devoted following there.

But they were never viewed as being part of the British Invasion that followed the enormous success of The Beatles.

In 2009, Cliff Richard and the Shadows brought their partnership to an end with the 'Golden Anniversary concert tour of the UK'. | But Cliff Richard is still singing. He still tours. Still sounds great. Still looks good. And if not exactly right up there with Sir Paul McCartney—is still pretty close. *Rock on, Sir Cliff.*

THE SHADOWS | Four-piece instrumental rock group
Hank B. Marvin (Brian Rankin) - Lead guitar | Bruce Welch (Bruce Cripps) - Rhythm guitar | Jet Harris (Terence Harris) - Bass guitar | Tony Meehan - Drums | 1961 replaced by Brian Bennett - Drums | The Shadows were *the* four-piece instrumental rock group in the UK—no question—and the first backing band to emerge as stars in their own right. | Originally called the Drifters, they were Cliff Richard's longtime backing group, even though they were contractually separate and received no royalties for any of the records on which they backed the singer.

In 1959, the Shadows (still called the Drifters) landed an EMI recording contract, with Columbia label record producer Norrie Paramor, and released three singles that same year—two of which featured vocals—but they found much greater success with their first instrumental hit 'Apache' which knocked Cliff Richard's 'Please Don't Tease' from off the No.1 spot.

The band followed up with several more major instrumental hits—including five UK No. 1s—including 'Man Of Mystery', 'FBI', 'Frightened City', 'Kon Tiki' and 'Wonderful Land'—a couple of which again knocked Cliff Richard off the top of the charts. | The Shadows continued to record and appear with Cliff Richard and wrote many of his hits.

Tony Meehan left the group in 1961 to become a record producer at Decca Records. | Jet Harris left to go solo in 1962 and hit the charts for Decca with 'Besame Mucho' and 'Main Title from *The Man with the Golden Arm*'. | The two paired up as a rock duo in 1963—and topped the chart with 'Diamonds'— followed up with 'Scarlett O'Hara' and 'Applejack'. | Brian Locking (1962–63) and John Rostill (1963–68) replaced Harris as the band's bass player.

The Shadows disbanded in 1968. | Marvin and Welch formed a vocal–guitar trio with John Farrar, as Marvin, Welch & Farrar, but people clamoured to hear the original Shadows' hits. | The Shadows reformed in 1973; Brian Bennett again on drums; continued to record and tour; finally disbanded in 1990. | The band reformed in 2004 - 2005 for a special UK and European tour. Then reformed again, for the final time, in 2009–2010, for the '50th Anniversary Reunion Tour' with Cliff Richard.

| Side Bar | The Shadows' Walk | Much imitated at the time, as it became a sure indicator of a music group's professionalism as performers. Later much lampooned by The Beatles. | It had its genesis in a 1958 Jerry Lee Lewis UK concert tour when Bruce Welch saw the black American band, the Treniers, perform. He was much taken by the way the saxophone players moved in unison to the beat. It looked fantastic. And he and Hank Marvin decided to do something similar, so as to look more interesting on stage, and developed a number of different 'step' sequences; swaying their bodies and guitars in tempo with the music. The most eye-catching and memorable, the soon to be iconic Shadows' Walk: Step forward. Step over. Step back. Pause. Repeat.

| Side Bar | The Shadows and The Beatles | Hank Marvin was 'famous' for wearing thick-rimmed glasses. John Lennon once said the reason he didn't wear his glasses on stage was in case anyone thought he was trying to copy the Shadow's guitarist—or worse—Buddy Holly. | Hank Marvin was also the first British rock musician to play a Fender Stratocaster solid-body electric guitar; brought back from the US for him by Cliff Richard; and so closely was it associated with him, that The Beatles didn't play Fender guitars until 1965. | Jet Harris acquired his Framus electric bass; also one of the first such guitars in Britain; when he'd toured with Tony Crombie and The Rockets, prior to joining the Drifters. | The Shadows were also the first rock band to feature VOX, amplifiers and echo units, which Brian Epstein took as a mark of excellence and approval, and he personally arranged with VOX for The Beatles to always use and feature the

same equipment. | Following The Beatles' failed audition with Decca Records, on 1 January 1961, the company's Head of A&R, Dick Rowe, did all he could to placate Brian Epstein, one of his company's biggest retail clients, and suggested that The Beatles group might do much better working with a professional record producer and he offered the services of Tony Meehan; all studio and production expenses, of course, to be met by Mr. Epstein. | The Beatles' manager and ex-Shadow turned record producer, duly met at Meehan's office at Decca's West Hampstead recording studios. But Brian Epstein was again kept waiting, and he didn't at all like what he later described as Meehan's patently uninterested and patronizing attitude. And on his return to Liverpool he wrote to Dick Rowe declining his offer. Makes you wonder 'What if?' | Lastly, some six months later, in Hamburg, when The Beatles backed Tony Sheridan at the 'My Bonnie' recording sessions for Burt Kaempfert, on 22-24 June 1961, they chose to do an instrumental; credited to Lennon-Harrison, no less; called 'Cry For A Shadow', in the style of The Shadows.

| **Side Bar** | **Yet another 'What if?'** | Norrie Paramor had just signed Cliff Richard to EMI in 1958 when the original Drifters—pre-Hank Marvin—were contracted to play BBC television's hot new weekly pop series *'Oh Boy!'* | Paramor tasked talent scout Johnny Foster to find and recruit a more accomplished, more exciting guitarist for Cliff's backing group. Foster duly ventured down to the 2i's Coffee Bar in Soho, the known place for hot new musical talent, in search of guitarist Tony Sheridan. Only, Sheridan wasn't playing that particular night. Instead, Foster's attention was drawn to young Hank B. Marvin, who could not only play guitar rather well, but also wore Buddy Holly-style glasses; a tailor-made solution to Norrie Paramor's problem; so he snatched up the young guitarist for Cliff and the Drifters. | It makes you wonder how different the music world might have been if Tony Sheridan had been at the 2i's that night and gone on to become a Drifter, and then a Shadow, and not later ventured out to Hamburg where he became 'The Teacher' and one of the singular influences on the savage young Beatles.

BILLY FURY | Pop Singer | Actor

Halfway To Paradise | Jealousy | I'll Never Find Another You | Last Night Was Made For Love | Once Upon A Dream | Like I've Never Been Gone

Born Liverpool. | 17 April 1941 - 28 January 1983 | Real name Ronald Wycherley | Before The Beatles hit the scene—Billy Fury was by far the biggest rock 'n' roll star to come out of Liverpool. | In 1955 fresh out of school he took up the piano and the guitar—worked on a Mersey tugboat to make money—and formed his own skiffle group. In 1958 studio he cut several songs in a small studio in Liverpool—sent a demo tape and photo of himself to impresario Larry Parnes—and then turned up unannounced at a Larry Parnes 'Pop Extravaganza Show' at the Essoldo cinema-theatre, Birkenhead, and managed to get an impromptu audition. | Parnes liked the young man's style but—as was always his distinctive 'trademark touch' with his new pop protégés—gave a new stage name laden with raw emotion and so Ron Wycherley became Billy Fury.

Fury joined Larry Parnes' London-based stable of 'hand-produced' teen-idol rock stars and became one of Britain's—and Decca Record's—top selling artists—with over two-dozen records in the UK Hit Parade between 1961 and 1966—racking up a total of 268 weeks. His run of hits included—'Halfway To Paradise', 'Jealousy', 'I'll Never Find Another You', 'Once Upon A Dream', 'Like I've Never Been Gone', 'Last Night Was Made For Love', 'Wondrous Place' and 'In Summer'.

10 May 1960. Allan Williams arranged for The Silver Beetles—and Gerry & The Pacemakers, Derry & The Seniors, Cass & The Cassanovas, Cliff Roberts & The Rockers—to audition for Billy Fury and his manager Larry Parnes at the Wyvern Club—later the Blue Angel—in Seel Street, Liverpool. Billy Fury liked the rough and ready rockin' Silver Beetles the best—but Parnes was put off by the group's untidy appearance, as well as the age of their drummer, Tommy Moore (who'd turned up late after Johnny Hutchinson of the Big Three had sat in for him). | In the

end none of the groups got to back Billy Fury, but The Silver Beetles did get hired to back Johnny Gentle, another of Larry Parnes' stable of stars, on a 9-day tour of Scotland. It didn't turn out to be too much of a success for the proto Beatles, but it was start. | It's telling that a couple of years later, on Sunday 21 October 1962, prior to their Cavern appearance that same evening, John, Paul, George, and Ringo, went to the Empire Theatre, Liverpool, to see Billy perform, backed by The Tornados.

Billy Fury made his film debut in 1962 in Michael Winner's *Play It Cool* and later also starred in *I've Gotta Horse* released in 1965. | Having been plagued by ill health since he was a child—when rheumatic fever had left him with a weak heart—the singer had to cancel several tour appearances due to his recurring heart problems. It led to him being hospitalized on a number of occasions and he ceased doing live performances altogether in 1967. He retired and spent his time breeding horses.

In 1973 he appeared with Ringo Starr and pop singer David Essex in the wonderful little gem of a film *That'll Be the Day*; produced by David Puttnam and scripted by Ray Connolly. In his cameo role as teen idol 'Stormy Tempest', Billy performed 'Long Live Rock', a number specially written for him by Pete Townshend. | Legend has it that during filming there was a jam session with Ringo on lead guitar, David Essex on bass, Graham Bond on drums, Harry Nilsson on tambourine, and Billy Fury on vocals. Oh, to have been a fly on that studio wall. | Billy Fury's heart finally gave out on Friday 28 January 1983. He was in the process of recording a new album and had just had a new single enter the UK pop charts. 'Halfway To Paradise'—all over again.

THE TORNADOS | Billy Fury's backing band | Joe Meek's 'in-house' instrumental group | 1962-1963 | Classic line up of The Tornados from the early years: Clem Cattini - Drums (1960-1965) | Heinz Burt - Bass guitar (1960-1963) | Norman Hale - Keyboards (1962) | Alan Caddy - Lead guitar (1962-1965) | George Bellamy - Rhythm guitar (1962-1965) | Stuart Taylor - Lead guitar (1964-1965) | Jimmy O'Brien - Keyboards (1964-1965) | The Tornados also acted as the 'in-house' instrumental group for many of record producer Joe Meek's productions and had several chart hits in their own right. Including UK and US No.1 'Telstar'; the startlingly new, all-electronic sounding, resoundingly infectious, 'ear-worm' of a tune composed and produced by Meek to honour the world's first communications satellite; also rather fittingly the very first US No.1 hit single by a British group. | The band's follow-up disc 'Globetrotter' reached No.5 in UK Singles Chart. Their next Meek produced composition, 'Robot', reached No.14. | The Tornados' chart success waned with the rise of The Beatles and the 'Mersey Sound'.

In mid 1963 Joe Meek plucked The Tornados' bassist, Heinz Burt, out from obscurity; had him dye his hair 'bottle blonde'; an early touch of 'punk rock'; and launched him on a solo career with 'Just Like Eddie', a tribute song to Eddie Cochran; and a hit. | Bit by bit The Tornados lost force as a band and slowly broke apart—and by1965 not one of the original line-up remained. | The Tornados' recording swansong—the theme tune to *Stingray* Gerry Anderson's TV puppet animation series. | A 'new' Tornados band came together to back Billy Fury in 1965. | The band re-formed as 'The New Tornados' in the early 1970s as the backing group to Billy Fury and Marty Wilde—and other British rock 'living legends'—on a year-long UK Rock 'n' Roll Tour.

MARTY WILDE | Pop singer | Songwriter
Honeycomb | *Endless Sleep* | *Fire of Love* | *Sea of Love* | *Bad Boy* | *Sea of Heartbreak* | *Ever Since You Said Goodbye*

Reginald Leonard Smith | Born Blackheath, London. | 15 April 1939 | One of Britain's first real rock 'n' roll singers. One of the first teen idols created and managed by London pop impresario Larry Parnes. | Parnes spotted Smith performing as 'Reg Patterson' at London's Condor Club in 1957. | Parnes liked the singer's raw wild energy and re-christened his new protégé 'Marty Wilde'. | The singer was signed to Philips Records. For the next couple of years, backed by a band called The Wildcats, he was right up there with Tommy Steel and Cliff Richard. | Marty Wilde appeared regularly on BBC Television's *6.5 Special* and was a headliner on ITV's breakthrough pop music show *Oh Boy!*

Marty married Joyce Baker-Smith—one of the Vernons Girls—one of Britain's first all-female vocal ensembles that also appeared regularly on *Oh Boy!*—thereby breaking the one inviolable law of all 'teen idols'—being 'openly available' for girl fans to dream about. | Undeterred—Marty became more and more of an all-round entertainer—always viewed by Larry Parnes as being a singing star's next move—appearing in musicals—most notably as Conrad Birdie in the original West End production of *Bye Bye Birdie*. | He starred in a number of films—all good old solid British entertainments: *'Jet Storm'* (1959), *The Hellions* (1961), *What a Crazy World* (1963). But jump to 1974 and you get a very different kettle of fish when Marty Wilde appeared with David Essex and Adam Faith in the luminous *Stardust*. The sequel to the terrific 1973 rock 'n' roll film *That'll Be the Day* that also starred David Essex in the lead role; that time alongside Billy Fury and an absolutely brilliant Ringo Starr. *Stardust* also very memorable for its tagline: "*Show me a boy who never wanted to be a rock star and I'll show you a liar.*"

Among Marty Wilde's 'British Rock Star' UK Hit Singles—some of them original—some of them covers—'Endless Sleep', 'Donna', 'A Teenager in Love', 'Sea of Love', 'Blue Moon of Kentucky', 'Bad Boy', 'Little Girl', 'Rubber Ball', 'Jezebel'. | Marty's first LP—*'Wilde about Marty'*—catchy title—was released in 1959. Followed up in 1960 by the LPs *'Marty Wilde–Showcase'* and *'Versatile Mr. Wilde'*; both equally catchy titles for some reason. In 1961 he released the LP of *'Bye Bye Birdie'*—after which nothing more until 1968 and the LP *'Dr. Dolittle'*. You really can't blame him for that—Sammy Davis Jnr. also recorded songs from the film—arguably some of Anthony Newley and Leslie Bricusse's finest work. One or two of them still sung to this day by the luminous Diana Krall. | Marty had a run of success as a songwriter himself and even wrote a hit for Lulu.

He continued to perform in 'Nostalgia Tours'—both in the UK and overseas—rock nostalgia never knowing any bounds. | In 2007 he celebrated 50 years in show business with another UK Tour—made extra special as it also featured his youngest daughter Roxanne Wilde—and the release of the album: *'Born To Rock And Roll–The Greatest Hits'* | The tour culminated in a concert recorded at the London Palladium—made additionally notable for reuniting all the remaining Shadows: Hank Marvin, Bruce Welch, Jet Harris, Brian Locking and Brian Bennett. | Marty Wilde is the father of pop singers Ricky, Kim, and Roxanne Wilde. | What a wonderfully wild ride he's had. (And just in case you're wondering that really is a deliberate play on words. Wild, eh?)

THE WILDCATS | Marty Wilde's backing band. | Big Jim Sullivan - Lead guitar | Tony Belcher - Rhythm guitar | Bobbie Clarke - Drums| Brian Locking - Bass guitar| Brian Bennett - Drums | Both Bennett (1961) and Locking (1962) later left the band to join The Shadows.

THE VERNONS GIRLS | An all-female vocalist ensemble made up of girls that originally worked the typing pool at Vernons 'football pools' company in Liverpool. | In 1958 and 1959—as a 16-piece vocal group—just count them—they made regular appearances—singing with the house band—on the ITV pop show *Oh Boy!* And over the three year life of the TV show released a number of hit singles for Parlophone. | In 1961—led by singer Maureen Kennedy—the group downsized to five girls and then three—and signed with Decca Records—where they specialized in doing covers of American hits. Their recordings of 'Lover Please' and 'You Know What I Mean'—originally by the US group The Drifters—were both hit singles. | As session singers for Decca, the Vernons Girls were the female backing voices on many hit records during the 1960s—one of the first being Billy Fury's 'Maybe Tomorrow'. | The trio of Jean Owen, Frances Lea, and Maureen Kennedy appeared in the 1962 Billy Fury film *Play It Cool* and on the 1964 TV film special *Around The Beatles* starring none other than The Beatles | The girls made the US LP charts with the release of the first ever Beatles tribute album—*'We Love The Beatles'*. And then—under the name 'The Carefrees' for some carefree reason—went back for a second bite with 'We Love You Beatles'—which was a hit in the US singles charts. | Of the many singing groups that came out of The

Vernons Girls perhaps the best known were The Ladybirds—formed by Maggie Stredder—with Marian Davies and Gloria George. The trio had a long association with *The Benny Hill Show* on BBC TV. They also supplied backing vocals on BBC television's weekly pop show *Top of the Pops*. | The Ladybirds also performed the backing vocals on the Jimi Hendrix Experience's first single—'Hey Joe'.

| Side Bar | The Vernons Girls and The Beatles - and other tidbits | Joyce Baker-Smith married Marty Wilde and they became the parents of pop singers Ricky Wilde and Kim Wilde and Roxanne Wilde. | Lyn Cornell married drummer Andy White—immortalized for being the session musician George Martin brought in as a steady-handed replacement for Ringo Starr at The Beatles' third recording session at Abbey Road Studios. The reason there are two versions of 'Love Me Do'—one released as a single—one as a track on The Beatles' *'Please Please Me'* LP. The single features Ringo Starr on the drum stool. The album version has Andy White—with Ringo on tambourine. | Vicky Haseman married pop singer Joe Brown. And later formed the breakaway group The Breakaways. Their daughter Sam Brown is also a well-known singer. | One or two members of The Vernons Girls went on to have solo careers—notably Jean Owen under the name Samantha Jones—while other ex-Vernons Girls banded together at various times—as singing duos and trios—as The Breakaways. The Redmond Twins. The Carefrees. The Pearls. The Two Tones. The DeLaine Sisters. And The Ladybirds. | What a remarkable pool of talent the Vernons Girls turned out to be.

JOHNNY GENTLE AND THE SILVER BEETLES | Rock Impresario Larry Parnes signed three Merseyside singers: Billy Fury, Lance Fortune... and Johnny Gentle. | Real name John Askew | 1936 Born in the Scotland Road area of Liverpool. (Not far from where Cilla Black was born) | In 1957 was an apprentice carpenter. He made his own guitar from a series of articles in a woodwork magazine and took up guitar lessons. | He teamed up with a friend and the duo made appearances at local social clubs singing Everly Brothers hits—'Bye Bye Love', 'Wake Up Little Susie', Bird Dog'—while regularly auditioning for talent agents looking to book acts for Merseyside's working men's clubs. | Worked on a cruise liner. Entered various talent contests. (Just as Tommy Steele had done.) | Won first prize at the Locarno in London, which led to an audition with Larry Parnes and a six-record contract with Philips Records. It was Parnes who dubbed him Johnny Gentle. | His first record—'Wendy'—failed to make the charts. His follow up—'Milk'—reached No. 28.

In 1960 Larry Parnes promoted Eddie Cochran and Gene Vincent's highly successful UK Tour. It went down such a storm when it played the Liverpool Empire that local entrepreneur Allan Williams—owner of the Jacaranda club—arranged to co-promote a repeat event at Liverpool Stadium. But before it could take place Eddie Cochran was killed in a road accident in the west of England. | 3rd May 1960 Gene Vincent chose to go on with the show even while still recovering from injuries sustained in the car crash. In an effort to bridge the gaping chasm left by Cochran—Williams also featured local bands Rory Storm & The Hurricanes, Gerry & The Pacemakers, and Cass & The Cassanovas. | Parnes was impressed enough by the Liverpool bands to think one of them might make a perfect fit as a backing band for Billy Fury. The rest might even be candidates to back one or more of his other singers when they went out on tour.

10 May 1960. Allan Williams arranged for Parnes and Billy Fury to audition groups at the Wyvern Club—later the Blue Angel—in Liverpool. | None of the bands that auditioned got to back Billy Fury, but the Silver Beetles were later selected to back Johnny Gentle on a nine-day Scottish tour. The group comprised John Lennon, Paul McCartney, George Harrison, Stuart Sutcliffe, and Tommy Moore—their combined fee £120. | 20 May 1960. Billed as 'Johnny Gentle and His Group'—the tour took in the towns of Alloa, Inverness, Fraserburgh, Keith, Forres, Nairn, and Peterhead. | Thinking they were about to hit the big time—three members of the band decided to adopt stage names: Paul became Paul Ramon; George called himself Carl Harrison; and Stuart answered to Stuart de Stael.

The repertoire for the Johnny Gentle Scottish Tour consisted of: 'It Doesn't Matter Anymore', 'Raining in My Heart', 'I Need Your Love Tonight', 'Poor Little Fool', 'I Don't Know Why I Love You But I Do', 'Come On Everybody' and 'He'll Have To Go'. | Gentle always maintained afterwards that he thought a great deal of the Silver Beetles and was most disappointed when they weren't available for his second tour of Scotland, when he was backed by Liverpool group Cass and The Cassanovas.

July 2 1960. Johnny Gentle appeared with the Silver Beetles just one more time. At the end of his second Scottish tour, he visited Merseyside and dropped by the Jacaranda club and was told the group was appearing that night at the Grosvenor Ballroom, Liscard. He drove over to the gig and joined them on stage and they reprised all the songs they'd played on the tour. | Some time later the singer asked Parnes to book the Silver Beetles as his backing band again—but they were away—in Hamburg—playing the Indra Cabaret Club for Bruno Koschmider. And the rest, as they say, is Beatles' history.

JOE BROWN | Pop Singer | Guitarist | Entertainer | Actor | Radio and TV Personality | 'Cockney' Pride and Joy
Joseph Roger 'Joe' Brown MBE | Born Swarby, in Lincolnshire. 13 May 1941 | Parents moved to Plaistow, in the East End of London, when he was aged two—which is why he's long been cast as a 'chirpy Cockney'.

Great 'personal favourite' of none other than Messrs. George Harrison and Brian Epstein. (And, truth be told; one of mine, too.) | As with so many early British rock 'n' rollers he began by forming a 'skiffle' group—he called his The Spacemen—in 1956.

In 1958 he was spotted by television producer Jack Good, who hired him to be lead guitarist in the band he put together for his new TV pop series, *Boy Meets Girls*.

In between TV work Joe backed Gene Vincent and Eddie Cochran—and a number of other celebrated US musicians—on their UK tours. | His first single—'People Gotta Talk'—was issued by Decca Records in 1959. | In 1960 he signed a management deal with London rock impresario Larry Parnes. His record, 'The Darktown Strutters Ball', went to No. 34.

1960. Performed on the Gene Vincent and Eddie Cochran UK Tour—at the end of which Cochran was killed in a road crash outside Bristol. Brown later said he learned a huge amount—as a rock guitarist—from Eddie Cochran.

In 1961 he moved over to the Piccadilly label and over the next couple of years had a number of UK Top Ten hits—most notably 'A Picture of You' (No. 2), 'It Only Took A Minute' (No. 6) and 'That's What Love Will Do' (No. 3) | In 1962's *NME* poll he was voted the UK's 'Top Vocal Personality'. | During the 1960s the indefatigable Joe appeared in half-a-dozen films, did TV and pantomime, and graced a number of stage musicals. Particular standout films: 1963's rockin' *What a Crazy World*—with Marty Wilde—and 1965's musical comedy *Three Hats For Lisa*—with Una Stubbs and Sid James.

From 1965 to 1968 he starred in the West End hit musical *Charlie Girl*—alongside Dame Anna Neagle. | He then went on to present the series *Joe & Co* for BBC Television and did three seasons of *The Joe Brown Show* for ITV.

Joe's long been widely viewed as being 'a musician's musician'—is highly regarded in and out of show business. And is ineffably likeable even when playing against type, which he did when he played a cameo as Dudley, a crooked club owner, in the 1986 film *Mona Lisa*, with Bob Hoskins, Cathy Tyson, Robbie Coltrane and Michael Caine.

In the 1980s he presented a daytime quiz show—*Square One*—for Granada TV. And presented a much-lauded series on the history of rock 'n' roll for BBC Radio 2. | In 2005 he co-wrote the musical, *Don't You Rock Me Daddio*, with songwriter Roger Cook.

In 2008, to mark his 50th Anniversary in show business, Joe undertook a 37-date 'Spring Tour'. Appeared at an 'all-star' Anniversary Concert at London's Royal Albert Hall—with Mark Knopfler, Dave Edmunds, Jools Holland, Chas & Dave, his daughter Sam Brown, and many others. And followed that up with a 36-date 'Autumn-Winter Tour'. That same year, he was awarded a UK 'gold album' for sales over 100,000 copies of *'Joe Brown-The Very Best Of'*.

To top all that, he was appointed Member of the Order of the British Empire (MBE) for "services to music" in the 2009 Queen's Birthday Honours List.

In now almost sixty years in the business he's released almost 50 singles and over 30 albums. | He's still at it. Still appears on TV. Still tours regularly. And, if that's not enough, he's nearly always at work on a new album. 'Chirpy' doesn't even begin to cover the half of it; he's an unabashed force of good nature.

THE BRUVVERS | Originally a collection of session musicians—dubbed 'the Bruvvers' by Jack Good—so as to give the notion of Joe Brown having his own backing band for record releases. In 1962 Joe needed an actual band to back him on tour and so 'Joe Brown and the Bruvvers' was made real. Two of its members—brothers Pete and Tony Oakman—had been in Joe's original skiffle group—The Spacemen—and had worked alongside Joe again in the rock band Jack Good created for his *Boy Meets Girls* TV show. In 1972 Pete Oakman joined 'Brown's Home Brew'—a band created by Joe to play a mix of rock 'n' roll, country, and gospel music—that also featured Joe's first wife, the singer Vicki Brown—a member of the original Vernons Girls.

| **Side Bar** | **Joe Brown and The Beatles** | Friday July 27, 1962 | The Tower Ballroom, New Brighton | With 'Picture of You' riding high in the UK Hit Parade, Brian Epstein put on 'A Bob Wooler Show' featuring 'Joe Brown with his Bruvvers' as headliners to 'the sensational Beatles'. | To plug the event, The Beatles sang their own version of 'A Picture of You' in every gig the played the week before the show. | In the two-day run-up to the show Joe Brown and his Bruvvers were mobbed when they made an appearance at NEMS record store to sign autographs. The group then packed out The Cavern for two lunchtime sessions. | Just before the start of the show at The Tower, George Harrison, ever the guitar buff, was passing Joe's dressing room and saw his Gibson ES-355, a thin, twin-cutaway, semi-hollow-body electric guitar, complete with Bigsby vibrato, and asked Paul McCartney's brother, Mike, to take a photograph of him holding the guitar. He did. George looks a little awestruck in

Mike McCartney's terrific, full-length, black and white photo. Apparently, Joe only learned of the photo years later and—tickled beyond measure—it only served to strengthen his by then very close friendship with George Harrison. | Joe played mandolin and sang backing vocals on two songs on George Harrison's 1982 Dark Horse Records album *'Gone Troppo'*.

In 2000 George Harrison was best man at Joe Brown's second marriage; Vicki Brown, his first wife having died of cancer in 1991. | Joe also played acoustic guitar on one track—and his daughter Sam Brown sang backing vocals on another—on *'Brainwashed'*—George Harrison's final album.

Following George Harrison's death from lung cancer on 29 November 2001, Joe appeared along with The Bruvvers at the Royal Albert Hall tribute *'Concert for George'* and sang 'Here Comes the Sun', 'That's The Way It Goes', and the haunting 'I'll See You in My Dreams'. A magical moment when he accompanied himself on the ukulele; a musical instrument he'd introduced to George Harrison a few years earlier and that the Beatle had developed an immense fondness for. And, believe you me, after Joe's gentle, heart-wringing performance there wasn't a dry eye in the house.

ADAM FAITH | Pop Singer | Actor | Entrepreneur

What Do You Want? | *Poor Me* | *Someone Else's Baby* | *How About That* | *This Is It* | *Don't You Know It* | *Don't That Beat All* | *Baby Take A Bow*

Terence Nelhams | Born Acton, West London | 23 June 1940 - 8 March 2003 | Singer with The Worried Men skiffle group who were given a residency at the 2i's Coffee Bar in Soho, London. | Spotted by TV producer Jack Good who booked him to appear on BBC TV's weekly pop show *Six-Five Special* and arranged a recording contract with HMV. | Adopted stage name Adam Faith. | First two records failed to chart. Good hired Adam to appear in the stage version of *Six-Five Special* | Booked to appear in TV series *Drumbeat*; the initial three scheduled appearances extended for entire 22 shows. | He was dropped by HMV label. Failed to chart again on the Top Rank label. But his residency on *Drumbeat* won him a contract with Parlophone in 1959.

His next disc—'What Do You Want?' went straight to No.1—as did his follow up single 'Poor Me'.

He had a run of 24 Hits over the next seven years—racking up a total of 260 weeks in the UK Charts including—'Someone Else's Baby', 'How About That', 'This Is It', 'Don't You Know It', 'The Time Has Come', 'Lonesome', 'As You Like It', 'Don't That Beat All', 'Baby Take A Bow', 'What Now', 'Walkin' Tall', 'The First Time', 'Message To Martha', 'Someone's Taken Maria Away' and 'Cheryl's Going Home'.

1967 married long-time girl friend, dancer Jackie Irving. They had a daughter, Katya.

1970 Adam Faith began a very successful second career as an actor. Appeared in the title role of the highly rated UK television series *Budgie*. Made film appearances in: *Beat Girl*, *Never Let Go*, *What A Whopper*, *Mix Me A Person*, *Stardust*, *McVicar*, *Yesterday's Hero* and *Foxes*. | He also launched 'Faith', a financial management consultancy for celebrity clients. Wrote financial columns for the *Daily Mail* and *Mail on Sunday* newspapers.

He managed the singer Leo Sayer for a time. | He returned to acting with a major role in the UK TV series *Love Hurts*. | In 1996 he published his autobiography *'Acts Of Faith'*. | In 1997 he embarked on a nine-month stage tour of the UK as the lead in *A Chorus Line*. | In 2002 appeared in the BBC TV series—*The House That Jack Built*.

In 1989 Adam Faith set up and funded the Faith Foundation Rhino Rescue—to help protect the species in danger of extinction from rhino horn poachers. He talked often of his desire to immigrate to South Africa so he could devote more time to his passion—but kept on working to keeps the funds flowing.

He suffered a major heart attack in his dressing room while touring in the play *Love And Marriage*—and died. He was a spritely 62 years of age, still with all the stage charm of his much younger self.

JOHNNY KIDD | Rock Singer

One of Britain's leading rock 'n' roll stars at the beginning of the Sixties. | Frederick Heath. Born Willesden, London. | 23 December 1939 - 7 October 1966 | Formed his first group—Freddie Heath and The Nutters—during the UK skiffle boom.

In 1959 he changed his name to Johnny Kidd—dubbed his backing group The Pirates—and his debut record for EMI—'Please Don't Touch'—reached No. 25 in the UK charts. | Johnny made good on the Pirates' name, by wearing 'swashbuckling' leather gear and a black eye-patch over his left eye. It soon became his distinctive trademark. | His next single—'You Got What It Takes'—also reached No.25 in the charts.

Johnny Kidd's first 1960 release sailed to the No.1 spot—the instant classic—'Shakin' All Over'. | He quickly followed up with—'Restless'—that reached No.22. | He had several other hits, notably the timeless rockers, 'A Shot Of Rhythm And Blues' and 'I'll Never Get Over You'. | 14 May 1962. Johnny Kidd & The Pirates appeared for a week at the Cavern, Liverpool. | 10 August 1962 they headlined the bill—above The Beatles—on 'The Riverboat Shuffle' on the Mersey Ferry *Royal Iris*'.

7 October 1966. Tragedy strikes again... *and only the good die young.* In the midst of a hectic schedule of one-nighters—Johnny Kidd was killed in a car crash at Radcliffe, Lancashire. He was just 26 years old.

THE PIRATES | The original crew of Pirates were made up of Brian Gregg on bass guitar, Art Caddy on lead guitar, and Clem Cattini on drums. But in 1961 they mutinied and abandoned ship to become The Tornados—variously Billy Fury's backing band and Joe Meek's in-house band. | Johnny Kidd then took on Cuddly Dudley's former backing band—and formed the backing trio that was to leave a considerable mark on future British rock bands—Mick Green on guitar, Johnny Spencer on bass, and Frank Farley on drums.

BRIAN POOLE | Singer | Guitarist | Performer

Born Barking, East London. 2 November 1941. | Brian Poole was the lead singer of 1960s London-based beat band the Tremeloes (1957–1962) that Decca deftly renamed 'Brian Poole and the Tremeloes' (1962–1967). | In the early years of the band—the Tremeloes took their inspiration almost completely from Buddy Holly & the Crickets. They played small venues—grew in accomplishment—and began to develop a close-harmony singing style. | Brian Poole's Buddy-Holly-style glasses and the Tremeloes' increasingly upbeat look and sound helped the band grow a wider and wider following—and they became one of London and the southern counties' top dance-hall attractions.

1 January 1962. New Year's Day. The Tremeloes auditioned at Decca Records' West Hampstead, London, recording studios in the afternoon, all but on the heels of The Beatles who'd also auditioned for Decca that very morning. | Mike Smith—Decca's recording engineer for both auditions—liked both groups, but ultimately chose The Tremeloes over The Beatles because they were a London-based band and would be much easier to keep in close contact with and therefore less costly to record. | As a condition of signing, Decca Records insisted the band bill themselves as 'Brian Poole and the Tremeloes'. The classic: 'named singer plus named backing band' combination, being still very much the preferred rock 'n' pop group format in London's 'Tin Pan Alley'.

The group made a number of early recordings for Decca—with little or no result—and also performed as the backing band for a number of other Decca recording artists. | In June 1963 the group had its first major chart entry with 'Twist and Shout'—the volcanic Isley Brothers' song that'd all but become a 'teenage anthem' in dancehalls throughout the land since the release of The Beatles LP *'Please Please Me'* in March of that year. | The Brian Poole and the Tremeloes version of 'Twist and Shout' rode the wave and reached No.4 in the UK singles chart—with over 1 million sales.

In September 1963 Brian and the band released the dancehall crowd pleaser 'Do You Love Me', which also reached No.1 in the UK Charts. It knocked The Beatles' second No.1 hit—'She Loves You'—from off the 'top spot'—and what's more stayed there for three whole weeks!

Brian Poole and the Tremeloes went on to produce more UK hits for Decca—with 'Candy Man' that reached No.6—and 'Someone, Someone' that reached No.2. | And then a slow fade. Until—in 1968—the band officially broke up and went their separate ways—and Brian Poole began to pursue a solo career.

THE TREMELOES | Brian Poole met Alan Blakley and Alan Howard when they were all at secondary school together. When they discovered they all had a shared interest in rock 'n' roll—like so many other teens up and down the country—they decided to form a rock band. | The original line-up consisted of Brian Poole - vocals and lead guitar, Alan Blakely - guitar, Alan Howard - bass, and another mutual friend—Graham Scott—who also played guitar. | 1957 Dave Munden joined the band - on drums. Alan Blakley then switched to lead guitar—as Brian Poole, his Buddy Holly spectacles fully to the fore, became lead vocalist and The Tremeloes' 'front man'.

PART TWO – MUSIC INFLUENCES. THE MEDIA.

4 – UK Rock 'n' Pop Media

BRITISH ROCK 'N' POP MEDIA IN THE EARLY 1960s

BBC RADIO SHOWS
'Pick of the Pops' | *'Saturday Club'* | *'Easy Beat'* | *'Pop Go the Beatles'*

RADIO LUXEMBOURG | *"208 on your radio dial"*

BRITISH TV SHOWS
'Six-Five Special' | *'Oh Boy!'* | *'Juke Box Jury'* | *'Thank Your Lucky Stars'* | *'Ready Steady Go'* | *'Top of The Pops'*

PIRATE RADIO STATIONS | Radio Caroline | Radio London

NATIONAL MUSIC NEWSPAPERS
New Musical Express | *Melody Maker* | *Disc* | *Record Mirror*

THE SIXTIES! | The Sounds of The Sixties presented a very different 'musical' media landscape than is experienced today; particularly in the UK It's easy to forget; even for someone who was a teenager at the time; just how unbelievably restricted and controlled everything was. Especially when compared to the instant access to music—of all genres—as well as information and data of all sorts—that we enjoy today. | The very first experimental communication satellites—Telstar 1 and 2—were launched July 1962—but it would be years before the technological advance they represented would benefit any self-respecting teenager. | The one technological breakthrough that helped take music out of the home and out into the street—or even from the family living room and into the privacy of one's own bedroom—was the transistor radio. And what a delight that was; to be able to turn on, tune in, and listen to your own music when and where you wanted to. | The very idea of the Internet was something out of science fiction. And any thought of a two-way wrist based communication device was safely locked away within the frames of '*Dick Tracy*' and '*Batman*' comics.

It wasn't until July 1979 that Sony first introduced the Walkman portable cassette player. Apple released the first iPod in October 2001. (And even those two technological breakthroughs in personal 'music audio' now things of the past.) | There were no cell or mobile phones of any kind—certainly no iPhone (June 2007). | It was pre-Google. Pre-YouTube. There was no Apple iTunes. No Amazon. No Beats. There was no Sirius or digital Internet radio. No music streaming Apps of any kind. | The Sixties were a musical desert as far as being able to hear any sort of music you loved—on demand. Is it any wonder then the thirst there was back then to hear good rock 'n' roll.

There were three main US television Networks: CBS, NBC, ABC, but multiple commercial local AM Radio stations that offered different genres of popular music and 'talk' radio. FM broadcasting stations being used primarily to simulcast whatever was played over their AM sister stations. | In the UK the only alternative to the BBC's three national radio networks was Radio Luxembourg. At least until the first 'Pirate Radio' ships took to the airwaves in March 1964.

The BBC was also the only national TV channel until 1955, when the first commercial Independent Television Network (ITV) began. Soon followed by a second BBC TV channel and even more regional ITV networks. | Every British TV programme was still only transmitted and received in black and white. Colour TV was slowly emerging in the US, but England didn't burst into colour until much later in the decade. Again— the demand for more colour in our lives seemingly ushered in by The Beatles. | Also, please note, this is by no means a definitive description of the 1960s British media landscape; it's merely meant to introduce you to some of the key rock 'n' pop radio and TV shows and music newspapers that always tend to pop up when delving into the early days of The Beatles.

BBC Radio Shows | British Broadcasting Company

In the early Sixties—in Britain—there was no commercial radio or local radio as we know and enjoy them today. There were just three national radio networks: The Light Programme; The Home Service; The Third Programme; all broadcast by the British Broadcasting Company; the BBC. | The BBC had strict formats for music radio, which resulted in officially sanctioned programme playlists and severely restricted 'needle time' of current commercially available record releases. | Instead, the various regional BBC Radio Orchestras, together with a stable of featured singers, covered the popular music 'Hits' of the day—and yesteryear. | The only way for any British teenager with a pulse and/or yearning for rock 'n' roll was to find a jukebox; visit a local dancehall; buy the record; or try tune in to Radio Luxembourg broadcasting from the European mainland. The 'evening only' broadcast signal from the tiny principality of Luxembourg always notoriously difficult to tune into, as it was always affected by atmospheric conditions, and faded in and out, in and out, in and out, as if a signal from a distant galaxy.

Brian Epstein, The Beatles' manager, realised very early on just how essential radio coverage would be in introducing and promoting the group to audiences outside of Merseyside. And in January 1962 he wrote to BBC Manchester asking for an audition. | Monday 12 February 1962. The Beatles auditioned at the BBC's Manchester studios. | BBC producer Peter Pilbeam wrote on their audition report: *"An unusual group, not as 'rocky' as most, more country and western with a tendency to play music."*

The group passed the audition. Pilbeam recorded The Beatles at a session at the Manchester Playhouse 7 March 1962—for broadcast on *'Teenager's Turn'* at 5:00 pm the following evening. | John sang 'Memphis Tennessee', 'Please Mr. Postman', and 'Hello Little Girl' (not broadcast). Paul sang 'Dream Baby'. George Harrison on lead guitar and vocal harmonies. Pete Best on drums. Their breakthrough onto British radio occurring seven months before the release of the group's very first 45rpm single 'Love Me Do'.

'*Pick of the Pops*' | Pop Music Radio Show | BBC Light Programme | From September 1957; when DJ Alan Dell began playing the Top Ten singles from the week's Top Ten Record Charts (drawn from various UK music papers) plus new entries to the Top 20; '*Pick of the Pops*' quickly became essential teenage listening for two glorious hours every Sunday evening.

29 March 1958. '*Pick of the Pops*' switched to Saturdays when DJ David Jacobs introduced the first official BBC 'Top 20'. | September 1961. DJ Alan Freeman took over hosting duties. | 7 January 1962. The show moved to its 'new' regular 4 PM Sunday slot. | Freeman split the programme into four: Chart Newcomers; New Releases; LPs; The 'Top 10' | '*Pick of the Pops*' always attracted a large listening audience due to the BBC's restrictions on "needle time" of commercially available recordings. | Freeman continued with the show when it moved to BBC Radio 1 and stayed until the programme ended in September 1972. | The show's theme tune, from 1961-1966, was 'At the Sign of the Swingin' Cymbal' written and performed by Brian Fahey and his Orchestra. | 1982-1997. Freeman revived '*Pick of the Pops*' and the show went through various iterations'; moved back and forth to Capital Radio, a London based commercial radio station; before finally returning to the BBC. | 1997. '*Pick of the Pops*' now firmly ensconced on BBC Radio 2 | 2000. Freeman retired. DJ Dale Winton took over. | Ex-radio London DJ Tony Blackburn then took over from him in 2010 and hosted until 2016. | '*Pick of the Pops*' continues to this day, 2017, and is presented by Paul Gambaccini, one of the UK's more gifted and accomplished pop writers and music commentators.

'*Saturday Club*' | Radio program broadcast on the BBC's 'Light Programme', later 'Radio 1', between 1957 and 1969. | One of the earliest and for many years almost the only radio program in the UK to broadcast 'pop music'. | BBC producer Jimmy Grant initially proposed a series: '*Skiffle Session*'. BBC management was dubious about a radio show 'specifically aimed at teenagers' but finally agreed to a weekly program. '*Saturday Skiffle Club*' was first broadcast 1 June 1957 with Brian Matthew as announcer and newsreader. | Lonnie Donegan—the country's top skiffle star—performed on the show. | October 1958. The program was extended to two hours, from 10 AM to 12 PM, Saturday mornings. "Skiffle" was dropped from the title; its budget increased; and a wider range of music styles and performers invited to appear that included Cliff Richard, Adam Faith, Marty Wilde, Terry Dene, Vince Taylor, Johnny Kidd, and Bert Weedon.

The show consisted mainly of pre-recorded 'live' performances due to official 'needle time' restrictions on the number of records that could be played by the BBC. Programs had four 'live' acts; five or six 'record requests'; and three 'new record releases.' By the end of its first year *Saturday Club* was regularly attracting a listening audience of two to three- million. After a Musicians' Union ban on performances by non-British musicians ended; the show began to feature performances by American artists on tour in the UK including Eddie Cochran, Gene Vincent, Duane Eddy, Bobby Darin, Jerry Lee Lewis, the Everly Brothers, Chris Montez, Tommy Roe, and Bo Diddley. | 1960. '*Saturday Club*' LP issued on Parlophone; the record label The Beatles would sign with two years later. | From January 1963, The Beatles regularly pulled in UK audiences of around 10 million on "Saturday Club" and a myriad of other BBC pop shows, until they received the ultimate recognition when the BBC gave them their very own show, '*Pop Go The Beatles*'. | For most of its run, *Saturday Club* was presented; with charm, aplomb, and good humour; by the legendary Brian Matthew.

| **Side Bar** | '*Saturday Club*' **and The Beatles** | The Beatles appeared on the program ten times. First on 26 January 1963, two weeks after the release of 'Please Please Me', when they performed 'Some Other Guy', 'Love Me Do', 'Please Please Me', 'Keep Your Hands Off My Baby' and 'Beautiful Dreamer'. | Their other appearances: 16 March, 25 May, 29 June, 24 August, 5 October, and 21 December 1963; 15 February, 4 April, and 26 December 1964. | The '*Saturday Club Fifth Anniversary Show*'—5 October 1963—starred The Beatles, the Everly Brothers, Tommy Roe, Frank Ifield, Kathy Kirby, Clinton Ford, Roy Orbison, Joe Brown and his Bruvvers, and Kenny Ball's Jazzmen.

'Easy Beat' | 1960 - 1967 | BBC Radio pop music program broadcast nationally on the 'Light Programme' between 10:30 - 11:30 AM on Sunday mornings. | Recorded at the BBC's Playhouse Theatre, London | The show's guest artists recorded 'live' in front of a studio audience. | One of the earliest BBC programs to broadcast pop music. It was initially presented by Brian Matthew; also the very popular presenter of BBC's *Saturday Club*; later by Keith Fordyce—and David Symonds.

| Side Bar | *Easy Beat* and The Beatles | The Beatles appeared on four occasions in 1963. | 7 April, they sang 'Please Please Me', 'Misery', 'From Me to You' | 23 June, they sang 'Some Other Guy', 'A Taste Of Honey', 'Thank You Girl', 'From Me to You' | 21 July, they sang 'I Saw Her Standing There', 'A Shot of Rhythm and Blues', 'There's a Place', 'Twist and Shout' | 20 October, they sang 'I Saw Her Standing There', 'Love Me Do', 'Please Please Me', 'From Me To You' 'She Loves You'.

'Pop Go the Beatles' | 30 April 1963. BBC producer, Vernon Lawrence, suggested The Beatles be given their own weekly radio series. The BBC commissioned four programs—with an option for a further eleven if successful. | May 1963. The Beatles recorded their first *'Pop Go the Beatles'* at the Aeolian Hall, New Bond Street, London. | Later episodes were recorded at the BBC's Paris Studio, Lower Regent Street, and Maida Vale Studio, London—and at BBC Manchester's Playhouse Theatre. | As well as 'hosting' the show The Beatles were required to play six or seven songs for each episode. | Each episode also featured a guest group chosen by the BBC and recorded in a different session—one of which was none other than Brian Poole and The Tremeloes who Decca Records had chosen to sign instead of The Beatles. | The first four shows were presented by Lee Peters—rechristened "Pee Litres" by John Lennon—and featured a mix of great Beatles' music and good natured Beatles' banter. | Each show began and ended with a 'Beatles-style' take on the nursery rhyme 'Pop Goes the Weasel'.

THE BEATLES IN LIVERPOOL, HAMBURG, LONDON

The first episode of *'Pop Go the Beatles'* was broadcast on the BBC's 'Light Programme'—Tuesday 4 June 1963 at 5:00 PM | The Beatles performed 'From Me', To You 'Everybody's Trying to Be My Baby', 'Do You Want to Know a Secret'. 'You've Really Got a Hold on Me', 'Misery', and 'The Hippy Hippy Shake'. | The Beatles' "own radio show" ran for 15 weeks—and was a huge success with fans. | The group performed many songs they never recorded for EMI—covers of songs by Chuck Berry, Carl Perkins, Arthur Alexander, Ray Charles, and other rock 'n' roll legends—hard-rockin' R&B songs upon which they'd built their fan following in Hamburg and Liverpool. | The Beatles' *'Pop Go the Beatles'* BBC sessions, in many cases, the only surviving recordings of songs from the group's early, pre-*Beatlemania* repertoire. The last show was broadcast 24 September 1963.

| Side Bar | The Beatles at 'The Beeb' | Between March 1962 and June 1965—The Beatles performed 52 times—on 16 different national and regional BBC Radio shows. The group sang and recorded a total of 88 different songs—many from the extensive song list the group had compiled over the previous years performing at clubs in Liverpool and Hamburg.

Thirty-six songs sung by The Beatles—and recorded by the BBC—were never officially issued by EMI-Parlophone. A fab selection of these and other songs can be heard on the double-CD box sets: *The Beatles: Live At The BBC Volumes 1 & 2*.

The BBC Radio shows that featured The Beatles as performers were: *The Beat Show* (x1) | *Easy Beat* (x4) | *From Us To You* - holiday specials (x4) | *Here We Go* (x4) | *The Ken Dodd Show* (x1) | *On The Scene* (x1) | *Parade Of The Pops* (x1) | *Pop Go The Beatles* (x15) | *Saturday Club* (x10) | *Side By Side* (x3) | *Steppin' Out* (x1) | *Swinging Sound '63*—broadcast live from Royal Albert Hall (x1) | *The Talent Spot* (x2) | *Teenagers Turn* (x1) | *Top Gear* (x2) | And for the last and final time on 'The Beeb'—a radio special entitled—*Ticket To Ride*.

UK Commercial Radio

RADIO LUXEMBOURG | *Winged messenger of Rock 'n' Roll* | *"This is Radio Luxembourg - Your Station Of The Stars - 208 on your radio dial."* | Privately owned commercial radio station based in the Duchy of Luxembourg on the European mainland—but with studios in London. | 1951. Radio Luxembourg began beaming popular entertainment programs—a mixture of drama, comedy, variety, sports, music—to UK and Ireland—on 208 metres on the 'Medium Wave'. | Mid-1950's the station began to increasingly feature pop music specifically to target Britain's growing teenage populace.

Long before pirate radio and modern commercial radio the English language service of Radio Luxembourg broadcast to the British Isles as an effective way for companies to advertise their wares. | British government legislation prohibited all forms of advertising over the domestic radio spectrum up until 1973. This gave the BBC a strict monopoly of radio broadcasting throughout the entire UK | And all very nice and good—for some—but for the longest time the BBC didn't play commercially released pop records over the radio. And so—unless you knew of a coffee bar or a club that had a jukebox— haunted the listening booths at some record store—visited a local dancehall or even a travelling fairground where they'd play rock 'n' roll over loudspeakers to get you into the mood to have fun—or as a very last resort plonked down the hard-earned six shillings and eight-pence and bought yourself a precious 45rpm disc of your latest rock 'n' roll flame and played it into the mat of your record player—there was absolutely no way to hear real good rockin' rock 'n' roll at the simple push of a button.

It all seems so very archaic now, but if you were into rock 'n' roll and the Top Twenty there was really only one sure way; you turned your radio wavelength dial to '208 metres' on the 'Medium Wave' and waited for the sounds of Radio Luxembourg to come wafting in. | The station sign-on time at dusk varied between summer and winter to allow maximum benefit from night-time atmospheric conditions. All of which meant the in-

THE BEATLES IN LIVERPOOL, HAMBURG, LONDON

coming radio signal could be weak or strong or somewhere in between. | The sounds of rock 'n' roll coming in in waves—as if a signal beamed down from some far distant planet. | The only thing that never waivered—at least for any British teenager with a pulse—was the absolute need to hear American DJ Alan Freed present *"Rock 'n' Roll"* on Saturday nights—each week's specially pre-recorded half-hour programme flown in from the States—and the UK Top Twenty hosted by Barry Alldis every Sunday night between eleven and midnight (from midnight till one o' clock during wintertime). | Jack Jackson also deserves a special mention—as he was the first British DJ to start playing authentic R&B records regularly on his Radio Luxembourg show—which he also later did on his BBC radio programme.

The secret password for all would-be audio voyagers to star sound No. 208: *"'Keynsham', spelled K-E-Y-N-S-H-A-M!"* (That's an in-joke for anyone that ever had to suffer through all the times the radio commercial, for a patented system for predicting football results, was repeated *ad nauseum*.)

Programs were presented by a team of 'resident' disc-jockey-announcers, from the studios in Luxembourg City; complimented by shows pre-recorded in the company's studios at 38 Hertford Street, London W1. | Radio Luxembourg and the BBC never referred to the existence of the other on air—although many famous disc jockeys of the time appeared on both stations. Among them: Jack Jackson, Brian Matthew, David Jacobs, Pete Murray, Keith Fordyce, Alan Freeman, Sam Costa, Alan Dell, Tony Hall, Shaw Taylor, Jimmy Young; and Muriel Young, quite the sweetest sounding of them all.

| **Side Bar** | **Radio Luxembourg and The Beatles** | The Beatles—John, Paul, and George—always talked avidly about listening to Radio Luxembourg in their early days in Liverpool. The one programme never to be missed if they could possibly help it—*"Rock 'n' Roll"*—Alan Freed's half-hour show featuring the latest US rock 'n' roll and R&B records by original artists—broadcast between 9:30 pm and 10:00 pm on Saturday nights—specially taped in US for re-broadcast across Europe and Britain. | Some Beatles people believe Alan Freed's professional nickname

"Moondog" was what prompted John to rename his group the Quarrymen—'Johnny and The Moondogs'—when in October and November 1959 they auditioned for Caroll Levis' *TV Star Search* show in Liverpool and Manchester. With "Moondog" having no other correlate in contemporary British popular culture, and knowing of John's propensity for word-play and his love of authentic rock 'n' roll, I have to agree. | The Beatles also later recalled that whenever they listened to Radio Luxembourg they always dreamed of one day hearing a record of their very own being played over the radio. | I allude to it in my mystery novel—*The One After 9:09*—that's based around the early days of The Beatles in Liverpool. Hamburg, and London. | There was a big billboard approaching the eastern entrance to Liverpool's Mersey Tunnel for 'Hessy's Music and Radio'. Neil Aspinall—their ever faithful roadie, would bang out the beat on the transit van's horn, as all three Beatles; this was before Ringo when Pete Best was still their drummer; chorused the billboard's headline, with added staccato emphasis on the last word: *"Hessy's Music and Ra-di-o!"* | It still speaks volumes to me that John, Paul, and George all fondly remembered such a singular magical moment. It plays to the fact that we all have impossible dreams when we're teenagers—even The Beatles.

British TV Shows | BBC - British Broadcasting Company | ITV - Independent Television Network

'Six-Five Special' | 1957-1958 | Roll film: Train speeding along the tracks. Opening credits. Cue audio. Music intro: *"The 6.5 Special's steamin' down the line...The 6.5 Special's right on time..."* | Both television and rock 'n' roll were in their infancy in Britain when the *'Six-Five Special'* thundered down the line and onto British television sets on Saturday evening 6 February, 1957. | BBC TV's first attempt at a real, live, rockin' rock 'n' roll program; its format was an innovation, much imitated since. No attempt was made to hide the cameras—the audience was part of the show—and the air of excitement was very real. | It was

called *'Six-Five Special'* as it was broadcast live at 'five past six' on Saturday evenings. | Pete Murray to camera: *"Welcome aboard the Six Five Special. We've got almost a hundred cats jumping here, some real cool characters to give us the gas, so just get on with it and have a ball...It's time to jive on the old six five."* | Originally scheduled for six weeks—the 55-minute show ran for 96 weeks. Hosted by 'Radio Luxembourg' disc jockey Pete Murray, co-producer Josephine Douglas, former champion boxer turned TV personality Freddie Mills, and singer Jim Dale. | Initially conceived by BBC executives as a general interest magazine—the show produced by the extraordinarily prescient Jack Good presented a mix of general interest and sports related items, traditional jazz, and—rock 'n' roll.

The show was an immediate hit—mostly because of Jack Good having his finger firmly on the pulse of Britain's growing army of teenage rock 'n' roll music fans. The show was once even broadcast 'live' from the 2i's Coffee Bar, in London's Soho. | The show's resident band, Don Lang and his Frantic Five, backed the show's guest stars. Among those who appeared: Kenny Ball & his Jazzmen, Chris Barber's Jazz Band, George Melly, Lonnie Donegan, Tommy Steele, Marty Wilde, Terry Dene, Adam Faith, Petula Clark, Cleo Laine, Johnny Dankworth, Joan Regan, Russ Hamilton, Wee Willie Harris, and the Dallas Boys. | An LP of the show was issued on the Parlophone label in 1957. | Yet given the still hugely conservative tenor of the times in post-war Britain it perhaps shouldn't come as a surprise that the 'breakout' success of *'Six-Five Special'* on national TV led to some degree of discomfort along the BBC's upper corridors of power. Increasing pressure was brought to bear on the show's co-producers to reduce the emphasis on rock 'n' roll and to increase the number of 'educational and sports' pieces so as to bring the program back more into line with the BBC's mandate to offer comprehensive 'public-service' programming. | After fighting the good fight for weeks on end, Jack Good finally resigned in early 1958, which hardly surprisingly led to a huge drop in audience figures. | The series finally hit the buffers and came to the end of the track on 27 December 1958.

| **Side Bar** | *'Six-Five Special'* **and The Beatles** | Don Lang's real name was Gordon Langham and some years later he was to play trombone on 'Revolution No.1' on The Beatles' *White Album*. | Singer and actor Jim Dale moved to New York—was a huge hit on Broadway—and was later the brilliant and often truly-inspired narrator of the 'Harry Potter' audio books.

'Oh Boy!' | 1958 - 1959 | Produced by ABC Television, for ITV; Britain's independent television network. | Half-hour pop music TV show. | After he was fired from the BBC's *'Six-Five Special'*, Jack Good joined rival ABC Television; one of a number of independent commercial television companies established in the UK during the 1950s; to create *'Oh Boy!'* | The show earned a regular Saturday evening slot across the country's entire independent television network after two initial trial broadcasts in the Midlands region. |*'Oh Boy!'* featured non-stop pulsating music. Eschewed all the sports, general interest, and public-service items. | It had speed and energy. Moved from artist to artist at a fast clip. It was hip. It was cool. It was 'the rock 'n' roll show' as he'd always imagined it. And it was just what Britain's teenage television audience had been waiting for. | The chance to see and hear Britain's top rock stars: Cliff Richard, Marty Wilde, and Billy Fury, was an irresistible lure for its chosen audience. The fact it was broadcast 'live' only added to all the energy and excitement. | The program even attracted top US music acts such as The Inkspots, Conway Twitty, and Brenda Lee—a sure sign of the show's rock 'n' roll credibility. | Backing for all the music acts was provided by Lord Rockingham's XI—a 13-man rock band of session musicians recruited specially for the show by Jack Good and music arranger Harry Robinson—who named the band as a play on the words *'rocking 'em!'* The band's rockin' guitarist, none other than the preternaturally gifted, Joe Brown. Word was that Jack Good, no mean slouch as a musician, often got into the act, too. | **"It's the most exciting thing I've ever seen on television; the lighting, the camera work, are great; the music swinging,"** said a *'TV Times'* music critic. | *'Oh Boy!'* trounced *'Six-Five Special'* in the ratings.

'Juke Box Jury' | 1959 -1967 | A BBC Television music show, hosted by 'DJ' David Jacobs, where each week a panel of four celebrity guests reviewed new record releases. | First broadcast 1 June 1959. | The show originally aired Monday evenings, but due to its immediate popularity was moved to the prime Saturday evening time slot on 3 September 1959. | The show was normally broadcast from the BBC TV Theatre, Shepherd's Bush Green, in London. | Each 25-minute program featured around seven or eight records. | The show was sometimes extended to an hour, and featured even more of the very latest platters, for special Christmas-editions. | Each week the host would ask the four celebrity 'Jurors'; normally comprised two male and two female guests; to judge a number of newly released records played on his jukebox; an actual Rock-Ola Tempo II; and forecast which of them would be a 'hit' or a 'miss'; each juror's decision accompanied by the ringing sound of a bell for a 'hit' or a klaxon hooter for a 'miss'. Should the guests' decision eve result in a deadlock—a panel of three audience members voted the tie-breaker by holding up a large circular disc with 'Hit' on one side and 'Miss' on the other. | Most every week a performer of one of the featured records would be hidden behind a screen only to emerge; sometimes with a stone-faced smile; to 'surprise' the panel once their verdict had been rendered.

The panel of judges changed week on week and featured current stars from the worlds of music, television, and film. | 'Skiffle King' Lonnie Donegan appeared as a 'Juror' several times. As did 'Goon' Spike Milligan and the sparkly singer—and close friend of The Beatles—Alma Cogan. Pop singers Lulu and Cilla Black appeared as Jurors on numerous occasions. US singing stars Roy Orbison and Johnny Mathis graced the Jury. Intriguingly, so did film director Alfred Hitchcock and actor David *Man from UNCLE*' McCallum. | 4 July 1964 the five members of the Rolling Stones made up the panel; the only time the show featured more than four 'Jurors'. Keith Richards later wrote of the group's appearance on the show: *"We really didn't give a shit.... We just trashed every single record they played."* | 27 September 1967. Falling ratings prompted the BBC to move the show from its prime time Saturday evening spot into the hinterland of an early Wednesday evening time slot. Three months later they removed *'Juke Box Jury'* from its schedule altogether. The show's last broadcast was on 27 December 1967.

| Side Bar | *'Juke Box Jury'* and The Beatles | 7 December 1963 | All four Beatles were 'Jurors' on *Juke Box Jury*. | Later, on different occasions, George Harrison and Ringo Starr appeared as 'Jurors'. As did The Beatles' manager Brian Epstein, who appeared twice. | By October 1959 *Juke Box Jury* reached a weekly audience of 9 million viewers. It grew to over 12 million viewers by early 1962. In contrast, The Beatles appearance on 7 December 1963 garnered an audience of 23 million. Makes you think: What was it about those four lads from Liverpool that could all but double a well-established TV show's viewing figures?

'Thank Your Lucky Stars' | 1961-1966 | British pop music variety show made by ABC Television who'd also produced the groundbreaking pop TV show *'Oh Boy!'* | *'Thank Your Lucky Stars'* was originally conceived as a rival to the BBC's already well-established *'Juke Box Jury'*, but it broadened the pop show genre significantly. | The program was broadcast on ITV: Britain's national network of independent television companies. | The show was recorded 'live' on a Sunday afternoon at the ABC Alpha Studios in Aston, Birmingham, for nationwide transmission the following Saturday evening. Some recorded material was also produced at Teddington Studios, in London. | *'Thank Your Lucky Stars'* soon became essential Saturday evening viewing for millions of British teenagers. | It was the first British TV show to showcase top US pop music stars on a regular basis. And many of Britain's top bands made their national TV debut on the show. | All the acts mimed to whatever was their latest 45rpm record release—there were no plugged-in guitars or microphones—drumming was no more than a frenzied stick-laden hand jive. The television audience was seduced into focusing solely on a pop star's 'ravishing look and recorded sound'.

There were a number of presenters over the life of the show: including Keith Fordyce, Pete Murray, Kent Walton, Sam

Costa, Jimmy Young, and Brian Matthew. | One of the show's most popular features—'Spin-a-Disc'—called for a guest DJ and three teenagers drawn from the 'live' audience—to review three newly released singles and award each of them 'points out of five'. | Gene Vincent was the first American artist to appear on the show. Many others followed: including Brenda Lee, The Ronettes, and sublime The Supremes. | 13 April 1962. The Shadows were the first British group ever to be awarded a Gold Disc and had the golden platter—for 'Apache'—presented to them on the show. | 7 July 1963. The Rolling Stones made their very first UK television appearance miming their very first single for Decca, 'Come On'. | In 1966 artistes were required to—heaven forefend—perform live. By coincidence it was the program's last year. | Over three thousand different music artistes—from both sides of the Atlantic—appeared on the show during its all-too-brief five-year run. | The final episode of the show—'*Goodbye Lucky Stars*'—was broadcast Saturday 25 June 1966 and was presented by pop singer and actor Jim Dale.

| **Side Bar** | **'*Thank Your Lucky Stars*' and The Beatles** | 19 January 1963. The show was The Beatles' first ever appearance on national TV. They mimed to their second 'single'—'From Me To You'. The episode was recorded a week earlier on 13 January and broadcast in black and white—which somehow seemed to fit them and their sound and their look to a 'T'. | This first vitally-important national television exposure had been arranged by music publisher Dick James to show Brian Epstein he had all the necessary pull to publish and promote the songs of John Lennon and Paul McCartney. | At their very first meeting in James' tiny London office, he'd picked up the telephone right in front of the sceptical Beatles' manager—called Philip Jones the show's producer—and secured the group their slot on the prime time pop show. It certainly impressed Brian Epstein—he later awarded Dick James the publishing rights to all future Beatles' songs. | 29 June 1963. '*Summer Spin Liverpool Special*'—an 'all-Liverpool' show starring The Beatles, The Big Three, Billy J. Kramer and The Dakotas, Gerry and The Pacemakers, Lee Curtis and the All Stars, The Vernon Girls, and The Breakaways. The program

drew 6 million viewers. | ABC always quick on the up-take introduced an additional seasonal replacement program with the memorable title—'*Lucky Stars Summer Spin*'—made even more memorable as Liverpool's very own Billy Fury was a regular performer on the show. | 21 December 1963. '*Lucky Stars On Merseyside*'—a second 'all-Liverpool' show starring: The Beatles, Gerry and The Pacemakers, Cilla Black, Billy J. Kramer and The Dakotas, The Fourmost, and The Breakaways. | The 'Spin-a-Disc' segment featured the inimitable Mr. Bob Wooler, the Cavern Club's very own DJ, as guest compere.

'Ready Steady Go!' - RSG! | *"The weekend starts here!"* | 1963 -1966 | British rock 'n' pop music television program. | Produced by Associated-Rediffusion—the weekday ITV contractor for London—but soon networked nationally. | First broadcast 9 August 1963 | The show went out 'live' early Friday evening— from the tiny Studio 9—located in the television company's Kingsway headquarters in the heart of central London. | It was transmitted in black and white; colour television being then but a dream in Britain; even as broadcasting companies in the US—ABC, CBS, NBC—were converting to colour.

The program was introduced with a knowing voice over: *"The weekend starts here!"* The words intoned over the sounds of the Surfaris' pulsating instrumental 'Wipe Out'. | There was no scenery—no costumes—no make-up—little or no choreography—television cameras were ever present. | The show was defiantly youth-orientated and much more informal than anything you might see on the BBC.

RSG! was immensely popular with would-be 'hip' young people—and had a particular following among 'Mods'—the 'cool style'-oriented youth subculture of the 1960s; into sleek Italian mohair suits and motor scooters, cycling jerseys, pork-pie hats; R&B, Tamla Motown, Ska, and Modern Jazz. '*Take Five*' anyone? | The entire *RSG!* studio was the stage. Artists would appear everywhere and anywhere—on mini-stages dotted around the studio—on studio gantries and stairs—even on the studio's main floor. The artists always closely surrounded by the audience milling around them or more often than not dancing expertly to the music. | The show's producers haunted London clubs—picking out the most fashionably dressed or best dancers to be in the audience. Always to ensure there was a 'hip' audience in tune with the times and—importantly—the very latest in hairstyles and fashions.

The show was notable for allowing artists to perform the full version of their songs rather than shortened versions demanded by other shows. All of which added to the pop show's 'authenticity' even though the artists all still mimed—at least for the first year or so until a new ruling by the Musicians Union banned 'miming to records' as being injurious to their members' livelihoods. | Opening title music for later editions of *'Ready Steady Go!'* was '5-4-3-2-1' by Manfred Mann; which gave way to the group's 'Hubble Bubble, Toil and Trouble'; and in the last season of the show to the Rolling Stones, 'Goin' Home'.

Some early shows were introduced by the luminous Dusty Springfield. The show's best-known presenters were DJ Keith Fordyce and 'typical pop fan recruited when she responded to a newspaper advert' Cathy McGowan. | Towards the end of 1964 a number of artists were actually allowed to perform live. | In April 1965 the show switched to all-live performance format. Moved to Studios 5a and 5b; located at the television company's much larger studios in Wembley, west of London; thus enabling artists to perform 'live' with the backing of a full orchestra.

'Ready Steady Go!' always endeavoured to feature the top recording artists of 'the time' including: The Beatles, Rolling Stones, the Who, Kinks, Dusty Springfield, Helen Shapiro, Cilla Black, Lulu, Sandie Shaw, Supremes, Temptations, Shirelles, Marvin Gaye, Otis Redding, James Brown & the Famous Flames, Beach Boys, Walker Brothers, Jerry Lee Lewis, Bobby Vee, Gene Pitney, P.J. Proby, Burt Bacharach, Billy Fury, Gerry and the Pacemakers, Searchers, Fourmost, Merseybeats, Animals, Hollies, Dave Clark Five, Zombies, Yardbirds, Them, Small Faces. | The 'Dylan-esque' British folk singer, Donovan, was first 'discovered' on *RSG!* | The immortal Jimi Hendrix made his first ever British television appearance on *'RSG!'* with an earth-shaking solo performance of 'Hey Joe'. After which, his London

club tour immediately sold out and he was very quickly added to a nationwide tour headed by the Walker Brothers. | April 1965. Dusty Springfield, a huge fan and 'vocal promoter' of the music of Motown, devised and introduced the *'RSG Motown Special'*: featuring Stevie Wonder, the Miracles, Martha and the Vandellas, and the Supremes, who all but stopped London traffic with their sublime 'Stop! In the Name of Love' to-camera dance routine. | October 1966 *'Ready Steady Who'*, a special *RSG!* episode performed entirely by The Who; who made 18 appearances on the show, more than any other artist or group.

As the 'beat boom' began to fade into the night the program was taken off the air—despite calls for it to continue. | The last *RSG!* show went out 23 December 1966. Fridays and weekends were never the same again.

| **Side Bar** | *'Ready Steady Go!'* **and The Beatles** | The Beatles appeared on several occasions. | During the 4 October 1963 episode—The Beatles' first appearance—Paul McCartney judged four teenage girls miming to Brenda Lee's 'Let's Jump the Broomstick'—somewhat ironic as the group had been but a support act to Brenda Lee on their first UK Package Tour. The ever-charming Paul chose 13-year-old Melanie Coe to be the winner. Three years later teenage-angst ridden Melanie ran away from her middle-class home—*"we gave her everything money could buy"*—and her disappearance was reported in the national newspaper —*The Daily Mail*. Paul was unaware of their previous connection when he used the newspaper story of Melanie leaving home as the basis for his still hauntingly beautiful 'She's Leaving Home'. |*'Ready Steady Go!'* gained its highest ever ratings on 20 March 1964. The Beatles were interviewed in between performing 'It Won't Be Long', 'You Can't Do That', and their then current hit—'Can't Buy Me Love'.

'Top of The Pops' - TOTP | 1964-2006 |The BBC—not to be outdone by the more pop-oriented independent TV channels—launched 'an exciting new pop television program' of its very own—the venerable *'Top of The Pops'*. | Created by BBC producer Johnnie Stewart. Inspired by the huge popularity of Radio Luxembourg's *Top Twenty Disc Club*. Produced at BBC TV's Manchester studios. | The show focussed exclusively on the UK Top Twenty Singles Chart. | First broadcast 6:35 pm Wednesday 1 January 1964. | Later that year the broadcast time was moved to 7:35 pm and the show moved to what became its regular Thursday evening program slot. The show was also extended by 5 minutes to 30 minutes.

Each *'TOTP'* episode featured 'mimed' performances from some of the week's best-selling pop music artists—as well as a rundown of that week's UK | An additional 'special edition' program was broadcast each Christmas Day. | The show quickly drew a large audience who kept coming back for more; as much for the fact, I suspect, that there was really nothing else on Thursday night to touch it. *'Ready Steady Go!'* already had the lock on Friday night. *'Thank Your Lucky Stars'* had Saturday.

'Top of The Pops' would always end the program with the week's best selling No.1 single—the only record that could 'appear' in consecutive weeks. The show also included the week's highest 'new entry' and—if it hadn't already been featured the previous week—the 'highest climber' in the charts. Any song that had gone down in the charts was of course already a distant memory. | For the first three years the show was presented by DJs Alan Freeman, David Jacobs, Pete Murray, and Jimmy Savile in weekly rotation. | To distance the show from the BBC's other pop program *Juke Box Jury*; instead of a jukebox's circular armature selecting and placing the chosen disc onto a turntable; *TOTP*'s current 'disc girl' would place a 45rpm record onto a turntable—set the stylus arm—*et voila*—the camera would cut to the next artist to appear 'live' miming to their latest hit.

In 1966, after mimed performances were banned by the Musicians' Union, the show moved from Manchester to London—and ultimately into the BBC TV's Lime Grove Studios, which were large enough to accommodate the new 'Top of the Pops Orchestra' led by Johnny Pearson; now a necessity for real 'live' performances. | After a few weeks of less than stellar performance by various artists, who couldn't reproduce anything like the sound on their records, a compromise was reached with the

Musicians' Union that allowed for the use of specially pre-recorded backing tracks; just as long as all the musicians who played on the track were later present in the studio and paid accordingly. | During its heyday *'Top of The Pops'* attracted over 15 million viewers each week. | The show proved to have extraordinarily enduring appeal—over forty years—and since its inception in 1964 it went through many changes in style, design, format, fashion—and music. | The show's final broadcast in the United Kingdom was on 30 July 2006. As The Beatles themselves might have sung: *'And in the end... Top of The Pops really was 'the toppermost of the poppermost'*

| Side Bar | *'Top of The Pops'* and The Beatles | 1 January 1964 | As holders of that week's No.1 spot The Beatles were the last artists to appear on the first *'Top of The Pops'* with 'I Want to Hold Your Hand'. | The Rolling Stones opened the show with 'I Wanna Be Your Man'—a song given to the group by John Lennon and Paul McCartney. | The other artists on that very first *TOTP* were: Dusty Springfield, the Dave Clark Five, the Hollies, and the Swinging Blue Jeans. | Due to the BBC's early policy of erasing video-taped recordings of old TV programs the vast majority of *TOTP* episodes prior to 1976 have been lost forever—including The Beatles only 'live' appearance on the show.

'Pirate Radio'
Marine-based Commercial Radio Stations

RADIO CAROLINE | *'The boat that rocked the music business'* | 28 March 1964 | Radio Caroline was the first of a number of pirate-radio stations anchored off the coast of England during the 1960s—all of them put to sea with the single purpose of getting around overly restrictive UK government broadcast regulations. | Radio Caroline— the brainchild of Irish businessman Ronan O'Rahilly—launched at noon on Saturday, 28 March—on 197.3 metres—and began regular daytime commercial radio transmissions to southern England from the motor vessel MV *Fredericia*—renamed MV *Caroline*—anchored just over three miles off the coast of Felixstowe, Suffolk, England—in the North Sea. And thereby in international waters and beyond the legal reach of British authorities. | Launched in a blaze of publicity Radio Caroline was an unmitigated success with its target daytime audience—not British teenagers this time but British housewives and any one at work—office or factory—that could have radio on during the day. | Its music-to-the-ears slogan: **"Your all-day music station"** a remarkable case of truth in advertising as the station initially broadcast from 6AM-6PM—seven days a week.

Even the jingly up-beat American-style radio commercials aired on the station; many of them voiced by American or Canadian-born DJs; proved a huge attraction. Nothing like them had been heard before on radio; not even Radio Luxembourg. | Without serious competition, Radio Caroline gained a regular daytime audience of around 10 million. | It wasn't long before it did rather well in the hours of the night, too. After the station's 6PM close-down—it quietly returned to the airwaves again at 8PM and continued on until after midnight—its target market teenagers with an ear for the latest pop music—its ship-to-shore signal much stronger than Radio Luxembourg could produce. | Other pirate stations soon sailed to sea—broadcasting mostly from locations off the Essex coast or the Thames Estuary. | Many of Britain's biggest bands, such as the Rolling Stones, The Who, The Dave Clark Five, all got their first real exposure on the pirate radio stations.

The British Government reacted with fury and outrage at the success of Radio Caroline and responded with a flurry of Acts; all of which proved s ineffective. They asked Panama to revoke the ship's registration. Blocked ship-to-shore communications. Warned off advertisers. | The chairman of EMI even suggested the British record industry should buy a ship of its own to jam Radio Caroline's signal. The British Copyright Council, the Musicians' Union, and Phonographic Performance Ltd all went on the attack by issuing writs, right, left, and centre.

Even Britain's General Post Office; issuers of the mandatory annual Radio and TV license, got into the act; telling listeners that they were liable to a £10 fine, and £50 more, for any repeat offences, simply for listening.

In 1967 the British Government—played its trump card—the 'Marine & Broadcasting Offences Act'—which made it illegal for any British subject—which of course included any and all advertisers—to associate with 'any unlicensed offshore broadcaster'. It was the death-knell for all commercial pirate radio stations

Yet the pirates, and the oceans of rock 'n' pop music they'd played, had found a home; changed public opinion; and shaped public demand. The BBC launched its very first fully dedicated national 'pop' radio station, Radio 1; modelled largely on the successful offshore station Radio London; barely a month after the 'Marine & Broadcasting Offences Act' had gone into effect.

The BBC Light, Home, and Third programmes also instantly updated to Radio 2, Radio 3 and Radio 4 on the radio dial. And if that wasn't victory enough, many of the pirate radio station's now beached disk jockeys were quickly pressganged into working for their former foe, 'Auntie' BBC.

It wasn't for another six years that the British Government would allow commercial radio stations to begin to operate in the country—in 1973.

Capital Radio, anyone?

RADIO LONDON | *'The boat that rocked...the BBC'*
1964-1967 | 'Radio London'—a.k.a *'Big L'* and *'Wonderful Radio London'*—was a 'Top Forty' commercial radio station that operated from a ship anchored in the North Sea—three and a half miles off Frinton-on-Sea, Essex, England.

'Radio London' was the brainchild of Don Pierson—an American businessman and entrepreneur from Texas—after he'd read a report in *The Dallas Morning News* about the launch of Radio Caroline in the UK | With his American 'know-how' and business contacts he was convinced he could to create a bigger and better 'pirate radio' station. | He commandeered; okay, he bought the USS *Density*; a former Second World War US Navy minesweeper, and renamed it the MV *Galaxy*.

The ship was fitted out for radio broadcasting in Miami; sailed across the Atlantic to the Azores; the antenna erected; then positioned off the Essex coast. | The station had its business office in London's West End—at 17 Curzon Street—just off Park Lane. | It was probably there that Don Pierson was forced to walk the plank after disagreements with his fellow investors, as he was definitely no longer on board when 'Radio London' began broadcasting 23 December 1964.

Radio London disc jockeys included: Tony Blackburn, Pete Brady, Tony Brandon, Dave Cash, Ian Damon, Chris Denning, Dave Dennis, Pete Drummond, Graham Gill, Duncan Johnson, Lorne King, Ed Stewart, Tommy Vance, the inimitable Kenny Everett, the great and much-missed John Peel, and the station's main newsreader, Paul Kaye.

At its peak the station boasted 12 million listeners across the UK plus a further four million in the Netherlands, Belgium and France. | And in the end—despite a number of politicians and influential people having fought hard to oppose it—the UK 'Marine & Broadcasting Offences Act' was introduced with the single intention of forcing all pirate radio stations to cease broadcasting. | The owners of Radio London chose not to defy the law and decided instead to close down—but did so in their own inimitable way.

'*Their Final Hour*'—a one-hour pre-recorded show was broadcast from 2 PM to 3PM on the station's last day. Complete with recorded greetings of remembrance and farewell from some of the UK's top recording stars—including Dusty Springfield, Cliff Richard, and Mick Jagger. | The 2:30 PM mid-program news bulletin read by Paul Kaye was the last 'live' item on the station. Followed half an hour later by his pre-recorded final announcement: "'*Big L' time is three o'clock. And 'Radio London' is now closing down*". | By which time all involved had abandoned ship. | Radio London lived on in spirit—as it was widely observed that the BBC's first ever 'all pop music' radio station—Radio 1—was modelled exclusively on the 'Top 40' format first introduced by the pirate radio station—with many of its former disk-jockeys taking up duties at BBC Radio.

| Side Bar | Radio London and The Beatles | The 'Top Forty' disc play format—all but ubiquitous in US commercial pop music radio stations of the time—was called "The Fab 40" in obvious allusion to 'The Fab Four'. | August 1966. The Beatles embarked on what would turn out to be their last US concert tour. It was the group's first trip to the US since the 'disc-cum-book burning' storm John Lennon's *"The Beatles are more popular than Jesus now..."* comment had caused in the US 'Bible Belt'. Just how the group would be received in America was a cause for much media speculation—and unpaid for PR—and Brian Epstein arranged for a number of British journalists to accompany the group on the tour. Radio London disk jockey Kenny Everett—a fellow Liverpudlian—was one of them.

Everett's task was to call Radio London with his report on The Beatles—each and every day of the group's 40-day US tour. But as the UK's General Post Office—the country's only telephone service provider—had cut ship-to-shore communication with all pirate vessels, Everett had to call a telephone number on the English mainland. | Fellow Radio London disk jockey Paul Kaye would go ashore—take the call in Harwich—tape the conversation—then head back to the ship— where the recording was edited and music inserted to make a 30-minute program—broadcast each evening at 7.30 | The program was sponsored by Bassett's, whose Jelly Babies were widely reported to be The Beatles' favourite candy.

In 1967 Radio London was given an eight-day exclusive on *'Sgt. Pepper's Lonely Hearts Club Band'*—the album not available in UK record stores until 1 June 1967. | *'Sgt. Pepper'* was played in its entirety countless times—adding to the tidal wave of the album's pre-orders. | Ringo Starr was one of the stars heard giving a final farewell on *'Their Final Hour'*—the station's final program. | *'Their Final Hour'* was followed by the last track ever played on the station—The Beatles' already anthemic—'A Day in the Life'. | One of the last swashbuckling acts enjoyed by the pirate station's army of avid listeners before it closed down for good at 3 PM on 14 August 1967.

| Side Bar | The Pirate Radio Stations and The UK's 'Marine & Broadcasting Offences Act' | 14 August 1967 | The British Government's purposefully draconian 'Marine & Broadcasting Offences Act' made it a crime for any British subject to supply music or programme commentary, fuel, food, or water—or any other form of assistance—except for lifesaving—to any ship, offshore structure—or any such entity used for broadcasting—without a license from the regulatory authority in the UK | The Act—even more significantly—also prohibited any British company—or any other foreign-based company with offices or products for sale in the UK—to advertise with any such aforementioned banned entity. | The Act went into effect at midnight 14 August 1967. And as was intended—it sounded the official death-knell for all pirate radio stations operating at the very edge of UK waters.

British National Music Newspapers & Magazines

New Musical Express | *"NME"* | British music newspaper | Originally published in tabloid format on standard newsprint. | 14 November 1952—took cue from US magazine *Billboard*—created the first UK Singles Chart—a list of the 'Top Twelve' best-selling singles—sourced by the *NME* from 'disc sales' in UK regional record stores. | In the early 1960s the *NME* started championing new British groups and in 1963 began vigorously promoting The Beatles. Frequently featuring The Beatles on the front cover. | In the mid 1960s the *NME* was primarily dedicated to pop, while its 'older' rival *Melody Maker* was known for its more serious music coverage. | By comparison—*Record Mirror* championed American rhythm and blues. *Disc* focused on 'UK Chart' news. | Competition between *Melody Maker* and *NME* intensified greatly and by the early 1970s *NME* had lost ground to its main rival. *NME* responded by recruiting a whole new team of—what turned out to be—arguably—the most extraordinary team of pop music journalists ever assembled; one of them the great and much missed Ian MacDonald. *

By early 1974 *NME* was selling nearly 300,000 copies per week—far outstripping *Melody Maker, Disc, Record Mirror,* and *Sounds*—and became Britain's best-selling music newspaper. | In the 1980s *NME* moved toward a magazine format. | An online version of *NME—NME.com*—was launched in 1996, which became the world's biggest standalone music site, with over seven million users per month | *NME.com* launched in USA in 2007. | *NME* magazine re-launched September 2015 as a nationally distributed free publication. | March 2018 ceased all print editions. *NME* now digital only. | * Ian MacDonald's book *Revolution In The Head* should be on the bookshelf of every Beatles' fan.

| Side Bar | *New Musical Express* and The Beatles | The '*NME* Poll Winners' Concert' was an annual music event produced to reflect the votes cast by *NME*'s readers as to which artist(s) were the most popular the previous year.

The Beatles appeared at the *NME* Poll Winners' Concert at 'The Empire Pool and Sports Arena, Wembley' on four separate occasions | 21 April 1963 | 26 April 1964 | 11 April 1965 | 1 May 1966, which turned out to be the very last concert appearance by The Beatles in the UK | *NME* Poll Winners' Concerts took place every year from 1959 until 1972; and each year featured between fifteen and twenty artists who had won in different music categories.

2002. *NME* started publishing a series '*Special Edition*' themed magazines made up of vintage articles, interviews, and reviews from the *NME* archives, entitled *NME Originals*. The top sellers, more than 30 years after the break up of The Beatles, was an edition covering the group's history; the other, an edition dealing with: 'The solo years of The Beatles'.

Melody Maker | "*MM*" | British music newspaper | Founded in 1926 as a magazine for dance band musicians. | One of the world's first music weeklies. | *Melody Maker* originally concentrated on big band jazz and Trad-jazz, was exceedingly slow to cover rock 'n' roll, and lost a lot of sales ground to the *New Musical Express—NME—*which began in 1952.

MM began its *'Melody Maker'* LP Charts in November 1958—some two years after the *Record Mirror* published the first 'UK Albums Chart'. | By the late 1960s, *MM* had recovered from its drop in sales by targeting an older market segment than the teen-oriented *NME*. | 2000. *Melody Maker* was purchased by IPC and merged with its 'long-standing rival'—*New Musical Express*.

| Side Bar | *Melody Maker* and The Beatles | 6 March 1965. *MM* called for the British Government to honour The Beatles. Somewhat surprisingly, all four Beatles' names then showed up on the Queen's 'Birthday Honours' list when it was announced 11 June 1965. | 26 October 1965. John, Paul, George, and Ringo all went to Buckingham Palace to receive their 'Member of the Most Excellent Order of the British Empire' medals; MBEs; from Queen Elizabeth II. A number of previous MBE honourees returned their decorations in disgust, even though it was Prime Minister Harold Wilson, who represented the Liverpool suburb of Huyton, who had lobbied the Queen to honour the group.

Paul later said he thought MBE really stood for 'Mr. Brian Epstein'. | 25 November 1969. John Lennon sent his MBE back:

"Your Majesty, I am returning my MBE as a protest against Britain's involvement in the Nigeria-Biafra thing, against our support of America in Vietnam, and against 'Cold Turkey' slipping down the charts. With love, John Lennon of Bag."

Ray Coleman, former editor-in-chief of *Melody Maker*, wrote well-received biographies on The Beatles and their manager: *Lennon: The Definitive Biography* | *McCartney: Yesterday and Today* | *Brian Epstein: The Man Who Made The Beatles*

Disc | British music 'magazine' | First published 1958 to compete with *Record Mirror*. | *Disc* gained a reputation for its emphasis on pop music—as reflected in the music charts—as opposed to its more music-industry-focused rivals *Melody Maker* and *New Musical Express* | *Disc*'s pop music charts were based on its own sample of shops, initially no more than 25 in number, but expanding to about 100 by the mid-1960s | From 1959 until 1973—*Disc* awarded silver discs for UK sales of 250,000—and gold discs for UK sales of 1,000,000. All awards based on sales figures submitted by the record companies, themselves. | From 5 December 1964 until 16 April 1966 it was re-titled *Disc Weekly* | 1966. It was incorporated with *Music Echo* magazine—itself previously taken over by *Mersey Beat*. The new magazine now known as *Disc* and *Music Echo*

| **Side Bar** | ***Disc* and The Beatles** | The photo on cover of *The Beatles in Liverpool, Hamburg, London* shows the group receiving a *'Silver Disc'* for UK sales of 250,000 at the Slough Adelphi on 18th May, 1963 | It was the first day of The Beatles' Third UK Tour. | Fellow Liverpudlian, Gerry Marsden, lead singer of Gerry and The Pacemakers, who was also on the bill, as was the American singer, Roy Orbison, presented the *'Silver Disc'* to John, Paul, George, and Ringo. | I was there and stomped and clapped and cheered The Beatles along with every other single person in the audience. | June 1966—under the cutting headline—*'Beatles: What a Carve-up'*—*Disc* was the first magazine to feature the notorious Beatles' 'butcher cover' for the US album 'Yesterday and Today' in colour.

Record Mirror | **British weekly music newspaper started in 1954 for pop fans and record collectors** | Launched two years after the *NME*, it never attained anything like the circulation of its rival. | Decca Records had a substantial share in the paper's ownership. | 22 January 1955 *Record Mirror* followed *NME's* lead and published a 'UK Singles Chart'. The chart recorded a 'Top Ten' calculated from postal returns from 24 record stores in major towns around the country. | 8 October 1955 the chart expanded to a 'Top Twenty' and the following year the number of record stores being sampled increased to sixty. | 28 July 1956. *Record Mirror* published the first UK album chart. | April 1961. A sharp increase in operation costs caused the music paper to phase out its 'Charts'. And on 24 March 1962 the paper began using the record sales charts calculated by *Record Retailer*, which had started publishing in March 1960.

During the 1980s *Record Mirror* was the only 'consumer' music paper to carry the official UK Singles and UK Albums charts—used by the BBC for Radio 1 and *Top of the Pops*—as well as the US *Billboard* Charts. | *Record Retailer* was the first UK publication to feature the Rolling Stones, the Searchers, the Who, and the Kinks. | *Record Mirror* was the first music paper to print in full colour. It was a success, buoyed circulation, and the paper continued with the same format throughout the 1960s.

| Side Bar | *Record Mirror* and The Beatles | *New Record Mirror* was the first national publication to publish an article on The Beatles. | November 1963 the music paper returned to its earlier name *Record Mirror* and featured a full colour picture of The Beatles on the cover, and the first run of 120,000 completely sold out. The following issue, minus The Beatles on the cover, fell to 60,000; a lesson that countless magazines have taken to heart ever since.

Wanting to stand out from all the other London music newspapers, *Record Mirror* went straight to the source and had Bill Harry, founder and editor of *Mersey Beat*, write a regular column on Liverpool's beat music phenomenon for the paper.

Which was probably the reason why, Dezo Hoffmann, *Record Mirror's* head staff photographer, got sent a letter by a reader in from a Liverpool fan bitterly complaining that the press were ignoring the 'fab' new group called The Beatles and that someone should come up to the city right away and photograph them.

Dezo did—and spent three days with savage young Beatles up in Liverpool—and it turned out to be a life changer for him. He was the first professional photographer in Britain to really capture the group's unique style and zany humour and The Beatles took to him and trusted him. Which explains why he was there with them at their first audition at Abbey Road Studios; was with them all around England and during their first visit to America; and at the recording and filming of *A Hard Day's Night*. With the result that his work is widely acknowledged as being the most complete documentation of The Fab Four from 1962 to 1964. When he died, in 1970, Apple Corp. purchased the rights to Dezo Hoffman's entire collection of Beatles' photographs.

PART THREE – QUINTESSENTIAL BEATLES

Quintessential Beatles | Q&A

Even after all these years—fifty years and counting since they first burst onto the scene—The Beatles are one of the most popular search topics on the Internet. Most of the enquiries now coming from young people born long after the group disbanded. A whole new generation newly come to 'The Fab Four' who've sensed there's so much more to explore and understand about The Beatles and their astonishing musical legacy.

The allure of the group just keeps on growing; the search for more answers seemingly never-ending.

The Beatles in Liverpool, Hamburg, London focuses in the main on the early years of the group and takes you from the birth of The Beatles all the way through to the global phenomenon that was *'Beatlemania'*—but of course there's much more to the story of The Beatles.

Quintessential Beatles Q&A deals with the entire time the group were together to provide additional depth to the **Preface: The Beatles - In Brief**. It consists of a kaleidoscope of twenty-four 'Questions & Answers'—facts, thoughts, and musings—from the day when John and Paul bonded over *'Be-Bop-A-Lula'*... through to *'Beatlemania'* and beyond. All the way to *Sgt. Pepper* and *The White Album*... to *Abbey Road* and *Let It Be*... and to the long, slow, sad break up of The Beatles in 1970.

1 - Who were The Beatles?

The Beatles were four working-class men from northern England who formed a rock group while still teenagers.

The Beatles—John Lennon, Paul McCartney, George Harrison, and Ringo Starr—were a 'beat' group from Liverpool, England—that came together in August 1962 to record for EMI's Parlophone label—at Abbey Road Studios, in London. Over the next seven years they went on to compose, record, and release an astonishing body of work; more than two hundred, highly original 'pop' songs; the energy and inventiveness of which still resonate with millions of people to this day.

So great was their appeal that in a little under a year of them first working together—they went from playing in relative obscurity in cellar clubs, jive hives, and ballrooms in Liverpool—and night-clubs in Hamburg's notorious red-light district—to a run of No. 1 Hit singles and albums in the UK charts that propelled them—seemingly overnight—into a national obsession—then a global sensation.

The sudden tidal wave of enthusiasm for 'The Fab Four'—as they soon came to be called—the extraordinary and ever growing allure of their brilliantly-inspired 'pop' music and their 'larger than life' personalities; the unbridled excitement and euphoria they generated among hordes of screaming teenage girls whenever and wherever they appeared; the like and scale of which had never been witnessed before; led Britain's newspapers to dub the phenomenon: "*Beatlemania*".

As musicians, and personalities, The Beatles seemed to blend with one another perfectly: a veritable Earth, Air, Fire, and Water. John Lennon's wonderfully assertive rhythm guitar, Paul McCartney's dramatically melodic bass guitar, George Harrison's bright rockabilly lead guitar, Ringo Starr's always distinctive drumming; all augmented by their unique voices and sublime three-part harmonies; everything coming together to create extraordinary music that somehow always seemed to be new and exciting—even daring and challenging.

The music of The Beatles was singularly joyful, endlessly creative, and uncommonly full of hope. Their songs were instantly recognizable and uniquely unforgettable. The melodies and lyrics touched people, often very deeply, and in the most positive of ways. Imbuing their young fans—in Britain—in America—then all around the world—with an undeniable sense of optimism. Whatever they sang about, everything seemed to say: "*Hey... come along with us... everything's going to be okay.*"

Yet it wasn't only their music that caused them to have such a huge influence on seemingly an entire generation of young people. The Beatles were also regarded as thought and style leaders—smart, witty, rebellious—and endearingly idealistic. They were irreverent, self-deprecating, playful, and fun. Never more so than when they were dealing with the world's media with whom they adamantly refused to be taken for or treated as fools. Their answers to questions were always dryly mischievous or memorably surreal. And should circumstances ever demand it, being past masters of the good old Liverpool 'put down', they'd deliver a barbed rejoinder that marked the inquirer as silly, uninformed, or just plain wrong. Regardless. The world's television and press corps simply couldn't ever get enough of them.

In always questioning everything worth questioning; be it music, recording techniques, business, art, life, love, society, politics, religion, or even themselves, The Beatles became inextricably linked with the very ideas of 'change' and 'new ways of being'. And never more so than when in mid-career they revealed they'd experimented with marijuana and LSD as ways to open the doors of perception, inspire creativity, and espoused the practice of mantras and meditation as aids in the quest for greater spiritual fulfilment. *"Hey... all we are saying... like... is that it works for us. Nothing more."*

Little wonder then that, as they always seemed to be at least one step ahead of everyone else in everything they said or did, The Beatles came to be seen as heralds of such newly emerging 'counterculture' ideas as sexual freedom, sexual-identity, feminism and gender equality—experimentation with drugs and transcendental religion—even environmentalism and vegetarianism. Ideas still very much in play and still being fought over to this day.

All of which went to make The Beatles one of the most significant cultural forces of the second half of the Twentieth Century.

The Beatles officially disbanded in 1970—but their musical influence was—and still is—immense. They are universally acknowledged to have been the most important—most influential rock band—of all time.

| Side Bar | Feminism and gender equality | Young girls on both sides of the Atlantic seemed to 'get' The Beatles implicitly. Saw immediately that the boys in the group offered an entirely transgressive view of 'masculinity' and what it meant 'to be a man'. And even though in the early Hamburg days The Beatles had adopted the leather look and trademark 'Pilzenkopf' Beatle haircut of Klaus Voormann and other 'Exis' they'd met and then had their image 'cleaned up' by Brian Epstein; wearing matching collarless jackets and newly washed hair; they 'represented' in the true twenty-first century meaning of the word an entirely new and different model of the modern man. A million miles away from the T-shirt and jeans tortured reality of existing masculine youth icons James Dean and Marlon Brando. No urban cowboys they. The cowboy boots John, Paul, and George had bought in Hamburg were swapped for Cuban-heel elastic-sided boots bought from London boot-makers to stars of stage and screen, Anello and Davide. All of which added up to: New. Different. Modern. Male. And the girls in the audience knew it and totally grasped it even if they couldn't yet put word to thought. They reacted intuitively, instinctively, and with such unfettered immediacy; the volume of their screaming and shouting, calling out and applauding, once likened to the full-on roar of a jet airliner; they shook the very foundations of the music and entertainment business. All but redefining youth culture and—yes—sowing the very seeds that would later flower into new notions of sexual identity and gender equality, and help bring the nascent female liberation movement into full bloom.

2 - What did The Beatles achieve as a group?

During their heyday as a rock group, The Beatles released twelve studio albums, thirteen EPs ('extended play' 45 rpm discs that could hold two songs per side), and twenty-two hit 'singles' in the United Kingdom.

More than two hundred startlingly original, all but perfect 'pop' songs written and composed by John Lennon and Paul McCartney; and George Harrison; and, yes, even by Ringo Starr. An astonishing feat of sustained creativity displaying ever-new heights of inspired musical invention; breaking rules and pushing boundaries in recording techniques. Changing the very idea of what a 'pop' song could be.

The Beatles not only forever changed the course of popular music; they also helped shape the hopes, dreams, and aspirations of millions of young people in the UK, the US, and all around the world.

Even though the group's first single in Britain—'Love Me Do'—was released way back in October 1962, no pop group or artist, before or since, on either side of the Atlantic, or anywhere else in the world for that matter, has come anywhere near to matching all The Beatles did and achieved. And even today, with the rise and rise of 24/7 music-streaming services and veritable multitudes of musical performances, amateur as well as professional, readily available on YouTube and other media platforms, it's all but impossible to believe that the creative quality and output of The Beatles, in all that they produced during their '*Seven Glorious Years*', will ever be equalled, let alone surpassed.

3 - Why is it crucial to understand Liverpool for one to fully appreciate The Beatles?

The plain fact is The Beatles couldn't have come from any place else. Honest. The Beatles' '*charm*' and '*cheekiness*'—essential elements of the fabled '*charisma*' that was so often key to their success—weren't simply traits unique to the group, but essential qualities of Liverpool '*culture*' itself.

Paul Du Noyer; that most excellent British music journalist and author—and a Liverpudlian, to Bootle—once wrote:

"Liverpool is more than a place where music happens. Liverpool is a reason why music happens."

Liverpool, like all great maritime cities, has long drawn people from far and wide, near and far, has long been multi-ethnic in character, and home to a populace of every race, colour, and creed. And it's this singular awareness of Merseyside having been a long bubbling cultural 'melting pot' that's given Liverpool an all but indestructible sense of itself. An inner strength that, whether it manifests to outsiders as a cock-sure confidence or feisty obstinacy, enables Liverpool to look out at the world without ever losing sight of its own special place in it.

Liverpudlians—or 'Scousers' as they like to call themselves in deference to Liverpool's distinctive 'Scouse' accent and dialect—have always tried to be self-sufficient; have always sought their own entertainments, created their own style of humour and music; most especially their music.

An ever-present "sound of the city"—a stew of songs and sounds and rhythms and melodies and modalities that could do nothing but reflect Liverpool's long multicultural history. And that's long made Liverpool a city unlike any other in Britain.

The 'melting pot' allusion all but bursting onto the scene during the late Fifties and early Sixties when Liverpool took the best of American rock 'n' roll and R&B and rockabilly and made the sound its very own: 'Merseybeat'.

A time when Liverpool was host to hundreds and hundreds of 'beat' groups—as well as hundreds of folk groups, Trad-jazz bands, R&B groups, black groups, and 'all girl' singing groups. Brass bands, too. Merseyside was also home to the UK's oldest and largest 'Country and Western' scene—nowhere else ever came within a lasso's length of it. The city also boasted hundreds and hundreds of venues of all shapes and sizes—including the Tower Ballroom—the biggest dancehall in the entire country capable of holding well over four thousand people. No wonder then Liverpool was also the birthplace of world's first bi-weekly 'all entertainments' newspaper—Bill Harry's aptly named *Mersey Beat*.

All of which underscores Du Noyer's canny claim that it's no accident the 20th Century's most important 'pop' group hailed from Liverpool. And reason enough, surely, for Liverpool to lay strong claim to being *"the Fifth Beatle"*—as it was the one place on earth where all the essential elements of 'Nature' and 'Nurture' could combine together to produce the fantabulous Beatles.

Many years later, when John Lennon lived with his wife Yoko, at the Dakota, on the Upper West Side of Manhattan, in New York City, one of his most treasured possessions was a wooden chest full of photographs and mementoes. One word hand painted on the lid: '**LIVERPOOL**'.

| Side Bar | The Beatles' Multicultural Liverpool | During the 19th and early 20th centuries, Liverpool gave safe harbour to large Jewish, Norwegian, Polish, German, and Greek communities. And was home to the oldest Chinese community in Europe. There's also been a significant 'black' community in Merseyside for over a hundred years: the oldest one in Britain, in fact. | The almost continual waves of Welsh and Irish migrants—all looking for work—earned Liverpool the title, *"the true capital of Ireland"... of Wales*, too, for that matter. | Little wonder, John Lennon and Paul McCartney could both claim Irish heritage. Or that The Beatles' first booking-agent-cum-manager Allan Williams, owner of the Jacaranda coffee bar, who booked them into their first club residency in Hamburg, was Welsh, or that his wife, Beryl, was Chinese. | Of note, because it was Beryl and her brother, Barry Chang, who huddled together with all five Beatles—John, Paul, George, Stu, and Pete—in the back of the campervan Allan drove all the way to Hamburg. | Also in the van with them, was Allan Williams' black business partner, 'Lord' Woodbine; club owner, entrepreneur, calypso singer, songwriter, and bandleader. Who, although originally from Trinidad, was the very first 'Scouser' to 'discover' the financial possibilities of Hamburg's nightclub scene; having recently had great success performing there with his Royal Caribbean Steel Band. | Liverpool's black community again playing an important role in The Beatles' story with Derry Wilkie, the black lead singer of Derry & the Seniors, the very first Liverpool 'beat' group to play Hamburg. Derry, proving such a hit with German audiences that Bruno Koschmider, owner of the Kaiserkeller, immediately wanted to hire more Liverpool rock 'n' roll groups for his club. Thereby opening the way for The Beatles to play Hamburg. | Also noteworthy, the black, Somali-Irish rhythm guitarist and singer, Vinnie Ismail, a stalwart of numerous black Liverpool groups who, amongst other things, taught John Lennon and Paul McCartney how to play the 'magic' string-bar-seventh chord.

4 - How does Gene Vincent's *'Be-Bop-A-Lula'* mark the birth of The Beatles?

When The Beatles first started they covered whatever songs most took their fancy. Especially rock 'n' roll: the "new sound" coming out of America. And Gene Vincent's instant classic, 'Be-Bop-A-Lula', has a particular significance. It wasn't just the first record Paul McCartney ever bought for himself; in a 2017 interview he remembers simply *"playing it to death"*; it was also one of the songs that brought John Lennon and Paul together.

The day it all began; Saturday, 6 July 1957; when the almost seventeen-year old John Lennon met the barely-fifteen-year old Paul McCartney at St. Peter's Parish Church Garden Fête, in Woolton, a suburb of Liverpool. Paul, his guitar slung across his back, standing amidst the milling afternoon crowd, having cycled to the event at the suggestion of his grammar school friend, Ivan Vaughan, who'd known John since infant school.

John's six-man 'Skiffle' group, The Quarrymen: Eric Griffiths on guitar; Ron Davis on banjo; John's best friend, Pete Shotton, on washboard; Len Garry on tea-chest bass; Colin Hanton, on drums; all bunched together atop the temporary wooden stage, already well into their first set. John standing, legs firmly planted, at the microphone, with his *'guaranteed-not-to-split'* guitar; already the centre of all eyes; singing 'Skiffle' and rock 'n' roll favourites 'Cumberland Gap', 'Maggie Mae', *'Be-Bop-A-Lula'*, and 'Come Go With Me'. Inventing lyrics on the spot if the proper words happened to elude his ever-questing mind. But working up an authentic sweat; saturating everything with the rawness and heat; the drive and beat; the very *feel* of rock 'n' roll.

John's performance more than enough for Paul to realise that here was a *bona fide* brother rock 'n' roller; someone that obviously felt the same way he did about the 'new' music. Someone he'd perhaps never thought to find in all of Liverpool. The very idea of it so compelling that right after The Quarrymen had completed their second afternoon set and sat together in a circle of chairs; relaxing, eating, drinking, smoking; at the church hall across the road; biding time before their two half-hour sets at the evening's 'Grand Dance'; an impromptu audition took place.

Ivan introduced Paul. Nods were exchanged. Silence reigned. So Paul picked up his guitar and 'rocked it up' with Eddie Cochran's 'Twenty Flight Rock' and Gene Vincent's *'Be-Bop-A-Lula'*, before ripping into a medley of Little Richard hits. He wrote out the words to 'Twenty Flight Rock' and *'Be-Bop-A-Lula'* for John, showed him how to tune a six-string guitar, properly, and then he left. Silence reigned a second time, each Quarryman alone with his thoughts, but John was utterly entranced by what he'd seen and heard.

John later discussed the matter with his best mate, Pete Shotton: *"This young bloke, Paul, plays guitar much better than me. He's got a great voice, too, and might just try and rival me as leader. And yet... he'd make the group that much stronger."*

Years later John fondly recalled that he sang *'Be-Bop-A-Lula'* the day he met Paul. Paul's also spoken of the song's importance to him and John. Gene Vincent's instant classic—a secret handshake between two rock 'n' roll mad Liverpool teenagers—signalling their mutual love of the "new music"—and the beginning of one of music's greatest ever song-writing partnerships.

5 - Who was Stuart Sutcliffe?

Stu Sutcliffe was The Beatles' original bass player and John Lennon's closest friend. He met John and Bill Harry, the founder and editor of *Mersey Beat*, at Liverpool College of Art and they all became fast friends. Stu's 'cool' James Dean look and demeanour, and his talent as a fine artist, impressed John hugely. It was John who persuaded Stu to use the money he got from selling one of his paintings at a biennial Liverpool art exhibition to buy a Höfner electric bass guitar and join his group—then called Johnny and The Moondogs—even though he couldn't play a note. Stu persisted but never really mastered the bass.

He did however come up with the name—'Beatals'—in homage to Buddy Holly and The Crickets. Stu's idea struck a chord but they soon embellished it and played under the name 'The Silver Beetles'.

In August 1960 John persuaded Stu to leave Art College and go to Hamburg with him and the group, now at last called The Beatles. And Stu duly played bass during the gruelling, all-important, first 16-week stint at the Indra and Kaiserkeller clubs. It was while playing the Kaiserkeller that Stu was introduced to the beautiful young German photographer, Astrid Kirchherr and her two closest friends—art students Klaus Voormann and Jürgen Vollmer—all three of who would later have a huge effect on the look and style of The Beatles.

Astrid Kirchherr and Jürgen Vollmer took the documentary style black and white photographs of the group in Hamburg—the first of their kind for any pop group. Soon Stu and Astrid became engaged. It was Astrid who first cut Stu's hair into the 'French style'—the look that later became universally regarded as The Beatles' iconic 'mop top' hairstyle. After the group's second season in Hamburg Stu left the group to stay on in Hamburg with Astrid and take up painting again. When The Beatles next returned to Hamburg, to play the newly opened Star-Club, John, Paul, and Pete Best bumped into a very distraught Astrid at the airport and she told them Stuart had died of a cerebral haemorrhage. John was utterly distraught. He'd already lost his mother. And now he'd lost his best friend, too. Years later, John said in an interview: *"I looked up to Stu. I depended on him to tell me the truth."*

6 - In what way was Litherland Town Hall a real 'turning point' for The Beatles?

The Beatles' first 16-week stint in Hamburg, playing the Indra and Kaiserkeller clubs, all but ended in disaster. George Harrison was deported for being underage and not having a proper work permit. Paul McCartney and Pete Best were ordered to leave Germany immediately afterwards, on a trumped-up charge of arson; later rescinded. Stu Sutcliffe decided to stay on in Hamburg with his new girlfriend Astrid Kirchherr. And John Lennon travelled home, alone, by train and cross-Channel ferry; his guitar-case in one hand, his suitcase in the other, his amplifier strapped to his back.

For the first couple of weeks of December 1960, everyone kept to themselves and licked their wounds. Paul even got himself a temporary job as a delivery van driver to help with the

Christmas rush. Then John resurfaced. The group played a couple of evenings at the Casbah Coffee Club, owned by Pete's mum, Mona Best. The posters on the walls, hand-drawn by young accountancy student Neil Aspinall, the group's new part-time roadie, proclaiming: *'Direct from Hamburg'*. But the momentum and drive The Beatles had built up as a group playing the Indra and Kaiserkeller had essentially stalled.

It was then that their booking agent-cum-manager Allan Williams, in another of his still relatively unsung all-important acts, given its later significance, introduced the group to 28-year-old Bob Wooler; itinerant disc jockey and *compère extraordinaire*. Wooler listened to The Beatles' tales of recent woe; developed a liking for the young lads in the group; and offered to help get them some bookings. And he contacted promoter Brian Kelly, for whom he sometimes acted as compère, and for the agreed-to princely fee of £6; about $18 at the time, but still £2 short of what he'd originally asked for; set The Beatles up as last minute additions to Beekay Promotions' *'Post-Boxing-Day'* dance, scheduled to take place at the Litherland Town Hall ballroom, located some five miles north of Liverpool city-centre.

The Beatles grasped hold of the opportunity with four sets of hands. But with Stu Sutcliffe still in Hamburg they still had to convince Chas Newby, then a college student, to fill-in on bass. (Chas had been the bass-player with Pete's original Casbah Coffee Club band, The Blackjacks, before he'd suddenly disappeared off to Hamburg with The Beatles.) The Beatles all spent Christmas with their respective families; did a quick rehearsal with Mr. Newby; and on the evening of Tuesday, 27th December, 1960, donned their leather gear and got ready to rock 'n' roll.

Meanwhile, posters proclaiming The Del Renas, The Deltones, and The Searchers were already up, so Bob Wooler, ever the professional, was busy pasting overlays with *'The Beatles - Direct from Hamburg'* across as many of them as he could. It's hardly surprising that many in the audience thought John, Paul, George, and Pete were German. Especially when they first saw them in their black leather jackets and trousers and cowboy boots. What they made of tweed-jacket wearing Chas Newby, filling in for the still absent Stu Sutcliffe, is anybody's guess.

But right from the start, when Paul nudged Bob Wooler off the microphone before he could even finish his mellifluous be-hind-the-stage-curtain introduction: *"Ladies and Gentleman... direct from Hamburg... the Be..."* and started belting out the opening words to Little Richard's 'Long Tall Sally', The Beatles stunned the crowd. No one had ever seen or heard anything like it. The group's hard rocking, hard-hitting, boot-stomping 'Hamburg' sound was so new, so raw, so loud, and so very, very different; it blew everyone and everything else away.

All the dancers in the ballroom; there were over a thousand people there that night; just stopped, turned, and rushed the stage to get closer to the action; again totally unprecedented. The Beatles' nonstop set of rock 'n' roll and R&B classics was an absolute smash. It instantly established The Beatles as a top 'live' draw all around Merseyside. Brian Kelly immediately booked them for two months straight. And every other Liverpool promoter, worth his salt, scrambled to book the group to do more gigs. From this point on the group never really looked back; only ever forward, towards the future, and reaching *'the toppermost of the poppermost'*.

The Beatles played 19 dates for Brian Kelly and an ever-growing number of other local promoters in January 1961. They played 31 dates in February, including their first lunchtime sessions at the Cavern Club and appearances at the Cassanova Club. They did 37 dates in March; three bookings in a single day increasingly the norm; including the first 'all-nighter' at the Iron Door for Sam Leach and their first evening appearance at the Cavern. The Beatles played Litherland Town Hall for Beekay Promotions fully 19 times during 1961; although never again as last minute additions, only ever as 'top of the bill' headliners.

"Up to Hamburg we'd thought we were OK, but not good enough. It was only back in Liverpool that we realised the difference and saw what had happened to us while everyone else was playing Cliff Richard shit." — John Lennon

7 - If The Beatles were only a back-up band when they recorded 'My Bonnie' in Hamburg... what's the big deal?

'My Bonnie' was The Beatles' first commercially released disc, but it also played a hugely pivotal role in the group's fortunes as it brought them to the attention of Brian Epstein, the man who would become their manager.

As the resident group at Hamburg's Top Ten club The Beatles not only had to perform their own series of 90-minute sets each and every night, they also acted as the backing group for the club's 'Star' attraction; English rock 'n' roll singer and musician Tony Sheridan. Famed German record producer and bandleader Bert Kaempfert saw them all performing together at the club, very much liked what he heard, and signed Tony Sheridan and The Beatles to separate contracts with his company Bert Kaempfert Productions.

Kaempfert arranged to record his "new music" group in a two-day session at Hamburg's Friedrich-Ebert-Halle on 22-23 June 1961. Tony Sheridan took lead vocals. John, Paul, and George, Stu Sutcliffe, and Pete Best did their utmost best to back him. And the motely group of Britisher musicians recorded rock 'n' roll cover versions of 'My Bonnie' and 'When The Saints Go Marching In'; both songs, conveniently, long out of copyright.

'My Bonnie' with 'The Saints' on the B-side—both credited to 'Tony Sheridan and The Beat Brothers'—was released as a single on the Polydor label in West Germany in October 1961. It made No. 4 on Hamburg's local singles chart, but peaked at No. 32 in the German hit parade. More importantly, George Harrison got a copy of the disc into the hands of DJ Bob Wooler back home in Liverpool, who played and promoted it over and over again at the Cavern. After all, it was a 'first' for a favourite local group.

Legend says it was Liverpool teenager Raymond Jones who first then walked into Brian Epstein's city-centre NEMS record store one Saturday afternoon, in late October 1961, to ask for a copy of 'My Bonnie'; a record he'd heard played again and again at the Cavern. But not only did Brian Epstein not have it in stock, he'd never even heard of it or the local group who'd recorded it. And as he prided himself on NEMS always having all the latest releases in stock, he immediately set himself the task of sourcing the missing record as soon as humanly possible. Thus setting into motion the series of events that led him to becoming The Beatles' manager in December that same year.

'My Bonnie' was released in Britain on 5 January 1962; this time credited to 'Tony Sheridan and The Beatles'. And was a great hit with Liverpool fans; still the only ones, at the time, in all of Great Britain to have even heard of The Beatles.

"It's just Tony Sheridan singing... with us banging in the background. It's terrible. It could be anybody." — John Lennon | Reflecting on 'My Bonnie', in 1963 – *The Beatles Anthology*

Even so, it wasn't just 'anybody' that made arrangements to see The Beatles at the Cavern; drawn there by the 45rpm record of 'My Bonnie'; it was Brian Epstein. And the rest, as they say, is music history. And a 'bonnie' wee tale it makes, too.

8 - What on earth was '*Beatlemania*'?

In a little under a year The Beatles went from playing in relative obscurity in cellar clubs, jive hives, and ballrooms in Liverpool, and former strip-clubs in Hamburg's red-light district, to a recording contact with one of Britain's 'Big Four' record companies and appearances at two of London's most prestigious venues. Added to which they had a string of No. 1 Hits in the UK 'Pop' Charts and two No. 1 albums. Made numerous appearances on British national television. Undertook four nationwide tours. And were catapulted into national fame.

Such was the immediacy of the tidal wave of enthusiasm for the group; the ever growing appeal of their brilliantly-inspired 'pop' music and 'larger than life' personalities; the unbridled excitement and euphoria they generated among hordes of screaming teenage girls whenever and wherever they appeared; the like and scale of which had never before been witnessed; the British press dubbed the phenomenon—"*Beatlemania*".

The two major incidents in 1963 that set the whole national craze into motion: When The Beatles first appeared on Britain's highest rated TV variety show *Sunday Night at the London Palladium* (13 Oct) and took the country by storm. Followed within weeks by their appearance at a Royal Command Performance (4 Nov) in front of members of Britain's Royal Family and the country's elite; later televised nationally; again to all but universal acclaim. (The time John Lennon famously asked the audience: **"Would the people in the cheap seats just clap your hands—and the rest of you simply rattle your jewellery."**)

"Beatlemania" grew into an unprecedented global phenomenon. Within another year The Beatles, both in person and with their first film, *A Hard Day's Night*, not only conquered the US 'pop' charts—as well as the hearts and minds of America's youth—but were catapulted to worldwide fame, international acclaim, and unparalleled success. And what had begun as a simple teenage music craze amongst fans in Liverpool, Hamburg, and London turned into a multi-generational, multicultural force the likes of which the world had never seen before and, in all probability, will never see again.

9 - What made The Beatles so different?

The Beatles were so very different to all the 'pop' artists who'd gone before them, certainly to British eyes and ears, as they were totally new in both look and sound. It didn't matter whether you were a boy or a girl, young people just couldn't seem to get enough of them or take their eyes off them. The Beatles were simply everywhere: in newspapers and magazines, on television and on film. And whatever 'it' was; they had 'it' in spades and to spare.

Then, of course, there was the odd looking hairstyles that John, Paul, and George all wore; so very different from the still popular Elvis-like, swept-back, Brylcreem-laden hairstyle or the 'short-back-and-sides' of almost every other young boy in England. And yet in the beginning it was their very 'everyday scruffiness' that had first endeared them to local fans at cellar clubs such as the Casbah, the Cavern, and the Iron Door. It made them 'normal'. Showed they were devoid of any 'stuck-up' airs or graces. And fans felt all the closer to them for it.

Even when their manager Brian Epstein stepped in and told them to: "clean up their act a little". Told them to stop smoking and eating and drinking on stage—stop making jokes and talking to the audience. Get rid of their leather jackets and scruffy jeans. Wear something a little more tasteful; grey tweed stage suits that a little tailor he knew would run up for them. They still looked different to everyone else. The looked like a real group, beholden to nobody but themselves.

Another thing that set The Beatles apart from all other groups—until seemingly everyone copied her unique style— were the iconic black and white photographs Astrid Kirchherr took of them in Hamburg; a number of which Bill Harry used to great effect in *Mersey Beat*. They were so very distinctive, so new, so authentic, and so very effective, that Brian Epstein later had other photographers try to capture the same documentary grittiness; only with The Beatles now dressed in smart suits. And even in a now famous suite of photos taken of them in broad daylight on an abandoned Liverpool bombsite; surrounded by rusted bicycles and prams, even an old motor car; they looked terrific. Striking images that stood out from all the studio-lit and shot, 8x10 '*Spotlight*' photos of artistes and bands that usually appeared in all the music newspapers and girls' magazines. And, later, when they appeared on TV, they always looked so striking, so sharp. It was almost as if they'd been tailor-made for black and white newspaper and magazine photography, television, and film.

What was even stranger; they really did look like a group, with no discernable leader. And that was different. They looked alike, dressed alike, and sounded alike. Shared the same dry sense of humour. Were tight-knit. Were always more than ready to take on all-comers. In which, they resembled nothing so much as a teenage street gang, only a very hip and cool one. Not for them the music industry norm of handsome teen-idol standing out in front of an all but interchangeable backing band. The Beatles set themselves up as a group from the very start—with each one able to act as lead singer. If a song called for it, their voices blended seamlessly in two or three-part harmonies. Or if singing 'call and response' their voices played off one another to brilliant effect. As a group of musicians they played together wonderfully. The three guitarists—lead guitar, rhythm guitar, and bass guitar—complemented each other superbly, the drummer always able to add just the right touch. No one ever needing to push to the front or stand out from the others; all and everything only ever in service to the song they were playing. All of which in time would become clearly recognisable signatures of a Beatles' song.

Even the way they arranged themselves on stage looked totally new and different. It helped, of course, that with Paul being left-handed and John and George right-handed, they could stand at the microphones with their guitars pointed in opposite directions. So everything balanced perfectly. Added to which the actual make and design of the guitars they each played was so very new and eye-catching. And however happenstance or serendipitous their acquisition, it all turned out to be extremely fortuitous: John's American-made Rickenbacker guitar and Paul's German-made Höfner violin-shaped bass guitar—both purchased in Hamburg—and George's US-made Gretsch 'Country Gentleman'—bought off a merchant seaman for cash in Liverpool—soon became iconic in their own right. And rightly so, as hardly anyone in Britain, save for the odd professional musician or two, had ever seen anything like them.

All of it all the more extraordinary when you consider that all four members of The Beatles were barely in their 'twenties when they became world famous.

10 - Were The Beatles really so charismatic? Or was it all just media hype?

Brian Epstein, the young Liverpool businessman who went on to become the group's manager, said that the very first time he saw them at The Cavern Club in Liverpool: *"I was immediately struck by their music, their beat, and their sense of humour on stage... and, even afterwards, when I met them, I was struck again by their personal charm. And it was there that, really, it all started."*

The Beatles were all so very witty, cheeky, and charming. When confronted by reporters they were fast with a quip and self-deprecating at the same time; an irresistible combination as it turned out. And were quick to win both hearts and minds for the simple reason they were always such fun to be around. They were extraordinarily magnetic. Whenever they entered a room, took to the stage, or appeared on screen; all eyes were immediately drawn to them. And when they came together to perform, they were even more magnetic, and uncannily so, the whole even greater than the sum of the parts. Even close friends or people who worked closely with the group remarked on the phenomenon.

As a group they just seemed to belong together. Were complete in themselves. Not in need of anything from anyone, certainly not anyone's approval. Which only served to make them all the more appealing, both individually and as a group. To the eyes of the young they appeared to possess magical abilities, some 'special knowledge'. And to some observers it really did seem that The Beatles could not only see the future, they could help shape it, perhaps even bring it into being. There was simply no one else like them. No one. They were utterly unprecedented. True originals. They were The Beatles, and no one else was or could ever be them; they were and would forever remain unique.

George Martin, the head of the Parlophone record label and their record producer, later said of The Beatles: *"They had this great charm... great cheeky charm. A charisma... that when you are with them, you are all the better for being with them... and when they leave... you feel a loss. I fell in love with them. It's as simple as that."*

11 - What was the big deal with The Beatles writing their own songs?

Back in the early Sixties rock 'n' roll bands didn't compose their own songs—it was rare even amongst solo artists. A very select few did. Buddy Holly. Chuck Berry. Little Richard. The Everly Brothers sometimes did. But they were very much the exception to the rule. And the brilliant singer-songwriter Bob Dylan had yet to appear on the scene. So it was an enormous stroke of good fortune when record producer George Martin elected to sign The Beatles to a recording contract with Parlophone Records. He was, arguably, the one record producer in all of London, at the time, who could help nurture the group's raw talent—and not dampen or discourage—or worse kill it stone dead. What's more he had the wit and grace and vision to let the group record songs they'd written themselves.

His decision all the more extraordinary when, as time would tell, it turned out there were three world-class songwriters in the group. All the more astonishing when you consider that none of The Beatles had any formal musical training whatsoever. They were all entirely self-taught. And yet were so intuitive, so imaginative, so extraordinarily gifted, they went on to produce music that more-formally educated musicians and composers would never have even allowed themselves to imagine, let alone create.

The Beatles 'coloured outside the lines' in every which way, imaginable. By always challenging accepted norms, always pushing boundaries, always seeking to develop new song structures and styles, always experimenting with new recording techniques, sounds, and modalities, they expanded the very idea of what popular music could encompass, what it could be. And as they grew as songwriters, as musicians, and as people, their songs reflected those changes and as a result changed 'pop' music forever.

In the very beginning, though, they were essentially a cover band, covering classic American rock 'n' roll, rockabilly, and rhythm and blues songs; many of which though would've sounded obscure even to American ears. They took whatever they considered were the best songs from whatever source: Sun Records in Memphis; Chess Records in Chicago; Atlantic Records; RCA-Victor; Detroit's Tamla-Motown; New York's Brill Building; and reinterpreted them and made them indelibly their own. They weren't even above using a song from a Broadway musical. Anything and everything that would help *"make a show"* even more memorable and exciting was up for grabs. The breadth and variety of which; they had close to three hundred covers in their repertoire before they began to record and play their own songs; would have given them an impressive grounding as to every element of composing a 'Hit' pop song.

"What kept the Beatles head and shoulders above everyone else is that they were prepared to change... do different things."
— George Martin

12 - Why was The Beatles' original drummer, Pete Best, sacked from the group?

Pete Best, the son of Casbah Coffee Club owner Mona Best, was The Beatles' drummer from the summer of 1960 through until the summer of 1962; playing nightclubs in Hamburg and venues of all sorts and sizes in Liverpool.

Some people said at the time that Pete was the most popular Beatle amongst Liverpool fans. The Cavern's DJ Bob Wooler referred to him as being: *"mean, moody, and magnificent... in the Jeff Chandler tradition"* (the actor Jeff Chandler was a major Hollywood movie star). Those same people also suggest that John, Paul, and George pushed Pete Best out simply because they were jealous of his good looks and his immense popularity with the group's girl fans.

I don't subscribe to that view. Even so, the way Pete Best was sacked, after having helped build the group's reputation—gig by gig by gig—for two hard-slog years, isn't exactly The Beatles' finest hour. The how and why of it, still a bone of contention with many people, but it had nothing at all to do with Ringo Starr, the man who would eventually replace Pete as the group's drummer. In fact recent research now suggests Ringo was but one of several drummers who were initially asked to replace Pete Best. *

The facts of the matter as stark now as they were then; when on Thursday, 16 August 1962, Pete Best was summarily fired by Beatles' manager, Brian Epstein: *"Pete, I've got some bad news for you. The boys want you out. And Ringo in."* Pete said later: *"It came as a complete bombshell... right out of the blue."*

Mersey Beat ran a cover story on the sacking in their very next issue. Word quickly spread. Hundreds of fans sent letters of protest to the magazine. Fans picketed NEMS music store. Someone scratched Brian Epstein's brand new Consul motorcar, after which he thought it prudent to hire a bodyguard. And even then, in a melee, with jostling fans a Cavern gig; George Harrison got given a black eye. Pete's fan weren't at all happy about it all. And not to condone any of it, but it should all be put into context. Few people were happy about it all.

Yet The Beatles were desperate. They needed to find a new drummer, a good one, and quickly. They'd been thinking about nothing else since their 6 June visit to EMI's Abbey Road Studios for their Parlophone 'artists' test' cum audition with George Martin. After the end of the session the record producer had quietly taken Brian Epstein aside and told him Pete Best's drumming wasn't suitable for recording purposes; his drum 'beat' apparently wasn't rock steady enough; and they'd need to employ a session drummer for any and all future studio work. Brian kept the news to himself at first, and only told John, Paul, and George a day or two later when they got back to Liverpool. And even then they didn't tell Pete.

The whole thing would have put John, Paul, and George into a complete and utter spin. They didn't have a signed contract. Every other recording company in London had already turned them down; some, several times, over. And if Pete wasn't a good enough musician, what did it say about the three of them. It might well spell the end of everything. It looked like their very last chance of a recording contract, the one thing in the entire world that they desired the most, was about to go up in smoke. As far as they saw it, their careers were on the line. And there was no other option, but to get themselves a new drummer, the very best drummer they could find, and have Brian sort out any legal wrangles later on.

After the sacking, Brian Epstein offered to help Pete get situated with another fast-rising Liverpool group, The Merseybeats. But Pete flat-out declined. He'd had more than enough of Mr. Epstein's business management, thank you very much. But Brian, being Brian, persisted, as he hadn't wanted to fire Pete; it was the other three Beatles who'd insisted on it. And so Brian quietly pulled some strings and, through the agency of his close personal friend, Joe Flannery, managed to get Pete set up with Lee Curtis and the All Stars. Then in 1963, when Lee Curtis left the group, they renamed themselves the Pete Best All Stars. The group made a record, for Decca, but were later dropped because of poor sales; the eventual fate of many a Merseyside group.

* See David Bedford and Garry Popper's excellent *'Finding The Fourth Beatle'*

13 - What impact did the arrival of Ringo Starr have on The Beatles?

It's often been said that Ringo Starr was the luckiest guy in the world to join The Beatles just before they became world famous. Though no less a person than John Lennon maintained that when Ringo joined The Beatles, he was even more famous around Merseyside than they were. Ringo was certainly one of Liverpool's best-known and best-liked drummers. Rory Storm and the Hurricanes—with Ringo Starr on drums—were the biggest band in Liverpool in 1960, everybody said so. And when early in October 1960 The Beatles moved from the Indra to the Kaiserkeller club, midway through their first season in Hamburg, the 'headline' beat group they found themselves in competition with each night, for the next eight weeks, was none other than Rory Storm and the Hurricanes. The Beatles hadn't long acquired their own novice drummer, Pete Best, and so they could have done nothing but admire, have even been jealous of, the skills of the far more accomplished and much more experienced Ringo Starr.

The two Liverpool groups got on famously together; The Beatles getting better all the time; thriving on the nightly competition to see who could put on the best show. John, Paul, and George even got to play with Ringo after a couple of weeks, when 'Lu' Walters—The Hurricanes' bass-player—asked them to sit in on a session he'd arranged and paid for himself at a tiny Hamburg recording studio. The first time the four future Beatles played together and a moment they all no doubt remembered.

So when a couple of years later John and Paul asked Ringo to join The Beatles, by now firmly established as Merseyside's top group, he wouldn't have felt at all intimidated or outclassed. You could even make the case The Beatles needed Ringo much more than he needed them, as they were desperate to find a drummer who could pass muster with record producer, George Martin.

And even though it now seems Ringo was but one of several drummers initially asked to replace Pete Best, as subsequent events have proved, unequivocally, he was *the* drummer The Beatles needed. He was everything his predecessor wasn't. He could play multiple different styles; not just a thudding four/four beat. Perhaps even more importantly he had an immediate rapport with the other three Beatles, both as an individual and as a musician. He shared the same whacky sense of humour. His personality fit theirs like a glove. So even though Pete Best might well have been a good drummer, even a great drummer, Ringo was all that and more—plus he also possessed that indefinable quality that also made him *an outstanding Beatle*.

One further thought, and no pun intended here, but with the virtue of hindsight, one can honestly say that everything happened for the best.

Pete Best played with The Beatles during the early days when they were essentially a rock 'n' roll cover band. And a bloody great one they were, too, by all accounts. Pete developed a really big, heavy bass drum sound; a full on 4/4 "atom" beat that really hit home with fans in the close confines of the clubs. And perfect for the needs of the time.

Ringo Starr was an altogether different kind of drummer, more nuanced, more accomplished, more versatile. And even though he also wasn't perhaps as steady as 'metronome-like' session player, Andy White, he could play in multiple different styles and deliver whatever beat was called for; always expertly and seemingly effortlessly.

And even if George Martin didn't exactly recognize it at the very beginning, the record producer soon came to realise, as did everyone else, that Ringo had a particular knack and feel for playing just the right drum pattern required for each and every new song that The Beatles composed. Always seemed to be able to add just the right touch. Playing only whatever was called for to lift a song and drive it forward, towards excellence, and no more. Very much like what George Harrison always did with his lead guitar work.

Ringo Starr turned out to be the missing piece of the puzzle for The Beatles—*"the full fulfilment of the missing part"*—across multiple dimensions, in life as well as music.

George Harrison later reflected on Ringo's debut with the group, after only a two-hour rehearsal on the evening of Saturday, 18 August 1962, at Hulme Hall, Port Sunlight, Liverpool: *"From that moment on... it just gelled... The Beatles went on to a different level."*

14 - Why was America so instrumental to The Beatles' success?

America wasn't simply the birthplace of Rock 'n' Roll it was also the biggest record market in the entire world. And as the song says, even though it was specifically written to celebrate New York, it's the same difference: *'If you could make it there... you could make it anywhere'*.

Britain's 'Skiffle King', Lonnie Donegan, had had a No. 1 Hit in the US Charts, but almost every other British act that had ever tried to break into the US market had failed utterly. Cliff Richard being the prime example. Even so, when Brian Epstein, riding the wave of *'Beatlemania'* in England, moved his NEMS offices from the centre of Liverpool down into the very heart of London's West End, he immediately set his sights on America. The utter indifference of the US music industry to British 'pop' recording artists didn't deter him one bit, he was determined "his boys" would succeed where all others had failed; that one day they'd even be bigger than Elvis Presley. The continued refusal of Capitol Records, in the US, to release any of The Beatles' first UK Hits, no doubt, uppermost in his mind.

Yet the door into the very heart of America had already begun to swing open. Even then it was the result of a chance encounter at London's Heathrow Airport when Ed Sullivan and his wife, returning to New York after a vacation, witnessed hordes of young people atop airport buildings obviously awaiting the arrival of some 'very important person' or other. At first Sullivan and his wife thought it must be for returning British Royalty. But when informed that the tumultuous scenes of screaming girls were for a pop group from Liverpool, and that the VIPS were in fact The Beatles returning from a brief tour of Sweden, the host of America's most prestigious 'prime time' television variety show quickly took note... *"This act could be of great interest to my TV audience. I should book them,"* or words to that effect. And all without once setting eyes on them.

When Ed Sullivan arrived back in New York he soon brokered a deal with Brian Epstein that brought The Beatles to the USA and led to the group's astonishing breakthrough into the all-important American market. The Beatles' first appearance on CBS-TV's nationally syndicated *The Ed Sullivan Show*—on the evening of 9 February 1964—was watched by over 73 million people and broke all previous 'TV audience viewing' records. The artist, whose appearance on *The Ed Sullivan Show*, had held the record before, none other than Elvis Presley.

"We knew America would make us or break us as world stars. In fact, she made us." — Brian Epstein

15 - Why are The Beatles' albums in the UK and USA so very different?

The Beatles' UK albums were just as the group intended them to be; the US albums weren't. A sad legacy of Capitol Records stubbornly refusing to release The Beatles' initial records in the US, despite being a wholly owned subsidiary of EMI the British recording conglomerate that owned Parlophone, The Beatles' UK record label.

The plain truth is Capitol Records couldn't or wouldn't hear the 'new' sound coming out of Britain. After all, nothing of any real consequence, musically speaking, ever came out of Great Britain. True. The Brits had had one or two successes, but nothing to write home about. Lonnie Donegan had a couple of 'Top Ten' Hits on the Billboard charts way back in 1956 and 1959. Mr. Acker Bilk had a No. 1 with 'Stranger On The Shore' in May

1962. The Tornadoes did the same with 'Telstar' in December 1962. But they were one-offs. Anomalies. Capitol Records knew what would and wouldn't sell in the US market; ask anyone.

And so despite the rise and rise of *'Beatlemania'* in the UK, Capitol Records flatly refused to release any of The Beatles' early singles or albums in the US. The sole reason the group's first UK singles finally appeared on US independents Vee-Jay and Swan Records, to no effect. Then, rival United Artists secured a three film—*three soundtrack*—deal with the group. The Beatles were booked to appear on CBS-TV's top-rated, primetime *The Ed Sullivan Show* and play concerts in Washington and New York's Carnegie Hall. The dam broke. The Beatles simply couldn't be ignored any longer. Brian Epstein flew to America and demanded and got Capitol Records to fund an unprecedented $50,000 promotional campaign: *'The Beatles Are Coming!'*

Beatles' records went out to American radio stations up and down the east coast and DJs began playing them non-stop, which in turn led to a huge wave of demand from "hip to the groove" transistor toting teenagers.

Then on 24 December 1963, Capitol Records finally got with the program and released 'I Want To Hold Your Hand' b/w 'I Saw Her Standing There'. The single hit No. 1 on *Billboard's* Hot 100 Chart on 18 January 1964. A week later 'She Loves You' took over the No. 1 spot. The Beatles arrived at New York's JFK airport on 7 February 1964 and two days later were catapulted into the living rooms, and hearts and minds, of America with their first appearance on *The Ed Sullivan Show*.

After which Capitol Records were suddenly forced to play catch-up. They ransacked The Beatles' back catalogue, mashed together a new sequence of singles and albums, to create their own versions of Beatles albums, with different playing orders and different sets of songs. That meant the contents of the US albums differed substantially from the UK releases, even when they bore the same name. And they carried on doing so with little or no regard as to the original intentions of the group or record producer, George Martin. Over time, releasing more Beatles' albums in the US than were ever released in the UK

UK albums consisted of 14 tracks; 7 tracks per side; as opposed to the 'universally accepted' US offering of 11 tracks. And as US albums were almost always built around 'singles', Capitol not only reduced the number of songs on their Beatles' albums, they also crammed on as many existing singles as they dared. A practice frowned upon by The Beatles as they thought it cheated the fans. *Please, Please Me*, the only UK Beatles' album ever to feature already existing 'Hit' singles: 'Love Me Do' b/w 'P.S. I Love You' and 'Please, Please Me' b/w 'Ask Me Why'.

The Beatles had major input with all their UK albums, everything from the final song compilation and track sequencing on both Sides One and Two, to front and back cover design, and all artwork, photographs, and text. Not so with Capitol. Like 'The Joker' they just did as they pleased. A 'smash and grab' attitude that meant the contents of the US albums differed substantially from the UK releases, even when they bore the same name. It wasn't until the 1967 release of *Sgt. Pepper's Lonely Heart's Club Band* that everything finally got onto the same track, as it were.

Yet even though the Capitol single and album releases do not, in the main, follow 'the canon of work' as was laid down and preferred by The Beatles themselves, there are countless Beatles' fans in the US who still hold to the song sequencing of the US releases. It was how they first heard the group; the exact order in which they got to know and love 'the canon', however mangled, forever etched in their hearts. The only possible response to which must be: '*to each, their own... you pays your money and you makes your choice*'. After all it's The Beatles we're talking about here. And you know that can't be bad.

| **Side Bar** | **The Beatles on Capitol Records** | Quick shout out for American Beatles' scholar Bruce Spizer; the one person to turn to for anything to do with The Beatles' Capitol catalogue. His epic, two-part *The Beatles' Story on Capitol Records* is now a collectable in its own right. If 'The Beatles in the USA' rocks your boat, anything by Mr. Spizer is tops! His book *The Beatles Are Coming!* is really an exceptional read on US '*Beatlemania*'.

16 - Why did The Beatles stop touring? Isn't that how rock bands make all their money?

After nearly four years of global *'Beatlemania'*—performing and touring nonstop—with nigh on sixty concert appearances in the USA, and more than fourteen hundred in the UK and around the world, The Beatles had had enough. They were exhausted. Touring was no longer enjoyable; it was an absolute chore. Their concerts had grown so large they were always full of unforeseen hassles.

They couldn't be heard in the vast sports stadiums and auditoriums that US concert promoters now expected them to play in and always fill to capacity. They couldn't hear themselves 'live' on stage because of the incessant screaming of tens of thousands of fans. Their amplifiers—'state of the art' at the time—were woefully inadequate. The stadium PA systems, designed for in-game commentary or announcements, were incapable of producing anything like true sound fidelity. Everything was horribly distorted. Nevertheless, every night they ran through the same 'set list' of old 'hits' knowing only too well it was technically impossible for them to duplicate in 'live' performance, the studio-based soundscapes of their just released album—*'Revolver'*. The Beatles feared they'd already lost their edge as performing musicians. Even more critically; they'd started to fear for their very lives.

Security had always been of prime concern for The Beatles' US Concert Tours. They'd first arrived in the country just a few months after the assassination of President John F. Kennedy. And so from the very outset had felt uneasy about threats to their personal safety. The situation made all the more intense during their Third US Tour, given the storm of protest and continued backlash to John Lennon's reported remark about The Beatles being *"more popular than Jesus."* A cynically contrived uproar in a mint julep cup that had resulted in the banning and burning of their records and memorabilia by 'evangelical' radio stations and mobs of former fans, and the picketing of their concerts in the American 'Deep South' by the Ku-Klux-Klan. All followed, of course, by the inevitable death threats.

Little wonder then that after their last 'live' concert at San Francisco's Candlestick Park, on August 29 1966, that marked the end of their fourteen-city American tour, The Beatles decided to give up touring for good. And instead retreated to the comparative safety of the recording studio, where in future they'd now only perform for themselves.

Three months later, in November 1966, The Beatles began work at Abbey Road Studios on the album that would revolutionize 'pop' music all over again and see them universally hailed as the world's most innovative recording artists—with yet another 'pop music' first—the concept album: *Sgt. Pepper's Lonely Hearts Club Band*.

17 - Why all the fuss over *Sgt. Pepper*? Will people ever get over it?

Sgt. Pepper's Lonely Heart's Club Band was The Beatles' eighth studio album. They began work on it, at Abbey Road Studios, in November 1966. And it took an unprecedented five months for them to complete the album. During which time the world could only impatiently watch and wait and wonder whether The Beatles still had it in them to surprise and delight or not.

The irony, of course, that the very first thing The Beatles did, on giving up touring, for good, and starting anew as a studio-based band, was to hide in plain sight and recast themselves as band of 'alter ego' touring performers: *'The band you've known for all these years... Sgt. Pepper's Lonely Heart's Club Band.'*

Released 1 June 1967 in UK and 2 June 1967 in US, it was an absolute sensation. So innovative and so revolutionary in concept and realisation it was an immediate and massive commercial and critical success. It was the top UK Album for 27 weeks and in all spent 148 consecutive weeks in the charts; selling more than 250,000 copies in its first week of release and by the end of June over half a million. It was No. 1 in *Billboard*'s US Chart for 15 weeks. And went on to become one of the best-selling, most critically acclaimed albums of all time and a landmark in 20th century music.

It had an extraordinary effect on young people; the excitement it caused seemed to pervade the very air. Released on a Thursday, just three days later, the great Jimi Hendrix had already taught himself the title track *Sgt. Pepper* in time to play it as his opening number at a show put on at Brian Epstein's recently leased Saville Theatre, on Sunday night, 4 June 1967. Paul McCartney and George Harrison as stunned as everyone else in the audience by the bravura display and "ultimate compliment" paid by the electrifying Mr. Hendrix.

In the weeks following its release it seemed everyone, everywhere, was listening to of *Sgt. Pepper*. American writer, Langdon Winner, recalled, driving across country: *"In each city the melodies wafted in from some far-off transistor radio or portable hi-fi... For a brief while, the irreparably fragmented consciousness of the west was unified, at least in the minds of the young."*

The album seemed to usher in a distinct season of hope, joy, and optimism amongst the young, on both sides of the Atlantic, and on the West Coast of America, especially in San Francisco. The album's fantabulous lyricism and kaleidoscopic soundscapes quickly became the universally accepted soundtrack to 1967's psychedelic-inspired *"Summer of Love"* and the rise of the 'Hippy' counterculture, and self-expression, and *"do your own thing... man,"* and feminism, and gay liberation. All of which were startlingly new avenues of thought and 'sounds' heard all around the world.

Famed British theatre critic Kenneth Tynan, never an easy man to impress, later spoke of *Sgt. Pepper* as being: *"a decisive moment in Western civilization."*

Some 45 years after it was first released *Rolling Stone* magazine, also born in 1967, named it *'The Best Album Of All Time'* and wrote: *"Sgt. Pepper... is the most important rock & roll album ever made, an unsurpassed adventure in concept, sound, songwriting, cover art and studio technology by the greatest rock & roll group of all time."*

The Beatles, together with record producer George Martin and studio engineer Geoff Emerick, pushed the available recording technology to its very limits. Recording techniques—universal now—had to be painstakingly developed, newly invented, to meet the ever-more inquisitive demands of the group. The Beatles' extensive use of multi-tracking, utilizing then state-of-the-art twin four-track machines, constructing tracks instrument by instrument, layer by layer, in pursuit of whole new vistas of sound-colour and instrumentation, effectively transformed studio recording forever after.

They brought a wealth of different musical influences to their songs: rock, folk, military brass band, old time British music hall, even music of the circus; as well as Western European and Indian classical music forms. The message abundantly clear: that everything, whatever musical genre or musical instrument, was up for grabs in the pursuit of recording excellence.

The Beatles' inventiveness also extended to their songs. The lyrics drawn from everyday events, be they funny or tragic, uplifting or sad, inspired by an old vaudeville poster, a newspaper story, a television advert, uniformed officialdom, or scenes from childhood memories or family life. All of it baring little or no resemblance to the eternal standbys of Tin Pan Alley's "love and lost love and longed for marriage". Yet it uncannily mirrored feelings that resonated with listeners of any age.

The album's artwork was extensive and unprecedented and changed the rules of what a 'pop' album could be or should be. The album's cover photo of The Beatles, dressed as Sgt. Pepper's Lonely Heart's Club Band, utterly resplendent in brightly coloured silk Victorian-style military band uniforms, all four stood in front of a cardboard-cut-out audience of their favourite historical figures and 'pop' culture heroes, as well as life-size waxworks of their earlier 'Mop-top' selves—created by the noted British 'pop' artist Peter Blake—elevated the album cover to a work of art. And is one of the most enduring images of the whole psychedelic era that was the late Sixties. But there was even more to delight the unsuspecting fan. The gatefold album had a pull out sleeve—also designed by Peter Blake—of 'cut-out' Sgt. Pepper memorabilia. It was also the first rock album to include the complete lyrics to all of its songs on the back cover; a real revolution, at the time.

All of it due to the courage, the utter audacity, of The Beatles' decision in August 1966 to give up touring for good and, instead, to concentrate on creating music in the studio. Freeing themselves to create music unrestricted by the need for it to be re-created later 'live' on stage in some far-off stadium somewhere. A decision seen as a likely career-ending disaster at the time, as it was the only accepted way for a band to get fans to buy their records, but yet another example of The Beatles' brilliance in inventing and then reinventing all aspects of 'pop' music and the music business. All of which, surely, is something still well worth the fussing over.

18 - People all act like The Beatles invented rock music. Seriously?

The Beatles were the first real rock *group*, as it were, with no discernable 'star' or leader standing out in front of an all but nameless backing group. A real 'group' a far more common occurrence in 'pop' music ever since then, but it was revolutionary at the time. It made The Beatles look totally 'new' and 'original' in press and PR photographs—and on stage and on TV—even before you'd heard them sing or play a single note.

The Beatles also seemed to work harder than any other band or group. They were never afraid to demand more and more of themselves and to play as many gigs as they could. And did so even before they signed with their manager Brian Epstein. Then with his support and encouragement, and his unshakable belief in them, they upped their game all the more; worked ever harder and harder; travelled up and down the country; did everything they could do to keep moving forward; right up until the time they were signed by George Martin of Parlophone Records. All of it done with the single-minded intention that if luck should ever find them, it would always find them working.

Even after the release of their first single—'Love Me Do'—The Beatles responded to any and every request for an interview or a photo-op or to appear on a radio or television show; while still keeping up a hugely punishing schedule and sometimes playing three bookings in a single day.

All the while demanding ever more of themselves. Never settling for 'good enough' but always pushing for something more, something 'better', something even more 'original'; be it in composing and writing their own songs, pushing the boundaries of their musicianship, or pushing for new sound effects and recording techniques in the recording studios of Abbey Road.

A new Beatles LP was always a massive event for Beatles' fans as it not only meant new songs, new instruments, new 'kinds' of music, but also, invariably, new ideas, new 'ways' of thinking—even new 'ways' of living. And so as The Beatles grew, it really did seem that we, their fans, also grew with them. Year by year—from the beginning of 1963 until the end of 1969—the measured release of their singles and albums was a veritable road map on how to grow up; how to be.

As the world's leading authority on The Beatles, the matchless Mark Lewisohn, says: *"They were always original, and that's thing that comes across from the beginning to the end. These people thought differently from everybody else, and that's why they made it to the very top."*

19 - Why wasn't there any cover art on the *White Album*? Did someone screw up?

The Beatles, the group's self-titled double album, was their ninth official UK album release and their *fifteenth* US album. It was also the group's first studio album in almost eighteen months. It went on sale on December 1, 1968 in the UK and went straight to No.1. In the US, the album opened at No. 11; the following week made No. 2; then in its third week finally hit No. 1.

'*The White Album*', as it universally came to be called, was the first real album project the group had undertaken since the death of their manager, Brian Epstein, in August 1967. And, arguably, represented nothing so much as a new beginning, a clean slate, a *tabula rasa*; it certainly came as a huge surprise after the four-colour-laden, eye-popping extravaganza of *Sgt. Pepper*.

The album stood out for its very starkness. It was minimalist, to say the least. It had no graphics or text anywhere, front or back, other than the group's name embossed on its plain white double-sleeve. And each and every album of the first pressing was also individually numbered.

Again, almost five months in the making, with 30 different tracks, this time, eschewing any pretence of a unified concept or theme, it clocked in at almost 94 minutes in length.

The result? A diffuse assortment of musical styles reflecting every conceivable train of thought, it was as nonsensical as it was poetic. Count you in? No. Count me out. And as each Beatle directed the recording of each particular song or ditty he'd written, 'The White Album' has often been described as the most diverse record in 'pop' history. Which is neither here nor there for being such, but extraordinarily intriguing, all the same, as it'd effectively blown the bloody doors off! All bets were off. And anything and everything now up for grabs.

Lester Bangs, *Rolling Stone*'s much missed, mercurially minded, music journalist and critic, hit the proverbial nail on the head when he said: *"The first album by The Beatles or in the history of rock by four solo artists in one band."*

Nevertheless, *The White Album* went on to become The Beatles' best selling album ever—with certified sales of over 20 million. And so 'new beginnings' or 'new departures' it was certainly no screw up, more a shape of things to come and the sad, yet now all but inevitable unwinding of The Beatles.

"There was a lot of friction during that album. We were just about to break up... and that was tense in itself."

— Paul McCartney

20 - Is it true that a woman broke up The Beatles... one of the wives? Yoko Ono?

It's a little more complicated than that. As the end of the Sixties approached, The Beatles had already achieved the impossible. And they simply wanted more, but not the same, they wanted different. They wanted change. They'd all been together, creating astonishing music and composing amazing songs for "seven glorious years"; John, Paul, and George, who'd been together since they were teenagers, for far longer than that. Now they were grown men. Four parts of the whole, locked together, having succeeded in giving everything the world had ever demanded of them. And they needed a break. They each wanted to pursue their own musical or artistic or spiritual endeavours—outside of The Beatles.

During their time recording *The White Album*—from May to October 1968—and throughout the months following, The Beatles made numerous comments; dropped various hints about the future of the group. There were rumours of growing differences; of a potential split. Ambiguous statements, in the main, that could be read as coded messages to one another or not. But nothing really definite; nothing the newspapers could write home about. The only thing for sure, to George Martin and the recoding engineers at Abbey Road Studios, and people close to them, was that the members of the fabled Beatles weren't at all happy—with each other or even with themselves.

There were any number of probable causes for the break-up, but no single earth-shattering event. It was a long time coming, even though to outsiders it appeared to happen in no time at all. One likely starting point was when The Beatles gave up touring for good in August 1966. Another, the unprecedented success of *Sgt. Pepper* in 1967; how on earth could any group conceivably top that, even if you were The Beatles? It cast a giant shadow.

As did then the accidental death of their manager, Brian Epstein, from a prescription-drug overdose soon afterwards. A truly tragic event that greatly shocked and affected them all, John Lennon most especially. It left a huge hole in all their lives.

Paul was the first to try and fill the void by initiating various projects for the group, some successful, some less so. And for a time John and George and Ringo gamely went along with it all, but they became increasingly disturbed by Paul's growing dominance within the group. It began to feel more and more like it was 'Paul McCartney and his backing band'. Inevitably conflicts arose; initially everything attributed to musical differences; but then things got personal.

At various points, during 1968 and 1969, George Harrison and Ringo Starr each left the group, with both Beatles eventually returning. And although John Lennon privately informed the other Beatles, in September 1969, that he was leaving the group, there was never any public acknowledgement of the break-up. And by 1970 all four Beatles had begun to work on solo projects.

Ultimately, the growing animosity between John, George, and Ringo on one side, and Paul on the other, fuelled for the most part by increasing business and financial differences, made it impossible for the group to continue working together. And then on 10 April 1970 Paul McCartney put out a press release in the form of a series of pithy "Questions & Answers" about The Beatles and himself in order to promote his new debut solo album *McCartney*.

Paul's remarks were somewhat ambiguous and said nothing definite either way about the future of The Beatles, but the world's press pounced on them and soon proclaimed in banner headlines: "*McCartney Breaks Off With Beatles.*" And whatever might have been his original intent, Paul only succeeded in driving a further wedge between himself and the other three Beatles. In an interview in *Rolling Stone*, the following month, an embittered John Lennon lashed out at Paul in a way he'd never done before; at least not publicly: **"He can't have his own way, so he's causing chaos... I put out four albums last year, and I didn't say a fucking word about quitting."**

By the end of the year, their differences grown even more rancorous, Paul formally filed suit to dissolve The Beatles' business partnership. At long last making official the 'unofficial' breakup that'd been in process for years.

| **Side Bar** | **Let it be Yoko** | And, no, it wasn't simply Yoko Ono—then his girlfriend, and later his wife—being in constant attendance in the recording studio, during the filming of *Let It Be*, and afterwards, that broke up The Beatles. She was merely a symptom of a group already in the process of disbanding. Yoko would have been here, there, and everywhere simply because John insisted she be there. And whatever John wanted, invariably came to pass... as in the end all things must.

21 - Forget for a moment about The Beatles changing the world for the better... How exactly did they change the music industry?

The Beatles transformed 'pop' music with every record they released. They are the group against which every other group, band, or artist—that came after them—is measured. Their boundless creativity demonstrated—again and again—that rock 'n' roll could embrace "*a limitless variety of harmonies, structures, and sounds.*" In doing so they helped change people's very attitude to 'pop' music—gave it greater credence—a greater role—made it more meaningful in people's lives.

It's hardly surprising then that within a relatively short period The Beatles went on to change the music business itself—from beginning to end. From sound recording to album cover design—from recording techniques to sound sampling and sound design. They were also the first group to produce song-specific pop videos for broadcast on TV—long before the advent of MTV in 1981 or YouTube in 2005.

The Beatles even changed the very nature of the 'pop song', taking it from their first brilliant two-and-a-half minute "instant 'pop' classics" of 'love and lost love', such as 'I Saw Her Standing There' and 'Can't Buy Me Love' and 'I Want To Hold Your Hand', to songs of greater depth and complexity; about life and death and childhood and aging and taxes and pain and self-doubt and loneliness and revolution and world politics and meditation and mind expansion and the universe within and without.

Everything from 'Eleanor Rigby' and 'She's Leaving Home' and 'Strawberry Fields' and 'Penny Lane' to 'Lucy In The Sky With Diamonds' and 'Tomorrow Never Knows' and 'Across the Universe' and 'A Day In The Life'.

And more than two hundred other much-loved and revered Beatles' song classics; many of them works of rare beauty and of lasting significance in people's lives.

The Beatles were the first rock group to have to play a concert in a sports stadium, simply to meet the unprecedented demand for tickets.

They were the first group to give up touring as the only way to promote their songs and sell records. They were the first group to become a studio-based band, in effect turning the recording studio into the sole arena for all their new work.

They were the first 'rock' band to adopt and adapt a wide profusion of other musical styles into their studio productions: folk, country, rockabilly, blues, 'British music-hall', 'military brass band', Jamaican 'reggae' rhythms; as well as Western European and Indian classical forms. The first to feature new and exotic musical instruments not normally associated with 'pop' or 'rock' music: harpsichord, clavichord, piccolo trumpet, French horn; string quartet and forty-piece orchestra; Indian sitars and tablas et al. Even an early form of sound synthesizer—an electro-mechanical, polyphonic, tape replay keyboard known to enthusiasts, such as Princess Margaret and the actor Peter Sellers, as a Mellotron. (The mind boggles. Who knew?)

For 'Tomorrow Never Knows' John Lennon wanted his voice to sound like the Dalai Lama standing on a mountaintop. The sound ultimately achieved courtesy of Abbey Road sound engineer Geoff Emerick's magical touch. Which made The Beatles the very first to push and record a vocal through a rotating Leslie speaker cabinet normally used to give a reverb effect and added dimension to a thumping great Hammond organ.

They were also the first rock group to 'sample' other audio sources and add them to the mix, a whole cornucopia of soundscape effects, even snippets of 'spoken word' taken randomly from radio broadcasts or film. The first rock band to feature electronic feedback as part of the desired sound design. The first to employ repeating 'tape loops'—random tape loops edited together—and pre-recorded tapes played backwards. Anything and everything was grist for their sound mill.

The Beatles were and, probably, will always be the only universally loved and admired rock group ever to disband at the very height of their creative powers and global appeal. And simply walk away from it all... to pursue other things.

22 - How on earth could The Beatles possibly have influenced an entire generation?

To all those who followed and idolized them it was as if The Beatles were always moving at the speed of light; constantly venturing into new worlds; inhabiting a different universe to everyone else. They seemed to grow and change with every new single and album they released. Opening up doors to new sounds, new possibilities of thought; even ways of being. And even as cool and as hip and as stylish as they undoubtedly were, more and more did it come to seem that they saw something, knew something, even possessed a special kind of wisdom.

The Beatles constantly reinvented themselves—musically as well as sartorially. As a group and as individuals they were always complete nonconformists. And were the first to introduce into 'popular consciousness' many of the ideas that would later be labelled "counterculture." Even the way they wore their hair, combed fully down over their foreheads into "the Beatle cut" was a mark of youthful defiance; a gentle kick against the rigid rules of conformity that held sway in post-war Britain. And even though their iconic eye-catching display of semaphore on the cover of their album *'Help!'* had no real meaning—their stances spell out the letters N U J V not H E L P—in everything else they said or did they signalled feelings of 'optimism' and of 'a new hope'; catalysts for a social revolution already in the making.

In their continued search for new ways of thinking, they experimented with mood and consciousness expanding drugs—marijuana and LSD—and flirted with Transcendental Meditation and other practices of Eastern mysticism. Their long hair, ever-changing fashion styles, even singing falsetto to add colour and tone to their songs, challenged accepted norms of 'masculinity' and began to blur the lines between the sexes simply by questioning gender stereotypes.

On first appearance, at least in the very beginning, it was very hard to tell The Beatles apart; they all seemed to resemble one another. A matter of hairstyle and clothes and Beatle boots and the odd-sounding Liverpudlian accents, but as their fans soon learned, they were all so very different.

For many people the characters of John, Paul, George, and Ringo were forever frozen in time after they saw The Beatles' first feature film *A Hard Day's Night*. John was "the witty and brainy one." Paul "the cute and romantic one." George "the very quiet and serious one." Ringo "the funny, lovable one."

And although John later railed against being typecast in so simplistic a fashion and later cut his hair short and took to wearing "Working Class Hero" glasses and unfashionable work clothes; by the simple act of The Beatles always wanting *to find* themselves; *to be* themselves; each of them always pushing the boundaries of their music, their thinking, and their very *'being'*; The Beatles helped an entire generation *"find themselves"* too.

And, all things considered, perhaps The Beatles' greatest accomplishment, their sublime body of work none withstanding, was not that they ever insisted, in song or in word or in deed, that the world *should* change, but that it *could* change, and change into something better for the good of one and all.

"We were all on this ship in the Sixties, our generation, a ship going to discover the New World. And The Beatles were in the crow's nest of that ship."
— John Lennon

23 - Were The Beatles ever a serious political force?

Not in the traditional sense, but as everything The Beatles said or did helped expand young peoples' awareness of new social and cultural possibilities they were a political force, of sorts; for how could they not be. Especially when they became more and more involved—and identified—with the counterculture and its emerging ideas. After all, they were the undisputed voice of the new generation: harbingers of the brave new world to come. Which made them a force to be reckoned with, on both sides of the Atlantic. And yet even with all that The Beatles were never overtly political; their message was only ever "the word is love."

It's true, though, that after the break up of the group and his marriage to Yoko Ono, John Lennon became more of a political activist—or rather an active pacifist—and used his popularity and notoriety as an ex-Beatle to advance numerous issues. John and Yoko making world headlines with their performance art "baggism" and "Bed-In For Peace" semi-political media events, and the later Plastic Ono Band 'Live Peace' concerts. Followed by worldwide campaign of giant billboards proclaiming "War Is Over! If You Want It." erected in 12 major cities including New York, Hollywood, Toronto, and London.

Then in the early 1970's when the couple moved to New York, they began to openly speak out against the Vietnam War and to sympathise with a number of 'radical' political personalities and left-wing groups; providing financial support by appearing and playing at various 'benefit' concerts. All very much to the concern, it seems, of then President Nixon who feared the peace-loving ex-Beatle might one day call for the youth of America "to rise up in armed protest." Which then, of course, led to the increased involvement of J. Edgar Hoover's FBI and other Federal agencies. And the US government actively seeking ways to deny John's permanent resident 'green card' status and have him deported from the country. A case John and Yoko fought with magnificent tenacity. The US Court of Appeals finally overturning the deportation order on October 7, 1975.

And so while it's no exaggeration to say The Beatles truly were a global phenomenon, with avid fans the world over, they were never counted as a serious political force other than perhaps in the countries behind the "Iron Curtain" where the music of The Beatles was officially banned.

"Iron Curtain" a metaphor first introduced by Winston Churchill in a speech he made at Westminster College, in Fulton, Missouri, 5 March 1946. An imaginary line that marked the 'Cold War' ideological and political 'divide' between post-war Capitalism and Communism. One that notionally separated the USSR and the East European block countries under its control on one side and the USA, the UK, Western Europe and much of the rest of the "free" world on the other. A divide made physical reality on August 13, 1961 when boundary walls were erected across much of Europe. The most famous example, the vast, concrete barrier: enforced by tanks, minefields, and armed guards; that divided East and West Berlin.

And yet... and yet... as later events proved when the 'Berlin Wall' finally came down on 9 November 1989, after nearly three decades, the daunting political edifice hadn't been at all an effective barrier against the music and message of The Beatles.

Mikhail Gorbachev, former President of the Soviet Union, who introduced *'Perestroika'* in the 1980s; a political movement calling for major reform within the Soviet Union's ruling Communist Party, along with the attendant policy of *'Glasnost'* or "openness to reform"; said as much: *"More than any ideology, more than any religion, more than Vietnam or any war or nuclear bomb, the single most important reason for the diffusion of the Cold War was... The Beatles."*

Sentiments echoed by Russian journalist and music critic Artemy Troitsky: *"The West spent millions on undermining communism but it had much less impact than The Beatles. The Beatles, Paul, John, George, and Ringo have done more for the fall of Communism than any other western institution. They alienated a whole generation of young, well-educated, urban Soviet kids from their communist motherland."*

Russian author and Beatles' fan Yury Pelyushonok; now living in Canada; says much the same: *"The Beatles were considered the big capitalist threat during the Cold War. You could bring Rolling Stones albums into the country, later on, but not The Beatles. You know why? I think it's because The Beatles were an event. The Rolling Stones were a rock band; but The Beatles were the cultural event of our century."*

"Da... Da... Da!"

24 - Why are The Beatles still so very popular, even after all these years?

True. The Beatles officially disbanded in April 1970 and, after seven years of unprecedented and unparalleled creativity, went their separate ways. All four former band-mates seeking to prove themselves, creatively, in their own right; looking to find their own path to music immortality. It's a common maxim the works they created individually never quite matched the sustained brilliance of what they'd achieved working together as a group. Yet as with all 'great art' it still all comes down to one's personal taste. You either like what each of them produced after the break-up or you don't. For it's undeniable John, Paul, and George—and even Ringo—each showed flashes of genius in the years following. At least, one thing almost everyone still seems able to agree on is that The Beatles were the greatest and most influential rock group of all time; and so well worthy of a listen.

Greater accessibility, arguably, one of the main reasons the essence of 'Beatlemania' is as alive today, as ever it was. The Beatles' in concert, on TV, in scenes from their films, the interviews they gave, all there on YouTube. Their music available: 24/7 on any number of streaming services or *The Beatles Channel* on SiriusXM; their vast music catalogue always ready to be downloaded from Apple iTunes. Or still enjoyed on recording platforms such as CD, DVD, and Blu-Ray, even though as audio-video technologies they are increasingly assuming 'classic' status. Or having gone round and round and already come back again, listened to on re-issued 33⅓ rpm vinyl disc—The Beatles' very first retail-recording medium. And there's still a huge aftermarket for the original vinyl LPs. Nothing, it seems, can stop or stem the flow of Beatles' music into the world.

But it's not only the music of The Beatles that continues to live on and on and on and on. Many of the concepts and ideas they helped bring to light in The Sixties—as individuals and as a group—still affect the generations that have followed. The Beatles pointed to "doors of thought" as well as perception. They did it in song. They did so in action. They did it in the lives they lived and, whether successful at the time or no, they never stopped trying to find new and better ways of being.

The word 'question' never once appears in any of the songs The Beatles wrote. Yet they inspired generations of young people to do exactly that: *To question | To never to take anything as gospel, but to be ever sceptical and cautious | Not to follow the crowd, but to think for yourself | To be unafraid | To dare to be different | To do your own thing | And to be your best self… not just for your own good… but for the good of all.*

This unabashed Beatles' fan is forever grateful that John, Paul, George, and Ringo—and Yoko, too, for that matter; and even Linda McCartney up on stage singing her heart out with Wings—all cared enough to put word to thought, put feelings of hope into song and deed, and put forward the very idea that: *'Change for the better was possible; without violence; without revolution; without war.'* And that *"All you need is love."*

All and everything offered in the simple unguarded hope that people would come join them and help try to improve the world for the good of one and all—and ultimately the world itself.

Reasons enough for The Beatles still to be so hugely popular even after all these years.

"The thing The Sixties did was to show us the possibilities and the responsibility that we all had. It wasn't the answer. It just gave us a glimpse of the possibility." — John Lennon

| Side Bar | The Magical Mystery Tour that every fan of The Beatles must take at one time or another | The truly magical thing about The Beatles and their music is that every new generation discovers them anew. Each generation, always finding something telling in the songs of 'yesterday': words, ideas, sounds that still seem to have some extraordinary relevance to their brave new world of 'today'; whether it be ten, twenty, thirty, forty, or even fifty years after the group broke up.

And all those new Beatles' fans, in turn join the millions and millions of existing unabashed Beatles' fans… of all stripes… of all generations… all around the globe… who all still happily attest… The Beatles are the best rock 'n' roll band that ever was… has ever been… or likely ever will be. *Yeah. Yeah. Yeah.*

The last line… of the last song… on the group's last album… a fitting reminder as to why The Beatles would seem to be… *like 'Love' itself*… eternal.

'And in the end the love you take is equal to the love you make'

PART FOUR – THE BEATLES TIMELINES

Extended Timeline

THE EARLY YEARS | PEOPLE | PLACES | EVENTS

BIRTHS
1926 January 3 - George Henry Martin - Highbury, London
1934 September 19 - Brian Samuel Epstein - Liverpool, England
1939 September 10 - Cynthia Powell born Blackpool, England
1940
June 23 - Stuart Fergusson Victor Sutcliffe - Edinburgh, Scotland
July 7 - Richard Starkey (Ringo Starr) - Liverpool, England
October 9 - John Winston Lennon - Liverpool, England
1941 November 24 - Randolph Peter Best - Madras, India
1942 June 18 - James Paul McCartney - Liverpool, England
1943 February 25 - George Harrison - Liverpool, England
1948 | The **'LP'** | Invention of two-sided multi-track Long Playing record | Plays at 33⅓ revolutions per minute (rpm) on a record-player turntable | The 12" vinyl disc is soon referred to as an "album" | It could play up to 60 minutes of music in total
1949| The **'45'** | Perfect for recording 'a single' pop song on each side | 45rpm 7" vinyl disc a huge success in jukeboxes | Plays up to 5 mins. music per side | Quickly supersedes old 78rpm discs

1951 May 28 - September 20 | *The Goon Show* (née *Crazy People*) | Spike Milligan | Peter Sellers | Harry Secombe | Michael Bentine | British radio comedy programme broadcast 'live' over the BBC Home Service | Surreal humour | Ludicrous plots | Larded with puns, catchphrases, bizarre sound effects | 'The Goons' satirised British politics, diplomacy, education, the class structure, the military, the police, show business, commerce, industry, art, literature, film when it was most definitely not proper to do so | The show continues to be broadcast until 1960. | John Lennon, Paul McCartney, George Harrison all huge fans.

1955

January — '**Rock Around the Clock**' by Bill Haley and The Comets reaches No. 17 on UK Singles Chart.

March — *Blackboard Jungle* | Released in US | Brings Hollywood into the Rock 'n' Roll era | 'Rock Around the Clock' plays under opening credits of the film | The response by small gangs of teenagers—to seeing 'themselves and their very own rock 'n' roll music' portrayed larger than life up on the big screen—overflows into minor vandalism. It's more than enough though to spark newspaper headlines. The die is cast: rock 'n' roll is "jungle music" for rebellious, ungrateful teens.

March — *Rebel Without A Cause* | Starring the soon to be immortal James Dean | Released in US | Teenage rebellion suddenly has a face and a look—the hair—the T-shirt—the blue denim jeans—the black and white Converse sneakers. | All it needs now is its own sound.

July — *Blackboard Jungle* | Released in UK | 'Rock Around the Clock' played under opening credits of the film | Originally refused a cinema certificate—***"filled as it is with scenes of unbridled hooliganism"***—but is later passed with heavy cuts as an 'Adults Only' X–certificate | When shown at a cinema, at the Elephant and Castle, in south London, the teenage **Teddy Boy** audience begins to riot, tearing up seats and dancing in the aisles. | Riots continue to take place around Britain wherever the film is shown.

September — UK | New 'Independent Television Network' starts to broadcast | Dubbed ITV to indicate its independence from the British Broadcasting Company—BBC—who up to this time have had a monopoly on broadcasting | September 22-24 | Associated-Rediffusion & Associated Television broadcast to London Region | February 17-18 1956 | ATV & Associated British Corporation broadcast to Midlands Region | May 3-5 1956 | Granada Television & ABC broadcast to North of England | The stages now set for The Beatles to one day appear on British TV

November — 'Rock Around the Clock' re-enters UK charts | Three weeks at No. 1

1956

January — "Rock Around the Clock" hits No. 1 in UK charts for two more weeks.

January — **Lonnie Donegan** | 'Rock Island Line' | An 'earth-shaking' hit in UK

March — UK | The 'Skiffle Craze' takes hold of the country's youth | Simple 3-chord style played with easy to get instruments: guitar, banjo, washboard, tea-chest 'bass'.

March - April — John buys 'Rock Island Line' as his first ever 78rpm single disc.

May 8 — *'Look Back in Anger'* | Play by John Osborne | Opens at London's Royal Court Theatre | *"Kitchen-sink"* drama takes post-war British theatre by storm | And gives birth to the term *"angry young man"* to describe an intelligent, educated young man of working-class origin who nevertheless feels hugely disaffected | Sets the stage for angry young John Lennon.

June — The authentic 'sound' of rock 'n' roll is heard at last | **Elvis Presley** | **'Heartbreak Hotel'** makes its debut on the UK Singles Chart | Peaks at No. 2 in June and stays on the charts for a further 22 weeks.

| *"When I first heard 'Heartbreak Hotel', I could hardly make out what was being said. It was just the experience of hearing it and having my hair stand on end."* — **John Lennon**

October 9 — On his 16th birthday, John buys two 78rpm single discs: Elvis Presley's twin-hit **'Hound Dog'** b/w **'Don't Be Cruel'** and The Goons' 'The Ying-Tong Song'

October 31 — Paul McCartney's mother, Mary, aged 47, dies unexpectedly from breast cancer. Paul is just 14 and is, understandably, deeply traumatized. | It's shortly after this that he writes his first song 'I Lost My Little Girl'.

1957

March — Still inspired by Lonnie Donegan and still all shook up by Elvis Presley's 'Heartbreak Hotel', John and school friend Pete Shotton start a skiffle group—The Blackjacks (The name later used by Pete Best's combo at the Casbah Coffee Club) | John plays guitar—bought for him by his Aunt Mimi—from Hessy's Music Stores.

May — John's skiffle group—now comprised of Pete Shotton, Colin Hanton, Rod Davis, Eric Griffiths, and Len Garry—all schoolboys at Quarry Bank High School—changes its name to '**The Quarrymen**' as referenced in the school song.

June — *The Girl Can't Help* | The movie's influence on Rock 'n' Roll music is huge. John and Paul both saw the movie when it played Liverpool—though they didn't see it together as they hadn't yet met. | Even as schoolboys they worshiped American Rock 'n' Roll stars and were both knocked out by the cameo performances of **Little Richard**, **'Fats' Domino**, **Eddie Cochran**, and **Gene Vincent and His Bluecaps**—all the better seen in Technicolor and on a huge Cinemascope screen. | Legend has it that on Wednesday September 18, 1968, The Beatles interrupted recording 'Birthday' at Abbey Road Studios, so they could nip back over the zebra-crossing to Paul McCartney's house to watch the British TV premiere of *The Girl Can't Help It*—and it wasn't just Jayne Mansfield doing things to milk bottles that they all wanted to see over again.

July 6 - Saturday — **The day 16-year old John Lennon met 15-year old Paul McCartney.** | The Quarrymen appear at the Woolton Parish Garden Fête at St. Peter's Church | The group scheduled to perform twice—on the back of a flatbed truck in the afternoon—on stage in the church hall in the evening

| *"The day I met Paul I was singing Gene Vincent's 'Be-Bop-A-Lula' for the first time on stage...on the back of a lorry. There's a picture of me with a checked shirt on, holding a little acoustic guitar...and I'm singing 'Be-Bop-A-Lula'."*

— **John Lennon**

| Paul is as impressed by John's singing ability, as his knack of making up lyrics to songs he doesn't know the proper words to.

| *"That was my first sight of John—his ingenuity with words and his stage presence."* — **Paul McCartney**

| Afterwards—'backstage' in the church hall—where the Quarrymen' are 'taking five' before their scheduled evening performance—Paul McCartney is introduced to John Lennon by mutual friend, Ivan Vaughn. | Paul picks up John's guitar and starts to play. | John is suitably impressed by Paul's ability to not

only tune the guitar properly, but also that he plays real guitar chords—even though, as Paul is left-handed, he has to play the instrument upside down. | The clincher—Paul plays 'Twenty Flight Rock'—sounding just like Eddie Cochran in *'The Girl Can't Help It'*—and what's more knows he knew all the right words too—then to top that he goes over to the old upright piano and belts out a number of Little Richard songs.

| *"He not only knew all the proper words, he could play the guitar properly, too. And if he was in the group, it'd make it that much stronger. So that's really all there was to it—he was in."*

— John Lennon

Two songs from The Quarrymen's evening performance are recorded, without the band's knowledge, on a suitcase-sized, reel-to-reel tape recorder and hand-held microphone. | Lonnie Donegan's 'Puttin' On The Style' and Elvis's 'Let's Play House' |

| A couple of weeks later, via his school friend, Pete Shotton, John extends an invitation for Paul to come join The Quarrymen. Paul ponders awhile and then accepts.

August 7 — The Quarrymen skiffle group plays the 'trad-jazz-only' Cavern Club—minus Paul McCartney who is away on holiday with his family.

September — Having failed all his 'O' level exams—John Lennon is granted an interview at Liverpool Art College to show his drawings and is accepted. And at the start of the Autumn Term—in full rockin' Teddy Boy gear and swept-back hairstyle with attendant quiff—he meets fellow art students Stuart Sutcliffe and Bill Harry—and his future wife Cynthia Powell—for the first time.

September — UK Hit Parade | **Elvis Presley** | **'Jailhouse Rock'**

September — UK Hit Parade | **Buddy Holly** | **'That'll Be The Day'**

October - December — The Quarrymen, with Paul McCartney now teamed with John Lennon on guitar and vocals, play half-a-dozen or so local workingmen's and social club engagements.

1958

February — UK | The Buddy Holly and The Crickets Tour

February - March — Memories differ as to exactly when or even exactly where—but after a seemingly impromptu display of note-perfect guitar artistry playing the Bill Justis instrumental rocker 'Raunchy' in front of John Lennon—legend says on the top deck of a double-decker bus—the moment artfully stage-managed by Paul McCartney. Despite John's earlier reservations about him being much too young—fourteen-year-old **George Harrison** is invited to join The Quarrymen. The young guitarist grins a toothy grin and is in the group.

March — Elvis Presley is drafted into the US Military (March 1958 – 1960)

March 20 — John and most all The Quarrymen see Buddy Holly and The Crickets at the Empire Theatre, Liverpool

March – December — No paid engagements, but The Quarrymen play at various Harrison family gatherings and functions.

July 15 — Julia Lennon, John Lennon's mother, is knocked down and killed by an off-duty policeman, still learning to drive, not a hundred yards away from 251 Menlove Avenue—where John lives and is being brought up by his Aunt Mimi—Julia's elder sister. John is utterly devastated by the loss—and it haunts him for the rest of his life. *"I was in a blind rage for two years after that. I was either drunk or fighting."* — John Lennon

| *"That became a very big bond between John and me, because he lost his mum early on, too. We both had this emotional turmoil, which we had to deal with and, being teenagers, we had to deal with it very quickly. We both understood that something had happened that you couldn't really talk about to anyone else."*

— Paul McCartney

Late Summer — The Quarrymen—John, Paul, George, Colin Hanton, and John Lowe—record 'That'll Be The Day' and 'In Spite Of All The Danger' (a song written by Paul and George) onto a shellac 78rpm demo disc, at a home-based recording studio, in Liverpool.

Late Autumn — The Quarrymen's drummer, Colin Hanton, quits the group.

1959

February 3 — US | Flying from one music gig to the next—part of a gruelling 24 concerts 'The Winter Dance Party' tour—Buddy Holly, Ritchie Valens, and J.P. Richardson—known as 'The Big Bopper'—all die in a small plane crash. | A great tragedy in the history of Rock 'n' Roll music; remembered on both sides of the Atlantic as *'The day the music died'*.

August 29 — The Quarrymen play at the opening night of **The Casbah Coffee Club**, Hayman's Green, West Derby. They return to play another six times in September and October.

Mid-October — John, Paul, and George adopt the name '**Johnny and The Moondogs**'—an allusion, no doubt, to Alan Freed, the American DJ who first gave name to "rock 'n' roll" and who called himself 'Moondog' on his pre-taped *'Rock 'n' Roll'* radio show broadcast every Saturday night on Radio Luxembourg. | The three future Beatles audition as 'a trio'—George and Paul on guitars, either side of John *sans* guitar—for the Carroll Levis *'TV Star Search'* show at the Empire Theatre, Liverpool. They succeed in getting through the first and second rounds of the competition.

November 15 — Johnny and The Moondogs travel by train to Manchester—Hippodrome Theatre—for the *'TV Star Search'* show's third and final round. However, as none of the group can afford to stay the night, they all take the last train home to Liverpool and are unable to appear 'on-stage' for the final judging by *'clap-o-meter'*—a hand-controlled device designed to indicate the volume of the audience's enthusiasm and applause.

November 17 —Second Biennial John Moore's Exhibition at Liverpool's Walker Art Gallery | **Stuart Sutcliffe**—John Lennon's closest friend at Liverpool Art College has oil painting, *Summer Painting*, selected for Biennial John Moore's Exhibition.

1960

January 17 — Stuart Sutcliffe sells *Summer Painting* to football pools magnate and arts patron, John Moore for £65.00. | John Lennon urges fine artist/non-musician Stu to use money to buy bass guitar. Stu buys Höfner 'President' bass guitar from Hessy's music store; joins Johnny and The Moondogs as bass-player.

February — Eddie Cochran and Gene Vincent begin UK Tour
March — **The Everly Brothers** begin UK Tour
March — John, Paul, George, and Stuart start to record their band rehearsals on a Grundig reel-to-reel tape recorder loaned from a friend of Paul's. Apart from the usual rock 'n' roll favorites, they also record early versions of songs by John and Paul | 'One After 909' | 'When I'm 64' | 'I'll follow The Sun' |

March. Monday 14 - Saturday 19 — Eddie Cochran and Gene Vincent headline *'The Sensational Double Star Attraction In Person'* UK Pop Package Show at the Liverpool Empire for London impresario Larry Parnes. A smash hit. | Local entrepreneur Allan Williams immediately contracts with Parnes to co-promote a follow-up concert at the Liverpool Stadium and schedules it for May 3.

April—Liverpool club-owner and promoter **Allan Williams** meets Hamburg club-owner **Bruno Koschmider**—quite by chance—at the famed **2i's Coffee Bar** in Soho, London. | Koschmider having travelled from Germany in the hope of hiring a Britisher Rock 'n' Roll group to play his Kaiserkeller club as **The Jets**—the London group he'd hired a month or two earlier—had already been poached away by a rival Hamburg club owner. | Williams contracts for Liverpool group **Derry and The Seniors** to go out to Hamburg.

April 17 — Eddie Cochran killed in car crash in Cheltenham on way to London Heathrow airport after a week of shows in Bristol. Gene Vincent badly hurt in same crash.

May 3 — Gene Vincent goes on with Liverpool show while still recovering from injuries. To bridge gaping chasm left by Cochran's death—Alan Williams also features local bands—Rory Storm & The Hurricanes, Gerry & The Pacemakers, Cass & The Cassanovas. | Larry Parnes impressed by quality of groups. Potential candidates as backing band for his singer Billy Fury—or one of the other 'pop idols' in his stable.

May 5 — Now named the **'Beatals'**—Stu Sutcliffe's idea as an homage to Buddy Holly and The Crickets | The 'Beat' in 'Beatals' meant to imply the group could 'see off' all competition. (Bill Harry's *Mersey Beat*—Merseyside entertainments newspaper—

that gave name to the whole beat boom still just over a year away from publication.)| The group play their first gig at the Jacaranda coffee bar for Allan Williams. | John Lennon asks Allan Williams to help manage them. | Williams is somewhat wary, but agrees to take on the role of agent and 'part-time' manager.

| *"I thought The Beatles were a right load of layabouts...there seems to be something about my personality that attracts the losers and fringe people of the world, and The Beatles just seemed to be part of that crowd."* — **Allan Williams**

May 10 — Allan Williams hates the name 'Beatals' but warms to the idea of '**The Silver Beetles'** | He arranges for them and several other Liverpool groups to audition in front of pop-star Bill Fury and his manager—the London impresario, Larry Parnes—to become the singer's new backing group. | The audition takes place at the Wyvern Social Club—that Williams later famously renames The Blue Angel. | The Silver Beetles turn up without a drummer and so Johnny Hutchinson of The Big Three—another group auditioning for the job—sits in for them. | In the end none of the Liverpool bands get chosen to be Billy Fury's next backing group.

May 14 — The Silver Beetles play a gig at Lathom Hall for promoter Brian Kelly—but he's not overly impressed.

May 16 — UK | Unopposed 'Second Reading' of a Parliamentary Bill to curb the disgusting and riotous activities of Teddy Boys. However, no law is ever passed.

May 20-28 — The Silver Beetles offered the job of backing Johnny Gentle—another teen-idol from Larry Parnes' stable of singers—on a nine-day tour of Scotland. They jump at the chance. They tour as 'Johnny Gentle and His Band'.

May 23 — Johnny Gentle crashes the car in which everyone is travelling. Tommy Moore—stand-in drummer for The Silver Beetles—is concussed—loses several teeth and his willingness to continue playing with the group. The tour isn't a big hit.

May 30 — The Silver Beetles engaged to play the Jacaranda on Monday nights.

June 6 — The Silver Beetles play the Grosvenor Ballroom | Whitsun Bank Holiday 'Jive and Rock' session | It's the first time they share the bill with Gerry and The Pacemakers.

June 13 — Drummer, Tommy Moore quits the group after the gig at the Jacaranda—says he can't stand any more of John Lennon or his withering sarcasm.

July 2 — An exposé article in *The People*—a national tabloid newspaper published every Sunday—shows photos of John Lennon and Stuart Sutcliffe making the best of it in the squalid flat they shared in Gambier Terrace: **'The Beatnik Horror. Though they don't know it...they are on the road to hell!'**

July — The Silver Beetles reduced to playing two sets, each night, for a week—with Paul now on drums—as a backing group for 'Janice'—a stripper—at the New Cabaret Artists Club—an illegal strip club also owned by Allan Williams.

July — US | Chubby Checker introduces 'The Twist' at the Rainbow Club, New Jersey. It soon becomes a dance craze on both sides of the Atlantic. Before 'The Twist' phenomenon, grown-ups simply wouldn't be caught dead dancing to teenage music.

July — Allan Williams and Bruno Koschmider come to an agreement about booking more Liverpool rock 'n' roll groups to perform in his Hamburg nightclub. Williams offers The Silver Beetles the engagement if they can find themselves a drummer.

August 6 — A Saturday-night gig having fallen through, John, Paul, and George re-visit the Casbah Coffee Club—owned by **Mona Best**. The Blackjacks—a three-piece combo—are performing that night with **Pete Best**, Mona's son, playing a brand new drum kit. Mmmmm?

August 12 — The following Friday—Pete Best auditions for the group at the Wyvern Social Club—after which—surprise, surprise—he's hired as the band's drummer. The group finally changes their name to **The Beatles.**

| **The Name** | From this day forth the group is known as **The Beatles** | John changes the second 'e' in 'beetle' into an 'a' as a pun on the word 'beat'—as in a beat of music | There's since been speculation; the idea even posed in *The Beatles Anthology*; that the real source was Laslo Benedek's *The Wild One*, the notorious 'motorcycle gang' film starring Marlon Brando released in the US in 1955 | Lee Marvin, playing one of the bikers, says:

"All the beetles (the girls in the gang) **missed you. Come on, Johnny, let's you and I..."** | Unlikely, as *The Wild One* was refused a release certificate in Britain and banned as **"potentially dangerous on social grounds"** and wasn't classified for showing in the UK until 1967.

August 16 — Allan Williams, his wife, and two friends, drive The Beatles to Hamburg—via the Harwich–Hook of Holland ferry—in an old, green, Austin A152 campervan.

August 17 - October 3 — **Hamburg** | Tired and very weary The Beatles *et al* arrive at dusk | Bruno Koschmider puts The Beatles into squalid, cramped accommodation in a run-down porn cinema he owns—der Bambi-Kino—situated in St. Pauli's infamous 'red-light' district. The very same night he has them play at his **Indra Cabaret Club**—a strip club hurriedly converted into a music club | The Beatles play the next 48 nights at the club. *"Mach schau! Mach schau!"*—*"Make a big show!"*— Koschmider yells at them whenever the pace slackens.

| *"When you think about it, sensibly, our sound really stems from Germany. That's where we learned to work for hours and hours on end and keep on working at full peak even though we reckoned our arms and legs were about ready to drop off."*

— George Harrison

September — UK | Trad-Jazz craze sweeps the country

October — UK | Hit Parade | Acker Bilk and His Paramount Jazz Band | 'Stranger on The Shore' | Instrumental tune becomes UK's biggest selling single of 1962 | In UK pop charts for over 50 weeks | Peaks at No. 2 | May 1962 - First No. 1 single by a British artist in US | Ultimately is the biggest-selling instrumental single of all time | Kenny Ball and His Jazzmen also have a big hit with 'Midnight In Moscow'.

October 4 — The Indra Cabaret club is forced to close because of a noise complaint. Koschmider moves them to the **Kaiserkeller**—his other St. Pauli nightclub—as the support band to **Rory Storm and The Hurricanes** (drummer Ringo Starr)— and contracts The Beatles to play for a further two months. The two Liverpool groups playing alternate 90-minute sets—for 7 hours at weeknights—8 hours at weekends.

| *"Sure, we come from Liverpool, there are hundreds of groups there...many on an R&B kick...but it was all that work on various club stages in Germany that built up our beat. 'Hamburg Stomp and Yell' music might be more accurate than Merseybeat or Liverpool Sound."* — George Harrison

| October - November | Hamburg | The Beatles make an important friend in ex-boxer **Horst Fascher**—'head bouncer' at Bruno Koschmider's Kaiserkeller club | Fascher's fearsome reputation in St. Pauli enough to keep The Beatles—John, especially—from being beaten up and much worse. But Fascher and his crew soon leave the Kaiserkeller to go work for Peter Eckhorn, owner of the much more upscale **Top Ten Club**.

October 15 — John Lennon, Paul McCartney, George Harrison—together with 'Lu' Walters and Ringo Starr—bass-player and drummer with The Hurricanes—record | 'Summertime' | 'Fever' | 'September Song' | at Hamburg's tiny Akustik Studio—the disc only ever intended for private use | **It's the first time the four 'future' members of The Beatles play and record together.**

October 16 — The Reeperbahn | St. Pauli | Hamburg | On a whim—'walking off' an argument with his then girlfriend, Astrid Kirchherr—'Exi' art student **Klaus Voormann** visits the Kaiserkeller, on the Grosse Freiheit, and witnesses The Beatles for the first time. The band rocks his world—and then some.

| Within days, Klaus Voormann returns to the Kaiserkeller with his two closest friends—photographers **Astrid Kirchherr** and **Jürgen Vollmer**—and they and The Beatles soon become fast friends. Astrid begins to photograph The Beatles on location and in her 'home' studio. Astrid and Stu Sutcliffe gradually become romantically involved.

Late October - Early November — The Beatles start to jam regularly with British rock 'n' roller **Tony Sheridan** headliner at the **Top Ten Club**. At the urging of Horst Fascher, the club's owner, Peter Eckhorn, offers them full-time work. | Bruno Koschmider is infuriated. As he sees it The Beatles are in clear breach of the performance 'exclusion zone' portion of their contract and hits the group with a termination notice. The Beatles dutifully attempt to play out the remainder of their contract. But then Koschmider extracts his own brand of revenge by tipping off the police that George Harrison is underage and not allowed to work.

November 12 — George Harrison is deported from Germany after someone tips-off Hamburg police that he's underage and therefore not allowed to work.

November 29 — Koschmider accuses Paul McCartney and Pete Best of setting fire to their rooms behind the Bambi-Kino that he'd so generously provided for the ungrateful Britishers. They're both arrested, spend the night in a police cell and are deported from the country the following day.

November 30 — After playing 58 finger-blistering, Preludin-fuelled nights at the Kaiserkeller The Beatles' first series of Hamburg engagements comes to a sudden and ignominious end.

December 1 — After having been deported from Germany, Paul McCartney and Pete Best arrive back in England.

December 10 — John Lennon—having stayed on in Hamburg with Stu and Astrid—finally makes the long train journey home back to Liverpool—alone—his suitcase in one hand, his guitar in the other, his amplifier strapped to his back. Stu stays on in Hamburg with new girlfriend Astrid Kirchherr for the coming Christmas and New Year holidays—during which time they get engaged.

December 15 — Liverpool | John Lennon finally re-establishes contact with Paul, George, and Pete; who'd all been secretly thinking he'd given up on The Beatles for good.

December 17 — Casbah Coffee Club | Pete Best contacts Chas Newby, his old Blackjacks band-mate, to sit in as The Beatles' bass-player. They play a few dates; but the mojo's gone.

December 27 - Tuesday — Still somewhat unnerved by their deportation from Hamburg, The Beatles play this all-important 'Christmas Dance' at **Litherland Town Hall** put on by Liverpool promoter, **Brian Kelly**. The Beatles late additions to the bill thanks to the urging of local DJ and new fan **Bob Wooler**, | The existing posters for the event quickly pasted with overlays proclaiming: *Direct from Hamburg! The Beatles*

| *"In Liverpool, people didn't even know we were from Liverpool. They thought we were from Hamburg. They said, 'Christ, they speak good English!' Which we did, of course, being English. But that's when we first, you know, stood there being cheered for the first time."* — John Lennon

| The Beatles stun the audience from their opening number—Little Richard's 'Long Tall Sally'—teenagers stop dancing and flock to the foot of the stage and cheer. | Suddenly, no one can get enough of The Beatles hard-edged, Hamburg-honed rock 'n' roll; not Liverpool beat fans; not Liverpool promoters. | Brian Kelly books the group to play 36 nights for 'Beekay Promotions' over the next three months. Other local promoters, especially **Sam Leach**, rush to do the same. | As George Harrison would recall years later: *"It really was the start of it all."*

| **The start of it all?** | This doesn't diminish in any way the efforts of all the other Liverpool promoters or the significance of all the many other venues in and around Merseyside and the North of England; all the cellar clubs, coffee bars, and jive hives; the church, village, and town halls; the ballrooms, theatres, and cinemas; even the ice-rinks; that The Beatles played at, before they and their manager, Brian Epstein, moved to London, with the rise and rise of '*Beatlemania*'. | Every part and parcel of Liverpool contributed, in its own special way, to the success of The Beatles. As is revealed in 'Quintessential Beatles', they really couldn't have come from any other place on earth.

December 31 — Casbah Coffee Club | Chas Newby's last appearance as The Beatles' bass-player before he quits the music business and returns to college | The big question for The Beatles: *"Who's going to play bass until Stu returns to the group?"*

1961

January — John F. Kennedy inaugurated as US President—the youngest person ever to hold office. *"The torch has been passed..."*

January — Paul McCartney takes up the bass guitar, sort of; John and George having flatly refused to do so; and adapts his Rosetti *Solid-7* guitar, by taking off all six strings and substituting three piano strings. Not the best of instruments, but to encourage him, his band-mates say that he already sounds better on bass than Stu Sutcliffe ever did.

January — The Beatles play 19 dates in Liverpool in the first month of the year—for Brian Kelly and an increasing number of would-be 'jive hive' promoters.

February — **Neil Aspinall** buys an old beat-up van and becomes The Beatles' road manager — their 'roadie' — responsible for getting them and their gear to music engagements.

February 9 — On 'DJ' Bob Wooler's recommendation, The Beatles make their first lunchtime appearance at **The Cavern** | Club owner **Ray McFall** wants to test whether rock 'n' roll can find an audience at the normally 'jazz-only' club | Even though The Beatles performance isn't advertised it's a great success. The first of many such Cavern gigs.

February 11 — Cassanova Club | Sampson and Barlow's New Ballroom | The Beatles play their first of many lunchtime and evening gigs for rock 'n' roll mad promoter Sam Leach. The group also play 'the Cass' on February 14, 16, 21, and 28

February 17 — St John's Hall, Tuebrook | The Beatles play their first non-Casbah Coffee Bar gig for promoter Mona Best—Pete Best's mum.

February 21 — The Beatles play another lunchtime gig at The Cavern | In the evening, they play 'The Cass' as well as Litherland Town Hall | Three bookings in a single day now increasingly the norm.

February — The Beatles play 31 different gigs in 28 days

March 11-12 — **The Iron Door Club** | *'Rock Around The Clock'* 12-hour all-night gig | Liverpool's very first *'Saturday night and Sunday morning'* rock session for Sam Leach | Stu Sutcliffe; on a brief visit home tell to his mother of his engagement to Astrid Kirchherr; resumes duties as the group's bass-player.

March 21 — The Beatles make their third appearance at The Cavern Club and their first evening session as guests at 'The Blue Jeans Guest Night' | Bob Wooler now the club's resident DJ

March — The Beatles play 37 dates for Liverpool promoters during March.

March — Paul McCartney begins to fill in as The Beatles' bass-player when Stu returns to Hamburg.

April 1 - July 1 — Hamburg | **The Top Ten Club** | The Beatles play 92 consecutive nights on this visit | Apart from playing their own sets, The Beatles also appear as the backing group for The Top Ten's 'resident headliner' Tony Sheridan.

| This season at The Top Ten Club is the cause of the split between Allan Williams and The Beatles. | Allan Williams—as 'agent and manager'—expected his cut of whatever fee Peter Eckhorn had agreed to pay the band | The Beatles—having arranged the booking themselves—and having suffered the consequences of their earlier falling out with Bruno Koschmider because of it—didn't feel at all obligated to pay what they considered was an undeserved 'management' fee. | The band maintained forever afterwards that they never signed a management deal with Williams and that he never managed them. | Williams is none too pleased and extracts his own brand of revenge by banning The Beatles from his nightclub, The Blue Angel, a much favoured afterhours hangout for Liverpool beat groups. | The band are only admitted again when Brian Epstein later intercedes on their behalf.

| Astrid Kirchherr cuts Stu Sutcliffe's hair in the French 'Exi' (existentialist) style | The 'trademark' hairstyle later adopted by all the other Beatles—except Pete Best.

| Paul McCartney buys his first Höfner 500/1 bass at the Steinway store in Hamburg for 267 DM; about £30 at the time. As a left-handed bass player, he thought the symmetrical shape of the violin-look-alike bass would look "less daft" than him having to play a right-handed cutaway model 'upside down'.

| April — Hamburg | Purely by chance, Brian Epstein visits Hamburg and Hanover on a management course for thirty retail executives put on by Deutsche Grammophon.

June 22-24 — Hamburg | Friedrich-Ebert-Halle Recording Studio & Studio Rahlstedt | Under the direction of German producer and orchestra leader Bert Kaempfert, the Top Ten Club's resident British rock singer Tony Sheridan selects The Beatles, with Paul on bass, as his backing group in recording sessions for

Polydor Records, which takes place at two different studio locations. | The eight songs they record include: 'My Bonnie Lies Over The Ocean' | 'When The Saints Go Marching In' | 'Nobody's Child' | 'If You Love Me Baby...Take Out Some Insurance On Me' | 'Aint She Sweet, with John on lead vocal | And the instrumental 'Cry For A Shadow'; credited to Lennon-Harrison.

| Polydor signs The Beatles to a 1-year, 4-record contract

July 6 — **Bill Harry**—Art School friend of John Lennon and Stu Sutcliffe—publishes the first issue of *Mersey Beat—Merseyside's Very Own Entertainments Paper* | 'Beat' being a play on the area patrolled, regularly, and on foot, by an on-duty uniformed policeman and nothing at all to do with musical notation | Published fortnightly—the teenage music-culture focused newspaper is the first of its kind in Britain—is an immediate success—and sells out completely—even at NEMS, the record store run by Brian Epstein.

| *"Suddenly, there was an awareness of being young. Young people wanted their own styles and their own music—just at the time they were beginning to earn money and have real spending power. Mersey Beat was their voice. It was a paper just for them—crammed with photos and information about their own groups."* — Bill Harry

August 2 — The Beatles begin their long string of resident nights at The Cavern Club.

October 15 - Sunday — *'Star Matinee'* | Charity variety show promoted by Jim Gretty, at the Albany Cinema | Brian Epstein sees The Beatles perform a ten-minute set

October 23 - Polydor Records release the 45rpm single 'My Bonnie' b/w 'The Saints' in Germany | The disc is credited to 'Tony Sheridan and The Beat Brothers' | The name changed because 'Beatles' sounds too much like *'Peedles'*—German slang for penis | The disc reaches No.32 on Germany's *Musikmarkt* chart

October 28 - Saturday - 3:00 p.m. — **Raymond Jones** goes into **NEMS** and asks to hear **'My Bonnie'** by The Beatles. | Legend says this is the first time **Brian Epstein** is even made aware of the Liverpool band | Bill Harry, founder and editor *Mersey Beat*, recalls events somewhat differently.

November 9 - Thursday — Brian Epstein—accompanied by his personal assistant, Alistair Taylor—goes to The Cavern to see The Beatles play a lunchtime session. | The visit arranged—so neither of them have to queue up outside with all the fans—by Bill Harry | Legend says it's the first time the group's future manager sees and hears them.

"I immediately liked what I heard. They were fresh, and they were honest, and they had what I thought was a sort of presence...a star quality...charisma." — Brian Epstein

November 10 - Friday — | New Brighton | **The Tower Ballroom** | **'Operation Big Beat'** | 7:30 p.m. to 1:00 a.m. | Sam Leach launches 'Big Beat' music on a grand scale with Merseyside's 'Top Five Groups' | The Beatles | Rory Storm and The Hurricanes | Gerry and The Pacemakers | The Remo Four | Kingsize Taylor and The Dominoes | Over 4,000 beat fans brave dense fog and travel through the Mersey Tunnel to get to the venue—some ten or so miles from Liverpool's city centre | A delighted, Tom McCardle, manager of The Tower Ballroom, informs Sam Leach it's broken all previous attendance records.

'Operation Big Beat' starts at 7:30 p.m. | The Beatles go on at 8:00 p.m. | Neil Aspinall then has to drive the group back through the fog to appear for Mona Best at Knotty Ash Village Hall before returning them for their second scheduled appearance at midnight.

November 11 - Saturday — The Beatles attend a special late-night party at the Iron Door Club thrown by Sam Leach to celebrate the unprecedented success of 'Operation Big Beat' | The promoter's secret hope that it will help convince The Beatles of his viability of being the group's manager as and when he finally throws his hat into the ring.

November 24 - Friday — | Tower Ballroom | New Brighton | **'Operation Big Beat II'** | Same line-up as before | With surprise appearances by American singer Davy Jones and Emile Ford | Another huge success for rock 'n' roll mad promoter Sam Leach

December — Brian Epstein—now increasingly interested in becoming The Beatles' manager—seeks advice and counsel from friends as well as people in the record retail business.

| After learning of Allan Williams' previous involvement as their agent and part-time manager he asks Williams outright whether he still has any claim to them.

"I wouldn't touch The Beatles with a fucking bargepole, Brian. They diddled me. They'll diddle you. You can have them. And good riddance." — Allan Williams

December 1 — New Brighton | Tower | The Beatles head the bill featuring six of Merseyside's top beat groups at another Leach Entertainments 'Big Beat' show.

December 3 - Sunday — John, George, and Pete arrive at Brian Epstein's office at NEMS for a scheduled 4:30 p.m. meeting | Epstein intent on discussing the possibility of him becoming their manager. | Epstein is concerned by Paul's absence and he asks George to call his home from a telephone in his outer office. | George does so, returns, and tells everyone that Paul's just got up and is having a bath. | Epstein is nonplussed: "But that means he'll be very late in arriving, now." | "Yes, says George, "but he'll be very clean, though, won't he?" | It's Brian Epstein's first real step into the world of Beatles. | When Paul finally does arrive, Epstein takes all the by-now-very-hungry Beatles to a local milk bar to discuss his business proposal. The Beatles are intrigued, but remain noncommittal | Epstein suggests a follow-up meeting after their coming Wednesday lunchtime gig at the Cavern | It impresses The Beatles that he already knows their work schedule.

December 6 - Wednesday — Early closing-day at NEMS and so it's supposed to be just Mr. Brian Epstein and The Beatles. | Epstein is surprised to see they've brought Bob Wooler with them as their "trusted advisor". | It's all somewhat awkward, but Brian Epstein presses on and presents The Beatles with a bleak overview as to their true financial situation: *"You're always working flat out, but really getting nowhere."* | He offers to become their manager.

December 8 — New Brighton | Tower | | The Beatles again head the bill of Merseyside's top groups at this 'Big Beat' show also featuring Danny Williams who has a hit in the British charts with 'Moon River' | A Leach Entertainments promotion.

December 9 - Saturday — Aldershot - 50 miles from London | The Palais Ballroom | *Liverpool v London - Battle of the Bands* | Another Sam Leach promotion; The Big Beat Session way down South this time. | Staged to introduce The Beatles to London impresarios and audiences. And to prove once and for all Sam's potential as The Beatles' manager. | It's a complete disaster as the local Aldershot newspaper has failed to run an ad for the event because Sam's 'non-local' bank cheque hasn't yet cleared. | The Palais Ballroom is utterly deserted. | Sam and The Beatles scour the town. And finally persuade 17 people to come dance.

December 10 - Sunday | The long drive back up to Liverpool, takes forever and The Beatles arrive very late for Bob Wooler's afternoon gig at Hambleton Hall. | Unexpectedly, Brian Epstein is there to see them play. Afterwards, he and The Beatles come to an informal agreement about him becoming their manager.

"Look, if you really want to succeed and get in to bigger places; make more money and be a bigger success; you're really going to have to change. And to start with: stop eating on stage, stop swearing, and stop smoking." — Brian Epstein

"We were in a daydream 'till Brian came along. We'd no idea what we were doing." — John Lennon

December 13 - Wednesday — The Cavern | Brian Epstein convinces Mike Smith, **Decca Records** A&R assistant, to travel up to Liverpool to see The Beatles...live! | The first step to securing The Beatles the all-important 'London' recording-contract

December 15 - Friday — New Brighton | The Tower | The Beatles top the bill of Merseyside's top groups, yet again, at this 'Big Beat Session' for Leach Entertainments.

December 17 — Brian Epstein meets with The Beatles at The Casbah Coffee Club to go over details of a prospective five-year management agreement to start in the New Year.

December 18 — A&R executives at Columbia and HMV—two of EMI's major record labels—inform Brian Epstein, by post, that having listened to the Polydor single 'My Bonnie' he'd sent them—regretfully decline the offer for them to sign The Beatles

December 23 — The Beatles perform at the first 'all-nighter' at The Cavern.

December 26 — New Brighton | The Beetles (sp.) perform with other top Merseyside groups at a special *'Boxing Night Big Beat Ball'* at The Tower for Leach Entertainments.

December 31 - Sunday — New Year's Eve | An uncomfortable 10-hour road journey from Liverpool to London—the four Beatles sitting hunched alongside their guitars, drums, and amplifiers in the back of Neil Aspinall's unheated van—the journey made all the worse by bitter cold and falling snow | As ever— Brian Epstein travels down to London by train.

1962

January 1 - Monday | A snowy and cold New Year's Day | **Decca Recording Studio** | West Hampstead | London | Scheduled for 11:00 am, the 'Artist Test' Audition starts late, as Decca 'senior assistant' A&R man, Mike Smith, is delayed. | The Beatles, and 'Eppy', as they now call Brian Epstein, are bags of nerves. | After repeated technical delays The Beatles; with Pete Best on drums; record 15 songs on Decca's two-track mono tape machines in little over an hour of studio time | Mike Smith congratulates the group on their effort and later has 45rpm 'Advance Test Recordings' made of the Lennon-McCartney composition 'Like Dreamers Do' for distribution to Decca Group executives.

January 4 — The Beatles voted 'Merseyside's Most Popular Group' in a *Mersey Beat* poll. The results announced in Issue No.13 with the front-page headline **'Beatles Top Poll!'**

January 5 — Polydor Records release 'My Bonnie' b/w 'The Saints' in the UK

January 12 - Friday — New Brighton | Tower Ballroom | The Beatles headline *Twist around The Tower* | Featuring a 'special guest' appearance by *Mr. Twist and the Twistettes*

January 19 —The Beatles headline at 'The Tower' again

January 24 — The Beatles sign a management contract with Brian Epstein at NEMS; witnessed by Alistair Taylor. | 'Eppy' doesn't append his signature to the document and won't, as a point of honour, until he gets "the boys" a recording contract with a major London label. Which in all probability will now be with Decca Records. | The management contract gives Epstein 10-15 per cent of the band's income for a period five years.

January 26 — New Brighton | The Beatles headline again at 'The Tower'

January 27 — Tony Barrow – album copywriter for Decca Records and record columnist – writing as 'Disker' for the *Liverpool Echo* – reports on The Beatles' Decca recording test: *'Decca disc producer Mike Smith tells me he is convinced that the label will be able to put The Beatles to good use.'*

January 31 — Decca Records rejects The Beatles | Decca signs London-based band, Brian Poole and The Tremeloes, instead. (A huge stroke of luck for The Beatles—as events would prove—not that they or anyone knew it at the time.)

February — Brian Epstein travels to London to visit Decca's head office, to appeal his case for The Beatles in a face-to-face meeting with the company's most senior recording manager, **Dick Rowe.** | *"One day The Beatles are going to be bigger than Elvis,"* proclaims Epstein at the lunchtime meeting in Decca's executive dining rooms, overlooking the Thames. | Rowe shakes his head. *"Pop groups are on the way out…guitar groups, especially. Your Beatles just won't sell, Mr Epstein. Why not stick to selling records, which you're very good at."* | Dick Rowe is known forever after as '*The Man Who Turned Down The Beatles*'.

February - March - April - May — Decca now having now firmly closed the door on The Beatles, over the ensuing four months Brian Epstein makes innumerable train journeys to London to try and secure the group a recording contract with the three other 'Big Four' recording companies | EMI | Pye | Philips | But he is repeatedly rejected. | Yet he continues on and on and sets up appointments with anyone who'll see him, however slight their connection to the recording business. | But few people even deign to listen to a single cut from the tapes of The Beatles' failed Decca audition. | Most don't even bother to give him the time of day and he's left to cool his heels in waiting rooms—large and small. | The secretary of one record company executive told Epstein: *"My boss is still out at another appointment, but you can play your music to our office boy, if you like, so you can get the opinion of a real teenager."* | Epstein declines the offer and leaves—fuming.

As Brian Epstein would later say: *"It wasn't just Dick Rowe that turned down The Beatles...everyone else in London did, too."*

| February - July — Also during this period, Brian Epstein carries on discussions with Polydor Records, in Germany, to try and arrange for The Beatles to be freed from their contractual obligations to Bert Kaempfert Productions.

February 8 - Thursday — One of Brian Epstein's earliest trips to London produces gold of a sort. | Having, again, been rebuffed—this time by Pye, as well as Oriole Records—he ventures into The **HMV Music Store**, on Oxford Street, *'The World's Largest Record Store'*—to pay a call on Bob Boast, the store's general manager, who he'd met on a Deutsche Grammophon retail management course, in Hamburg, the year before. | Boast can't help, directly, but does suggest that the tapes of 'the Decca audition' be converted to 78rpm acetate discs in the store's 'Personal Recording Department' by Jim Foy, the store's disc-cutter.

Foy likes what he hears on the tapes and when Brian Epstein informs him that three of the songs are, in fact, original compositions by two members of The Beatles, Foy produces two double-sided 10" discs: 'Hello Little Girl' b/w 'Til There Was You' | 'Love of The Loved' b/w 'Like Dreamers Do'

Foy suggests that Epstein should meet **Sid Colman**, general manager of Ardmore & Beechwood, one of EMI's music publishing companies, with offices in the same building. | Colman also likes what he hears and asks to publish the original Lennon-McCartney songs. | Brian Epstein is gratified, but explains he's looking for a recording contract, not just publishing. If Colman can help him to secure that; he can publish the songs | Colman puts in a telephone call to EMI's head-office and arranges for Brian Epstein to meet record producer, George Martin.

February 13 - Tuesday — EMI, Manchester Square | Soho | London | Brian Epstein's first meeting with **George Martin** | Head of Parlophone—EMI's smallest, least-important, subsidiary label—better known for light-classical, novelty, and comedy records | Brian Epstein plays the 78rpm acetate discs from 'the Decca audition' session | The EMI record producer isn't overly impressed, but says he'll think on it and get back to him | Almost three months pass before the two men get to meet again.

February 15 - Thursday — New Brighton | The Tower | *'The Pre-Panto Ball'* | The Beatles share top billing with Terry Lightfoot & his New Orleans Jazz Band | Sam Leach makes hay with Liverpool University's annual student *Mardi Gras*-like charity *'Panto Day'* and puts on his own very special pre-event ball | The event draws 3,500 people.

February 20 - Tuesday — Southport | Promenade | Floral Hall | Brian Epstein ensures The Beatles are seen to be going up in the world | The gig in a posh theatre for once | Also on the bill | Gerry and The Pacemakers | Rory Storm and The Hurricanes.

February — Little Eva does 'The Locomotion' | Songwriters Goffin and King's pint-sized former babysitter causes new national dance craze on both sides of the Atlantic.

March 2 - Friday — *'Mad March Rock Ball'* at The Tower | The Beatles headline another Leach Entertainments promotion

March 7- Wednesday — Manchester | Playhouse Theatre | *Teenager's Turn...Here We Go* | The Beatles record their BBC radio début wearing new suits made especially for them by Brian Epstein's personal tailor | In light of the fact the BBC had insisted for years that its newscasters wear formal dinner suits to read the news, not quite as mad as it sounds. It certainly has the desired effect; the show's producers think The Beatles look very professional | On the show with newly-smartened up Beatles is the renowned Northern Dance Orchestra, under the direction of Bernard Herrmann | The 'old world' of entertainment face-to-face with the 'new'; and not for the last time.

March 8 - Thursday — The Beatles first 'appearance' on the radio | *Teenager's Turn* is broadcast to listeners *'oop North* on the BBC Light Programme from 5:00 p.m. - 5:29 p.m.

March 17 - Saturday — Liverpool | Knotty Ash Village Hall | **'St. Patrick's Night Rock Gala'** | Sam Leach sets up a special **'Battle of The Bands'** between The Beatles and Rory Storm and the Hurricanes | Later friends and family attend a private party to celebrate Sam's engagement to Joan McEvoy | Brian Epstein and Bob Wooler among the guests.

March 31 – Saturday — Gloucestershire | Stroud | The Subscription Rooms | This time it's Brian Epstein's turn to see if The

THE BEATLES IN LIVERPOOL, HAMBURG, LONDON

Beatles can catch the eyes and ears of all those odd people who live far beyond the borders of Lancashire... *down South.*

April 6 - Friday — New Brighton | Tower Ballroom | *'A Night To Remember'* | *'Farewell Ball'* | Emile Ford and The Checkmates | The Beetles (sp.) | *Also Merseyside's Top 4 Groups* | Gerry and The Pacemakers | Howie Casey and The Seniors | Rory Storm and The Hurricanes | The Big Three | A rockin' Sam Leach send-off before The Beatles fly off for a two-month season in Hamburg | Not a dry eye or dry throat in the house.

April 9 — Beatles John, Paul, and Pete fly to Hamburg to play a residency at **Star-Club** | Grosse Freiheit | St. Pauli | for club owner and 'porn king' Manfred Weissleder.

April 10 — Stuart Sutcliffe, living at the Hamburg home of Astrid Kirchherr, his girlfriend, and now studying at the Hamburg College of Art, under the tutelage of Eduardo Paolozzi, collapses and dies of a cerebral haemorrhage.

April 11 — Beatle George (delayed as he's been ill with flu) and Brian Epstein fly to Hamburg on the same flight as Stuart Sutcliffe's distraught mother. On their arrival at the airport, they meet Astrid Kirchherr and Klaus Voormann and the three other Beatles, who've only just been informed of Stu's death. | John Lennon is utterly devastated by the death of the man he called *'his closest friend, his alter ego, and his guiding force'.*

Hamburg — The last week of April | The Beatles record two songs with Tony Sheridan so they can be released from their recording contract with Bert Kaempfert, two months early | 'Eppy' intent on clearing any and all road-blocks to success with EMI

May 9 - Wednesday — London | EMI Abbey Road Studios | Brian Epstein—still utterly frustrated at the extent of the delay—at long last meets George Martin | The record producer offers to conduct an 'Artist Test' for The Beatles sometime in the near future. | Fearing it might well be 'the Decca situation', all over again, Brian Epstein, nevertheless, takes it as a 'Yes' and sends a congratulatory telegram to The Beatles in Hamburg and another to Bill Harry and *Mersey Beat* in Liverpool:

Bill Harry c/o Mersey Beat Royal 0003 Liverpool.
Have Secured Contract For Beatles To Recorded For EMI On Parlaphone Label | 1st Recording Date Set For June 6th

May — New Brighton | Tower Ballroom Company | Tom McCardle, manager of The Tower Ballroom, gives in his notice, to go and open his own club—'The Valentine'—in Temple Street, Liverpool | Given the huge success of his Friday-night 'Big Beat' franchise at The Tower, Sam Leach is offered the job | It's a rock 'n' rollers dream come true.

May 17 — New Brighton | Tower Ballroom | *'Thank Your Lucky Stars'* | *Rhythm & Blues Spectacular* | *Starring 'Mr. Rock 'N' Roll' Himself* | **Jerry Lee Lewis** | *Plus a Galaxy of Ten Star Groups* | *A Bob Wooler Rockerscope '62 Presentation* in partnership with NEMS | But no sign of The Beatles—as they're still away in Hamburg—playing Star-Club.

The Echoes | Jerry Lee Lewis's backing band find themselves without a drummer | And—lo and behold—Ringo Starr of The Hurricanes steps in and fills the slot.

May 18 — George Martin sends an 'Application For Artiste Contract' through proper administrative channels to EMI's contracts department.

May 24 — A fully typed-up EMI 'Artiste Contract' is returned to Martin 'pre-dated' 4 June for him to forward on to Brian Epstein | The EMI producer receives the contract back from The Beatles' manager—duly signed and witnessed—on 5 June.

June 6 - Thursday — The Beatles to **EMI's Abbey Road Studios**—with Pete Best on drums | George Martin's first time with The Beatles as record producer | After the 'artists test' session Martin informs Brian Epstein he can't use Pete Best on drums for any future recording purposes—as his drum 'beat' simply isn't rock steady enough. | The Beatles are offered a one year—4-song contract—at a penny (1d) per record sold—'a farthing' (a quarter of one old penny) per Beatle—a derisory amount, but standard practice at the time in the British recording industry for as yet unproven talent.

June 7 - Friday — Brian Epstein and his brother Clive set up **NEMS Enterprises** | A management company to specialise in the entertainments business. | Ltd. Co. formalised June 26

June 11 - Monday | Manchester | Playhouse Theatre | The Beatles travel to Manchester by motor coach; accompanied by hand-picked members of the newly formed Beatles' Fan Club; to record their second 'appearance' on the popular *Teenager's Turn...Here We Go* radio show | And just as Brian Epstein had planned—the fans' squeals and screams of delight don't go unnoticed by BBC Radio producers | In the ensuing crush of fans, outside the theatre, after the show, the coach departs, leaving Pete Best stranded and—as if a grim augur of things to come—he has to make his own way back to Liverpool by train | The show is broadcast over the BBC's Light Programme on June 15.

June 21 - Tuesday | New Brighton | Tower Ballroom | *'Number One...Star Show'* | Brian Epstein's brilliant 'positioning' idea to have "his boys" as second-on-the-bill to a top-line act—preferably an international one | 'Hey! Baby' | Bruce Channel | Delbert McClinton *'Harmonica'* | *Direct from America!* | THE BEATLES | *Parlophone Recording Artistes!* | Branded 'for immediate authenticity' as *A Bob Wooler Show* | After the show McClinton shows John Lennon how to play the harmonica passage from 'Hey Baby' as well as giving him other pointers on how to play the blues on a chromatic harmonica. | When The Beatles later record 'Love Me Do' John employs McClinton's blues style to superb effect.

June 28 — Birkenhead | The Majestic Ballroom | *Merseyside's Luxury Ballroom* | The Beatles' first booking with the Top Rank Organisation | Very important to Brian Epstein as it could very quickly lead to more prestigious bookings for The Beatles.

June 29 - Friday — Tower Ballroom | New Brighton | Leach Entertainments Present **'Operation Big Beat III'** | *'A Cavalcade of Rock 'n' Twist'* | Merseyside's Top Ten Groups | *Starring Parlophone & E.M.I. Recording Artistes THE BEATLES* | And all for just 6/- (Six shillings then about the equivalent of $1.25)

June 30 - Saturday — Knotty Ash Church | Sam Leach marries Joan McEvoy | The Beatles attend the wedding, but not the reception as they're playing Heswall Jazz Club with The Big Three that night | Brian Epstein and Bob Wooler attend the reception | Gerry Marsden, Rory Storm, and Ringo Starr do, too. As do most Merseyside musicians of any note that aren't away playing in Hamburg.

July 27 - Friday | New Brighton | Tower Ballroom | A *Bob Wooler* Show | Promoted by NEMS | **Joe Brown and The Bruvvers** | The group from London headlines over The Beatles and all the other Merseyside groups | George Harrison doesn't mind as he's one of Joe Brown's biggest fans.

August 15 - Wednesday — The Cavern Club – lunchtime and evening sessions | Pete Best's last two performances as drummer with The Beatles.

August 16 - Thursday — In the early hours of the morning John and Paul drive across country to Butlin's Holiday Camp, in Skegness, to recruit **Ringo Starr** | Meanwhile, mid-morning at the NEMS office, Whitechapel, Liverpool, by request of the three other Beatles; and quite without warning; Brian Epstein sacks Pete Best from the group | Not The Beatles' finest hour; and only understandable in the light John, Paul, and George all thought that if they didn't act—and get a different drummer—they'd lose their hard-won Parlophone recording contract.

| Ringo agrees to join The Beatles—for £25 per week—but elects to play on with Rory Storm and The Hurricanes until the weekend | That evening Johnny 'Hutch' Hutchinson, of The Big Three, is drafted in as drummer for The Beatles' scheduled gig at the prestigious Riverpark Ballroom, Chester.

August 17 - Friday — With Pete Best now out of the picture for good, 'Hutch' sits in again as The Beatles' drummer for the evening gigs at the Majestic Ballroom, Birkenhead, and The Tower Ballroom, New Brighton.

August 18 - Saturday — Hulme Hall, Port Sunlight | After a two-hour rehearsal, Ringo Starr plays his first gig as a Beatle | **The first performance of The Beatles as everyone would come to** *know, know, know them...and love, love, love them.*

| Question: *"When you joined The Beatles, Ringo, they weren't quite as big as they are now, were they?"* | **"They were the biggest thing in Liverpool. In them days that was big enough."**

— Ringo Starr | *Playboy* | Interview | **28 October 1964**

August 19 - Sunday — Ringo Starr debuts as a Beatle at The Cavern | The Beatles are attacked by aggrieved Pete Best fans and George Harrison gets given a black eye.

August 22 - Wednesday — The Cavern Club | The Beatles' lunchtime session is filmed by Granada TV - the North's independent television company based in Manchester - for the program *'Know The North'* | However, the programme isn't transmitted until 1963.

August 23 - Thursday — John 'does the right thing' and marries **Cynthia Powell**, his girlfriend since art college, who is pregnant with his child – in a civil ceremony at a local registry office | Brian Epstein gives them the keys to his private flat in the city centre, as a wedding gift | In the evening, The Beatles play the Riverpark Ballroom, Chester, a second time.

September 4 - Tuesday — EMI Abbey Road Studios – The Beatles fly down to London for their second recording session | Their first with Ringo Starr on drums | Record 'Love Me Do', a Lennon-McCartney composition, and 'How Do You Do It' composed by reliable hit-maker, Mitch Murray | George Martin has reservations about Ringo's drumming, in particular his lack of time-keeping, but this time keeps his concerns to himself.

September 6 - Thursday — Liverpool | Toxteth | Rialto Ballroom | *The Beatles Show* Ringo Starr still on drums | Rory Storm and The Hurricanes (with a new drummer) | The Big Three | The Merseybeats | A Leach Entertainments promotion.

September 11 - Tuesday — EMI Abbey Road Studios – The Beatles' third visit. George Martin has the more reliable, rock-steady-time, session drummer, Andy White, already installed in the studio | Ringo Starr is relegated to playing tambourine and maracas | In the end, the producer directs Andy White and Ringo to each record a version of each song | 'How Do You Do It' is finally abandoned due to The Beatles' very unenthusiastic takes of the song | The Beatles re-record 'Love Me Do' | And then record two new Lennon-McCartney compositions | 'P.S. I Love You' | 'Please, Please Me'.

September 14 - Friday — *'Operation Big Beat V'* | The Tower Ballroom | Almost Sam Leach's last gasp at The Tower—but what a way to go | The Beatles | Rory Storm and The Hurricanes | Gerry and The Pacemakers | Billy Kramer and The Coasters

September 21 - Friday — *'Rory Storm's Birthday Night'* | New Brighton | Tower Ballroom | Very much Sam Leach's last hurrah at The Tower! | The Beatles | Rory Storm and The Hurricanes | The Big Three | Billy Kramer and The Coasters.

October 1 - Monday — The 'new' Beatles sign a new management contract with Brian Epstein just four days before the release of 'Love Me Do' | As John Lennon had said to 'Eppy'—months before, at the very beginning of their business relationship: *"Just get us a recording contract... down in London... 'Eppy'... and you can manage us."*

October 5 - Friday — **'Love Me Do'** b/w 'P.S. I Love You' released as a 45rpm single in UK | Legend has it that Brian Epstein orders 10,000 copies for NEMS music stores, thus ensuring the record hits the national 'pop charts'.

October — **Mal Evans**—one-time Cavern bouncer—hired to assist Neil Aspinall as 'second roadie' for The Beatles.

October 12 - Friday — **Little Richard** | *'The Quasar of Rock'* | At The Tower Ballroom | New Brighton | Yet another hugely original idea by Sam Leach | But the promoter is outmanoeuvred and outbid by Brian Epstein and the booking reverts to NEMS | The Beatles appear as second on the bill to Little Richard | 'With A Sensational Line Up of 10 Top British Rock Groups *including* The Beatles' | How could it fail—especially as one of those 10 acts is Lee Curtis and the All Stars appearing with their new drummer Pete Best.

October — Having lost out to Brian Epstein—and feeling he no longer has the full support of The Tower Ballroom Company—Sam Leach gives in his notice as manager of The Tower—and gives up his hold on the all-important 'Friday-night franchise'. The time-slot is very quickly taken over by business partners Brian Epstein and Bob Wooler.

October 28 - Sunday — Little Richard stars at the Empire Theatre, Liverpool | 'A NEMS Enterprises *'Pop Package Show'* | All Brian Epstein's idea this time | The Beatles again appear as second on the bill | Great publicity as it puts them on a near par to the more established rock star | And 'Good Golly Miss Molly' it's another rockin' NEMS success.

THE BEATLES IN LIVERPOOL, HAMBURG, LONDON

October 30 - Tuesday — The Beatles fly to Hamburg to play Star-Club again.

November 1-14 — Hamburg | The Beatles play Star-Club for a two-week residency | Share the bill, again, with Little Richard.

November 26 – Monday — London | EMI Abbey Road Studios | The Beatles' fourth session with record producer George Martin | The Beatles record 'Tip Of My Tongue' | 'Ask Me Why' | 'Please, Please Me' – the song completely reimagined by Lennon and McCartney since their September 4 recording session | George Martin so pleased, he tells The Beatles: **"Gentlemen, you've just recorded your first number one hit."**

November 28 — Liverpool | 'The Young Idea Dance' | *The 527 Club* on the top floor of Lewis's Department Store | A special Christmas treat for the store's young staff | The Beatles also play The Cavern that same night.

December 3 — Bristol | The Beatles appear 'live' on the television show *Discs-a-Go-Go*

December 4 — London | The Beatles appear 'live' on the children's television show *Tuesday Rendezvouz* | Broadcast from ATV's Kingsway Studio in central London.

December 5 — Liverpool | Back to The Cavern for lunchtime and evening gigs with Gerry and The Pacemakers.

December 7 — New Brighton | Tower Ballroom | The Beatles | A show for 'NEMS Enterprises'.

December 8 — Manchester | The Oasis Club

December 9 — Liverpool | The Cavern Club | George Martin attends The Beatles' evening gig to hear for himself whether he can record the group's debut album 'live' at the club | He decides against it as the acoustics in the cellar club's three-arched, low ceiling, brick-lined interior are wholly inadequate for recording purposes.

December 15 — Birkenhead | The Majestic Ballroom | The regular evening show is followed, at midnight, by *The Mersey Beat Poll Winners Show*. The Beatles voted 'Most Popular Group' for second year running. | The show runs until 4:00pm.

December 17 — Manchester | The Beatles play 'live' on Granada Television's *People and Places* show.

December 18 - December 31 — Hamburg | Grosse Freiheit | Star-Club | Thirteen more hard days' nights away from home over Christmas and the New Year | And Cynthia pregnant—with Julian—back in Liverpool | The Beatles fifth and final Hamburg club residency | Part of their New Year's Eve session is recorded on a portable Telefunken tape recorder by 'Kingsize' Taylor—who's also appearing at Star-Club with The Dominoes.

December 27 — 'Love Me Do' gets to No.17—its highest position—in the UK charts.

1963

January 11 — **'Please, Please Me'** b/w 'Ask Me Why' 45rpm disc released in UK

January 13 - Sunday — Birmingham | *Thank Your Lucky Stars* | The Beatles mime to their new single in front of a studio audience at ABC Television Studios | Their appearance on one of the country's top pop music shows arranged for them by Dick Rowe—who would go on to become The Beatles' song publisher

January 19 - Saturday — *Thank Your Lucky Stars* | Transmitted at 5:30 p.m. | The very first nationwide British television broadcast of The Beatles.

January 21 — The Beatles signed to Vee-Jay records in the US

February 2 - March 3 — The Beatles | **First UK Tour** | Supporting **Helen Shapiro** | 'Walking Back To Happiness' | Britain's youngest ever female chart topper.

February 11 - Monday — EMI Abbey Road | Studio Two | The Beatles record 10 songs for their début LP *'Please, Please Me'* in a throat-shredding 'one day' marathon session | 4 songs from The Beatles' first two singles added to complete the 14-track album

February 22 — **'Please, Please Me'** becomes **The Beatles' first UK No.1 single**

| Capitol Records | EMI'S US subsidiary still utterly unconvinced of The Beatles' relevance to the US market and refuse to distribute their records | George Martin signs deals with small independent labels Vee-Jay Records and Swan Records.

March 5 — EMI Abbey Road | Studio Two | The Beatles record their third single | 'From Me To You' | 'Thank You Girl'

March 9 – March 31 — The Beatles | **Second UK Tour** | Supporting double-bill of American chart-toppers Chris 'Let's Dance' Montez and Tommy 'Sheila' Roe.

March 22 — *'Please Please Me'* LP album released in UK

April 8 — John Charles Julian Lennon born Liverpool

April 11 — **'From Me To You'** b/w 'Thank You Girl' 45rpm single released in UK

May 11 - Saturday — The Beatles' LP *'Please, Please Me'* tops British album charts and remains 'top' for 30 weeks.

May 18 – June 9 — The Beatles | **Third UK Tour** | Supporting American singer and chart-topper **Roy Orbison** | 'Only The Lonely' | 'In Dreams' | 'Running Scared' | 'Dream Baby' | On hearing theatre audiences' incessant screaming for The Beatles, Orbison graciously moves to end the show's first half and cedes top billing to The Beatles.

June 14 – Friday — The Beatles final appearance at the Tower Ballroom | New Brighton | *'Mersey Beat Showcase'* | A NEMS Enterprises presentation | Also on the bill are Gerry and The Pacemakers | And five other Merseyside groups.

July 1 – EMI Abbey Road | Studio Two | The Beatles record their fourth single | 'She Loves You' | 'I'll get You'

July 8 – August 31 — The Beatles appear in a series of week-long engagements at a number of British seaside resorts.

July 18 – October 23 — EMI Abbey Road | Studio Two | The Beatles record tracks for *'With the Beatles'* their second LP

August 3 - Saturday — The Beatles make their last appearance at the Cavern. Sources differ as to the exact number of dates the group played at this famed Liverpool beat club, but it's estimated to have been at least 292 times.

August 23 — **'She Loves You'** b/w 'I'll get You' 45rpm single released in UK | Hits No.1 on advance sales alone | The first Beatles' single to sell a million copies | Biggest-selling record in UK until 1978, when it's surpassed in sales by 'Mull of Kintyre'; recorded by Paul McCartney's post-Beatles band Wings

October 4 — The Beatles 'mime' 'She Loves You' on their first appearance on *Ready, Steady, Go!* a rock/pop music programme transmitted live, every Friday evening, from ITV Television Studios in central London. An off-camera voice always starts the show off with *"The weekend starts here!"* then it's straight into 'Wipe Out' by the Surfaris.

October 13 - Sunday — The Beatles appear on ATV's **Val Parnell's Sunday Night at the London Palladium**. | The British equivalent of CBS's *The Ed Sullivan Show* | 13+ million television viewers watch the show | After newspaper photos emerge of screaming fans outside the theatre, before and after the show, the National Sunday papers dub it *"Beatlemania"*.

October 17 — EMI Abbey Road | Studio Two | The Beatles record their fifth single | 'I Want To Hold Your Hand' b/w 'This Boy' | First time using EMI's new 4-track tape machine.

October 24 - 30 — The Beatles tour Sweden | October 24 — *'The Beatles Popgrupp från Liverpool på besök i Stockholm'* | The Beatles tape a live, seven-song, concert in front of invited audience of teenage girls at Swedish National Radio's Karlaplan Studios. *Pop '63* program shows The Beatles on tip-top form.

October 31 — US TV celebrity Ed Sullivan, about to fly back to New York, sees hordes of teenagers at London Airport waiting to welcome The Beatles home and is hugely intrigued by the event; his first thought that it must be for arriving UK Royalty!

November 1 - December 13 — The Beatles **Fourth UK Tour**

November 4 - Monday — The Beatles appear at the hugely prestigious *Royal Variety Command Performance*, held annually at the Prince of Wales Theatre, in London. | Before belting out 'Twist And Shout' John Lennon makes his famous remark in front of the Queen Mother, Princess Margaret, and other members of the establishment | *"For our last number I'd like to ask your help. Would the people in the cheaper seats clap your hands and the rest of you, if you'll just rattle your jewellery."* After the show is broadcast on TV the following Sunday evening, *'Beatlemania'* engulfs all of Great Britain.

| The Beatles Official Fan Club set up to respond to growing tide of *'Beatlemania'* | Brian Epstein asks NEMS employee Freda Kelly to act as club secretary. A key role *"Good old Freda"* discharges faithfully for a further 10 years.

| Brian Epstein flies to the States to persuade Capitol Records to release The Beatles in the US; also meets with Ed Sullivan

THE BEATLES IN LIVERPOOL, HAMBURG, LONDON

November 22 — *'With The Beatles'* LP released in UK | Tony Barrow, now the group's press officer, writes the album's sleeve notes and uses the superlative *"the fabulous foursome"*; and the sobriquet **"The Fab Four"** is soon universally adopted.

'With The Beatles' only second album, in UK chart history, to sell million copies | *South Pacific* soundtrack album first in 1958.

November 29 — **'I Want To Hold Your Hand'** b/w 'This Boy' 45rpm single released UK

December 4 — Capitol Records; EMI subsidiary; finally take note of *'Beatlemania'* and announce they've signed The Beatles in the US market. | Mount unprecedented $50,000 PR campaign | Beatles' first Christmas record sent to Fan Club members.

December 24 - January 11 — Finsbury Park Astoria | London | *'The Beatles Christmas Show'* with Liverpool's Cilla Black | The Fourmost | Billy J. Kramer and The Dakotas

December 24 — 'I Want To Hold Your Hand' b/w 'I Saw her Standing There' 45rpm released in US | Tops the Billboard singles chart for seven weeks | The opening salvo in what would shortly come to be called: **"The British Invasion."**

1964

January — Capitol Records—at Brian Epstein's insistence—at last pulls out all the stops and launches a $50,000 marketing campaign across the US | *'The Beatles are Coming'*

January — 'I Want To Hold Your Hand' enters the US singles chart... *with a bullet!*

January 12 — The Beatles make their second appearance on the hugely popular ATV variety show *Sunday Night at the London Palladium* | Singer Alma Cogan is also on the bill; and she quickly becomes a close and trusted London friend of the group

January 16 - February 4 — Paris | The Olympia Theatre |The Beatles in concert with Trini Lopez and Sylvie Vartan | The concert series doesn't sell out | Also, there are more boys than girls in the audience, and not a single sign of *'Franco-Beatlemania'*.

| Paris | The Beatles record two of their songs in German—at EMI's Pathé-Marconi studios—especially for the German market *'Komm, Gib Mir Deine Hand'* b/w *'Sie Liebt Dich'*

February 1 — 'I Want To Hold Your Hand' reaches No.1 in the US singles chart

February 7-22 — **The Beatles in America**

February 7 - Friday — The Beatles fly in to New York's Kennedy airport to be welcomed by five thousand screaming fans | An airport official says it's unprecedented even for kings and queens | The Beatles' off-the-cuff banter at the press conference immediately following their arrival completely charms—and disarms—the US press corps of over 200 photographers and cameramen, and newspaper, radio, and television reporters.

| Question: *"What do you think of Beethoven?"* | Ringo: *"Great. Especially his poems."*

| Question: *"In Detroit, there's people handing out car stickers saying, 'Stamp Out The Beatles'."* | Paul: *"Yeah well, we're bringing out a 'Stamp Out Detroit' campaign."*

| Question: *"Are you for real?"* Paul: *"For real."* John: *"Come and have a feel."*

| Question: *"Would you please sing something?"* | Beatles: *"No!"* | John: *"No, we need money first."*

| Question: *"Why does your music excite people so much?"* | Paul: *"We don't know. Really."* | John: *"If we knew, we'd form another group and be managers."*

February 9 - Sunday — The Beatles appear on CBS-TV's *The Ed Sullivan Show* from studios in New York City. The event sets a new world record for the largest-ever TV audience. 73+ million people all across America watched the show. It smashes to pieces the previously held record—the television debut of Elvis Presley on *The Ed Sullivan Show.*

February 10 - 21. Concert at The Coliseum in Washington | Back to New York for two shows at Carnegie Hall | On to Florida to snatch a quick holiday | February 16. A second televised appearance on *The Ed Sullivan Show* from the famed Deauville Hotel, in Miami Beach | Another 70 million viewers tune in to see and hear The Beatles.

February 22 — America "re-conquered" The Beatles fly back to the UK

February 25 - April 16 — EMI Abbey Road | Studio Two | The Beatles record a four-track 45rpm EP | Start on the soundtrack for their first film *A Hard Day's Night*.

March 2 - April 4 — *A Hard Day's Night* | Film directed by Dick Lester | Shot in 8 weeks at a cost £189,000 (c. $400,000 in 1964) | London and West Country locations and Twickenham Film Studios | Post-production for film completed in another 8 weeks | In profit even before the film opens due to massive advance sales of soundtrack album (the only reason the film was originally commissioned by United Artists) and 'Special Preview' screenings in US

March 9 — NEMS Enterprises, now with a staff of twenty-five, moves from Liverpool to premises in Argyll Street, London | New office situated next door to the London Palladium.

March 19 — London | The Beatles receive their award as the ***Variety Club's Show Business Personalities of The Year***

March 20 — '**Can't But Me Love**' b/w 'You Can't Do That' 45rpm single released in UK

March 23 — John Lennon's first book *In His Own Write* published in UK

March 28 — The Beatles have 10 songs in the Billboard 'Top 100' singles chart.

April 4 — The Beatles now have 12 songs in the Billboard 'Top 100'—including all 'Top Five' spots.

June 1-3 — EMI Abbey Road | Studio Two | The Beatles record more songs for the soundtrack album of *A Hard Day's Night*

June 4 — The Beatles hold 'Top 5' spots on the Billboard Charts | 'Can't Buy Me Love' | 'Twist & Shout' | 'She Loves You' | 'Want to Hold Your Hand' | 'Please, Please Me'

June - July — The Beatles | The First Leg of Their First World Tour | 37 concerts | 27 days | Denmark | The Netherlands | Hong Kong | Australia | New Zealand

June 19 — Extended Play | EP released in UK | 'Long Tall Sally' | 'I Call Your Name' | 'Slow Down' | 'Matchbox'

July 6 - Monday — *A Hard Day's Night* | UK film premiere takes place at Pavilion Theatre, Piccadilly Circus, London W1 | Prestigious charity even attended by Princess Margaret and Lord Snowdon | *A Hard Day's Night* directed by Dick Lester | Written by Alun Owen | Filmed in black and white | Documentary-style | Influenced by French 'New Wave' | Chronicles *'Two Days In The Life'* of characters John, Paul, George, and Ringo | An unnamed British rock 'n' roll band (everyone knows who they really are) are all seeming prisoners of their own extraordinary success | One scene reminiscent of The Beatles' US press conference on their arrival at JFK | Piccadilly Circus closed to traffic for film premiere. Milling crowd of 12,000 Beatles' fans outside cinema bring central London to complete standstill.

| Question: **"Are you a Mod or a Rocker?"**
Ringo: *"Um, no. I'm a Mocker."*
| Question: **"Do you often see your father?"**
Paul: *"No, actually, we're just good friends."*
| Question: **"How did you find America?"**
John: *"Turned left at Greenland."*
| Question: **"I say... what would you call that hairstyle you're wearing?"**
George: *"Arthur."*

July 10 — '*A Hard Day's Night*' soundtrack album released in UK | First Beatles' LP to feature all Lennon-McCartney originals | Seven from the film | 'A Hard Day's Night' | 'I Should Have Known Better' | 'If I Fell' | 'I'm Happy Just to Dance With You' | 'And I Love Her' | 'Tell Me Why' | 'Can't Buy Me Love' | Flip Side | 'Any Time at All' | 'I'll Cry Instead' | 'Things We Said Today' | 'When I Get Home' | 'You Can't Do That' | 'I'll Be Back'

July 10 — 'A Hard Day's Night' b/w 'Things We Said Today' 45rpm single released UK

August 11 - Tuesday — US premiere *A Hard Day's Night* in New York | Andrew Sarris *The Village Voice*: *"...the Citizen Kane of jukebox movies."* | Film critic Roger Ebert later describes the film as *"...one of the great life-affirming landmarks of the movies."*

Global *'Beatlemania'* erupts as both the film and album of *A Hard Day's Night* are released to worldwide acclaim.

August 19 - September 20 — The Beatles Tour US and Canada | 23 cities | 30 concerts | 30 days | 10,000 to 20,000 fans attend each '30-minute' performance.

August-23 — Los Angeles | The Beatles play the Hollywood Bowl | Capitol record their performance with the aim of releasing a 'live' album. | The sound quality of the tapes proves inadequate for commercial release.

August 28 — New York | The Beatles meet Bob Dylan.

September - October — EMI Abbey Road | Studio Two | The Beatles record tracks for a new LP and single.

| October – *A Cellarful of Noise* | Brian Epstein's autobiography published in the UK | Ghost written by Derek Taylor from taped interviews | Taylor is recruited as Brian Epstein's personal assistant at NEMS Enterprises, London. | He later assumes the role of The Beatles' Press Officer.

October 9 - November 10 — The Beatles | **Fifth UK Tour** | *Special Guest Star direct from America*—**Mary Wells** | The Motown star—with her huge hit 'My Guy'—backed by Sounds Incorporated—closes first half of the show | Liverpool group The Remo Four opens second half.

November 27 — **'I Feel Fine'** b/w 'She's A Woman' 45rpm single released in UK

December 4 — **'*Beatles For Sale*'** LP | 'On Sale' at record stores everywhere in Britain.

December 24 - January 11 1965 — Hammersmith Odeon, London | The Beatles' second season of Christmas - New Year's holiday shows—'Another Beatles Christmas Show' with The Yardbirds | Freddie and The Dreamers | Elkie Brooks | Sounds Incorporated

1964

A Brief Coda to The Beatles' *'Annus Mirabilis'*:

"*If you look at our itinerary; we did maybe a tour of England; a tour of Europe; a tour of America; two albums; and about 4 EPs; and three singles; and made a movie; all in the same year.*"
— George Harrison

"*We were just on this roll and we were all in our early twenties and we were just going with it.*"
— Ringo Starr

| As UK one press report put it at the time: **'Their unimaginable success made The Beatles world figures... important enough for the Prime Minister and the Queen's consort to discuss, in news conferences.'**

| Question: "Have you ever met the Queen?"
John: *"No. She's the only one we haven't met. We've met all the others."*
Paul: *"All the mainstays."*
| Question: "Winston Churchill?"
Ringo: *"No, not him."*
John: *"He's a good lad, though."*
— The Beatles | Interview | *Playboy* | 28 October 1964

The Middle Years

'Braannnng!' | From the unforgettable opening chord of the opening track of **A Hard Day's Night** | G suspended 4th chord | Played by George Harrison on his new Rickenbacker twelve string guitar | To the thunderous sustained-beyond-all-measure final piano chord of **'A Day In The Life'** that brings **'Sgt. Pepper's Lonely Hearts Club Band'** to such a climatic *"I want it to sound like the end of the world"* close | The multi-layered sound produced by Beatles John, Paul, and Ringo—and George Martin and 'roadie' Mal Evans all simultaneously sounding an E-major chord on three separate pianos | Which Martin then augments with a harmonium | The random noises, voices, and sounds of backwards laughter heard on the run-out groove,

along with a high-pitched tone inaudible to human ears that could only be heard by dogs, an idea of John's. One more instance of how The Beatles continued to push the boundaries in audio; 'Revolution No. 9' arguably the ultimate example.

The Later Years
'The White Album' | *'Abbey Road'* | *'Let It Be'*

The End
30 January 1970 | Marked by the last fading chords of **'Get Back'** on the album ***'Let it Be'***—the very last song The Beatles played on the Rooftop Concert at Apple's Savile Row headquarters. | The silence... and the void... filled by the 'Solo' works of: John Lennon | Paul McCartney | George Harrison | Ringo Starr

And After
December 1970 | Jann Wenner — Founder & Editor of *Rolling Stone* — conducted a landmark "no-holds-barred" post-Beatles interview with John Lennon and Yoko Ono in New York City that first saw publication in **1 July 1971** edition of *Rolling Stone*:

| Question: **The Beatles were always talked about - and The Beatles talked about themselves - as being four parts of the same person. What's happened to those four parts?**

John: *"They remembered that they were four individuals. You see, we believed The Beatles myth, too. I don't know whether the others still believe it. We were four guys... I met Paul and said, 'You want to join me band?' Then George joined. And then Ringo joined. We were just a band that made it very, very big, that's all. Our best work was never recorded."*

| Question: **Why?**

John: *"Because we were performers in Liverpool, Hamburg... and other dance halls. What we generated was fantastic when we played straight rock... and there was nobody else to touch us in Britain."*

And On Into The Beyond:

John Lennon | 9 October 1940 - 8 December 1980
Murdered by a deranged—supposed former Beatles' fan. Shot dead outside his home in the Dakota apartment building, in New York City. | John's death caused worldwide mourning. A shocking moment that no true Beatles' fan can ever forget... or forgive.

George Harrison | 25 February 1943 - 29 November 2001
Died of throat cancer and was cremated | George's ashes later scattered upon the sacred waters of the River Ganges and River Yamuna in India as per Hindu tradition. | Much mourned. Much missed. | *Concert for George*. A tribute held at the Royal Albert Hall November 29, 2002 later televised around the world.

George Martin | 3 January 1926 - 8 March 2016
Sir George Martin | Appointed Commander of the British Empire (CBE) in 1988 | Knighted for 'Services to Music' in 1996 | Tributes were paid to him from all around the world.

From 'The Beginning' through to 'The End'

For a more detailed account of The Beatles; day-by-day, week-by-week, month-by-month, and year-by-year; one source will forever remain utterly indispensable: *The Complete Beatles Chronicle* by the seemingly indefatigable, world-renowned, British-born, Beatles' historian Mark Lewisohn.

The Chronicle is a large format book, suited for armchair, desktop, or library table. Which is why I also much enjoy turning to *The Beatles Diary: Volume One* by Barry Miles; a regular-sized book culled from a compendium of different sources; many of which are from Miles' own copious notes and research, but, as he himself attests; for the sake of accuracy regarding dates, times, and venues; the majority of information drawn directly from Mark Lewisohn. *The Diary* is great for reading at coffee bars and on trains and boats and planes.

Read On | Rock On | Roll On

PART FOUR—THE BEATLES TIMELINES

A Hard Day's Night

Trailer | Timeline | Reflections

A Hard Day's Night | Film Trailer

A Hard Day's Night | British 'musical comedy' film starring The Beatles - John Lennon, Paul McCartney, George Harrison, and Ringo Starr. | Producer - Walter Shenson | Director - Dick Lester | Scriptwriter - Alun Owen | Filmed in black and white | Documentary-style | Influenced by French 'New Wave' | Jump cuts. Fast edits. Interposed surrealism. | Chronicles two 'Days In The Life' of characters John, Paul, George, and Ringo—members of a British rock 'n' roll band—never called The Beatles in the film because everyone already knows who they really are—all seeming prisoners of their own extraordinary success. | Shot in under 8 weeks at a cost £189,000 (c. $400,000 at the time) | Filmed in London and West Country locations and Twickenham Film Studios. | Post-production for the film completed in a further 8 weeks. | Released by United Artists | July 6 (UK) and August 12 (US) during the height of *'Beatlemania'* | 85 minutes

> "Looking at the performances of The Fab Four it's hard to believe that John and Ringo are just 23 years of age, that Paul is 21, and George is barely 20—all of them so very assured and accomplished—even though the screenplay had been written expressly to reflect them and their individual characters, they can't help but transcend the material. The film seems 'ageless'— and however many time you see it, it always delivers 85 minutes of sheer, unmitigated joy. A uniquely 'fab' film experience."

A Hard Day's Night | Film Timeline

1963

September | London | Noel Rodgers; United Artists Records Representative; discovers EMI has neglected to secure any provision regarding film soundtracks in their contract with The Beatles. | Rodgers approaches 'Bud' Ornstein, Head of Production for United Artists European film division, with idea that UA should offer The Beatles a three-picture deal, so that UA can obtain the rights to three—highly lucrative—soundtrack albums.

October | London | Ornstein negotiates three-picture deal with Brian Epstein. | Tasks independent film producer Walter Shenson—an American also based in London—to produce a Beatles' film with enough new songs to make up a soundtrack album—director, script, and title to be determined. The film has to cost no more than £200,000 and be ready for release July 1964. | The subtext: Go produce a low-budget rock 'n' roll exploitation movie so we can get as much money out of teenage Beatles' fans' pockets; before the pop group fades into obscurity and the screaming stops. | Shenson taps Dick Lester to direct.

October 15 | 32-year old Dick Lester and Walter Shenson have their first meeting with The Beatles at the BBC Playhouse – Northumberland Ave, London, where the group are rehearsing for a radio broadcast.

October 24-30 | The Beatles tour Sweden

November | Johnny Speight, acclaimed British TV hit writer; Dick Lester's first choice as the film's screenwriter; is unavailable. Lester turns to actor-playwright Alun Owen, a Liverpudlian, he'd previously worked with on a BBC TV comedy show.

December 4 | Capitol Records at long last begin a wide scale release of Beatles' records in the US

November | Owen and Shenson meet. Owen asks: **"What's the idea for the film?"** | Shenson recalls a wild taxi ride he'd once had with The Beatles through the streets of London where the group drew crowds whenever they alighted from the taxi-cab. **"An exaggerated day in the life of The Beatles,"** he tells Owen.

November 6-8 | Alun Owen flies to Dublin with The Beatles to observe them up close on their 'Autumn Tour' and get a real feel for the character of each of the group's members.

November 7 | Owen sees the group perform twice at the Adelphi Cinema and after three days and nights of 'shadowing' the group returns to London with the 'vision' of the as yet untitled film's screenplay planted firmly in his head. | Owen tells Walter Shenson: *"They're prisoners of their success. They go from airport to hotel to theatre or stadium or concert hall; back to the hotel; then straight back to the airport. It's the same in every city they go to. They travel in a little cocoon of Liverpool. There's the manager, the road manager, the publicity man, the car driver, the guy that sets up and breaks down their equipment. That's all they ever see. Because they'd be mobbed; all but torn to pieces; the moment they got out of the car or hotel room or off the concert stage."*

Fear of being mobbed? Afraid of being torn to pieces? What? In 1963? No exaggeration on Alun Owen's part. As the year draws to a close *'The Fab Four'*, as the British media now call The Beatles, are the most popular musical artists in all the UK and all of Europe; the passion, enthusiasm, and excitement of their fans unprecedented. | The Beatles have had four No. 1 Hit Singles: 'Please Please Me' | 'From Me To You' | 'She Loves You' | 'I Wanna Hold Your Hand' | The Beatles' first LP: *'Please Please Me'*—released 22 March—hit the top of the UK Album Charts in May and remained there for 30 weeks, only to be replaced by the group's second LP—*'With The Beatles'*—released 22 November. | *'With The Beatles'* had advance orders of over 300,000— quickly sold over half a million copies—and topped the Album Charts for 21 weeks. | The Beatles topping the album charts for 51 consecutive weeks. | Again—all and everything is completely without precedent. Is it any wonder then the excitement caused by December's 'Official announcement' from film production company—Proscenium Films: 'The first ever film starring The Beatles is about to go into production in the New Year'. *What in the world could top that?*

December 26 | Capitol Records issue 'I Wanna' To Hold Your Hand' | The long delayed release of The Beatles in the US accompanied—at Brian Epstein's insistence—by a national $50,000 promotional campaign, which results in several million posters around the US all proclaim: *"The Beatles Are Coming!"*

1964

January 16 - February 4 | Paris | The Olympia | The Beatles in concert with Trini Lopez and Sylvie Vartan. | Brian Epstein telephones to tell them they have a No.1 record in the US

January 25-28 | Alun Owen and Dick Lester and Walter Shenson fly to Paris; stay at the same hotel as The Beatles, The George V | Owen's vision for the film is reaffirmed when Dick Lester hears a reporter ask John Lennon what he thought of Stockholm when the group made their recent trip to Sweden. And John replies: *"It was a plane and a room and a car and a cheese sandwich."*

February 1 | The Beatles top the US Billboard Top 40 Singles chart—week ending 1 February 1964—with 'I Wanna' To Hold Your Hand'—the official start of *'Beatlemania'* in the US

February 7 | The Beatles fly from London Airport aboard Pan Am 'Flight 101' bound for New York City | Brian Epstein, Neil Aspinall, Mal Evans; plus dozens of journalists and photographers; also on the flight. | The aircraft arrived JFK Airport 1.20pm. To be greeted by thousands of screaming fans.

| The Beatles utterly charm and disarm the US press corps at a scheduled airport press conference.

February 9 | The Beatles, after much anticipation and great fanfare, appear 'live' on the Sunday evening nationally televised **The Ed Sullivan Show**. Their appearance draws an estimated 73 million viewers; breaking all previous viewing records.

February 11 | The Beatles to Washington D.C. for first American concert at Washington Coliseum.

February 12 | The Beatles fly back to New York to perform Carnegie Hall.

February 13 | The Beatles fly to Miami Beach, Florida—for a few days holiday. | The press reporting their every move.

February 16 | The Beatles' second Sunday-evening appearance on *The Ed Sullivan Show*—broadcast 'live' from the Napoleon Ballroom - Deauville Hotel - Miami Beach.

February 22 | The Beatles fly back to the UK | They arrive at Heathrow Airport at 7:00 a.m. to be met by more than ten thousand screaming fans.

February 23 | The group's third appearance on *The Ed Sullivan Show*; 'taped' earlier in the day of the 9 February TV show.

February 24 | United Artists and Walter Shenson now have the hottest property in the world: The Beatles' first movie.

February 25 | George's 20th birthday

February 25-29 | EMI Abbey Road | Studio Two | The Beatles record new songs for the film.

February | Dick Lester decides to film in black and white—to get a heightened sense of documentary realism. Hires Gilbert Taylor as cinematographer | Robert Freeman—photographer who shot *With The Beatles* LP cover is hired to create the title sequence | George Martin—The Beatles' record producer—is appointed the film's musical director.

February 29 | Saturday | The Beatles see Alun Owen's film script for first time—the film unit set to begin principal photography the following Monday 2 March | Tentative film titles: *Beatlemania* | *Beatles No. 1* | *What Little Old Man?* | *Oh, What A Lovely Wart!* | *On The Move* | *Travelling On* | *Moving On* | *Let's Go* | *It's a Daft, Daft, Daft, Daft, Daft World*

March 1 | EMI Abbey Road | Studio Two | The Beatles record another song for the film—'I'm Happy Just To Dance With You'

March 2 | Dick Lester begins principal photography for the film at London's Paddington Station | Uses hand-held camera on the station platform when The Beatles are mobbed by crowds of screaming fans—as well as aboard the moving train—for added flexibility and to achieve *"a more fluid sense of realism"*.

March 2-6 | Dick Lester given tapes 9 new songs specially written for the film by John Lennon and Paul McCartney. He selects 7 songs for the film.

March 5 & 12 | Dick Lester shoots the film's 'opening' scenes at London's Marylebone Station.

March 10 - 20 | Filming at Twickenham Studios. With a brief foray to Les Ambassadeurs, London, for gambling club scenes.

March 23 - 2 April | Lester shoots concert sequences at Scala Playhouse.

April 4 | The Beatles have 12 songs in the Billboard 'Hot 100'—including all 'Top Five' spots: No. 1 'Can't Buy Me Love' | No. 2 'Twist and Shout' | No. 3 'She Loves You' | No. 4 'I Want to Hold Your Hand' | No. 5 'Please Please Me'

April 4-12 | The film's title, all now agree: *A Hard Day's Night*

April 16 | EMI Abbey Road | Studio Two | The Beatles record the film title song—'A Hard Day's Night'—written to order 'overnight' by John Lennon at request of Walter Shenson.

April 23 | Last day of shooting; Thornsbury Playing Fields, Middlesex.

April 24 | The filming wraps—and goes into post-production.

June 1-3 | EMI Abbey Road | Studio Two | The Beatles record more songs for the 13-track UK album *A Hard Day's Night*.

July 6 - Monday | *A Hard Day's Night* | Royal Charity Film Premiere attended by Princess Margaret and Lord Snowdon | London Pavilion Theatre | Piccadilly Circus | London W1 | A chanting crowd of 12,000 Beatles' fans outside the cinema bring central London to a complete standstill—echoes the wild celebrations that took place at the end of WWII.

July 10 | *A Hard Day's Night* soundtrack album released in UK | First Beatles' LP to feature all Lennon-McCartney originals | The title song: 'A Hard Day's Night' | Seven songs from the film: 'I Should Have Known Better' | 'If I Fell' | 'I'm Happy Just to Dance With You' | 'And I Love Her' | 'Tell Me Why' | 'Can't Buy Me Love' | 'You Can't Do That' | Plus the song Dick Lester omitted: 'I'll Cry Instead' | Plus 4 new originals recorded for the UK 13-track album: 'Any Time at All' | 'Things We Said Today' | 'When I Get Home' | 'I'll Be Back'

July 10 | Cheering crowds line the streets to welcome home The Beatles. | Civic reception at Liverpool Town Hall, complete with the Mayor and Mayoress, followed by Northern Charities Film Premiere of *A Hard Day's Night* at the Odeon Cinema.

August 2 | *A Hard Day's Night* goes on 'General Release' throughout UK

August 11 | US Premiere at Beacon Theatre, New York.

August 12 | US Release of *A Hard Day's Night* | Opens in 500 theatres across the country | The film in profit even before it opens due to massive advance sales of US soundtrack album and 'Special Preview' screenings in US

August - September | *'Beatlemania'* goes global as film and album of *A Hard Day's Night* are released to worldwide acclaim.

A Hard Day's Night | Reflections

That brilliantly bright, spectacular sounding, seemingly never-ever-heard-before opening chord, played by George Harrison on his shiny new 12-string Rickenbacker guitar, at the start of *A Hard Day's Night,* on both the opening of the film and the soundtrack album; *'Dm7 add11'* or *'Gm7 add11 dim 4',* the argument is still raging; heralded the start of 'The Sixties' for countless teenagers the world over.

| Directed with wit and élan by Richard Lester. Shot in black and white. *A Hard Day's Night* is a stunningly brilliant crystallization of *cinéma vérité,* documentary film, and rock 'n' roll movie; brimming with good-natured anarchy, irreverence, and comedic flare. The film is 85 minutes of pure joy and manages to capture a particular moment in time to perfection.

| *Time* magazine rated it one of the 100 greatest films of all-time. The British Film Institute thought much the same; ranking it at No. 88 of the *'Top 100 British films of the Twentieth Century'.*

It certainly proved to be an extraordinarily influential film; as it not only gave birth to a whole new generation of rock musicians; it also introduced young filmmakers to a whole 'new wave' approach that later burst onto the scene, and television screens, as the MTV pop music video revolution. There are any number of people who even see *A Hard Day's Night* as a catalyst to 'the whole cultural revolution' that was 'The Sixties'. The mop-topped 'Trojan Horse' that gave an aura of acceptability to the rebellious nature of 'rock 'n' roll' and that sowed the seeds of the "counter culture" that later took root in the UK and U.S.A.

| **Richard Lester** said in an interview some years after making the film: *"The general aim of the film was to present what was apparently becoming a social phenomenon in this country. Anarchy is too strong a word, but the quality of confidence that the boys exuded! Confidence that they could dress as they liked, speak as they liked, talk to the Queen as they liked, talk to the people on the train who 'fought the war for them' as they liked... [Everything was] still based on privilege—privilege by schooling, privilege by birth, privilege by accent, privilege by speech. The Beatles were the first people to attack this... they said if you want something, do it. You can do it. Forget all this talk about talent or ability or money or speech. Just do it."*

| **Roger Ebert**, the great, much lamented, American film critic, said in an interview to mark the film's first re-release: *"I don't think that people often go to the movies and have their ideas change. But I think people can go to the movies and have their feelings change. And those feelings lead to ideas. A Hard Day's Night is obviously not a political film in an overt way. Yet out of 'A Hard Day's Night' came The Sixties."*

| Heady stuff, indeed, in terms of cultural history, but also not easily dismissed. The film has proven itself to be a perfect distillation of a particular 'moment in time' in recent cultural history that still resonates with young and old alike—on both sides of the Atlantic. *A Hard Day's Night* is of The Sixties, but is in no way confined by them or is even defined by them. The ideas the film gave voice to; the questions it helped pose, even if only obliquely; still need answering. All of which is to say that *A Hard Day's Night*, although utterly of its time—if the last 50 years are anything to go by—is also very much forever.

PART FIVE-THE BEATLES | DISCOGRAPHY

The Beatles - On Record

From 'Be-Bop-A-Lula' to 'Beatlemania'

The arc of this book stretches from—the day John met Paul when they each sang Gene Vincent's 'Be-Bop-A-Lula'—a secret handshake that shouted: "*I dig 'Rock 'n' Roll', too!*"—all the way to the wondrous sounds of the only ever all Lennon-McCartney album *A Hard Day's Night*—that both signifies and celebrates the very height of *'Beatlemania'*. The sheer, unfettered joy of it all, there for all to see and hear, again and again and again, in their absolutely amazingly fab first film *A Hard Day's Night*.

From that point on the unending demands made upon the group—due to the speed and utterly unprecedented scale of their worldwide success—regularly caused The Beatles to stop and take stock of their situation. The 'irony', 'pandemonium', and 'pot' all reflected—consciously or unconsciously—in the titles of their next albums: *Beatles For Sale*—*Help!*—*Rubber Soul*. Hidden messages? The Beatles were famous for it.

As for The Beatles' other wondrous albums, I'll leave those for others to tell you about. There are certainly enough experts out there; on all aspects of The Beatles and their music; and I've recommended the very best of them; and many of their published works in: **'Reading The Beatles'** and **'Reading The Sixties'**. But here now with special emphasis on the years 1958 through to 1964 are the sounds *From 'Be-Bop-A-Lula' to 'Beatlemania'*

| **PART ONE** | Complete listing of the official and 'unofficial' recordings from The Beatles' 'Early Years' | 1958 - 1964
| **PART TWO** | Complete UK and US Discographies | 1962 - 1970

PART ONE

UK Parlophone Recordings | 1961 - 1964

The Singles: Love Me Do/P.S. I Love You (Oct 5, 1962) | Please Please Me/Ask Me Why (Jan 11, 1963) | From Me To You/ Thank You Girl (Apr 12, 1963) | She Loves You/I'll Get You (Aug 28, 1963) | I Want To Hold Your Hand/This Boy (Nov 29, 1963) | Can't Buy Me Love/You Can't Do That (Mar 16, 1964) | A Hard Day's Night/Things We Said Today (Jul 10, 1964)

The EPs: Twist and Shout (Jul 12, 1963) | The Beatles' Hits (Sep 6, 1963) | The Beatles - No. 1 (Nov 1, 1963) | All My Loving (Feb 7, 1964) | Long Tall Sally (Jun 19, 1964) | Extracts from the Film *A Hard Day's Night* (Nov 4, 1964) | Extracts from the Album *A Hard Day's Night* (Nov 6, 1964)

The Albums: Please Please Me (Mar 22, 1963) | With the Beatles (Nov 22, 1963) | A Hard Day's Night (Jul 10, 1964) | Beatles for Sale (Dec 4, 1964)

Non-Parlophone Recordings | 1961 - 1964

THE BEATLES WITH TONY SHERIDAN, HAMBURG
Polydor Singles: My Bonnie/The Saints (Jan 5, 1962) | Sweet Georgia Brown/Nobody's Child (Jan 31, 1964) | Why/ Cry For A Shadow (Feb 28, 1964) | 'Ain't She Sweet / Take Out Some Insurance On Me Baby (May 29, 1964)
Polydor EP: My Bonnie/The Saints/ Why/Cry For A Shadow (Jul 12, 1963) | **Polydor LP:** The Beatles First (Jun 19, 1964)

THE DECCA AUDITION TAPES
1 January 1962. The Beatles auditioned for Decca Records at Decca Studios, Broadhurst Gardens, in West Hampstead, north London. And recorded fifteen songs in a little over an hour. Decca ultimately rejected the band and instead selected London-based group Brian Poole and the Tremeloes. | Originally only

available on 'bootleg' recordings—a number of the songs from the audition were officially released on The Beatles' compilation album *Anthology 1* by **Apple Records** on 20 November 1995.

The fifteen songs recorded at the Decca Audition session: Like Dreamers Do | Money (That's What I Want) | Till There Was You | The Sheik of Araby | To Know Her Is to Love Her | Take Good Care of My Baby | Memphis, Tennessee | Sure to Fall (In Love with You) | Hello Little Girl | Three Cool Cats | Crying, Waiting, Hoping | Love of the Loved | September in the Rain | Bésame Mucho | Searchin'

LIVE! AT THE STAR-CLUB IN HAMBURG, GERMANY 1962
Adrian Barber recorded a number of the group's live performances during The Beatles' last ever week at Star-Club. And 'Kingsize' Taylor recorded The Beatles' final performance on New Year's Eve.

Given the astonishing success of The Beatles, many 'bootleg' versions have since appeared on the scene. To say the least—the audio quality is terrible. Not that that has ever stopped legions of Beatles' fans from searching out the recordings.

Featured songs: Hully Gully | I Remember You | Little Queenie | I Wish I Could Shimmy Like Sister Kate | Red Sails In The Sunset | Reminiscing | Talkin' About You | Sheila | My Girl Is Red Hot | What I'd Say | Your Feets Too Big | Falling In Love Again | Where Have You Been All My Life | Be-Bop-A-Lula

Apple Recordings | 1958 - 1965

LIVE AT THE BBC | 1962 - 1965
'Live' studio recordings broadcast on various radio shows on the BBC Light Programme from 1963 to 1965. | Released 1994. Apple Records. UK/US | **George Martin** chose 56 songs for the album—30 of which had never been issued previously by The Beatles—all interspersed with snippets of banter between the group and program hosts. | *Live at the BBC* peaked at No. 3 on the US *Billboard* album chart, but reached No.1 on the UK albums chart. During its first year of release the album sold an estimated 8 million copies worldwide. |

Time magazine said: "*as a time capsule, the set is invaluable.*" Anthony DeCurtis—for ***Rolling Stone***—described the album as "*an exhilarating portrait of a band in the process of shaping its own voice and vision.*" | 2013. A re-mastered *Live at the BBC* album was released along with a second volume of BBC Radio broadcasts: *On Air – Live at the BBC Volume 2*

Disc One: From Us To You | I Got A Woman | Too Much Monkey Business | Keep Your Hands Off My Baby | I'll Be On My Way | Young Blood | A Shot Of Rhythm And Blues | Sure To Fall (In Love With You) | Some Other Guy | Thank You Girl | Baby It's You | That's All Right (Mama) | Carol | Soldier Of Love | Clarabella | I'm Gonna Sit Right Down And Cry (Over You) | Crying, Waiting, Hoping | You Really Got A Hold On Me | To Know Her Is To Love Her | A Taste Of Honey | Long Tall Sally | I Saw Her Standing There | The Honeymoon Song | Johnny B Goode | Memphis, Tennessee | Lucille | Can't Buy Me Love | Till There Was You

Disc Two: A Hard Day's Night | I Wanna Be Your Man | Roll Over Beethoven | All My Loving | Things We Said Today | She's A Woman | Sweet Little Sixteen | Lonesome Tears In My Eyes | Nothin' Shakin' | The Hippy Hippy Shake | Glad All Over | I Just Don't Understand | So How Come (No One Loves Me) | I Feel Fine | I'm A Loser | Everybody's Trying To Be My Baby | Rock And Roll Music | Ticket To Ride | Dizzy Miss Lizzy | Kansas City / Hey-Hey-Hey-Hey | Matchbox | I Forgot To Remember To Forget | I Got To Find My Baby | Ooh! My Soul | Don't Ever Change | Slow Down | Honey Don't | Love Me Do

ON AIR - LIVE AT THE BBC VOL. 2 | 1962 - 1965
Features 39 more 'Live' studio recordings of BBC radio show broadcasts from 1963 to 1964. | Released 2013. Apple Records. UK/US | Again all previously unreleased tracks from The Beatles—and as before also has accompanying snippets of in-studio banter between the group and the different radio show presenters. | Includes different versions of several songs released

THE BEATLES IN LIVERPOOL, HAMBURG, LONDON 413

previously on *Live At The BBC*—simply to underscore the fact The Beatles recorded a number of their favourite songs multiple times for dear old "Auntie Beeb." | Most songs taken from The Beatles' first four LPs: *Please Please Me*, *With the Beatles*, *A Hard Day's Night*, and *Beatles for Sale*. Other songs are the group's covers of early rock 'n' roll classics by Little Richard, Chuck Berry, and Buddy Holly et al—most of which were never recorded in a studio or released on any Beatles' album. | During their many 'live' BBC radio broadcasts—from March 1962 through June 1965—The Beatles performed a total of 88 different songs. The album not compiled by George Martin this time, but by Messrs. Kevin Howlett and Mike Heatley.

Disc One: Words Of Love | Do You Want To Know A Secret | Lucille | Anna (Go To Him) | Please Please Me | Misery | I'm Talking About You | Boys | Chains | Ask Me Why | Till There Was You | Lend Me Your Comb | The Hippy Hippy Shake | Roll Over Beethoven | There's A Place | PS I Love You | Please Mister Postman | Beautiful Dreamer | Devil In Her Heart | Sure To Fall (In Love With You) | Twist And Shout

Disc Two: I Saw Her Standing There | Glad All Over | I'll Get You | She Loves You | Memphis, Tennessee | From Me To You | Money (That's What I Want) | I Want To Hold Your Hand | This Boy | I Got A Woman | Long Tall Sally | If I Fell | And I Love Her | You Can't Do That | Honey Don't | I'll Follow The Sun | Kansas City/Hey-Hey-Hey-Hey! | I Feel Fine

ANTHOLOGY 1 | **1958 - 1964**
A compilation album—the first of a trilogy—released 20 November 1995 by Apple Records UK/US as part of Apple's *The Beatles Anthology* multi-media project that comprised an eight-episode TV series and DVD release, a coffee-table book—*The Beatles Anthology by The Beatles*—and three double-album CDs: *Anthology 1-2-3*.

Anthology 1 features rarities, outtakes, and live performances; including material from John, Paul, and George's earliest days as **The Quarrymen**. And also includes tracks with original bass player **Stuart Sutcliffe** and drummer **Pete Best**, and songs from the 'failed' Decca audition, as well as outtakes from the *Beatles for Sale* recording sessions. The album topped the *Billboard* album chart and went 'Platinum' eight times over.

Disc One: Free As A Bird | That'll Be The Day | In Spite Of All The Danger | Hallelujah, I Love Her So | You'll Be Mine | Cayenne | My Bonnie | 'Ain't She Sweet | Cry For A Shadow | Searchin' | Three Cool Cats | The Sheik Of Araby | Like Dreamers Do | Hello Little Girl | Besame Mucho | Love Me Do | How Do You Do It | Please Please Me | One After 909 | Lend Me Your Comb | I'll Get You | I Saw Her Standing There | From Me To You | Money (That's What I Want)| You Really Got A Hold On Me | Roll Over Beethoven

Disc Two: She Loves You | Till There Was You | Twist And Shout | This Boy | I Want To Hold Your Hand | Can't Buy Me Love | All My Loving | You Can't Do That | And I Love Her | A Hard Day's Night | I Wanna Be Your Man | Long Tall Sally | Boys | Shout | I'll Be Back | You Know What To Do | No Reply | Mr. Moonlight | Leave My Kitten Alone | No Reply | Eight Days A Week | Eight Days A Week | Kansas City/Hey Hey Hey Hey!

PART TWO

The Beatles Complete UK Discography | 1962-1970
Just as The Beatles and George Martin intended

In the UK—from 1962-1970—The Beatles released 12 studio albums, 13 EPs, and 22 singles, on EMI's **Parlophone** record label and later on The Beatles' own **Apple Records**.

The Beatles' core catalogue of Lennon-McCartney and/or George Harrison compositions amounts to 217 songs and around 10 hours of music. All the group's musical works were originally released on vinyl as full-length Long-Play 33⅓ rpm albums (LPs) | Extended-Play 45 rpm records (EPs) | Two-sided 45 rpm singles. And most Beatles' albums were released in both mono and stereo versions.

The entire collection has been re-released a number of times on compact disc (CD)—original, re-issue, and re-mastered—as well as on the now long-discarded 'cassette' and '8-track' platforms. | 2018. The Beatles' can also now be accessed on Apple iTunes and a dedicated Sirius channel.

The original UK albums invariably had 14 tracks—as originally conceived by The Beatles and George Martin, their record producer. *A Hard Day's Night* the only exception has 13 tracks—but then again all of them were Lennon-McCartney originals. And other than the first LP *Please Please Me* none of the UK albums included songs already released as 'singles'—as neither The Beatles nor their producer wanted "to rip off the fans". In comparison the albums released by **Capitol Records**—never had more than 11 tracks per album and were liberally sprinkled with Beatles' singles—the only reason that more Beatles' albums were released in the US than in the UK In 1967—with the release of *Sgt. Pepper*—at the absolute insistence of The Beatles—releases on both sides of the Atlantic at last got into lockstep. | * 1968—in both the UK and US—starting with the single 'Hey Jude' and the album *The Beatles* (aka 'the White Album')—everything later recorded by the group was released on Apple Records.

UK Albums: Please Please Me (Mar 22, 1963) | With the Beatles (Nov 22, 1963) | A Hard Day's Night (Jul 10, 1964) | Beatles for Sale (Dec 4, 1964) | Help! (Aug 6, 1965) | Rubber Soul (Dec 3, 1965) | Revolver (Aug 5, 1966) | Sgt. Pepper's Lonely Hearts Club Band (Jun 1, 1967) | The Beatles (White Album) (Nov 22, 1968) | Yellow Submarine (Jan 17, 1969) | Abbey Road (Sep 26, 1969) | Let It Be (May 8, 1970)

UK EPs: Twist and Shout (Jul 12, 1963) | The Beatles' Hits (Sep 6, 1963) | The Beatles - No. 1 (Nov 1, 1963) | All My Loving (Feb 7, 1964) | Long Tall Sally (Jun 19, 1964) | Extracts from the Film *A Hard Day's Night* (Nov 4, 1964) | Extracts from the Album *A Hard Day's Night* (Nov 6, 1964) | Beatles for Sale (Apr 6, 1965) | Beatles for Sale - No. 2 (Jun 4, 1965) | The Beatles' Million Sellers (Dec 6, 1965) | Yesterday (Mar 4, 1966) | Nowhere Man (Jul 8, 1966) | Magical Mystery Tour (Dec 8, 1967)

| Side Bar | Polydor Records | Jul 12, 1963 | For obvious reasons—Polydor released My Bonnie—a quasi-Beatles' EP—the same day the Twist and Shout EP went on sale.

UK Singles: Love Me Do / P.S. I Love You (Oct 5, 1962) | Please Please Me / Ask Me Why (Jan 11, 1963) | From Me To You / Thank You Girl (Apr 12, 1963) | She Loves You / I'll Get You (Aug 28, 1963) | I Want To Hold Your Hand / This Boy (Nov 29, 1963) | Can't Buy Me Love / You Can't Do That (Mar 16, 1964) | A Hard Day's Night / Things We Said Today (Jul 10, 1964) | I Feel Fine / She's A Woman (Nov 23, 1964) | Ticket To Ride / Yes It Is (Apr 9, 1965) | Help / I'm Down (Jul 19, 1965) | Day Tripper / We Can Work It Out (Dec 3, 1965) | Paperback Writer / Rain (May 30, 1966) | Eleanor Rigby / Yellow Submarine (Aug 5, 1966) | Strawberry Fields Forever / Penny Lane (Feb 17, 1967) | All You Need Is Love / Baby You're A Rich Man (Jul 7, 1967) | Hello Goodbye / I Am The Walrus (Nov 24, 1967) | Lady Madonna / The Inner Light (Mar 15, 1968) | Hey Jude /Revolution (Aug 30, 1968) | Get Back / Don't Let Me Down (Apr 11, 1969) | The Ballad Of John And Yoko / Old Brown Shoe (May 30, 1969) | Something / Come Together (Oct 6, 1969) | Let It Be / You Know My Name (Look Up The Number) (Mar 6, 1970)

The Beatles Complete US Discography | 1964-1970
Just as Capitol Records intended... to make the most profit
Most of The Beatles' albums were released in the USA under different names—largely due to **Capitol Records** trying to play catch up and—to put it bluntly—issuing as many of their own Beatles' song compilations as they could get away with—regardless of the similarity of whatever title appeared on the album cover. A lamentable occurrence that only ceased with the release of *Sgt. Pepper's Lonely Hearts Club Band*. (Though Capitol did later manage to sneak in an additional album with *Hey Jude*—a collection of non-album singles and B-sides never released in the UK. Go figure.)

US Capitol Albums: *Meet the Beatles!* (Jan 20, 1964) | *The Beatles' Second Album* (Apr 10, 1964)| *A Hard Day's Night* (Jun 26, 1964) | *Something New* (Jul 20, 1964) | *Beatles '65* (Dec 15, 1964) | *The Early Beatles* (Mar 22, 1965 | *Beatles VI* (Jun 14, 1965) | *Help!* (Aug 13, 1965) | *Rubber Soul* (Dec 6, 1965) | *Yesterday and Today* (Jun 20, 1966) | *Revolver* (Aug 6, 1966) | *Sgt. Pepper's Lonely Hearts Club Band* (Jun 2, 1967) | *Magical Mystery Tour* (Nov 27, 1967) | *The Beatles* (White Album) (Nov 25, 1968) | *Yellow Submarine* (Jan 13, 1969) | *Abbey Road* (Sep 26, 1969) | *Hey Jude* (Feb 26, 1970) | *Let It Be* (May 18, 1970)

| Side Bar | *The Beatles' Story* | Nov 23, 1964
A rather ham-fisted, pseudo-documentary-style double-album compilation of 'compère cum radio-style commentary' snippets; at least to these ears; all jumbled together with interviews, press conferences, intermixed with all-too-brief fragments of original Beatles songs and/or orchestral pieces. And if not exactly *The March of Dimes* it does show Capitol at their money-grubbing worst—at least to these eyes. Still—even after all these years—I just had to buy it—and from Japan, too. Only for the very dedicated and/or deluded collector. Trust me.

| Side Bar | *Introducing... The Beatles* | Jan 10, 1964
The very first Beatles' album released in the US was on **Vee-Jay Records** (*"God bless 'em"*) a full ten days before Capitol's *Meet the Beatles!* | The Vee-Jay Beatles' album charted at No.2 behind Capitol's Beatles' album, but by late 1964 had sold over million copies.

US Capitol EPs: Four By The Beatles (May 11, 1964) | 4 By The Beatles (Feb 1, 1965)
US Capitol Singles: I Want To Hold Your Hand / I Saw Her Standing There (Jan 13, 1964) | Can't Buy Me Love / You Can't Do That (Mar 16, 1964) | A Hard Day's Night / I Should Have Known Better (Jul 13, 1964) | I'll Cry Instead / I'm Happy Just To Dance With You (Jul 20, 1964) | And I Love Her / If I Fell (Jul 20, 1964) | Matchbox / Slow Down (Aug 24, 1964) | I Feel Fine / She's A Woman (Nov 23, 1964) | Eight Days A Week / I

Don't Want To Spoil The Party (Feb 15, 1965) | Ticket To Ride / Yes It Is (Apr 19, 1965) | Help / I'm Down (Jul 19, 1965) | Yesterday / Act Naturally (Sep 13, 1965) | We Can Work It Out / Day Tripper (Dec 6, 1965) Nowhere Man / What Goes On (Feb 21, 1966) | Paperback Writer / Rain (May 30, 1966) | Yellow Submarine / Eleanor Rigby (Aug 8, 1966) | Penny Lane / Strawberry Fields Forever (Feb 13, 1967) | All You Need Is Love / Baby You're A Rich Man (Jul 17, 1967) | Hello Goodbye / I Am The Walrus (Nov 27, 1967) | Lady Madonna / The Inner Light (Mar 18, 1968) | Hey Jude / Revolution (Aug 26, 1968) | Get Back / Don't Let Me Down (May 5, 1969) | The Ballad Of John And Yoko / Old Brown Shoe (Jun 4, 1969) | Something / Come Together (Oct 6, 1969) | Let It Be / You Know My Name (Look Up The Number) (Mar 11, 1970) | The Long And Winding Road / For You Blue (May 11, 1970)

| Side Bar | Capitol *Starline* Singles: Oct 11, 1965
Multiple singles released on 'bargain' **Capitol** *Starline* label: Twist And Shout / There's A Place | Love Me Do / P.S. I Love You | Please Please Me / From Me To You | Do You Want To Know A Secret / Thank You Girl | Roll Over Beethoven / Misery | Boys / Kansas City - Hey Hey Hey Hey

| Side Bar | The Beatles on Capitol Records | The American Beatles' scholar **Bruce Spizer** is the man to turn to for anything to do with The Beatles' US Capitol catalogue. His epic—two-part—*The Beatles' Story on Capitol Records*—is a collectable in its own right. His book *The Beatles Are Coming!* is an exceptional read on US '*Beatlemania*'.

Reading The Beatles

MORE ABOUT JOHN | PAUL | GEORGE | RINGO

'To know, know, know them...'
Delve deeper into the extraordinary musical, social, and cultural phenomenon that was The Beatles with these recommended books and websites:

Beatles Books To Read

01 *The Complete Beatles Chronicle* | *The Beatles: All These Years: Tune In* (Vol. 1/3) — **Mark Lewisohn** | An astonishing body of work that always rewards repeated reading. Definitive. Indispensable. Inspired. From *The Beatles Live!* through to *The Beatles Recording Sessions* and the incomparable *The Complete Beatles Chronicle*—an essential read for any Beatles' fan. | *The Beatles: All These Years: Tune In*—The first of Lewisohn's three-volume magnum opus was 10 years in the writing—and it shows—in attention to detail and in the telling. As it says on the back cover: *"Let's scrub what we know, or think we know, and start over: Who really were these people, and how did it all happen?"* Simply superb and, again, essential reading for any Beatles' fan. | Personally, I can't wait to *Turn On...* (hopefully 2020) and then *Drop Out*.

02 *Revolution In The Head: The Beatles Records and the Sixties* — **Ian MacDonald** | A masterpiece—*sans pareil*. One of the very best books on The Beatles, their music, and 'their time'. Deserves to be on every 'Beatles bookshelf' right alongside the collected works of Mark Lewisohn. Another book that rewards repeated reading.

03   *Can't Buy Me Love: The Beatles, Britain and America* — **Jonathan Gould** | Essential reading. And very much a personal favourite. Hugely insightful views into The Beatles' music, as well as a very nuanced appreciation of the group's extraordinary influence and affect on post-war society in both the UK and US Another book to read and read again for the pleasure of Mr. Gould's wise and witty observations. Should be a standard university text for Beatles' studies—at any and every level.

04   *Mersey Beat: The Beginnings of The Beatles* | *Ultimate Beatles Encyclopaedia* | *Encyclopaedia of Beatles People - et al* — **Bill Harry** | Bill Harry's first-hand knowledge of many of the people he writes about is unbeatable—incomparable—beyond scholarly. Delve even deeper with his individual encyclopaedias on John, Paul, George, and Ringo. Ignore the occasional bits of errata that pop in some of the editions of his many books that some readers carp and complain about; Bill Harry's breadth and depth of knowledge simply can't be contested—or bettered. He's "the man" and is always a must-read for any serious Beatles' fan. And if you ever come across a copy of his *Book of Lennon*, grab it; it's another rare treat.

05   *"Love Me Do!" The Beatles' Progress* — **Michael Braun** | There's no better fly-on-the-wall account of the band's early days. A young American journalist does a double-take as the band sets out on its first, six-week British tour. Hard to find, but well worth hunting down a copy.

06   *The Beatles: The Authorised Biography* | *The Quarrymen* — **Hunter Davies** | The first and best 'inside story'. First published in 1968. Dismissed by some as being too sanitized—and having one too many unforced errors—they rather miss the point. Hunter Davies was there with The Fabs—with unrestricted access—at the very peak of the group's success. And the truth is he doesn't at all shy away from all the so-called 'gritty little facts'—and, rather more importantly, he doesn't make them up, either. It's also an elegantly written book—even though

written at speed. Later editions—always newly revised. | *The Quarrymen* offers intriguing insights into the formative years of John Lennon and Paul McCartney—and the 'Skiffle' band that was in every way the genesis of The Beatles. Nicely told.

| Side Bar | *The John Lennon Letters* - **Edited by Hunter Davies** Davies does a bang up job collecting, collating, and annotating around three hundred letters and postcards that John Lennon wrote to family and friends—and to people he'd never met—during his lifetime. Reveals much about the man and his magical, mercurial mind. Intimate. Informative. And often very inspiring.

07 *Shout! The True Story of The Beatles* | *John Lennon - The Life* | *Paul McCartney - The Life* — **Philip Norman** | I've included all three works here—as they bookend journalist Philip Norman's take on The Beatles and its two most prominent members: Lennon and McCartney. First and last words—as it were. | 1981. *'Shout!'* was the first unofficial 'all the dirt 'n' more' book about the group. Published within a year of John Lennon's murder... Paul McCartney rather famously re-titled it: **"Shite!"** No doubt because of Norman's assertion that: **"John hadn't been one-quarter but three-quarters of The Beatles."** And although still unloved by some—even after all these years—for its unapologetic bias—is exceptionally good on the group's early days in Hamburg. | *John Lennon - The Life* Hugely detailed, but draws its real strength from candid interviews with such key people as George Martin, Neil Aspinall, Yoko Ono... even Paul McCartney—as well as countless others—all of whom knew John intimately or had close dealings with him. The revelations from the interviews alone make the 800+ pages well worth the read. | *Paul McCartney - The Life* Again a series of interviews woven together and hugely detailed. Given the earlier antipathy, Norman as surprised as anyone that ex-Beatle Paul gave tacit approval for him to interview family and friends. Norman's biography of John probably the event that helped to rebuild burned bridges. The first of the many McCartney biographies to deal, extensively, with Paul's post-Beatles life.

| Side Bar | Other Paul McCartney biographies | For my money *FAB - An Intimate Life of Paul McCartney* – **Howard Sounes** | *Paul McCartney - Many Years From Now* – **Barry Miles** are much better reads. The latter because a good half of the book is told in Paul McCartney's own words; taken from a series of one-on-one, taped-interviews between two friends of long standing. And why am I not surprised by this; but with no axes to grind, it also paints a wholly respectful and warmly affectionate portrait of John Lennon.

08 *John Lennon*: Vols. I & II | *Brian Epstein: The Man Who Made The Beatles* — **Ray Coleman** | Of the many chroniclers of The Beatles, I developed a special affection for Coleman's work, especially in regard to his twin-biographies on **John Lennon** and his biography of **Brian Epstein**. The latter book, particularly, because it was what first keyed me in to 'the Sam Leach Affair'.

09 *The Beatles: The Biography* — **Bob Spitz** | It's often been said that: "The heart of the matter can best be seen from afar." Case in point. Mr. Spitz is yet another American with eyes firmly set on the prize. Only this time—The Beatles—from start to finish—in England and America. And very nicely done, too. At almost 1000 pages: a veritable treasure trove of a biography, nicely detailed, and nicely voiced.

10 *A Cellarful of Noise* — **Brian Epstein** | The autobiography of The Beatles' manager published in 1964. The words and thoughts are entirely his; even though it was 'ghost written' by Derek Taylor who went on to become a trusted confidante and Apple Corps insider. A compelling portrait of The Beatles' early days that very much goes to underscore Brian Epstein's absolute and untiring belief in the group.

11 *All You Need Is Ears* — **George Martin** | Warm, witty, wonderful. (*And what a pair of ears!*) But then I'm an unabashed fan of the man. Without whom etc. A gentle—but revealing amble through his extraordinary career as one of Britain's most accomplished record producers. His respect, admiration, and love of The Beatles, is evident throughout.

12 *The Rocking City* **(UK)** | *The Birth of The Beatles* **(US)** — **Sam Leach** | This is one of my all time favourite books about The Beatles. It puts you 'right there'—in the clubs and on the streets of Liverpool—in the very early days of the group. There's really nothing else quite like it—certainly nothing else to touch it. It's funny, untidy, funny, irrepressible, funny, exhilarating, funny—sometimes even sad—but bubbly and boisterous in the extreme. Much, as I suspect, was the author, Sam Leach, himself. | Unfortunately, Sam Leach is almost always written out of Beatles' history—and that's a crying shame. He's barely mentioned in *The Beatles Anthology* and given little or no credit for all he did. But I'm convinced that—along with such highly respected Liverpool luminaries as Bill Harry, Bob Wooler, and Ray McFall—he played a hugely important and significant role in the early life of The Beatles and a signal part in the rise of the whole Merseybeat scene. Sam Leach richly deserves to be applauded for that. | I urge you to read his book. It merits a much wider audience and an honoured place on every 'Beatles Bookshelf'. Long may he be remembered; and one day be regarded as the true Liverpool treasure that he was.

13 *The Man Who Gave The Beatles Away* — **Allan Williams (& William Marshall)** | Liverpool club owner and would be entrepreneur Allan Williams secured bookings for The Beatles in 1960 when nobody else would even look at them—let alone listen to them. Acting as their booking-agent-cum-unofficial-manager he got them an audition with a London pop music impresario and was responsible for sending them out to Hamburg. When I first read his book some years after it was first published in 1975, I dismissed it as merely opportunistic and Allan Williams as nothing more than a chancer. | Years later I read Mark Lewisohn's take on events in *The Beatles: All These Years: Tune In* which led to an abrupt change of heart on my part. I realised then how very blind, as well as ignorant, I'd been and simply had to take another look at Allan Williams and his book (which I still had on my shelves). And I'm glad I did. | Is it worth the read? Is Allan Williams worth your time? Absolutely. With the wisdom of hindsight, even if Williams's take on events sometimes stretches the truth, in many ways it bears noble comparison with Sam Leach's wonderful *The Rocking City*, as it's actually very revealing of the times and is often very, very funny and shows Allan Williams to have truly been one of the great Liverpool characters.

14 *Beatle! The Pete Best Story* — **Pete Best (& Patrick Doncaster)** | The book represents the first time that Pete Best, the original Beatles' drummer, put word to his side of what happened when—after having endured two hard slog years with the group in Liverpool and Hamburg—he was fired without warning on 16 August 1962. Pete Best was as open as it was possible for him to be in 1985 when the book was first published. And so it's an important read on lots of levels. | It was later followed by *The Best Years of The Beatles* — **Pete Best with Bill Harry**. More a celebration of the man with loads of photographs from Bill Harry's extensive *Mersey Beat* archives. A great step in re-framing Pete Best to the world. | Later came: *The Beatles - The True Beginnings* — **Roag Best with Pete & Rory Best.**
A coffee table book that does justice to the famed Casbah Coffee Club—situated in the basement of the Best family home—anecdotes and photographs, old and new, from the Best archives. Nicely done. | As new revelations came to light—the latest entry into the Pete Best saga saw the Liverpool author Spenser Leigh weighing in with his version of events. Variously entitled: *Best Of The Beatles: The Sacking Of Pete Best* and *Drummed Out!: The Sacking Of Pete Best*

15 *I'll Never Walk Alone - An Autobiography* — **Gerry Marsden (with Ray Coleman)** | Bright and breezy, cheeky and, sometimes, surprisingly gritty. And listed here because Gerry was not only a great friend, but also a keen rival of The Beatles. Another hard-driven boy from the hard Liverpool streets of the Dingle—just like Ringo Starr—who found his way up and out with music. Gerry and The Pacemakers—the second Liverpool beat group signed by Brian Epstein. And the first Liverpool group to get three No. 1 hits in a row on the UK charts with their first three singles releases.

16 *The Man Who "Framed" The Beatles - A Biography of Richard Lester* — **Andrew Yule** | If you're as much an avid fan of The Beatles' first film *A Hard Day's Night* as I am then this book is for you. If not—just go see the film again—and then come back and rethink the issue. It represents another one of those 'Lightning Bolts' I always go on about, when talking about The Beatles. One of those God-given collaborations between The Beatles and people who seemingly walk up from out the blue to best serve them on their journey. Dick Lester was one; the film's producer Walter Shenson was another; the film's scriptwriter Alun Owen, yet another. I could go on. And I do in Part Four of this book devoted to the production of the film. As ever Andrew Yule does a sterling job as a biographer, this but one of a number he's written.
| **Side Bar** | If you're at all interested in delving deeper into the making of the film there's a terrific book by **Stephen Glynn** for 'TCM Turner Classic Movies: British Film Guides' called, what else but, *A Hard Day's Night.* A little gem of a book.

17 *Here, There and Everywhere: My Life Recording The Beatles* — **Geoff Emerick** | A little off The Beatles' track for the purposes of my two books of the early years, up to and including '*Beatlemania*', as it deals more with the recording of the groundbreaking Beatles' singles: 'Strawberry Fields Forever' and 'Penny Lane' and the seminal albums *Revolver* and *Sgt. Pepper*—but an unabashed delight nevertheless—and one well worth the read. (The audio version voiced by Martin Jarvis—an unabashed joy.)

18 *Beatles' Gear* — **Andy Babiuk** | Just as it promises: everything The Beatles bought, touched, used; musical instruments, amplifiers, microphones *et al*; to make their magnificent music. Truly, a revelation; and such total fun to boot.

19 *A Day In The Life - The Music and Artistry of The Beatles* — **Mark Hertsgaard** | Another Beatles book by an American journalist. This one specifically designed to examine the musical art of The Beatles. It has great bones. It started as a *New Yorker* piece profiling Mark Lewishon and grew from there. Hertsgaard, only the second person, after Lewishon, to gain access to the EMI Beatles sound vaults. Insightful. Engagingly written.

20 *The Beatles Diary. Volume 1: The Beatles Years* — **Barry Miles** | A mostly 'all-text update' of his earlier large format and copiously illustrated *The Beatles Diary*; and in many ways all the better for it. 380+ pages—with just 16 pages of small black and white photos—but otherwise packed to the gills with cross-checked facts and details from a vast compendium of acknowledged sources. A most worthwhile resource.

21 *The Rough Guide to The Beatles* — **Chris Ingham** | A small book—but it packs an atomic four-four beat. A great little primer to The Beatles. Chris Ingham's nicely informed wit is ever at hand. It's like having a night out with your best friend down the pub and being continually amazed at just how much he knows about—and loves—The Beatles. Definitely worth the price of a round of drinks.

22 *Read The Beatles: Classic and New Writings on The Beatles, Their Legacy, And Why They Still Matter* — Edited by **June Skinner Sawyers** | A selection of writings from both sides of the pond - spanning the entire career of The Beatles. The first three parts devoted to The Early Years (1960-64). Followed by: The Middle Years. The End. Looking Back. The Beatles Apart. Why The Beatles Still Matter. All the pieces—Andrew Sarris' splendid review of *A Hard Day's Night* from *The Village Voice*—even a poem by Allen Ginsberg—nicely curated and edited. The 'Foreword' by Astrid Kirchherr is very touching. The editor's 'Introduction' is very good. With a detailed Chronology. And maps of Liverpool. What's not to like?

23 *How They Became The Beatles: A Definitive History of the Early Years 1960–1964* — **Gareth L. Pawlowski** | As untidily put together as The Beatles themselves undoubtedly were in the early days, but such fun. The lack of surface sheen only adds to the 'real feel' of the (re)telling.

24 *The Beatles: Anthology* – **The Beatles** | The Fabs in their own words; even if their memories do differ at various times. Still a delight, especially when perused alongside yet another viewing of *The Beatles: Anthology* box set of DVDs.

25 *The Beatles: 10 Years That Shook The World* — **Edited by Paul Trynka** | *MOJO* | The UK's premier rock music magazine, *MOJO*, gathered together a veritable 'Who's Who' of rock journalism. A truly outstanding group edited by Paul Trynka: Bill Harry, Mark Lewisohn, Hunter Davies, Spenser Leigh, *the late, much lamented* Ian Macdonald, Chris Ingham, Nick Kent, Mark Ellen, David Fricke, Andy Gill, Paul Du Noyer, Robert Sandall *et al*. There's also a treasure trove of noted rock musicians who reflect on The Beatles and their music. Most excellent.

Beatles Books To Delight The Eye

If "a picture is worth a thousand words"—then collections of contemporary photographs of the people, places, venues, and events that touched the lives of The Beatles more than deserve a special mention. And, in this, the original 'iconic' works of a few photographers stand supreme:

01 *Hamburg Days* — **Astrid Kirchherr & Klaus Voormann** | Astrid's iconic photographs and Klaus's drawings of The Beatles' early days in Hamburg, in the huge collector's book published by Genesis are a joy; incomparable. Her **'*Yesterday - The Beatles Once Upon A Time*'**, co-compiled with *Stern* photographer Max Scheler, is yet another timeless treasure. As, too, is **'*Astrid Kirchherr with the Beatles*'** - published by Damiani - March 2018

02 *The Beatles In Hamburg* — Jürgen Vollmer | The photographs of the early days of The Beatles in Hamburg reveal the real nitty-gritty of the city's infamous Reeperbahn red-light district. Puts you right there in the rock 'n' roll clubs with the savage young Beatles und *le blouson noir*. Terrific. Timeless.

03 *The Beatles | Yesterday - Photographs of The Beatles* — **Robert Freeman** | Freeman's work was iconic right from the very start; his album cover shot for **With The Beatles** both startling and new. And then of course he gave us the look and feel of *A Hard Day's Night*. His first giant sized coffee table book: **'The Beatles'** an event. His later **'Yesterday - Photographs of The Beatles'**, a real joy.

04 *Mike Mac's White and Blacks | Remember - the Recollections and Photographs of Michael McCartney | Thank U Very Much, Mike McCartney's Family Album* – Michael McCartney Photos, both candid and personal, of the early members of The Beatles. Even if only with the family's Kodak 'Box Brownie'; Macca's younger brother possessed a 'wonderful eye' and captured many magical moments from before and during and after the beginning of it all. Wonderful 'past joys' to savour of the young Paul McCartney, John Lennon, and George Harrison *et al*.

05 *With The Beatles. The historic photographs of Dezo Hoffmann* — Dezo Hoffmann | Another cracker from Omnibus Press. Edited and designed by Pearce Marchbank. Dezo was the first professional to photograph The Beatles—which means he was also the very first to be commissioned and paid accordingly. A treasure trove of the early Beatles.

06 *The Beatles' Files* – compiled by Andy Davis | *The Beatles' Unseen Archives* – compiled by Tim Hill & Marie Clayton A shout out for the *Daily Mirror* and *Daily Mail*—and these two resulting books of photos from their respective archives. True eye candy for all Beatles' fans.

Beatles Websites To Visit

Before we get to the list of recommended Beatles' websites, may I suggest you also check out: **The One After 9:09** 'SPECIAL FEATURES' website that presents The People | The Places | The Times | The Tides. Everything that helped shape: '*The Beatles. In Liverpool, Hamburg, London*' and '*The One After 9:09. A Mystery With A Backbeat.*' http://www.theoneafter909.com

There are hundreds of websites on the World-Wide-Web dedicated to all aspects of The Beatles, their music, and their times. *"Pepperland"* as some call it. And what it all says is that there's still a deep-seated fascination, a hunger even, to know more, and to draw more and more meaning and understanding from the unique phenomenon that was, and still is, The Beatles.

I stand in awe at the dedication and endeavour shown by so many people, all around the world. And whether it's been by recommendation or simply having stumbled across someone's website; it's invariably proven to be a veritable magical mystery tour. "Thanks to one and all. Love - Love - Love your work."

These are some of my favourite ports of call:

01 The Savage Young Beatles
http://www.beatlesource.com/savage/
So simple. Yet so right. Pure perfection. Original photographs and pithy captions. Always an education. Always such unmitigated fun. Hat's off to the person(s) behind the curtain. And should we ever meet in *"Pepperland"* —*"There will be beer."*

02 Beatle Links
http://www.beatlelinks.net/links/
A website justly positioned as: **The Beatles Internet Resource Guide.** The site doesn't sell or promote any products or services directly–but functions as an aggregator of Beatles related sites—and as such is priceless.

03 The Beatles Bible
http://www.beatlesbible.com
One of the great Beatles fan orchestrated sites; comprehensive; always compelling; clearly a labour of love. Always a joy to find myself here. Like visiting an old friend.

04 = Mersey Beat
http://www.mersey-beat.com
The one and only Bill Harry—founder and editor of *MERSEY BEAT—Merseyside's Own Entertainments Paper*—rocks the People—The Places—The Times —The Tides as only he can. His eye—and memory—for the telling detail will have you always coming back for more. Indispensable.

04 = Bill Harry's Mersey Beat Blog
billharry.co.uk
New 'blog' website (2015) from the indefatigable Bill Harry—still able to surprise—sometimes even shock—with his new takes on old times. Much warmer—when not wearing his Official 'Beatles' Historian' hat—and all the more revealing for that. This is already a must-read. *Keep on rockin' Mr. Harry—no one does it better.*

05 = The Beatles Connection
http://thebeatlesconnection.blogspot.com
A great Beatles' blog site—very worldly and comprehensive in its approach. Proves again that there's never a language barrier when it comes to loving The Fabs.

05 = The Daily Beatle
http://wogew.blogspot.com/2008/02/wogblog.html
Website about all things Beatles. For the last 10 years: Blogs. Postings. Articles. Galore

06 = *DM's Beatles Site*
http://www.dmbeatles.com
This knockout website from one—Dmitry Murashev. A singular labour of Beatles love—that's engagingly comprehensive—and has been years in the making. Another great thing about the site is that it's also a portal into the 'Top 100 Beatles Websites Worldwide'. Nice one, Dmitry.

06 = *Top 100 Beatles Websites Worldwide*
http://top.dmbeatles.com
A portal into the Top 100 Beatles Websites Worldwide (The actual number running around 180+ at Q4 2016) Oh, for more Beatles hours in the day. Thanks again, Dmitry.

07 *The Fest for Beatles Fans*
http://www.thefest.com
The Fest for Beatles Fans just has to be included here. The indomitable Mark Lapidos began "The Fest" way back in 1974. The three-day festival—honours all things Beatles—and takes place twice-annually in New York and Chicago. Musicians. Personalities. Authors. The festival regularly attracts the biggest stars in The Beatles' firmament. The festival and web site a great source for Beatles' music, books, and merchandise.

08 *The Beatles Website*
http://www.thebeatleswebsite.com
A very talented group of Beatles' fans created this comprehensive web portal about all things 'Beatles'—many of them noted 'Beatles' celebrities in their own right: David 'Liddypool' Bedford and Jude 'Lennon' Southerland Kessler among them. Nice folks.

09 *Beatles Forever*

https://m.facebook.com/BeatlesJohnPaulGeorgeRingoForever

facebook page run by the most excellent Jeff Pelkmans; a dedicated Beatles' fan who has managed in a matter of years to draw together an inspired array of editors and author-co-editors:

Beatles' People: Bill Harry - Founder and editor of *Mersey Beat* | Tony Bramwell - NEMS & Apple Corps senior executive | Pete Best - original Beatles' drummer & son of Mona Best - founder of the Casbah Coffee Club | Roag Best - Pete's younger brother & Neil Aspinall's son

Beatles' Friends: Leslie Cavendish–hairdresser to John, Paul, and George 1966 – 1975 | Michael Hill – school friend of John's | Fred Seaman - NY PA to John and Yoko

Beatles' Book Authors: David Bedford | Aaron Krerowicz | Jerry Hammack | Alex Cain | Robert Rosen | Mick Francis | Dennis Alstrand | Scott Cardinal | Tony Broadbent

Beatles' Bloggers *et al*: Jesse Vejar | Alex Barranco | Gary McKechnie | Brian Bess | Andre Homan | Tony O'Keeffe

10 *The Gilly*

http://thegilly.tumblr.com/archive

Not a functioning website—more a legacy—thousands upon thousands of curated images from all moments in Beatles' life, love, and lore. A website very close to my heart—a twin to *Savage Young Beatles* in many respects. Now no longer active, but still there to be enjoyed. Thanks *Gilly*—whoever you are or were. Another promise: *"There will be beer."*

PART FIVE – THE BEATLES | BOOKS

Reading the Sixties

THE SIXTIES: A SPIRIT OF CHANGE COUPLED WITH A WAVE OF OPTIMISM... *A VERY HEADY MIX*

Rock 'n' Roll | JFK | *South Pacific* | Cuban Missile Crisis | 45 rpm 'Singles' + 'EPs' + 33 rpm LPs | Teddy Boys | The Twist | Great Train Robbery | *My Fair Lady* | Mini Skirts | *Psycho* | Radio Luxembourg | *Saturday Night and Sunday Morning* | The Pill | 'Lady Chatterley's Lover' | Portable tape recorders | 'Profumo' Scandal | Credit cards | AM - FM Music Radio | Carnaby Street W1 | Transistor Radio | *The Sound of Music* | Stereo | Assassination of President John F. Kennedy | *Oliver!* | Long Hair for Men | *Beyond the Fringe* | Vietnam War | *'Beatlemania'* | Mods and Rockers | Michael Caine | Telstar | Fender Stratocaster | *The Avengers* | Civil Rights March | VOX Amplifier | Skateboards | *Avant-Garde* | 'She Loves You' | "I have a dream" | *Who's Afraid of Virginia Woolf?* | IBM's 'Selectric' Typewriter | The Sound of 'Merseybeat' | David Bailey | LSD | 'A Love Supreme' | *Star Trek* | *From Russia With Love* | Peter Max | 'The British Invasion' | *Private Eye* | Vidal Sassoon | Race Relations Act | Monterey Festival | Bob Dylan | *Bonnie and Clyde* | Peter Sellers | *Lawrence of Arabia* | Tamla-Motown | VOX Amplifiers | Marshall McLuhan | Terence Stamp | 4-Track Professional Recordings Machines | '*Sgt. Peppers Lonely Hearts Club Band*' | Pop Art | *Dr Strangelove* | Beach Boys | Mary Quant | *Breakfast At Tiffany's* | Abortion | *That Was The Week That Was* | Twiggy | *La Dolce Vita* | Sit-Ins | Jack Kerouac | 'To Kill A Mockingbird' | The Kinks | *A Hard Day's Night* | Feminism | 'Swinging London' | Len Deighton | Sidney Poitier | Habitat | The Doors | *Midnight Cowboy* | Grateful Dead | Jean-Luc Godard | *The Graduate* | David Hockney | Rolling Stones | *Hair* | *In the Heat of the Night* |

Concorde | *Ready Steady Go!* | 'The Spy Who Came In From The Cold' | Women's Liberation | 'In A Silent Way' | Assassination of Martin Luther King | *2001: A Space Odyssey* | Existentialism | Andy Warhol | 'Tapestry' | Jimi Hendrix | Ken Kesey | *Easy Rider* | The Who | Muhammad Ali | *A Man for All Seasons* | Woodstock | Neil Armstrong | *Rosemary's Baby* | 'The Sound of Silence' | Pirate Radio Ships | Assassination of Robert F. Kennedy | *Blow Up* | Hippies | *Monty Python's Flying Circus* | 'The Feminine Mystique' | Apple | Kurt Vonnegut | Altamont | François Truffaut | '*Our World*' Global Satellite Television Broadcast' - *All You Need Is Love*

ARTS & CULTURE | SOCIETY & POLITICS
'Nothing You Can Know That Isn't Known...'

The times... they really were a'changing... And they could do nothing but help shape events, worldwide. | Not everyone could put words to it, at the time, but most every teenager or young adult definitely felt that *change was in the air*... and that it could only be a force for good... *a change for the better.*

Books well worth the read if you want to find out more about 'the times' The Beatles lived through... played and created in... why they and their music had such a huge effect on the world's then emerging youth culture... and why they still do.

Books About The Sixties:
Rock 'n' Roll, R&B, Pop, Beat Music *et al*

01 *Mersey Beat: The Beginnings of The Beatles* — **Bill Harry (Compiled by "Miles")** | For the authentic feel of what was going on around Merseyside; on the streets, in the stores, as well as in the clubs; even who was off in Hamburg; there's no better place to start than with this compilation of replica pages from *Mersey Beat – Merseyside's Own Entertainments Paper*. From the very first fortnightly issue 6-20 July 1962 through to the last in 1964. | Whatever else you read about The Beatles was written years afterwards; Hunter Davies and Michael Braun the most notable exceptions; but even they wrote several years after the events that saw the birth of The Beatles. For a true sense of the real, raw, rockin' time and place nothing beats *Mersey Beat*.

This 'facsimile newspaper-size' compilation may be hard to locate, but it's more than worth it; you'll find yourself reading it from cover-to-cover, over and over again. Barry Miles and Omnibus Press at their very best. | **Author Note:** It's always struck me as extraordinarily fortunate, for all Beatles fans, that two such gifted 'chroniclers' as Bill Harry and Astrid Kirchherr were on hand to witness and record the early days of the biggest pop music phenomenon of the Twentieth Century and that they both did it so well, so convincingly, so very expertly. Everyone that came afterwards stands on their shoulders; no exceptions.

02 *Revolution In The Head: The Beatles Records and the Sixties* — **Ian MacDonald** | A simply wonderful record of 'the times'. And another book well worth a second mention; just so that you don't miss it. A masterpiece. *'Sans pareil'*. Astonishing. One of the very best books on The Beatles, their music, and their 'times'. Read it once, you'll read it twice, and then read it again and again for the sheer pleasure of it. | **The People's Music**, MacDonald's follow up book, journeys through the music of the Sixties and Seventies in a series of essays; the key one of which comprehensively argues that the emergence of The Beatles changed the world of music forever. Again, remarkably perceptive work from this much missed British rock journalist.

03 *Can't Buy Me Love: The Beatles, Britain and America* — **Jonathan Gould** | Another book that delves deep into 'the times' on both sides of the Atlantic. And again well worth the second mention so you don't miss it. Essential reading. Hugely insightful views into The Beatles' music, as well as a very nuanced appreciation of the group's extraordinary influence and affect on post-war society in both the UK and US. Another book to be read and re-read for the singular pleasure of Mr. Gould's always wise and witty observations. | 2017. Gould's glorious book *Otis Redding: An Unfinished Life*; as revealing and as compelling re 1950s, 1960s, 1970s African-American influence on US music and culture; another book that rewards repeated reading.

04 *Awopbopaloobop Alopbamboom* — Nik Cohn | The inimitable Nik Cohn. The first real rebel of rock journalism and his early thoughts and pronouncement on Rock 'n' Roll *et al* still need to be reckoned with—and seriously so—even after all these years. His collection of essays on Britain: *'Yes We Have No'* is another wonderful read. Great stuff.

05 *John Lennon 1940-1980* | *Stardust Memories* | *The Ray Connolly Beatles Archive* — Ray Connolly | Another favourite British 'pop' journalist. He wrote for the *London Evening Standard*, *The Sunday Times*, and other newspapers; always with a telling detail. He knew John. His biographies: **John Lennon 1940-1980**, published a year after John's death—though slim—still a book to treasure and **Being John Lennon - A Restless Life** published in 2018. He also wrote the screenplay, and book, for one of the very best Beatles' inspired films: **That'll Be The Day**. It has a performance from Ringo Starr that's a treasure in itself. | Connolly's book **Stardust Memories**; published pieces on pop culture celebrities of the time; is just the ticket to ride all the way back to the Sixties. | **The Ray Connolly Beatles Archive**: a newly published collection of his newspaper articles of the times; a treasure trove. | If you ever get the chance to read or hear his BBC radio play, **'Sorry, Boys, You Failed The Audition'** run don't walk to listen to what might have happened if record producer George Martin had turned the lads down. All lovingly realised by someone who knew them and loved who they were.

06 *The Beatles Diary Vol. 1: The Beatles Years* — Barry Miles | Journalist and Indica bookshop co-owner "Miles" was a member of The Beatles' inner circle during their London years. Which is to say he knew everyone worth knowing. It's also why his attention to detail is spot on. Drawn from his own journal notes and files; events, dates, and times reconfirmed by the best of other Beatles' books and sources; it's presented as a series of day-by-day, year-by-year diary entries of the decade. Makes for a very accessible one volume. Another cracker from Omnibus Press.

07 *The day John met Paul - An hour-by-hour account of how The Beatles began — Jim O'Donnell* | What's not to love? Told with real affection for the two young lads—and the city they both grew up in—by an American rock journalist who trod where lesser British angels might have perhaps even feared to tread. A nicely told tale that puts you at elbow's length from the young John and Paul as they find and recognise each other as true Rock 'n' Roll fanatics—to the sounds of Gene Vincent's 'Be-Bop-A-Lula'—Eddie Cochran's 'Twenty Flight Rock' and a whole medley of Little Richard hits. All really rather wonderful.

08 *The Beatles in Liverpool* | *The Beatles in Hamburg* — **Spencer Leigh.** | Both books "dead Fab" (in the true superlative Liverpool sense) and written by a real Liverpudlian, to Bootle; one who really knows his stuff. Leigh's also a constant presence on Merseyside Radio and the Liverpool 'Beatles' scene.

09 *Liddypool - Birthplace of The Beatles* | *The Fab One Hundred and Four (The Evolution of The Beatles from The Quarrymen to The Fab Four, 1956-1962)* | *Finding the Fourth Beatle* — **David Bedford** | *Liddypool*; the work of another real Liverpudlian and true Beatles' fan. A *Magnum Opus*, with 300-plus pages of photos, old and new, plus detailed notes, maps, and commentaries. As the author says: *"To understand The Beatles, you have to understand Liverpool."* Love for The Beatles and the City that gave them birth shines through on every page. | *The Fab One Hundred and Four* tells of every Liverpudlian musician who ever played with the group that grew into The Beatles. Nicely researched | 2018 will see the publication of *Finding the Fourth Beatle*; a book he co-authored with Gary Popper. The story of The Beatles from 1956-1970 told through the perspective of their 18 drummers! All entirely new to me.

10 *Liverpool - Wondrous Place - Music From Cavern To Cream* — **Paul Du Noyer** | Yet another real Liverpudlian, true music fan, and knockout rock journalist. He began with *New Musical Express*—became editor of '*Q*' magazine—and then helped found *MOJO* magazine. |

'Nuff said—the man certainly knows his stuff. As it says on the tin: *"Liverpool is the cradle of British pop, a city responsible for more number 1 hits than any other."* As you'd expect Du Noyer covers The Beatles, Gerry and The Pacemakers, Cilla Black, Billy J. Kramer, The Searchers *et al*—but it's the Liverpool he then takes you to that has you marvelling at the city and its seemingly never ending river of world class musicians. I thought I'd put the book down after reading about The Beatles—how wrong I was—and how right I was to keep on reading. The forward is by Sir Macca, himself. Most excellent.

11 *The Beatles In Hamburg* | *The Beatles Popular Music and Society* — **Ian Inglis** | Hamburg was hugely key to the development of The Beatles. And this book doesn't shy away from the intense difficulties the group faced even just in surviving their times in the city—but tellingly nowhere does it descend into tabloid sensationalism. It's a meticulously observed rockin' read. And its measured, nicely articulated approach is impressive and refreshingly illuminating. | Mr. Inglis having earlier caught my eye and ear—and trust—in the book that he edited: *The Beatles Popular Music and Society*

12 *The Beatles and Some Other Guys* | *The Restless Generation. How Rock Music Changed The Face of 1950s Britain* — **Peter Frame** | Frame's book of 'Rock Family Trees', *Some Other Guys*, is a never-ending magical mystery tour and an absolute delight. You follow the lines between musicians and the formation of groups. It's seemingly never ending. And such fun. | *The Restless Generation.* Frame's *magnum opus*. Majestic and magnificent in scope. An extraordinarily detailed journey through the birth of rock 'n' roll in post-war Britain. Brilliantly realised. A *tour de force*. Madly addictive in that it also rewards repeated reading.

13 *Hamburg - The Cradle of British Rock* | *Beat Merchants. The Origins, History, Impact and Rock Legacy of the 1960s British Pop Groups* — **Alan Clayson** | Alan Clayson takes you to post-war Hamburg—no holds barred. It's frank—sometimes brutal—and a bit of an eye-opener. But if you can keep your head about you while all around you on the Reeperbahn are seemingly losing theirs—it's well worth your time. Makes an excellent case for Hamburg truly being "The Cradle of British Rock." | *Beat Merchants* takes you from the first pre-war stirrings of pop all the way through to sounds of The Sixties and all who made them; or tried to. Clayson not only tells of the artists who went on to become world famous, but also, the many, many others from all over the UK who came and went with a whimper. As a former musician during those heady times he definitely knows about what and whom he speaks. | The ever-prolific Clayson has also written: *The Quiet One - A life of George Harrison* and *Ringo Starr - Straight Man or Joker*

| **Side Bar** | **Alan Clayson** and **Peter Frame** are in a class by themselves when it comes to the detailed accounting of British pop, rock 'n' roll, and R&B groups. Clayson gives you the feeling he was at every single gig, by every single band that ever played anywhere in the UK and is very generous with his manifold memories. | Frame has the draughtsman's keen and objective eye, and an astonishing head for the most obscure but still meaningful detail. Tremendous work from both authors.

14 *The Beatles' London - The Ultimate Guide To Over 400 Beatles Sites In And Around London (UK)* | *The Beatles' London - A Guide To 467 Beatles Sites In And Around London (US)* — **Piet Schreuders - Mark Lewisohn - Adam Smith** | Yes—that Mark Lewisohn. Book first published in the UK in 1994; US edition in 2009. Such unmitigated fun—from start to finish—and from cover to cover. Indispensable if you ever intend to visit London; just as indispensable if you don't; I keep a copy on both sides of the Atlantic just to be sure never to be without it.

15 *Beatlemania! The Real Story of The Beatles UK Tours 1963-1965* — **Martin Creasy** | Another winner from Omnibus—who also published *'Mersey Beat: The Beginnings of The Beatles'* by Bill Harry. *Beatlemania!* is the perfect companion to Michael Braun's great *"Love Me Do!" The Beatles' Progress* When read together, they give a 360-degree view—inside and outside the bubble—of The Beatles on tour. Creasy's book is an absolute delight for anyone that actually witnessed those early UK tours—the memories will come flooding back. For everyone else; the two books give a wonderful sense of having been there.

16 *Rock Odyssey - A Chronicle of The Sixties* — **Ian Whitcomb** Rock 'n' roll from inside the whirlwind. Ian Whitcomb had a rockin' hit, 'You Turn Me On', that got into the Top Ten charts in 1965, but turned out to be a proverbial 'one hit wonder'. A year later when the sound system, the amps, and all the lights had been turned off, Whitcomb took to writing about it all. An engrossing history of Sixties' rock 'n' roll. Takes the lids off both the London and West Coast music scenes and isn't at all shy about crashing them together. (Symbolism, anyone?) Merely a heads-up that Ian can get quite worked up at times—and good for him. Always a fun read, though, and very perceptive, his take on the Liverpool sound, very incisive.

17 *Meet The Beatles: A Cultural History of The Band That Shook Youth, Gender, and The World* — **Steven D. Stark** | This one from 2005 by 'a voice' I got to know listening to National Public Radio in the US. Of key interest to me; the all important question Steven Stark set himself: *To explore and explain the impact The Beatles had on popular culture—and to show how their music as well as their personal lives were inextricably entwined with revolutions in thought, spirituality, and social awareness.* All very engagingly done. My only complaint: that with the more than hundred interviews Mr. Stark undertook for the book; many of them in Liverpool; he failed to talk to Sam Leach or mention the Iron Door Club or The Tower at New Brighton; a crying shame.

18 *The Sound Of The City: The Rise of Rock and Roll* — **Charlie Gillett** | A particular favourite. When I read on the back cover what Ray Coleman (*Melody Maker*) had said about Gillett's book: 'That it could well be 'the definitive document on the social revolution that was rock'—it was enough for me to buy it right then and there. Glad I did, too. As a history of rock 'n' roll it can't be beat. Gillett's analysis of rock song lyrics is an on-going revelation as to the Times as they were a'changing. Another book that rewards repeated reading.

19 *Sonata For Jukebox - Pop Music, Memory, and the Imagined Life* — **Geoffrey O'Brien** | Reflections on how popular music infiltrates our lives and shapes the way we remember it. One man's odyssey through American music and pop culture. The chapter on The Beatles in America is outstanding. Very engagingly written. The kind of personal narrative that were you driving along in your automobile—all the way across America—would have you turning round at the coast and heading back for more. A never-ending delight.

20 *Flowers In The Dustbin – The Rise of Rock and Roll, 1947 - 1977* — **James Miller** | Another history of rock 'n' roll. Nicely written by a cultural historian and veteran music journalist. His somewhat disenchanted points of view, persuasively argued. All of which is to say, he knows where most all of the bodies are buried and in which dustbins of history they've been consigned to. Even so, you can tell he still loves 'real' rock 'n' roll.

21 *Twilight of The Gods* — **Wilfrid Mellers** | I for one like Mellers' book—a lot. And I learned more than a lot from this British academic. Even though it took me a number of reads, as well as a number of years to really appreciate what he was saying. The lack of comprehension was entirely mine, and no fault at all of Mellers. | Many people find *Twilight of The Gods* much too dry; especially when Mellers gets deep into the structure and theory of the music of The Beatles. I think it's more than worth the ticket to ride—even if only for his comments on the social phenomenon that was The Beatles—and their

Times. | Mellers was the first writer in my experience to ever allude to the mythic structure of The Beatles story; the first to touch upon the parallels to 'The Hero's Journey' that Joseph Campbell had written about in his seminal *The Hero With A Thousand Faces.* | A book for the ages.

22 *The Beatles as Musicians: The Quarrymen through Rubber Soul* | *The Beatles as Musicians: Revolver through The Anthology* — **Walter Everett** | Everett's two books venture into territory that some Beatles' fans might think they could easily skip; as they're not musicians, nor do they think themselves musically-minded; which would be a great pity. Everett's detailed analysis of the musical work of The Beatles is a revelation. His enthusiasm for the sheer artistry and brilliance of The Beatles' music is quite infectious. And, as with Ian MacDonald's superlative *Revolution In The Head,* you'll forever afterwards listen to the songs of 'The Fab Four' with renewed wonder.

23 *Tell Me Why - The Beatles: Album by album, song by song, the sixties and after* — **Tim Riley** | A very accessible analytical journey through The Beatles' entire musical catalogue of work—and its long term impact on popular music. It might tell you something that I bought both the earlier (1998) and later (2002) editions of the book—Riley is that good. Highly recommended. I'm also a great fan of his *Hard Rain: A Dylan Commentary*

24 *The Beatles - An Oral History* — **David Pritchard & Alan Lysaght** | Mostly drawn from long-form interviews undertaken for a 'documentary-style' radio show of the same name, together with research material sourced and gathered over the years. It's a treasure trove of 'aural history'. You might kid yourself you've heard it all before, but there's much here that will surprise and delight you; especially from people who you might have thought you've known for all these years. All in all a nice production by these two Canadian authors and program producers.

Books About The Sixties: Arts, Culture, Society, and Politics

01 *The Sixties* — **Arthur Marwick**
History professors are like wine. Some travel well. Some age well. Arthur Marwick does both. I first came across his work doing research for my series of historical-mystery novels about a cat burglar in post-war London; Marwick's slim volume *British Society Since 1945*, captured me. And so by the time he published *The Sixties*, I was already well and truly primed. At almost 1000 pages his book can appear daunting, but don't be put off. Even if only consulted selectively you'll find it becomes ever more definitive in your understanding of the decade.

02 *The Portable Sixties Reader* — **Edited by Ann Charters** | An anthology of essays from Penguin Classics; its US focus a good balance to the British view of the 1960s. The final chapter, *'Elegies for the Sixties'*, a tribute to ten individuals whose lives and deaths captured the spirit of the decade is very much worth the price of the book. As it says on the tin: *"A literary time capsule from the decade that changed the world."*

03 *All Dressed Up. The Sixties and the Counterculture* — **Jonathon Green** | A comprehensive overview of cultural and political events in Sixties' Britain. Engagingly perceptive. Nicely structured. Written with style and wit. (Green's *Days In The Life*, an oral history of Sixties 'counterculture', written a decade earlier, is also well worth the read.)

04 *In The Sixties* — **Barry Miles** | 'Miles' was at the centre of so much that happened in London in The Sixties. He knew almost anyone who was anyone and probably many you or I have never heard of; but should have. As ever, Miles is exceedingly warm and generous with his memories. It's always a pleasure to spend time with him; in all of his many books; whether he's talking about Ginsberg, Burroughs, Kerouac... or Paul McCartney... or The Beatles.

05 *Please, Please Me: Sixties British Pop, Inside Out* — **Gordon Thompson** | Written by an *Ethnomusicologist*, who knew? Thompson delves into the Sixties British music scene with a passion and perception that perhaps can only ever come from an outsider looking in. The social, economic, and political influences that shaped so much of post-war Britain are all given their proper due, to help give readers background and context, but it's cleverly done and with a light touch. History as seen through the eyes of the songwriters, musicians, A&R men, and record producers, as opposed to simply rounding up the usual suspects; PR stories and ghosted autobiographies of the 'pop stars'.

06 *Ready, Steady, Go! Swinging London and the Invention of Cool* (UK) | *The Smashing Rise and Giddy Fall of Swinging London* (US) — **Shawn Levy** | Like one long gossip column; that fillets 'the London scene' from 1961 to 1969. His discerning eye is smart, knowing, insightful and often very funny. He pins all the butterflies to the board, without breaking a single one of them on the wheel. A delightfully wicked read.

07 *Revolt Into Style. The Pop Arts In Britain* — **George Melly** | One of Liverpool's finest. Jazz singer, raconteur, columnist, TV celebrity. Melly was one of the first to take 'Pop' seriously enough to write about it in book length. From the early part of the decade, but no less perceptive for that, even though he didn't always 'get' The Beatles, he got a lot right about the swirling movements in the stream that helped give rise to 'The Fab Four'.

08 *1963 - Five Hundred Days* — **John Lawton** | John Lawton just happens to be one of England's best mystery writers (His Detective Inspector Troy series is simply superb: *Black Out | A Little White Death | Rip Tide et al*). Before that he was a journalist and TV producer of some considerable stature and that's when he wrote *Five Hundred Days*. A witty and wise and perceptive series of essays that form a compelling narrative of one of the more compelling years of the decade.

09 *Never Had It So Good 1956-63 – A History of Britain From Suez To the Beatles | White Fire 1963-69 – A History of Britain In The Swinging Sixties* — **Dominic Sandbrook** | Two volumes. Very engagingly written. Very readable. You'll learn much more about post-war Britain than you might originally have wanted to; and then go straight back for *more...please, sir...more*.

10 *A History of Modern Britain* — **Andrew Marr** | Andrew Marr is a staple on British TV. He's certainly one of the best political journalists and commentators of his generation. The book is the companion piece to the BBC TV series of the same name (As seen on PBS in US) that looks at Britain from the post-war years to the beginning of the new Millennium. His well-informed, seemingly effortless, narrative style makes for compelling television and a most enjoyable read.

11 *Modernity Britain - Book Two: A Shake of the Dice 1959-62* — **David Kynaston** | Kynaston's series of books on 'Modern Britain' are extraordinarily compelling. An on-going series of commentaries culled from contemporary diaries, letters, journals, newspapers—it is matchless in revealing the true voice of the times with all its attendant hopes and dreams and fears.

12 *Run It Down The Flagpole. Britain in the Sixties* — **Bernard Levin** | One of the great British columnists and broadcasters in The Sixties; and for many decades afterwards. Always perceptive. Ever passionate. Often extraordinarily persuasive. The newspaper columns collected in the book provide a marvellous time machine; touching on the great and good, the not so good, and the sometimes downright scurrilous. Levin, never less than piercing in his observations: ever witty; scrupulously erudite; and always a delight to read and re-read whatever the decade.

ACKNOWLEDGEMENTS

Author's Special Thanks

THE BEATLES in LIVERPOOL, HAMBURG, LONDON and *THE ONE AFTER 9:09*—the work of fiction based on The Beatles' early years in Liverpool, Hamburg, and London—would both have been impossible to write, but for the extraordinary wealth of memoirs, chronicles, and original research concerning The Beatles and their times that has been published over the last fifty years and more. Some estimates put it at around 2,000 books—others considerably more. All I can say is that I must have 500 or more titles in my very own Beatles' Library—and have read every one of them—some of them many times over.

I've recommended some sixty or so books in: '**Reading The Beatles**' and '**Reading The Sixties**' as I believe them to be the best of the best. As much for the sheer pleasure that comes from reading them—as the knowledge and scholarship they so generously impart. My debt of gratitude to all of the many individuals concerned—authors, editors, publishers, archivists, and curators—is total.

Yet I must single out a select few authors for special mention, as more than anything else it is they who have most helped to enlarge and shape my appreciation of The Beatles. And I hold them in the very highest esteem and regard. My thanks to Bill Harry, Mark Lewisohn, and Jonathan Gould, and to the late, much lamented Ian MacDonald and Sam Leach.

Other authors I also want to commend by name, as much for their framing of the Sixties as for their insights on The Beatles: Michael Braun, Hunter Davies, Philip Norman, Ray Coleman, Nik Cohn, Ray Connolly, Barry Miles, David Bedford, Paul Du Noyer, Spencer Leigh, Andy Babiuk, Geoff Emerick, Bob Spitz, Mark Hertsgaard, Chris Ingham, Jim O'Donnell, Ian Inglis, Peter Frame, Alan Clayson, Martin Creasy, Ian Whitcomb, Geoffrey O'Brien, Charlie Gillett, Wilfrid Mellers, Walter Everett, Steven

D. Stark, Tim Riley, Gordon Thompson, Arthur Marwick, Shawn Levy, Jonathon Green, Andrew Marr, David Kynaston, Dominic Sandbrook, George Melly, John Lawton, Bernard Levin.

I'm all too aware that far too many of the people I refer to have already 'left the building', so to speak, but all great work is timeless and calls for continued acknowledgement—and thanks.

I'd also like to acknowledge Dr. James McGrath's work on the influence of black musicians on the emerging Liverpool music scene of the early Sixties; especially his comments regarding the still unjustly unsung 'Lord' Woodbine and Vinnie Ismail.

And while we're at it, a special tip of the hat to UK music magazines: *MOJO*, *Uncut*, and *'Q'* for their many excellent articles and 'special editions' about The Beatles and their times.

Ditto *Rolling Stone* in the US for its oft-inspired journalism.

Many thanks, too, to the dedicated fanzines: ***Daytrippin'*** and ***Beatlefan***. And to the many blogs and websites devoted to The Beatles mentioned in '**Reading The Beatles**'.

Ever More Reasons To Be Thankful

The birth of The Beatles began with a sequence of *'five lighting bolts from the Gods'* that defies all probability: John meets Paul | Paul leads to George | George leads to Ringo | The Beatles lead to Brian Epstein | Brian Epstein leads to George Martin | Five signal events, without the occurrence of any one of which, The Beatles, as we knew and loved them, would never have existed.

And, so, thanks to the late **George Martin**; the *'fifth lightning bolt'*, even if not the fifth Beatle. Unique, in terms of both the times and place, he had the smarts, the skills, and importantly *'the ears'* to help produce, as well as introduce The Beatles and their music to the world. He was by all accounts, a true gentleman; and a most worthy 'Knight of The Realm'.

Thanks, too, to the late **Brian Epstein**, who by all evidence was a man of great charm and style and singular vision; as well as of extraordinary perseverance and dedication; and about whom Paul McCartney once declared: *"If anyone was the fifth Beatle, it was Brian."* 'Nuff said.

Thanks to the late **George Harrison**. What a lovely man he was. His musicianship, song writing, driest-of-dry wit, and 'unique soul' are forever inspiring. *"Namaste...George."*

Thanks to the one and only **Ringo Starr** for not only being uniquely and irrepressibly 'Ringo', but also for always being—and providing—the full fulfilment of the missing part. *"Thanks a million, Ritchie."* (Or rather—*Sir Ringo*. And about bloody time, too.) *"Keep on bashing those skins... er... Sir."*

And lastly: Thanks to **John Lennon** and **Paul McCartney** for their sublime body of work. My heartfelt thanks to both men: to the memory of the one taken from us all, all too soon; and to the other musical genius who—to everyone's delight—is still rockin' as hard as ever he did. Twin legends in their own time... in my life... and for evermore.

And... I Got By With A Little Help From My Friends

Especial thanks, too, to my 'Beatle Buddies' of long standing—John Morell and Andrew Tonkin—and new Beatle friend Joe Mallon—who all helped make sure I didn't stray too much or take too many detours on the long and winding road that was *The Beatles in Liverpool, Hamburg, London*. 'A little help from my friends'... doesn't even begin to cover half of it.

And in the end... all and everything dedicated to my dear departed music-mad, Beatles' loving, younger brother, Seth, who left the building far too soon for all who knew him... and love, love, loved him.

"*A perfect blend of fact and fiction*" — Bill Harry

THE ONE THAT STARTED IT ALL

The One After 9:09

REVIEWS

"A perfect blend of fact and fiction... a recreation of the Mersey scene as it happened, with the real people who made it happen, all placed in an exciting and enthralling mystery, an unmissable page-turner. Could well be true if my belief in an alternate reality was ever proved in quantum theory!"
  | **Bill Harry** | Founder & editor of *Mersey Beat* Liverpool Art College friend of John Lennon & Stu Sutcliffe. | Bestselling Author | World-Renowned Authority on The Beatles

"Loved it! Loved the writing. Loved the subject matter. Loved the story. Anyone who grew up loving rock 'n' roll and the Beatles will love The One After 9:09. Tony Broadbent skillfully captures a phenomena and the heartbeat of an entire generation. The One After 9:09 rocked. I rolled. And I dug it!"
  | **Robert Dugoni** | *New York Times* & #1 Amazon Bestselling Author

"There's nothing better than capturing the Liverpool of John Lennon and The Beatles accurately, and so often authors fail to properly understand the city The Beatles grew up in. However, Tony has done a fantastic job in capturing the time and the place, and the feel, of the city of the young Beatles at the turning point of Beatles' history. A great story, told really well, and a great read. What else could you want from a book?"
  | **David Bedford** | Author: '*Liddypool: Birthplace of The Beatles*' | '*The Fab One Hundred and Four (The Evolution of The Beatles from The Quarrymen to The Fab Four, 1956-1962)*' | '*Finding the Fourth Beatle*'

THE ONE AFTER 9:09 - *A MYSTERY WITH A BACKBEAT* | *'Rebel Without A Cause'* meets *'A Hard Day's Night'* |

A dramatic novelisation of 'The Birth of The Beatles' in the Liverpool, Hamburg, and London of yesterday.

A DISAFFECTED LIVERPOOL TEENAGER BECOMES INVOLVED WITH THE BEATLES WHEN HE'S HIRED TO HELP PREVENT THE MURDER OF THE GROUP'S MANAGER, BRIAN EPSTEIN.

Liverpool 1961. A city about to explode with the sound of raw-edged rock 'n' roll—reborn. Beat groups outnumber street gangs. Gangs of Teddy Boys terrorise dance halls and clubs with flick-knives and bicycle-chains. Gangsters demand protection money and firebomb clubs that don't pay. But nothing can stop the beat. The beat goes on. The demand for drink, cigarettes, sex, drugs, and rock 'n' roll just keeps growing.

But The Beatles are going nowhere fast—and they know it. Liverpool's grown much too small. Hamburg has become a drag. It's the same old grind—day in, night out. The big question: Who can get them a recording contract down in London—get them to *'the toppermost of the poppermost'*?

Only two men have vision enough to do it. Sam Leach—a pushy, local, rock 'n' roll mad promoter with towering dreams way beyond his means. And Brian Epstein—the sophisticated, urbane owner of a local record store.

A group of rival promoters are plotting to push Sam Leach out of the business for good. The man convicted of beating, robbing, and blackmailing Brian Epstein has not only vowed to kill him, but is about to be released from prison. Everyone, it seems, wants to spoil the party.

Into the swelling scene steps art student Raymond Jones, an angry young man desperate to find something—someone—to believe in after the death of his dad in a road accident. Picasso, Pollock, and de Kooning don't have the answers. Neither do Kerouac, Camus, or Sartre. So, just maybe, he'll find his salvation in rock 'n' roll.

THE BEATLES IN LIVERPOOL, HAMBURG, LONDON

PRE-TEXT

History tells us that an 18-year-old boy named Raymond Jones, walked into a store in Liverpool, around three o'clock on Saturday, 28th October 1961, and asked Brian Epstein, head of the record department, for a disc called 'My Bonnie'. "I'm afraid not," said Epstein, shaking his head. "Who's the record by?"

"A group called The Beatles," said Jones.

The fabled meeting is said to be what first prompted Brian Epstein to seek out the then relatively unknown Liverpool beat group, become their manager, and steer them on to worldwide fame and fortune.

However, an increasing number of people now say the meeting never took place and that Raymond Jones never even existed.

What's incontestable is that it was Brian Epstein who first recounted the story in his autobiography—*A Cellarful of Noise*—published in 1964 at the very height of '*Beatlemania*'.

Brian Epstein's influence on The Beatles was paramount and it's highly unlikely we would have ever heard of the 'Fab Four' were it not for him and all that he did for the group.

So what really did happen all those years ago? And why would Brian Epstein base the legend of The Beatles upon a lie?

Much of what you'll read in *The One After 9:09* is true...

'SPECIAL FEATURES' Website - Four Fab Blogs on The Beatles | Films | Books | Big Questions | Memories, Dreams, & Reflections | With additional commentary and photographs on **THE BEATLES** | **PEOPLE** | **PLACES** | **TIMES** | **TIDES** | All designed to accompany **THE ONE AFTER 9:09** and **THE BEATLES in LIVERPOOL, HAMBURG, LONDON**

| For educational purposes only | Simply to help increase everyone's enjoyment of The Beatles | **'SPECIAL FEATURES'** can be accessed at www.theoneafter909.com

TONY BROADBENT'S OTHER WORKS

Other Books & Stories

MYSTERY NOVELS

The Smoke. London Narrative No. 1
Spectres The Smoke. London Narrative No. 2
Shadows In The Smoke. London Narrative No. 3
The One After 9:09 - A Mystery With A Backbeat

SHORT STORIES

'As To: An Exact Knowledge of London' — *Studies in Sherlock -*
ed. Leslie Klinger & Laurie R. King
'The Remaining Unknowns' — *The Mystery Box*
ed. Brad Meltzer - Mystery Writers of America

FOR CHILDREN – OF ALL AGES

The Timeless Teachings of Guru Zuzu